D1648401

Building Web Services and .NET Applications

Lonnie Wall
Andrew Lader

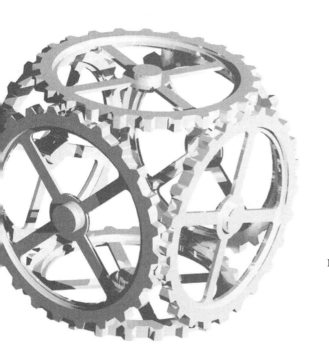

McGraw-Hill/Osborne

New York   Chicago   San Francisco
Lisbon   London   Madrid   Mexico City   Milan
New Delhi   San Juan   Seoul   Singapore   Sydney   Toronto

McGraw-Hill/Osborne
2600 Tenth Street
Berkeley, California 94710
U.S.A.

To arrange bulk purchase discounts for sales promotions, premiums, or fund-raisers, please contact **McGraw-Hill**/Osborne at the above address. For information on translations or book distributors outside the U.S.A., please see the International Contact Information page immediately following the index of this book.

Building Web Services and .NET Applications

1234567890 DOC DOC 0198765432

ISBN 0-07-213047-4

Publisher	Brandon A. Nordin
Vice President & Associate Publisher	Scott Rogers
Acquisitions Editor	Jim Schachterle
Project Editor	LeeAnn Pickrell
Acquisitions Coordinator	Tim Madrid
Technical Editor	Jon Louthian, Andrew Moore
Copy Editor	Marcia Baker
Proofreaders	Stefany Otis, Heidi Poulin
Indexer	Valerie Robbins
Computer Designers	Carie Abrew, Mickey Galicia
Illustrators	Michael Mueller, Lyssa Wald
Series Design	Roberta Steele
Cover Series Design	Greg Scott
Cover Illustration	Eliot Bergman

This book was composed with Corel VENTURA™ Publisher.

Contents

Acknowledgments

While writing this book, we learned that it takes hard work from a lot of different people to make a successful book. First and foremost, we'd like to thank Wendy Rinaldi for recognizing what we had to offer—a fresh outlook on designing applications using XML. Once Wendy got things started, Jim Schachterle took over and helped guide us through the rest of the development and writing process for this book. Jim was very helpful in the initial stages with guidance on the structure and format used by this series, along with helpful tips on the writing process. We also appreciate the patience and understanding that Jim showed when client work would impact the write schedule. We could not have completed this book without the encouragement and support that Jim provided.

Along with the support provided by Jim and Wendy, the rest of the top-notch editorial staff at McGraw-Hill/Osborne were instrumental in helping produce a high quality book. Timothy Madrid and LeeAnn Pickrell were responsible for routing chapters through the different development and production stages, while Marcia Baker applied her editing skills during the copyedit stages. LeeAnn was also very helpful in the copyedit stages with her experienced insight into technical publishing. Please take time to check out the rest of the Osborne team, listed near the front of this book. Without this team, this book would not have the editorial quality it has.

No technical book such as this can be published without the help of technical editors who are highly skilled in the topics discussed. For this book, we were fortunate to have the help of Jon Louthian and Andrew Moore. They were crucial in maintaining technical accuracy and focus.

Lastly, RDA Corporation, the company we work for, has been extremely supportive during the process of writing this book. As you can imagine, a book of this size and scope takes a lot of effort and time. RDA was willing to support us during that time and allowed us to include the book as part of our work objectives. The support and encouragement that we received from RDA is indicative of the principles that have made RDA what it is today and of the commitment to quality for which RDA consistently strives.

—the Authors

I'd like to thank my best friend and wife, Eleanor, for her encouragement and support through this writing process. I'd also like to thank my son, Justin, for understanding why I couldn't take him places or spend much time with him while I was working on "the book." The process of writing a book while working full time takes a lot of effort and doesn't leave much free time. My wife and son sacrificed a lot over the past year so I could concentrate on this, and I really appreciate their understanding. I also promise not to take a computer with us or do any work on our next vacation.

I'd also like to thank other co-workers at RDA, such as Mark Jones and John Keimig for reviewing some of the chapters and providing feedback. The different viewpoints and suggestions I received from these guys led to a better quality book for readers. Their insight was a very welcome addition.

—*Lonnie Wall*

I would like to thank those close to me for their support and encouragement. I would also like to thank McGraw-Hill/Osborne and RDA, without them this book would not have been possible. And lastly, I would like to thank several co-workers for their time and feedback, specifically Ray Barley, Dave Barnhill, Brian Berns, Mark Jones, and Russell McCullin.

—*Andrew Lader*

Introduction

Recently, Microsoft "bet the company" on a new approach to application design and deployment based on a Web services model. This new platform is called .NET, and it introduces a new set of servers, services, and client applications. For developers, this represents a new approach to designing applications with many different options and the associated challenges of determining how everything fits together. As a result, we have produced a book that starts with in-depth coverage of Web services and ends with the development of ASP.NET and Windows Forms applications.

Since the foundation of .NET is based on XML, we start with discussions on what XML is and how to use it in applications and Web services. Instead of focusing on language syntax and the mechanics of writing code, you learn how to design applications that take advantage of the power available with .NET. We also provide guidance on choosing when to use Web services in a design and how to build large-scale enterprise applications. This guidance and information comes from a combined 30 years of experience developing applications. As a result, we discuss "real world" issues and provide examples that come from applications in production today.

Our experience with building applications using .NET has been extremely positive and fun. We hope that you get a sense of just how easy and fun it is to develop applications with .NET. In addition, we hope you come away from this book with a solid understanding of how to design and build applications that use Web services and the .NET platform.

Who Should Read this Book

The information contained in this book is meant for all developers eager to learn how to design and build .NET applications. So, rather than using just one programming language, this book uses a mix of languages throughout its examples. We expect readers will have some experience developing applications, but we don't expect them to have any prior knowledge of the Visual Studio.NET development environment. All we ask for is some experience with application development and an open mind to new ideas.

What This Book Covers

Part I starts with an overview of the evolution from stand-alone applications to distributed .NET applications. Following the overview, we provide in-depth information on different XML-related topics that represent the foundation of .NET. Along the way, we discuss design techniques and provide benchmark information that demonstrates why XML is a great solution for distributed design. We end this part with our first look at Web services and how you can take advantage of this technique in distributed designs.

Part II starts with in-depth information on the .NET Framework that includes the Common Language Runtime (CLR), Common Type System (CTS), and Common Language Specification (CLS). By learning how the CLR works and the role that the CTS plays in developing .NET applications, developers will have a much better understanding of how everything fits together. This part also discusses how to take advantage of new features available in SQL Server 2000 and how to take advantage of the powerful new features in ADO.NET. We end this section with a discussion of DataSets and how to effectively use them in application design.

Part III focuses on actually building .NET applications using information discussed in the first two parts. The first two chapters in this section focus on developing ASP.NET Web services and Web Form applications. We then take you through the development of a stand-alone Windows Forms application and evolve that application into a distributed design that uses Web services. We look at how Windows Forms applications can interoperate with Java applications through the use of Web services. We wrap up with a chapter on debugging .NET applications. This chapter takes you through the steps needed to configure and use debugging features in .NET. You'll find that debugging is easier than ever and is integrated across all different layers of an application. In one session, it is possible to step from client code to server code and back to client script code all with very little effort.

Sample Code

The sample code and applications developed throughout this book can be downloaded free-of-charge from the McGraw Hill/Osborne Web site at **http://www.osborne.com**. Because this book is focused more on design rather than on writing code, you will not be required to download code in order to benefit from this book. If you do want to work along and review the actual code discussed, however, you will need to download the samples.

Overview of XML

OBJECTIVES

▶ Describe the evolution of Windows application development from the client/server model to distributed services with .NET.

▶ Gain a complete understanding of XML concepts with in-depth discussions on XML structure, XML schemas (XSD), XML Stylesheets (XSLT), and XPath and DOM specifications.

▶ Describe how DOM objects map to a real-world example of hierarchical data and how developers can take advantage of structured XML data to improve performance and scalability.

▶ Learn how to take full advantage of SOAP in applications, and how to implement a SOAP solution using ASP and HTML.

▶ Learn when to use Web services and how to design Web service–based architectures.

The Windows Distributed Platform

IN THIS CHAPTER:

Distributed Data

Distributed Components

Distributed Architectures

Distributed Services

Summary

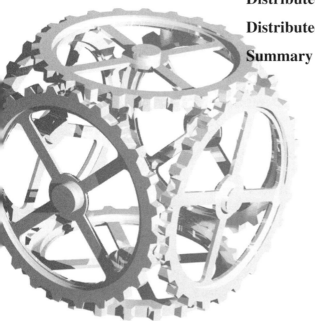

I n the past several years, the Microsoft Windows platform has evolved from a traditional client/server platform with distributed data to one capable of supporting heterogeneous distributed services. This chapter provides a high-level overview of that evolution, starting with distributed data in the client/server model and finishing with distributed services in the new Microsoft .NET platform. Along the way, we examine some of the issues developers faced and how those issues were resolved. The focus is on technologies that evolved to support distributed computing, which should help define exactly what distributed computing is. We then look at how XML and the *Simple Object Access Model* (*SOAP*) played a major role in facilitating the evolution of Windows into a true distributed services platform. The last section of this chapter also provides an overview of the .NET Framework topics that are covered in this book.

Distributed Data

From the late '80s to mid '90s, most development effort focused on client/server designs. A *client/server design* is typically considered an application with a user interface—the client—which accesses a database engine—the server. Important to note is a database engine doesn't represent data alone; it also represents the capability to perform various operations on the data, such as sorting and filtering. Another term for this type of design is *two-tiered*, which means two different layers are in the design: the client and the database server. This doesn't actually require two separate computers; a single computer can act as a client and a server. The two-tiered client/server model represents a design where database engines can be distributed across a network with multiple clients, as shown in Figure 1-1. As the Microsoft Windows platform evolved, new services were developed that improved the capability to work with distributed data.

During this evolution, the *personal computer* (*PC*) was finding its way into more and more business applications. Small businesses were starting to use PCs for accounting and office administration, large companies were finding uses for PCs where the power of a mainframe wasn't required. Client/server business applications were being developed for PCs that started replacing older mainframe systems. In addition, a need arose to provide shared access to database engines that didn't really exist in current PC technologies. All of this, along with advances in user interface development, resulted in several key solutions that were developed by Microsoft to solve some of these requirements. Two key solutions developed during this period were *open database connectivity* (*ODBC*) and *object linking and embedding* (*OLE*), which lead to the *Component Object Model* (*COM*).

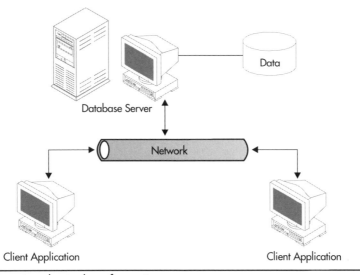

Figure 1-1   *Two-tier physical configuration*

Open Database Connectivity (ODBC)

Early client/server applications were designed with all the business logic encapsulated in the application. The database engine was typically used to store data and provide different views of the data based on operations performed. Each database engine had a different *application programming interface (API)* or *database management system (DBMS)*, which was typically located on the same machine as the application. Access to shared data was done through shared files or a proprietary DBMS developed for each database engine. This was difficult for developers. If the database engine they were familiar with didn't support required features, such as shared access to the data, developers were forced to learn a new interface. Along with a new interface, each DBMS also had its own version of query languages used to perform database operations. In 1992, Microsoft introduced ODBC, which resolved most of these issues.

ODBC was based on the X/Open Data Management Specification, SQL Call-Level Interface (CLI), and the ISO/IEC Call-Level Interface specifications. ODBC uses the *structured query language (SQL)* as a common language for relational database engines. This was accomplished with the use of drivers, developed for each DBMS, which act as a common interface between the application and the database engine. These drivers translate the SQL commands into DBMS specific commands and allow direct access to the underlying DBMS. On top of these drivers sits a *driver manager,* which is responsible for loading the drivers and processing requests from clients. The driver manager can also handle other database-related activity, such as connecting to the database, processing commands, and managing transactions. Because ODBC was based on industry standards, a large number of database vendors embraced the technology and developed drivers. Today, over 170 different ODBC drivers have been developed for relational database engines.

With the introduction of ODBC, Microsoft took one of the first steps toward distributed computing. ODBC made accessing different databases easier for developers by providing a common interface. As ODBC technology matured, new features were added that allowed for distributed transaction management, which allows different applications access to the same data while providing central management of that access. The driver manager, along with ODBC drivers, provided this functionality. The driver manager also allowed for run-time binding to different ODBC drivers, which made updating ODBC drivers or switching to different database engines without recompiling code easier.

Object Linking and Embedding (OLE)

Other major changes to application design and implementation during the early '90s included significant improvements to the *graphical user interface (GUI)*. User interfaces were becoming more sophisticated and services were being developed to help implement these interfaces. One of these services was the *Dynamic Data Exchange (DDE)* protocol, which the Windows clipboard uses to support cutting-and-pasting data from one application to another. DDE allowed applications to share data with other applications, but that was the limit of its usefulness. To provide a better solution with object-oriented access to common data, Microsoft developed object linking and embedding (OLE).

The initial version of OLE focused on supporting compound documents that contain embedded or linked data from another document. This linked or embedded data was actually an object that represented another document. As OLE started gaining acceptance in application development, the designers of OLE realized this same model could be applied to other objects, not only to documents. OLE provided a powerful programming model that supports the capability to assemble applications using data and behavior from other applications. Instead of only embedding documents within other documents, developers could embed other applications within the document. As a result, the OLE development team built an infrastructure that supported the capability to access the functionality of one application from another. This resulted in the birth of the COM, which was introduced with OLE 2.0 in 1993. At this point, OLE also stopped being used as an acronym for object linking and embedding and, since then, has simply referred to a technology called OLE, pronounced *oh-lay*.

Component Object Model (COM)

COM is probably one of the most significant technologies developed by Microsoft in the past decade. For years, developers have been able to include functionality developed by someone else into their application with *a dynamic-link library (DLL)*. An example of this is the previously discussed ODBC interface. A DLL exposes an API that can be used with any programming language that supports interfacing with a DLL. The DLL itself represents binary code that can be statically linked into an application at compile time or loaded into the application at run time in a shared implementation. In most cases, DLLs are shared among several different applications on the same machine. Microsoft had also developed a different kind of DLL called a Visual Basic eXtension (VBX), which provided common graphic interface components Visual Basic developers could use in their applications. Unfortunately, some major limitations and issues existed with this type of development. Developers were restricted to using languages supported by the DLL and not all languages, such as Visual Basic, could be used to develop DLLs. Deployment was also difficult; new versions of a DLL could break applications developed against an older version. COM addresses these issues and represents a significant step toward the capability to distribute and reuse common functionality.

Providing a detailed description of COM is outside the scope of this book, but a large number of books are devoted to that topic. You do need a basic level of understanding to see how COM affects distributed computing, however. The following high-level description assumes some knowledge of COM.

In general, COM defines a programming model that allows applications to use functionality from other applications or components without the limitations imposed by using DLLs. The programming interface used to access a component is defined using a separate language called the *Interface Definition Language (IDL)*, which is based on the *Distributed Computing Environment (DCE)* IDL definition, and extended by Microsoft. The IDL is compiled into a binary file called a *Type Library,* which can be read by any language that understands the IDL. The actual interface implementation is language-specific, but it must follow rules defined as part of the COM specification. This represents a complete separation between the interface definition and implementation. What this means is an application developed with any language can access COM components written in a different language as long as it understands COM.

For developers, the COM programming model also changed the way applications were being developed. Instead of building large, stand-alone applications that access a database engine, components were being developed that implement business functionality, which are then combined with user interface and utility components to produce applications. In reality, there is little more to application development with COM than simply plugging different components together to produce an application. Nevertheless, this describes the general concepts and makes it obvious that business components can be used in more than one application. This reuse of business components provide huge benefits to companies that develop internal business applications.

Another aspect to the COM specification deals with versions of component interfaces. Again, a detailed description of all the different interfaces in a COM component is beyond the scope of this book. Instead, we look briefly at some of the key identifiers and how they are associated.

With COM, all interfaces are required to have a *globally unique identifier (GUID)*, associated with it, called an *interface identifier (IID)*. A GUID is a 128-bit unique number that users can request from Microsoft or generate using tools provided by Microsoft. Several different types of GUIDs are associated with a COM object. The Type Library is identified with a *Library Identifier (LIBID)*; each interface has an IID; and a *Class Identifier (CLSID)* is used to create the COM object. Also, a different type of identifier is called a ProgId. The *ProgId* is a string that uses the application and component name, and may or may not contain a version number. The ProgId is used to retrieve the correct CLSID from the Registry when creating components. If a version number isn't included, then the current version is used; otherwise, the version-specific CLSID, if found, is used. One note of caution though: ProgIds aren't guaranteed to be unique, which requires careful attention to naming conventions used. Developers can also use CLSIDs and IIDs directly to create COM objects. With the use of ProgIds, CLSIDs and IIDs developers finally have control over the version of a component they want to use within their applications.

As new services were added and business applications matured, the traditional client/server model wasn't holding up. Database languages were maturing and applications were being developed to use a common data store accessible from multiple clients, which led to a change in the placement of business logic. Instead of putting all the logic in the application, developers were starting to put business logic in the database with the use of stored procedures and triggers. This allowed different components and applications to use the same data without having to duplicate business rules in all the components. As powerful as the new database engines were, though, they still didn't support some of the complex processing requirements that programming languages do. In addition, the processing overhead required to handle the business logic limited the data processing capability of the database. The time had come for a new programming model that allowed for distribution of business logic, as well as business data.

Distributed Components

During the last half of the '90s, development started changing from two-tiered client/server designs to an architecture that supports distributed components. Windows applications, using distributed data services, were starting to move business logic into the Data Services layer. The data layer of a two-tiered application isn't the best place to put business logic unless the rule being applied is data intense. If a business needed access to different database engines, it either had to duplicate the business rules or put them in the client. The traditional two-tier client/server architecture wasn't holding up. We needed a new architecture that would give clients the capability to share common business components along with the data. This led to the development of a new type of design paradigm called three-tier architecture.

In a *three-tier architecture,* we have client applications, business components, and database engines divided into three different layers. Figure 1-2 provides a static view of the three different layers. The significance of this architecture is that business components are treated as separate entities, used by different clients, who have access to different database engines. Several advantages exist to developing applications this way:

▶   Business components can be shared by different applications.

▶   Business rules are centralized.

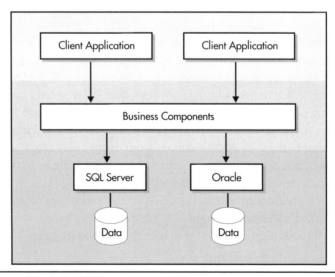

Figure 1-2   *Three-tier static view*

► Developers can use appropriate languages for the required tasks.

► Data can be shared by different business components.

► Application components can be distributed across several different machines.

► Provides better scalability when using a stateless design.

We could go on, but the advantages should be clear by now. To support three-tier architectures, the Microsoft Windows platform continued to evolve with new services that support remote access to components such as remote automation, *Distributed COM (DCOM)*, and *Remote Data Services (RDS)*.

Remote Automation

In 1995, with the release of Visual Studio 4.0, Microsoft deployed a new method for accessing OLE components across network boundaries. This new method, called *Remote Automation,* represented the first step toward distributed components, sometimes known as *distributed processing.* Remote Automation uses several different applications and DLLs, both 16- and 32-bit versions, developed by Microsoft to support remote access to OLE components. Although Remote Automation isn't a client/server architecture as discussed previously, it does still have clients and servers. The *client* represents a machine hosting the application that wants to access server components. The *server* represents a machine hosting components that provide the functionality other applications want to access. As with any client and server relationship, a single machine can host both types of components.

To support client requests, a *Remote Automation Server* is required to have an *Automation Manager* service running. During the installation of remote automation servers, another service, called a *Remote Automation Connection Manager,* is used to configure the security requirements and network protocol to use for communications. Once the server is configured, the Automation Manager is launched as a stand-alone application that uses Registry information set by the Connection Manager. The Automation Manager handles automation requests from clients to activate the server components. Once activated, the server component uses an automation proxy DLL to pack and unpack data for movement across the network.

The client uses an automation proxy DLL to instantiate the remote server component and handle the packing and unpacking of data passed across the network. The Remote Automation Connection Manager can also be installed on the client to modify configuration settings. To use Remote Automation with Visual Basic, the developer only needs to include AOL Automation as a reference and then use the CreateObject command to instantiate the object.

Remote Automation is still available today as a solution, but is usually only used with 16-bit applications. In reality, Remote Automation is difficult to configure, deploy, and maintain. The Automation Manager has to be launched on the server as an application, which makes it difficult for unattended server deployment. Remote Automation is also an add-on that needs to be installed on both client and server machines, which adds to the complexity of deployment.

Distributed COM (DCOM)

Less than a year later, Microsoft released Windows NT 4.0, which contained significant enhancements designed to support distributed computing. One of those new enhancements was an update to COM, which is actually an extension, called *Distributed COM* (*DCOM*). With DCOM, the applications and components required to support Remote Automation are built into the operating system. You no longer need to install additional components, and the server isn't required to run a separate application. In addition, because DCOM is an extension, existing COM components can be accessed remotely without any changes.

The actual implementation of DCOM is similar to Remote Automation. On a server, the *Service Control Manager* (*SCM*) takes over the duties the Automation Manager performed. The client also uses the SCM to instantiate a remote component. The SCM itself is responsible for determining where the component is hosted, and then communicating with the SCM on the server to instantiate the object and return connection information to the client.

The actual task of packing and unpacking the data for movement across the network is handled by COM itself. A separate automation proxy DLL no longer exists. A utility program named DCOMCNFG.exe is used to configure the location of the remote components. The DCOM configuration utility is also used to configure different security rights that control who can launch, access, or configure components on the server and client. Because a machine can act as both a server and a client, there is only one DCOM configuration application. For a client to access a remote component, the only requirement is to run DCOMCNFG.exe and configure where the remote component is hosted.

By late 1996, Microsoft had also developed and released DCOM for Windows 95, which is installed as a separate package. DCOM represents a programming model, which is much easier to implement than Remote Automation, and is the preferred method for 32-bit applications. Figure 1-3 shows the physical configuration of clients and servers in a three-tier architecture with DCOM used for the business server and clients.

Remote Data Services (RDS)

Around the same time, another team at Microsoft was developing a suite of components for data management called the *Microsoft Data Access Components* (*MDAC*). The most well-known MDAC component is the *ActiveX Data Object* (*ADO*), which provides a COM interface to database access components, such as ODBC and OLE DB. One of the objects included with ADO is a *Recordset object,* which represents a data set that can be manipulated by clients. With the second release of MDAC—version 1.5—a new interface was added that supports the capability to marshal the Recordset object across network boundaries. *Marshaling* is the process of packaging up data into a binary packet that can be sent across the network, and then unpacking that data on the receiving end. In reality, the actual

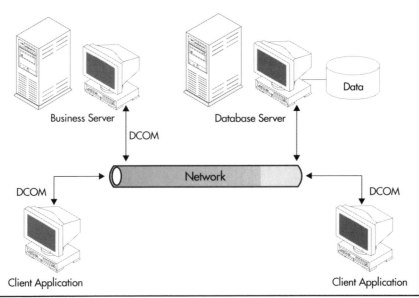

Figure 1-3   *Three-tier physical configuration*

Recordset object is not marshaled across; instead, the data is marshaled to a new instance of a Recordset object on the client.

The initial implementation with MDAC 1.5 was called ADOR, and then renamed almost immediately to an *ActiveX Data Connector* (*ADC*). With the release of MDAC 2.0, the component was renamed once more to *Remote Data Services* (*RDS*), which is the final name we have today. One of the interfaces or objects included with RDS is called a *DataSpace.* The DataSpace object is responsible for interacting with MDAC components on a server to instantiate a component remotely and provides access to the component, similar to Remote Automation. The original implementation was meant as a solution for HTML Web pages that used client-side scripting to instantiate the DataSpace object, which then used the HTTP protocol to marshal data between the client and server. With new releases of MDAC components, the DataSpace object has evolved to support the instantiation of an object locally or remotely, using either DCOM or the original implementation with HTTP marshaling.

One major caveat to using RDS for distributed components is the server object must be designed as a stateless component. We discuss stateless design considerations in more detail later in this chapter and in Chapter 6. For now, the main point to understand is this: with RDS, every call to the server component is made to a new instance of that component. The RDS interface, when using HTTP, isn't the most efficient way to access components remotely, but it also has one major advantage. Because the HTTP protocol is used, it's possible to access components remotely through firewalls that usually don't allow the use of DCOM.

Distributed Architectures

Once DCOM was implemented, the Windows platform was poised to move into the world of distributed computing. The timing was also good: modems were getting faster and the *Point-to-Point Protocol* (*PPP*) was allowing for richer content on something called the *World Wide Web* (*WWW*). The Internet was taking off; applications needed to support more users than ever before. Developers needed to be able to build systems that could handle these new requirements. Mainframe and midrange computers could handle the load, but they were expensive. The PC-based x86 computers that Windows NT ran on couldn't support the same number of users on a single computer. This was the time for a new programming model in Windows that defined how applications could be built for distribution across multiple computers. Microsoft realized this and they were ready with a new strategy called the *Windows Dynamic interNet Architecture* (*DNA*).

Windows Dynamic interNet Architecture (DNA)

Microsoft Windows DNA, originally described as the Windows Dynamic interNet Architecture, started out as a set of design guidelines based on Microsoft technologies. These technologies enabled the development, deployment, and management of distributed applications. When DNA was first introduced in 1997, it was described as an architecture for developing Internet applications. As businesses started taking advantage of Internet and intranet technologies, three-tier applications were being designed with each of the tiers distributed across several machines. Windows DNA both supported and encouraged this move toward distributed applications, and it has evolved into a suite of products, services, and tools that support the creation of distributed applications. Because of this evolution, Microsoft has also dropped the emphasis on Dynamic interNet Architectures and describes Windows DNA as a platform for Web solutions. One important point to remember is, even though the focus is Web solutions, Windows DNA still supports solutions that don't require Web services.

Before going further, we need to consider one other point: Windows DNA is based on COM. Always remember this statement when you think about Windows DNA. The architecture, as well as most of the products and services that Windows DNA represents, are based on the COM/DCOM programming model. However, Windows DNA isn't only about COM. Windows DNA supports open standards and represents a unified approach for building distributed applications. At the heart of Windows DNA is a three-tier architecture based on a set of design guidelines that use services and products with a common interface. That common interface is COM, which means COM services and products developed up to this point would be supported with Windows DNA. In addition, the investment developers have put into learning COM wouldn't be lost, in fact that knowledge is valuable. Windows DNA makes a lot of sense, is based on existing technologies, supports new technologies, and represents a unified model for building distributed applications.

Before we look at the details of the architecture, let's see what some of the different products and services are. When we talk about products, we mean applications and systems that provide different services, such as managing components and handling HTTP requests. Table 1-1 shows an example of some of these products and services, and where they fit into the three-tier architecture. This table is not complete and it doesn't attempt to show all available products and services.

Product	Services	Tier
Microsoft Access	Database Engine	Data
Microsoft SQL Server	Database Engine	Data
Oracle	Database Engine	Data
Internet Information Server (IIS)	ASP, HTML, Scripting, SSL	Business
Microsoft Exchange Server	MAPI, POP3	Data
Microsoft Transaction Server (MTS)	Distributed Transactions, Resource Management, Component Hosting	Business
Microsoft Message Queue (MSMQ)	Asynchronous Transactions, Messaging	Business
Microsoft Data Access Components (MDAC)	ADO, OLE DB, RDS	Presentation and Business
SNA Server	COMTI, Heterogeneous Data	Business
Internet Explorer	HTML, DHTML, Scripting	Presentation
Netscape Navigator	HTML, Scripting	Presentation
Visual Studio	Application Development	Presentation and Business
Windows Operating System	COM/DCOM, COM+, File Services, Active Directory, MSXML	All

Table 1-1   *Windows DNA Products and Services*

The design guidelines Windows DNA proposes are based on using a three-tier architecture. Figure 1-4 shows a Windows DNA Static View with the tiers labeled according to Windows DNA specifications. Each of the tiers, or layers, in the architecture has different requirements. The following descriptions define those requirements and should help provide a better understanding of how all this fits together.

Presentation Services

The *Presentation Services layer* represents the user interface. The user interface to a Windows DNA application can be a thin client deployed to a browser, or a thick client deployed as a stand-alone application. The functionality requirements of the

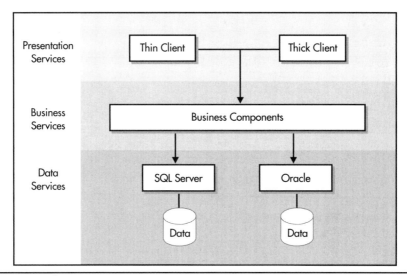

Figure 1-4   *Windows DNA Static View*

Presentation Services deal with providing an interface to the application for users. Thin clients developed for Internet browsers have limited resources compared to stand-alone applications. This may result in different presentation components developed for the same application. Each set of components is focused on managing the user interface and not the business operations behind the interface. Some of the services used at this layer are HTML, DHTML, Scripting, ADO, and RDS.

Business Services

The *Business Services layer* is responsible for managing the business operations behind the Presentation Services layer. Business components can reside on the same machine as the presentation components or on a separate machine. This is where COM and DCOM provide benefit. It doesn't matter where you put the component. Applications can link to it at run time using information from the Registry. Business components themselves handle processing requests, implementing business rules and providing a high-level Data Interface layer. It's important to understand that the Data Interface layer here is an abstraction or wrapper to the Data Services layer, which is discussed in the section that follows. Some of the services found at this layer include transaction support, component management, ADO, OLE DB, resource management, and messaging.

For the purpose of Windows DNA, all these services in the middle tier represent Business Services. As previously described, though, several different layers can be within the Business Services tier. This layering is sometimes referred to as an *n-tier design,* which means any number of tiers can be within the design. The main point here is, in the Windows DNA platform, these are all considered part of one tier or layer: Business Services. In alternate platforms, such as .NET, these different tiers can also represent different service layers.

Data Services

The *Data Services layer* represents database engines, file systems, and directory services. Database engines can be deployed to a single server or multiple servers. With Windows DNA, the database can also reside on a completely different platform. The Data Service components are responsible for managing the actual data store. With file systems, this means the management of physical data on a hardware medium. Directory Services include the capability to control and manage access to the data. Although some people consider components like ADO and OLE DB as Data Services, they really represent Business Service components that access Data Services in the Windows DNA platform.

One of the major design goals with Windows DNA was the capability to support scalability. As mentioned earlier, the three-tier architecture provides a good model for achieving this. Scalability can be considered the capability of an application to handle growth. Two common ways exist to scale an application: *scaling up* is accomplished by adding more hardware to a single machine, while *scaling out* is done by adding more machines. An example of scaling out is the use of Web Farms to handle a high volume Web site. For an application to scale out, the application logic must be distributable. What this means is we need to be able to spread the work an application has to do across multiple processes and machines for that application to handle more users. With a three-tiered architecture, the Business Services and Data Services can be designed so expansion is supported simply by adding additional processors—scaling up—and computers—scaling out—to handle the demands. If the system is designed correctly, using stateless concepts, then the Business Components and Data Services can be distributed across multiple computers with minimal configuration changes.

Stateless Design with XML

Finally, we reach one of the key concepts in this book, which is using the *eXtensible Markup Language* (*XML*) in distributed applications. Probably the most significant impact XML has on distributed development is the capability to pass state with function calls. This is significant with a distributed architecture and even more significant if using the RDS.DataSpace Interface to interact with remote components. With these types of components, understanding that each function call is invoked in a new instance of that component is important. This is different from standard object-oriented programming, where an object's attributes are set first, and then operations are performed on that object. With stateless distributed components all that object attribute information, or state, must be passed in with the function call.

When talking about stateless designs, one fact needs to be cleared up right away: even in a stateless architecture, state exists. *State* is data, modified at run time, that is used when processing requests. Actually, there are several different types of state, which we describe in the following list.

▶ **Persistent**   This is state information stored in nonvolatile storage, such as a database or file. Most distributed designs rely heavily on persistent data to store state information between calls. An example would be storing information about a user in one function, and then using that information in a different function. This type of data is available to any process with access to the data store, which has a lifetime that extends past the life of the application.

▶ **Application**   This is globally available state information, saved in some type of volatile data store. Examples of volatile data are public variables in a Visual Basic BAS module or data saved with the *Shared Property Manager* (*SPM*). In both cases, the lifetime of *Application State* is directly tied to the lifetime of the application. When the application is released from memory, the state is no longer available.

▶ **Instance**   This is state information associated with an instance of an object and is found in standard objects where attributes of an object represent the state of that object. An example of *Instance State* would be user information stored in a Person object. The lifetime of this type of state is tied directly to the lifetime of the object. When the object is released or destroyed, the data is no longer available.

▶ **Context**   This is state information available within the context of a specific function call. An example of *Context State* is a stateless component where all the data that would normally exist as Instance State needs to be passed in with each call. The lifetime of this state is tied to the function call. After returning from the function call, the data is no longer available.

If you haven't guessed already, Context State is where XML really provides benefit, but it can also be used with other types of state. One of the challenges that developers have faced over the years with stateless components deals with handling the Context Data. Until XML was available, several different methods were used to pass Context Data into functions. The easiest approach is to use individual parameters for each piece of data that needs to be passed in. This approach can be difficult to implement on large projects because of interface dependency issues that arise. Another approach is to use something called a *SafeArray,* which can be marshaled between COM components using standard automation. This works and it doesn't cause the same dependency issues. A SafeArray is difficult to use with some programming languages, however, and it's even more difficult to manage when dealing with hierarchical data. Another method of passing Context State is to use the ADO Recordset object. This object is designed to marshal the data across network boundaries and was actually the recommended method for passing data from a server to the client. Because a *Recordset* is a COM object, it's easier for applications developed in any language to manipulate the data. The biggest drawback to this approach is much more work is done than simply marshaling data across the wire, which results in fairly poor performance. When XML became available for handling Context State, it was a dream come true. Finally, a method exists for passing Context State in a hierarchical fashion, which can be easily used in any programming language.

We've seen how the Windows platform has evolved to handle distributed components. With the capability to distribute components across multiple computers, Windows applications are able to scale. This scalability was a key factor in the capability to handle the rapid expansion of the Internet. However, it's important to understand that a stateless design is one of the key components in building scalable solutions.

Even though we've focused on distributed computing, it's important to note that Windows has evolved in other areas as well. New Windows services were developed that improved interoperability, security, transaction management, deployment, and configuration management. The Windows operating system itself has shown it can handle 24/7 operations with services like the Microsoft Cluster Server. All these services and improvements are part of Windows DNA, which shows just how much Windows DNA encompasses.

For several years, it looked like Windows DNA was the answer to distributed computing. A problem existed, though; the COM/DCOM infrastructure didn't support the concept of Distributed Services very well. You have to know where a component exists to access that component. Nothing was in place to provide the capability to search for services. In a true Distributed Services environment, applications should be able to find a specific service without having to know where it exists in the first place. Once the Windows platform can support Distributed Services, we'll have a true Distributed Computing Platform.

Distributed Services

With the Windows DNA platform in place, businesses were starting to develop most of their applications as Web-enabled applications. Three different types of Web-enabled applications exist, which the following describes:

▶ **Internet**   This application is available to anyone on the Internet. The *Internet* is a global network consisting of millions of computers that provide different types of services. To access an Internet application, users must be able to access the network.

▶ **Intranet**   This application is available only on a closed network system. A *closed network system* is a network that either exists with no connections to the Internet or is connected to the Internet through firewalls that restrict access to the internal network. Most businesses have internal networks that can be used to host intranet applications.

▶ **Extranet**   This application can be accessed through the Internet, but is only visible to users who have rights to see the application. Typically, these represent intranet applications that users can access through the Internet. Extranets can be accessed by using a firewall that allows authenticated users past or by establishing a *virtual private network* (*VPN*) connection to the intranet using the *Point-to-Point Tunneling Protocol* (*PPTP*).

Probably the most attractive aspect to Web-enabled applications is they're easy to deploy and update. With traditional client/server applications, deployment isn't too bad, but it is difficult to perform updates and make sure all users have the correct version. Several different management systems handle automatic updates, but they're usually only found in large organizations. With Web-enabled applications, all the deployment and version information resides on the server. When users access the application, they can be updated automatically. Another benefit of Web-enabled applications is they are much more accessible to users and other applications, which means users on a UNIX platform can access applications on a Windows platform. This global visibility also allows businesses to provide services to other businesses, referred to as a *Business-to-Business* (*B2B*) interface or application.

The Simple Object Access Protocol (SOAP)

When designing B2B applications, one of the challenges developers face is providing a common interface between the business components. When talking about component interfaces, two different types generally exist: tightly coupled and loosely coupled.

With *tightly coupled interfaces,* the client component would need to bind to the server component at compile time. If the interface changes, then the client component needs to be rebuilt. Many people would argue that all interfaces should be tightly coupled because the action of compiling the application ensures the components can successfully interface with each other. This is baloney! All this means is the actual function call will be successful. It doesn't ensure the function implementation will be successful; you can always pass invalid parameters. When developing an interface between companies over the Internet, this is extremely difficult to manage. The business providing the component would have to maintain all previous interfaces, which is supported with COM.

Because COM is the best choice for tightly coupled interfaces, the application would also need to use the RDS.DataSpace Interface or modify transport protocols to get past most firewalls. This imposes a restriction on platforms that can host and use the business services. They would all have to support COM and have MDAC components installed. Even though COM is available in many different platforms, it still isn't supported everywhere. Businesses must be able to access services outside of COM to be considered truly distributed services.

With a *loosely coupled interface,* method parameters are passed in as a packet. Instead of defining parameters for each piece of data, typical implementations only require one parameter to handle the packet of data. This is much easier to implement in an environment where different teams and different companies interface with each other. What this means is the implementation can change at either end without affecting each other. In addition, with a loosely coupled interface, an intermediate transport can be used to pass the data between components. No need occurs for a client component to instantiate an instance of the server component, which can be handled by transport or processing components. In addition, with loosely coupled interfaces, application developers aren't restricted to using COM. This represents a much wider base of platforms that can host business services.

Because XML represents a common language supported worldwide, it provides the perfect solution for implementing loosely coupled interfaces. With this in mind, a group of industry experts developed an implementation of XML called the *Simple Object Access Protocol* (*SOAP*), which is designed with B2B interfaces in mind. The SOAP protocol is targeted at allowing rich interaction between applications using the Web infrastructure. Basically, SOAP includes header and processing information with the data that defines how the data should be handled. Chapter 7 contains detailed information on SOAP and Chapter 8 provides examples using SOAP.

Web Services

With SOAP in place, a new type of service has been introduced called a Web service. Technically, *Web services* are loosely coupled applications that use Web-based protocols and XML for the widest possible reach. Logically, these represent services that can be accessed from any platform using a common language. That common language is XML, which is implemented by SOAP and other specifications, such as the *Universal Description, Discovery, and Integration* (*UDDI*) specification and the *Web Services Description Language* (*WSDL*). By using SOAP, XML, and common transport protocols, Web services represent true distributed services that support a heterogeneous environment.

Both the UDDI and WSDL specifications are covered in Chapter 8. For this discussion, though, understanding how these work together can help. UDDI is used to publish information about available Web services using XML grammar. The UDDI interface is actually a Web service that applications can use to search for companies and discover the services available at each company. These services are not limited to Web services; a UDDI entry could contain a telephone number or links to documentation or to any other information that a company decides to publish. When a Web service is found, an application can retrieve the information that describes the Web service in the form of a WSDL specification. The WSDL contains information about the interfaces provided by a Web service along with information about the datatypes that are used by the service. In addition, the WSDL file contains information that describes the different message protocols supported, such as SOAP or HTTP POST, along with links to the actual Web service. Because XML is used to define the contract, a client can get all the information they need about the Web service prior to interacting with it.

Probably the most significant impact of Web services is they represent true distributed services and not just distributed components. By using HTTP as the main transport, firewall issues are resolved, making services available to more clients. In addition, clients won't need to target a specific computer to access this service as they do with DCOM. Instead, they only need a URL that can be obtained through discovery services. With distributed components, applications are tightly coupled to servers in a somewhat static environment. Although implementing distributed components in a dynamic environment is possible, this is difficult to do and much more difficult to maintain. With distributed services, applications are loosely coupled in a dynamic environment. This represents a much more robust application model, which is very scalable and, with the capability to access different services, much easier to build.

The Microsoft .NET Framework

With the introduction of SOAP and Web services, developers finally have a foundation for building true distributed applications. This is only a start, though. To build applications that take advantage of these new features, developers need additional tools and utilities. In addition, the COM programming model doesn't hold up well in a middle-tier implementation. Object interaction is complex, which often leads to performance and stability problems. Developers needed a new programming model that makes it easier to share functionality and use objects from different sources. This was the time for another change: COM and Windows DNA took us a long way, but lacked the scope and flexibility needed for distributed applications. As a result, with SOAP and Web services as the foundation, Microsoft created a new framework for developing applications called the .NET (DotNet) Framework, as shown in Figure 1-5. This framework replaces Windows DNA and represents a major change in application development.

Because the Microsoft .NET Framework is the preferred framework for building applications in Windows 2000 and Windows XP, we need to look at what this means.

Before we get too much further into the .NET Framework, however, let's step back and see where this fits in relation to the big picture view of Microsoft .NET. We need to consider several different aspects of Microsoft .NET. First, is the .NET

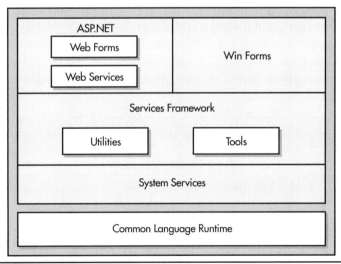

Figure 1-5   *The .NET Framework*

platform, which represents a complete infrastructure for building and implementing .NET applications. We also have .NET Products and Services, along with third-party Web services. Some examples of .NET Products and Services are Windows Server.NET, Visual Studio.NET, and My Services.NET. An example of a third-party Web Service would be an Insurance Quote service published by an insurance underwriter. When you put all this together in a collaborative environment, you get Microsoft .NET. Figure 1-6 shows an example of how some of these pieces fit together. As you can see, the .NET Framework works in collaboration with other products and services to implement custom applications or commercial products. In reality, the .NET Framework represents *a software development kit* (*SDK*) and Runtime Engine that developers can use to build applications.

When Microsoft first started putting together .NET, they called it the *Next Generation Windows Services* (*NGWS*). Early documentation for .NET referred to a NGWS SDK for building applications. That functionality is now part of the .NET Framework and the NGWS term is no longer used. As developers, we will spend most of our time working with the .NET Framework. We will also use .NET products, such as Visual Studio.NET, to help us build .NET applications, along with tools used to import and examine .NET components.

For now, let's look quickly at the new programming model that developers will use with the .NET Framework. Traditional APIs and COM interfaces normally used to build applications have been replaced with a set of classes that provide access to system and framework services. These classes, along with application classes, are hosted in a new Runtime Engine, called the *Common Language Runtime* (*CLR*). Standard development languages have also been modified to support a *Common Language Specification* (*CLS*) and a brand new language called *C#* (pronounced *see-sharp*), has been developed with the CLS in mind. The CLS allows for the

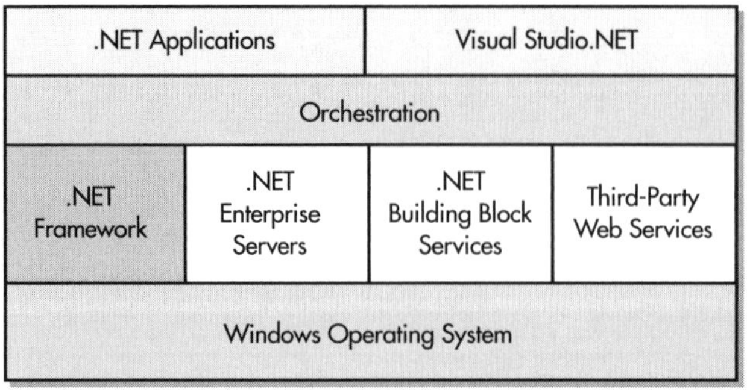

Figure 1-6 *Microsoft .NET*

generation of common code used by the CLR to implement and manage the classes. Applications developed within the framework can also use external services accessed dynamically during run time. This new programming model, rounded out with a new set of tools and utilities, make building .NET applications a snap.

We finish out this section with a closer look at developing .NET classes, compiler support available to developers, and a quick look at some important services in the .NET Framework. Remember, we also cover these topics in much more detail throughout the book.

Developing .NET Classes

Within the .NET Framework, we can have applications that access system services, interact with other services, and provide an interface for users. These services are accessed and interfaces are built using classes provided by the framework. The classes themselves represent a true object oriented-based approach to developing applications. As pointed out earlier, a major drawback to the COM programming model was the performance penalty and complexity of developing a middle-tier application with a deep object hierarchy. Normally, COM-based applications on the middle tier need a processor-based approach for performance and stability. With .NET, all those issues are resolved. In fact, COM isn't used, and developers no longer have to worry about the complexity and issues involved with using COM. COM isn't entirely dead, though. Many applications and services still use COM today. Microsoft wasn't about to ignore this, and it has developed utilities that can generate the information necessary for .NET objects to call COM objects and for COM objects to call .NET objects. All of this and more is discussed in detail in Chapter 6.

When a component is compiled by languages that support the CLS, *Microsoft Intermediate Language (MSIL)* code is produced, along with metadata that describes the component, its dependencies and datatypes used by the component. The MSIL code is simply optimized pseudocode, which the Runtime Engine, or CLR, uses to generate executable code that's compatible with the host operating system. This compilation of code is done when needed using a *just-in-time (JIT)* compiler inside the CLR. The CLR is designed to compile code only when needed, which allows for faster application start-up, but also adds some performance overhead. A precompiler can also be used on IL code to produce a binary for the target operating system, which also improves performance. However, the CLR has been designed with JIT compiling in mind and the performance hit is small. Once a component is compiled, it isn't recompiled. The CLR also handles other details of object management, such as memory management and validation, providing a safe run-time environment for applications.

The MSIL code and metadata, described previously, are all contained in an *assembly,* which represents the fundamental unit of deployment for a .NET application. The assembly is made up of four parts that can be contained in a single file or spread across multiple files. The first part is a *manifest,* which contains *assembly metadata* information. This information includes the name, version, and security requirements of the assembly. Additional assembly metadata information includes references to other assemblies and resources used by the application. The next part is *type metatdata,* which contains information about datatypes used by the application. The third section contains the MSIL code described previously. The last section contains actual resources, such as BMP files, used by the application. Chapter 9 covers these concepts in much more detail. One important fact stands out here, however, the "DLL Hell" issue has finally been resolved. Deployment with .NET allows assemblies to live side by side and actually binds shared components to assemblies in such a way that they won't be replaced by newer versions. The newer version is bound to assemblies that reference that version, and then is deployed on the same system as the older version.

Compiler Support with Visual Studio.NET

One of the most drastic changes for developers is the development environment. However, Microsoft has also gone out of its way to make this transition as easy as possible for the majority of developers building applications today. Instead of developing one language that supports the CLS and runs within the CLR, Microsoft modified its existing suite of development languages to support the CLS. What this means is developers familiar with Visual Basic can continue to use Visual Basic in the future with .NET. If an application needs some of the language constructs available in Visual C++, then that language can also be used. All components developed to run within the .NET run time are called *managed components.* Visual C++ is also the only language that supports the capability to write unmanaged code, which is code that runs outside the .NET run time. With Visual Studio.NET, Microsoft also introduces the C# language, which is a superset of C++ without the complexity of C++. The compilers for these languages all generate MSIL code based on the same CLS, which leads to one of the most significant improvements for developers. Classes developed in one language can be inherited and extended by classes developed in a different language. With a common class-based programming model, developers will find that building .NET applications are easier and more fun to develop. We no longer have to deal with all the issues and restrictions imposed by the COM-based programming model.

Important .NET Services

We also have two important services—ADO.NET and ASP.NET—that are part of the .NET Framework and available through framework classes. Chapters 12 and 13 provide much more detail on ADO.NET, while Chapters 14 and 15 cover ASP.NET. As a result, we only take a high-level look at both of them here. ADO.NET represents a significant improvement over previous versions of ADO. Along with the management of database elements, ADO.NET supports features such as an in-memory database and the capability to manage data using XML. The programming model in ADO.NET has also improved, using a DataSet centric approach to handling data instead of the Recordset approach. ASP.NET also significantly improves on the previous version of ASP. In fact, ASP has been completely rewritten from the ground up. This new version supports events, improved caching, and access to compiled components. It also provides the capability to host Web services and translate UDDI, WSDL, and SOAP requests. For Web-based applications, ASP.NET also provides a new set of services for developing the user interface called *Web Forms.* The Web Form classes are also available through the framework class model.

Up to this point, we focused primarily on Web-based services when it comes to presentation, but the .NET framework also provides for Windows applications. The service that represents the .NET recommendation for building applications is called *Win Forms.* Win Forms can also be accessed through the framework class model and are discussed in more detail in Chapter 16. For now, it's sufficient to know the .NET Framework supports both Web-based and desktop-based applications.

With SOAP and Web services, the Microsoft Windows platform can be considered a true distributed services platform. The Windows .NET Framework provides an environment for developing .NET applications while delivering the tools and utilities developers need. Also important to note is XML, as implemented by SOAP and Web services, plays a significant role in implementing the distributed services platform and Windows .NET, in general.

Summary

You've seen how the Microsoft Windows platform has evolved from a client/server platform with distributed data to something capable of handling distributed services. Although the discussion was high level and focused on a distinct set of technologies, the idea of distributed computing should be much clearer. The three main types of distributed services we discussed are listed in the following:

▶ **Distributed Data**   This is the model used by client/server applications. Data can be distributed to different computers and shared by multiple clients.

▶ **Distributed Components**   This is implemented when developing three or n-tier applications. In this model, the business components can be distributed to different computers and shared by multiple applications. The main difference here is distributed components are accessed using COM/DCOM, which isn't as flexible as a service-based design.

▶ **Distributed Services** This model is used in both three- and n-tier applications. The difference between distributed components and services is services represent objects that are dynamic and robust. They can still be distributed across multiple machines and go even further by supporting more platforms. Services can also be discovered and accessed without having any prior knowledge about the system where a service is hosted.

We've also seen how XML plays a significant role in distributed computing. Areas like stateless design, Web services, and discovery of Web services all benefit from the use of XML. We also looked at the Microsoft .NET Framework, which builds on XML concepts and provides a new programming model for developers. With Microsoft .NET and the .NET Framework, developers finally have the ability to develop heterogeneous distributed services and applications easily. The Windows distributed platform is finally a reality.

To summarize the chapter:

▶ The client/server model uses distributed data.

▶ ODBC, OLE, and COM evolved during the client/server evolution.

▶ Remote Automation, DCOM, and RDS played major roles in moving Windows to a three-tier distributed component platform.

▶ Windows DNA provides guidelines, products, and services for building distributed components.

▶ XML and SOAP play a significant role in supporting distributed components and services.

▶ The Windows .NET Framework, along with Visual Studio.NET, provides guidelines, products, and services for building distributed applications.

XML Basics

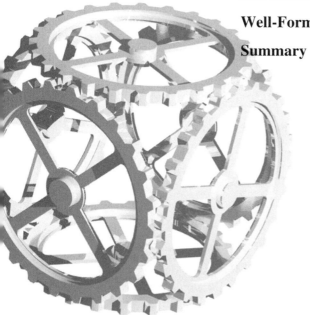

T he next four chapters provide an overview of XML, the eXtensible Markup Language, and its associated technologies. XML is an essential part of the Microsoft .NET Framework; therefore we use XML in our examples throughout the book. These chapters are not a complete reference; they are not intended to teach XML. Instead, these chapters provide an overview, highlighting the important features we use in our examples throughout the book.

What Is XML and Why Is It Here?

XML stands for *eXtensible Markup Language*. You should remember three things about XML: extensible, extensible, and extensible. XML doesn't have any tags of its own and it doesn't constrain you or limit you like other markup languages. Instead, XML defines rules for developing semantic tags of your own. The tags you create form vocabularies, which can be used to structure data into hierarchical trees of information. You can think of XML as a *metamarkup language* that enables developers, companies, and even industries to create their own, specific markup languages.

XML is derived from the *Standard Generalized Markup Language* (*SGML*), which is a rich language used mostly for huge documentation projects. The designers of XML drew heavily from SGML and were guided by the lessons learned from HTML. They produced a specification that was only about 20 percent the size of the SGML specification, but nearly as powerful. While SGML is typically used by those who need the power of an industrial-strength language, XML is intended for everyone.

One of the most important concepts to grasp in XML is about content, not presentation. The tags you create focus on organizing your data rather than displaying it. XML isn't used, for example, to indicate a particular part of a document is a new paragraph or that another part should be bolded. XML is used to develop tags that indicate a particular piece of data is the author's first name, another piece is the book title, and a third piece is the royalties made on the book.

For example, the following HTML snippet could easily be part of an XML document:

```
<p>
<H1>Mark Twain</H1>
<li>The Adventures of Huckleberry Finn</li>
<li>Tom Sawyer</li>
</p>
```

While the `<p>`, `<H1>`, and `<li>` tags would tell HTML how to display the information in a browser, these same tags in an XML document would only provide a way to demarcate the content of the document. Interpretation is left to the application that consumes the XML document. In other words, the `<p>`, `<H1>`, and `<li>` tags simply contain data and could mean anything. Most likely the owner of the XML document would rename them into something more meaningful. For example, the same snippet could be written using XML this way:

```
<author>
<name>Mark Twain</name>
<bookTitle>The Adventures of Huckleberry Finn</bookTitle>
<bookTitle>Tom Sawyer</bookTitle>
</author>
```

As you can see, this XML is much more readable and informative.

The question becomes this: why does so much hype surround XML? No special editors are needed to create XML documents, though an abundance of them are available. And no break-through technology is involved. Much of the attention swirling around XML comes from its simplicity. Specifically, interest has grown because of the way XML simplifies the tasks of the developers who employ it in their designs. Many of the tough things software developers have to do again and again over the years are now much easier to accomplish. XML also makes it easier for components to communicate with each other because it provides a standardized, structured language recognized by the most popular platforms today. In fact, in unveiling its new .NET platform, Microsoft has demonstrated how important XML is by using it as the underpinning of the entire platform. As you see in later chapters, .NET relies heavily on XML and SOAP in its framework and base services to make development easier and more efficient.

XML Process Overview

No special *Integrated Development Environments* (*IDEs*) or editors are required to create XML documents. Any simple text editor can be used. The governing body of the XML specification, the *World Wide Web Consortium* (*W3C*), has developed specifications for parsers to read XML documents. These parsers determine whether an XML document is well formed and valid.

NOTE

We describe well-formed XML and valid XML in the following sections—they aren't the same thing.

The W3C has also defined a specification for an object model for XML, called the *Document Object Model* (*DOM*). The DOM reads in the entire XML document, building a tree of nodes, one node for each element. These objects can be queried and manipulated, and then saved as a new XML document.

While the specification for DOM was being developed, the *Simple API for XML* (*SAX*), was created by Peter Murray-Rust, Dave Megginson, and members of the XML-DEV mailing list to provide a common event-driven API for all XML parsers. Unlike the DOM, it generates events for all the data it encounters as it processes an XML document. It doesn't generate a tree of objects like DOM; thus, it requires a smaller memory footprint and is typically faster than the DOM.

While the W3C defined the object models for these processors, it was left to companies like Microsoft and Sun to build their own versions based on these specifications. Here's the fantastic part to remember about all this: XML, which can be read and processed by Sun's Java processors, can also be read and processed in exactly the same way using Microsoft's processors. This means XML is truly platform-independent.

Self-Describing Data

The most powerful feature of XML is it doesn't define any tags. Creating your own tags is what makes XML extensible, however, defining meaningful tags is up to you. When creating tags, it isn't necessary to abbreviate or shorten your tag names. It doesn't make processing them any faster. But it can make your XML documents more confusing or easier to understand. Remember, developers are going to be writing code against your XML documents. On the one hand, you could certainly define tags like the following:

```
<H1>John Q. Employee
<p><b>Hired:</b>July 1, 1985</p>
</H1>
```

Using these HTML-esque tags might make it easy to be displayed in a browser, but they don't add any information to the document. Remember, XML is focused on content, not presentation. Creating the following XML would be far more meaningful:

```
<Employee>
  <FirstName>John</FirstName>
  <MiddleName>Q</ MiddleName>
  <LastName>Employee</LastName>
  <Hiredate>July 1, 1985</Hiredate>
</Employee>
```

The second example is far more readable in human terms, and it also provides more functionality and versatility to nonhumans. With this set of tags, applications can easily access the individual's first, middle, or last name without splitting any strings or searching for spaces. And, for developers writing code, searching for the last name in an XML document becomes much more natural when the name of the element is `lastName`, for example, rather than `H1`.

TIP

Indenting the tags in the previous example was done purely for readability and certainly isn't necessary in your XML documents. You may find, however, when you create your own documents, indentation helps you to read them.

Presenting the data shouldn't be a concern when you define your tags. An entire language is designed for processing XML documents into outputs—the *eXtensible Stylesheet Language* (*XSL*)—but we address this topic later, in Chapter 5. For now, focusing on the power that comes from naming your tags in a meaningful way is what's important.

Well-Formed XML

One of the more important jobs of an XML parser is to determine if a given XML document has been written correctly according to the W3C specification—in other words, determine if the document is well formed. To be well formed, all the tags and instructions must be correct syntactically. Note, this refers only to the way the document has been written and organized and says nothing about the actual tags you created or the data you placed within your document.

First and foremost, an XML document must contain one and only one root element. All other elements must be children of this root node. This element, referred to as the *root element* or the *root document element,* is the document's raison d'être.

Syntactically, XML documents look vaguely similar to HTML, but XML is far more strict. While you can create any tag you want, it must be enclosed in angle brackets (< ... >). And all tags must be closed by a terminating tag. So, for example, if you create the tag `<author>`, it must have a matching `</author>` tag. Note, the forward slash, `/`, is used to demarcate the terminating tag. Also, XML tags may begin with any letter or an underscore. Subsequent characters may be numbers, letters, underscores, hyphens, and periods. The tag name cannot contain any whitespace.

Like HTML, tags may be nested, but they cannot overlap. You can enclose a set of `<book>` ... `</book>` tags within `<author>` ... `</author>`, but you cannot terminate the book tags outside the author's termination tag. For example, the first half of Listing 2-1 is an example of a well-formed XML document, while the second half is not.

Listing 2-1   *Well-Formed XML Document Comparison*

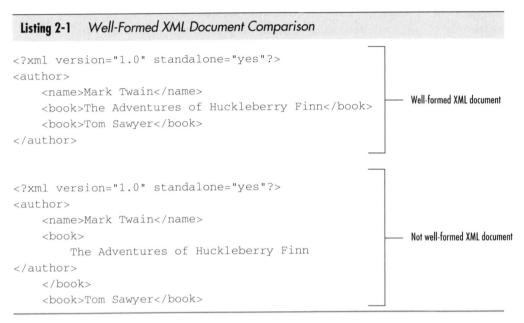

```
<?xml version="1.0" standalone="yes"?>
<author>
    <name>Mark Twain</name>
    <book>The Adventures of Huckleberry Finn</book>
    <book>Tom Sawyer</book>
</author>
```
Well-formed XML document

```
<?xml version="1.0" standalone="yes"?>
<author>
    <name>Mark Twain</name>
    <book>
        The Adventures of Huckleberry Finn
</author>
    </book>
    <book>Tom Sawyer</book>
```
Not well-formed XML document

NOTE

The first line of Listing 2-1 is called the XML declaration.

To summarize, here's the base set of rules used to determine if an XML document is well formed:

▶   It must have one and only one root element known as the document element; all other elements must be children of this root node.

▶   All element tags must be properly terminated.

▶   Empty elements using a single tag must end with / >.

▶   Elements must nest completely within their parent node.

▶   Isolated markup is not allowed.

▶   Attribute values must be contained within single or double quotes.

▶   XML is case-sensitive, so consistent use of case is required.

XML Declaration

Let's examine the first line of Listing 2-1, which is an XML declaration. An XML declaration is a *Processing Instruction* (*PI*), which indicates the version of XML used and the encoding for the document, along with other information. This is placed in the beginning of the XML document in the portion called the *XML Prolog*.

The prolog signals the beginning of the XML document proper and may contain an XML declaration, other processing instructions, comments, and a document type declaration. The XML declaration, along with any other processing instructions, is optional, as are the comments and document type declaration. Thus, the prolog can be entirely empty.

NOTE

A Document Type Declaration may contain a Document Type Definition (DTD), which can be used to provide some validation of the actual XML document's content. This book doesn't use DTDs; instead, we use XML Schemas, so DTDs aren't discussed here. XML Schemas are used heavily in the .NET platform and provide much more information about the structure of data than is possible with DTDs.

PIs provide the parser with information and hints on how to interpret the document. All PIs are demarcated with a beginning `<?` and a terminating `?>`. The XML declaration instruction is shown using two attributes: `version` and `standalone`. The `version` attribute indicates to the parser the version of the XML specification it was written against. The `standalone` attribute, which is optional, lets the parser know whether the document is dependent on an outside schema or DTD. A third option, `encoding`, is also optional and can be used to designate the character encoding for the document.

Attributes

Attributes are used within elements and are name/value pairs separated by an equals sign. The value is always enclosed in single or double quotation marks. In this example, the `version` attribute of the XML declaration indicates this document conforms to the W3C 1.0 specification. The `standalone` attribute is optional and defaults to `yes`, meaning this document isn't dependent on an external DTD. A third attribute, `encoding`, not shown here, is optional and instructs the parser as to the type of character encoding used for the document (for example, ANSI, UTF-8, or UTF-16).

Attributes are used not only in processing instructions, but also in elements. Both instructions and elements may have as many attributes as necessary. When using a schema to define elements, you have the flexibility to define which attributes are required, which are optional, and what the default values are for each element used in the document.

Elements

Referring back to the well-formed XML in Listing 2-1, the `author` tags, along with everything inside them, are referred to as an element. Elements consist of begin and end tags (`<author>` and `</author>`) and the content between them. In this case, the content is the name element and two book elements. By now, you should be able to recognize that the content of the name element is `Mark Twain`, and the contents of the book elements are `The Adventures of Huckleberry Finn` and `Tom Sawyer`, respectively.

Elements are the main staple of XML documents. They ultimately contain the information of the document. As we've said, elements can have attributes, but they may also contain text, elements, or a combination of both. *Empty elements* are a unique type of element because they have no content or text of their own, but they may contain attributes. In the case of book elements, they could be simplified to look like this:

```
<book title="The Adventures of Huckleberry Finn"/>
<book title="Tom Sawyer"/>
```

This `/>` notation at the end of the tag indicates the element has no content of its own, that is, it's empty. In this example, however, it does have one attribute, `title`.

TIP

As a rule of thumb, when trying to determine which data should be element content and which should be attributes, it's often easier to think of elements as nouns and attributes are adjectives.

Entities

In addition to elements, XML documents can contain entities. *Entities* can be thought of as replacements of text or data. They can be used to abbreviate long, repeatable text or they can be used to replace difficult to write text. Entities can also reference external data located in files.

For example, if you want the following copyright notice—copyright 2002 Acme Corp—at the bottom of all your Web pages, it would be much easier to use an entity like the following:

```
&copyright;
```

Note, the & and the ; are required. When the XML document is processed, each time that entity is found, it's replaced with the text *copyright 2002 Acme Corp.*

This straightforward entity falls under the heading of *general entities*. Other types of entities include parameter entities and external entities. *Parameter entities* are just like general entities but, instead of being used in the XML document, they are used within the Document Type Declarations to help define other attributes, elements, and entities. Instead of using the &, they use the % character.

External entities are used to import files of text or data. For example, they could be used to include another XML document or an image file. Their syntax is the same as general entities.

CDATA

Sometimes, you may want some parts of your XML document to be ignored by the parser and not processed at all. To force the parser to ignore sections of your document, you can enclose them in character data sections. For example:

```
<![CDATA[
  Ignore this data please.
]>
```

Often, CDATA sections are used to enclose code for scripting languages like VBScript or JavaScript.

Syntax Summary

Tables 2-1, 2-2, and 2-3 summarize XML declarations, elements, and entities:

Syntax	Explanation
`<?xml version="1.0" encoding="UTF-8" standalone="yes"?>`	The XML declaration
`<?name string?>`	Processing Instruction (PI)
`<!-- string -->`	XML comment
`<![CDATA[ … ]]>`	Unparsed character data

Table 2-1 *Declarations and Processing Instructions*

Syntax	Explanation
`<tag>`	An element's start tag
`</tag>`	An element's end tag
`<tag attribute="value">`	A start tag with an attribute
`<emptytag/>`	An empty element tag
`<emptytag attr_one="value" attr_two="value"/>`	An empty tag with two attributes

Table 2-2   *XML Element Syntax*

Our discussion of well-formed documents has centered on the syntax of the elements and entities, but not of the data contained within. To address the validity of the data, XML requires an agreement or contract between those creating the document and those consuming the document. Chapter 3 discusses XML Schemas and how they are used to validate XML content.

Syntax	Explanation
`&#decimal;`	Represents a character in decimal format either unavailable from the keyboard or that will cause interpretation problems by the XML parser. Examples are * and &169;
`&#xhex;`	Represents a character number in hexadecimal notation, for example, 
`&entityname;`	Represents a user-defined entity (five predefined entities exist: &, <, >, ', and " representing &, <, >, ', and ")

Table 2-3   *XML Entity Syntax*

Summary

Much more can certainly be written about XML and a number of books have done just that. We began this chapter by stating we would provide an overview of XML, highlighting important features used later in this book. Chapters 3, 4, and 5 continue this overview, focusing on particular parts of XML.

To summarize this chapter:

► XML is extensible. It provides a specification for creating your own tags. XML is a metamarkup language.

► You have the ability to create your own tags, so make them meaningful. Because XML doesn't define any tags, creating tags that make sense to other developers is crucial.

► The W3C provides parsers to determine if a document is well formed. This is a simple test that returns a Boolean pass or fail.

► Two object models exist for processing the content in any XML document: the Document Object Model (DOM) and the Simple API for XML (SAX). The DOM allows random access and the capability to modify, delete, and replace nodes in the XML hierarchy. SAX provides a simple, efficient way to process large XML documents.

► To be well formed, XML must essentially conform syntactically to the W3C specification, and all elements within the document must be children of one and only one document element.

XML Schemas

IN THIS CHAPTER:

Namespaces

XML Schemas

Summary

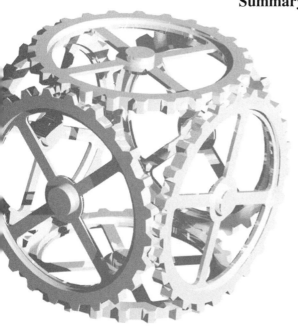

I n the previous chapter, we discussed how XML enables you to create your own tags, which form vocabularies. The word "vocabulary," though, is vague. Used in this way, vocabulary seems to infer some established set of XML elements and attributes that is known to people and their documents everywhere, and that somehow, any document can draw from this set of tags to describe its data.

But data requires structure, organization, and relationships, and, up until now, we haven't discussed any way to describe such things. *Structure* is an essential ingredient to conveying information. It lets computers and people know where to put data and where to look for data. Applications consuming data rely on the *relationships* between the individual pieces of information. Certainly, someone writing XML could form the data into some rational arrangement based on common sense, but this would have to be done repeatedly for each document. Moreover, it isn't commonplace for individuals to write XML themselves. That isn't to say this doesn't happen, but more often than not, XML used by business applications is generated by computer programs, usually pulling information from some data source. How can structure and organization be conveyed to a computer program so it generates the XML in the desired configuration? And how can these configurations be communicated to other applications?

The word "vocabulary" hints that some way might exist to do this, but it doesn't elaborate. And, even if some loose structure was established between the XML document designer and the application developer, no intrinsic way would exist to verify, or validate, that the XML used by either was, indeed, in accordance with this agreed-upon format. Imagine one application that consumes the XML generated by another application—a common scenario in the business world. How would one or the other agree the XML it was processing was organized and structured properly? Who would be right?

To answer these needs, the W3C first developed *Document Type Definitions* (*DTDs*). The DTD specification was inherited from SGML. DTDs offer the capability to organize the elements and attributes into structured hierarchies, as well as to perform validation checks to make sure the XML follows the rules. DTDs have several limitations, though. Among the complaints was DTDs weren't powerful enough to capture all the unique requirements of organizing data into hierarchies. Nor were they very extensible or easy to interpret. And DTDs had no support for datatypes. Finally, DTDs looked nothing like XML (they use Extended Backus Naur Form). These weren't trivial concerns. To address these issues and others, the W3C developed XML Schemas.

XML Schemas offer a common way for developers to design structured XML. Using a rich language, XML Schemas define elements, attributes, cardinalities, relationships, and the basic organization of XML data. They also provide a way to communicate this information to other applications and, equally important, XML Schemas provide a way for these applications to validate the XML that's passed to their components.

Namespaces

Before diving right into schemas, we should discuss namespaces. For XML to use schemas, it must provide a way to indicate certain elements and attributes belong to a particular schema. Therefore, schemas rely on the capability to group related elements together into domains. To understand schemas, you must first understand how to group elements together.

A *namespace* groups elements together by partitioning elements and their attributes into logical areas and providing a way to identify the elements and attributes uniquely. Namespaces are also used to reference a particular DTD or XML Schema, but this is discussed in more detail later.

As mentioned, a namespace is a set of XML elements and their constituent attributes. Before identifying the syntax for namespaces in XML, let's elaborate on them. Namespaces establish recognized groups of elements that are often used together. This is accomplished by prefixing each member element and attribute with a name, uniquely identifying them as part of that namespace. Grouping elements into a namespace allows them to be referenced easily by many XML documents and allows one XML document to reference many namespaces.

Reuse

Namespaces can allow any number of XML documents to reference them. This allows namespaces to be reused as needed, rather than forcing developers to reinvent them for each document they create. Returning to our common business scenario, consider the two applications: the server that generates the XML, relying on a particular namespace, and the client that consumes this XML, which also must rely on the same namespace. Rather than generating two namespaces—one for each application—a single namespace can be referenced by both applications in the XML they generate.

This lets namespaces be reused, which is an important feature. Just as in software development, reuse eliminates having to reinvent the wheel each time the same need arises, saving valuable development time. Not only can namespaces be reused by different parts of one application, they can be reused by different parts of any number of applications. Therefore, investing in developing a well-thought-out namespace can pay dividends for some time.

Multiple Namespaces

Just as multiple XML documents can reference the same namespace, one document can reference more than one namespace. This is a natural by-product of dividing elements into logical, ordered groups. Just as software development often breaks large processes into smaller procedures, namespaces are usually chunked into smaller, more logical groupings, like modules. Creating one large namespace with every element you think you might need doesn't make sense. This would be confusing to develop and it certainly would be confusing to anyone who had to use such a cumbersome apparatus. Rather, smaller, more natural namespaces should be developed to contain elements that belong together.

These namespaces could be used as building blocks, assembled together to form the vocabularies required by a large program. For example, an application might perform services that help users to buy a house. This application would require elements that define builders, mortgage companies, and title companies. Namespaces make it possible to include these vocabularies inside one XML document, pulling from each namespace as needed.

Ambiguity

Sometimes, namespaces can overlap and contain identical elements. This can cause problems when an XML document relies on the namespaces in question. An example of such a collision might be a namespace containing elements for book orders and another with elements for book inventories. Both might use elements that refer to a book's title or an author's name. When one document attempts to reference elements from both namespaces, this creates ambiguity for the XML parser.

Namespaces solve the ambiguity by uniquely identifying each element and attribute used in the document. If, as in the previous example, an element of one namespace references a book title, it is demarcated clearly as part of that namespace. Thus, when later on in the same document, an element identical in name also references a book's title, it makes use of the other namespace and no collision occurs.

Qualified Names

Elements and attributes that belong to a particular namespace are identified as such, so they don't conflict with other elements and attributes sharing the same name. This solves the previously mentioned ambiguity. By prefacing a particular element or attribute name with the *namespace prefix,* a parser can correctly reconcile any potential name collisions. The process of using a namespace prefix creates *qualified names* for each of the elements and attributes used within a document. The following sections describe the proper syntax for creating qualified names.

Namespace Syntax

As an example, let's use a fictional `author` vocabulary. We could rewrite the XML from the previous chapter using namespaces:

```
<author:author xmlns:author="http://my_url/author.xsd">
    <author:name>Mark Twain</author:name>
    <author:book>The Adventures of Huckleberry Finn</author:book>
    <author:book>Tom Sawyer</author:book>
</author:author>
```

You declare a namespace inside the element tag of the element the namespace describes using the following syntax:

```
xmlns:author="http://my_url/author.xsd"
```

The `xmlns` keyword is a special kind of attribute, which indicates we're about to declare an XML namespace. The name following the colon—`author` in this case—represents the *namespace prefix.* And the information between the quotes is the *Uniform Resource Identifier* (*URI*), pointing to the actual namespace—in this case, a schema. The URI is a formal way to differentiate between namespaces; it doesn't necessarily need to point to anything at all. The URI is used only to demarcate elements and attributes uniquely. The `xmlns` declaration is placed inside the element tag using the namespace.

NOTE

A URI is a unique name recognized by the processing application that identifies a particular resource. URIs include Uniform Resource Locators (URL) and Uniform Resource Numbers (URN).

Each element in the previous example is prefixed with the namespace prefix, `author`, and separated by a colon. The combination of the namespace prefix and the element or attribute name form a unique moniker. So, in this example, `author:author`, `author:name`, and `author:book` are all qualified names.

Multiple Namespaces

One of the more important reasons for having namespaces is so XML parsers can reconcile different vocabularies that might otherwise prove ambiguous. To declare multiple namespaces in your element tag, you would use the following syntax:

```
<order:customer_order xmlns:order="http://my_url/order.xsd"
            xmlns:inventory="http://my_url/inventory.xsd">
```

After this declaration, elements and attributes defined in the `order` and `inventory` vocabularies can be interspersed as long as they use qualified names. For example, `order:partNumber` might be a qualified name for an element in the `order` namespace, while `inventory:partNumber` could be a qualified name in the `inventory` namespace. If used in the same document, neither instance of the `partNumber` element would cause any problems for the XML parser because both would be properly qualified.

Default Namespaces

Default namespaces are simply a tool to make XML documents more readable and easier to write. If you have one namespace that will be predominant throughout your document, then it's easier to eliminate prefixing each of the elements with that namespace's prefix. When declaring the namespace, simply avoid using the prefix in the declaration and the parser then uses that namespace as the default for your document.

For example, the following code declares the XSL namespace as the default for the document.

```
<xsl:stylesheet version="1.0"xmlns="http://www.w3.org/1999/xsl/Transform
```

Default namespaces save time when creating large documents with a particular namespace; however, they don't eliminate the need to use prefixes for attributes.

XML Schemas

As previously stated before our detour into namespaces, XML Schemas have evolved as a response to problems with the W3C's first attempt at data validation, *Document Type Definitions* (*DTDs*). DTDs are a legacy inherited from SGML to provide content validation and, while DTDs do a good job of validating XML, certainly room does exist for improvement. Some of the more important concerns raised about DTDs are the following:

- ▶ DTD uses Extended Backus Naur Form syntax, which is dissimilar to XML.
- ▶ DTDs aren't intuitive, and they can be difficult to interpret from a human-readable point-of-view.
- ▶ The metadata of DTDs is programmatically difficult to consume.
- ▶ No support exists for datatypes.
- ▶ DTDs cannot be inherited.

   To address these concerns, the W3C developed a new validating mechanism to replace DTDs called *XML Schemas*. Schemas provide the same features DTDs provide, but they were designed with the previous issues in mind and thus are more powerful and flexible.

Processing Schemas

In the previous chapter, we discussed how vendors develop parsers against the W3C XML specification. This is also true of XML Schemas. The W3C has provided the specification for XML Schemas, leaving it to the individual vendors to implement the actual validation in their parsers.

   However, while well-formedness is always checked, parsers must be directed to perform validation. This is done by specifying the XML Schema using a namespace reference. Once the parser has completed its initial check for well-formed XML, it determines if any schemas are specified. If so, the parser loads them and performs the validation on the XML content and structure.

   Schemas are stored as text files. Typically, their filenames use the extension *.xsd*. Because they are standard XML files, though, they could also use *.xml*. Parsers load them exactly as they might another XML document.

   Schemas are referenced in XML documents using namespaces. Sometimes, a hint is given as to the exact location of the schema files to help the parsers locate and process them using a URI. For example, the following element references a schema called `mySchema`:

```
<my_schema:rootElement xmlns:my_schema="http://Schemas/MySchema">
```

   Because the URI in the `xmlns` attribute doesn't actually need to point to anything in particular, however, how would the parser find and load this schema? To help parsers locate the exact location of a schema document, a schema was developed by the W3C that offers a solution. To reference this schema, include the following namespace reference in your XML:

```
xmlns:xsi="http://www.w3.org/2000/10/XMLSchema-instance"
```

The exact location for this schema is **http://www.w3.org/2000/10/XMLSchema-instance.xsd**, though this Web site doesn't provide the actual definitions for the attributes. It does allow a schema to be assigned to a specific XML document, however. For example, assigning a schema to the previous example using `XMLSchema-instance` would contain the following hint:

```
< my_schema:rootElement
    xmlns:my_schema="http://Schemas/MySchema"
    xmlns:xsi="http://www.w3.org/2000/10/XMLSchema-instance"
    xsi:schemaLocation="http://Schemas/MySchema
                        http://MyServer.com/Schemas/MySchema.xsd">
```

This assumes, of course, that http://MyServer.com/Schemas is a viable URL that can be accessed by a parser.

The attribute `schemaLocation` is part of the `xsi` namespace. Its value actually contains two parts, which together tie the namespace reference used in the `xmlns` attribute (that is, `xmlns:mySchema="..."`) with the actual location of the schema document. Now, the parser can load the schema and validate the XML.

Examining Schemas

The first thing you notice about schemas is they look just like XML. The second thing is schemas are usually longer than a DTD; typically, schemas are longer because they contain more information.

Let's examine schemas by first looking at a sample XML document that describes errors in a system, as shown in Listing 3-1.

Listing 3-1   *Sample XML Document Containing a List of Application Errors*

```
<?xml version="1.0" encoding="UTF-8"?>
<errorList>
    <error severity="info">
        <number>-100</number>
        <message>The application failed to load the information.</message>
        <source>LoadBankAccount.asp</source>
```

```
    </error>
    <error severity="warning">
        <number>-1000</number>
        <message>The connection string does not appear to be valid.</message>
        <source>Bank.dll</source>
        <module>C:\Project\Account.cpp</module>
        <lineNumber>3456</lineNumber>
    </error>
    <error severity="critical">
        <number>54654</number>
        <message>A connection to the database failed.</message>
        <source>GenericDataServices.dll</source>
    </error>
    <error severity="fatal">
        <number>-1</number>
        <message>An unknown error occurred.</message>
        <source>LowLevel.dll</source>
        <module>C:\Project\LowLevelModule.cpp</module>
        <lineNumber>65</lineNumber>
    </error>
</errorList>
```

This example contains four errors and their respective information. Each `error` has a `severity` attribute. This attribute can take on one of four values: `info`, `warning`, `critical`, and `fatal`. Each `error` element also has three child elements: a `number`, a `message`, and a `source`. In addition, some `error` elements also have a `module` element and a `lineNumber` element, referring to the actual line and source file where the error was generated. All of this is contained within the `errorList` document element.

Therefore, we need something that provides this structure, defines the sequences of the elements along with their cardinalities, and defines possible values for the attribute `severity`. The schema shown in Listing 3-2 provides all the information needed to validate the XML in Listing 3-1:

Listing 3-2   *Sample XML Schema for Lists of Errors*

```
<?xml version="1.0" encoding="UTF-8"?>
<xsd:schema xmlns:xsd=http://www.w3.org/2000/10/XMLSchema
            elementFormDefault="qualified"
            targetNamespace="ErrorList.xsd"
            xmlns:erl="ErrorList.xsd">
    <xsd:element name="errorList">
        <xsd:complexType>
            <xsd:sequence>
```

```
                    <xsd:element name="error" type="erl:errorType" maxOccurs="unbounded"/>
                </xsd:sequence>
            </xsd:complexType>
        </xsd:element>
        <xsd:complexType name="errorType">
            <xsd:sequence>
                <xsd:element name="number" type="xsd:integer"/>
                <xsd:element name="message" type="xsd:string"/>
                <xsd:element name="source" type="xsd:string"/>
                <xsd:element name="module" type="xsd:string" minOccurs="0"/>
                <xsd:element name="lineNumber" type="xsd:integer" minOccurs="0"/>
            </xsd:sequence>
            <xsd:attribute name="severity" use="required">
                <xsd:simpleType>
                    <xsd:restriction base="xsd:NMTOKEN">
                        <xsd:enumeration value="critical"/>
                        <xsd:enumeration value="fatal"/>
                        <xsd:enumeration value="info"/>
                        <xsd:enumeration value="warning"/>
                    </xsd:restriction>
                </xsd:simpleType>
            </xsd:attribute>
        </xsd:complexType>
</xsd:schema>
```

XML Schema Preamble

Let's dissect the schema shown in Listing 3-2, starting at the top with the preamble. A *schema preamble* is found within the element, schema. All XML Schemas begin with the document element, schema. The first xmlns attribute is used to reference the namespace for the XML Schema specification; it defines all the elements used to write a schema. The second xmlns attribute declares the namespace for the schema we're creating, in this case, erl. Three letters is usually good for a namespace, but it can be longer. XML Schemas can independently require elements and attributes to be qualified. The elementFormDefault attribute specifies whether or not elements need to be qualified with a namespace prefix. The default value is "unqualified". This schema, like most schemas, assigns the value of "qualified", which means that all locally declared elements must be qualified. This attribute also allows schemas to be used as the default schema for an XML document without having to qualify its elements. The attribute attributeFormDefault specifies whether locally declared attributes must be qualified. Its default value is "unqualified". Because it is not specified in this schema, locally declared attributes do not need to be qualified with a namespace prefix. The targetNamespace attribute indicates the namespace and URI of the schema being defined.

NOTE

*The current version of .NET uses the xsd namespace: xmlns:xsd=***"http://www.w3.org/2001/XMLSchema.**

NOTE

The attribute `targetNamespace` *is important because it's used to indicate this schema belongs to the same vocabulary as other schemas that reference the same namespace. This is how large vocabularies can be built, stringing them together with the schema keyword* `include`. *Including and importing schemas are discussed later in this chapter.*

Complex Types

Note, the schema itself looks just like XML. This example defines a root element called `errorlist`. The child elements beneath the one declaring the element `errorList` define its children. Based on the declarations of the child element named `complexType`, `errorList` has only one child. The `complexType` element is used by schemas to define other elements. Here it uses the next element, `element`, to define the child for `errorList`. To summarize, the one child of `errorList` is defined by the information contained in the `complexType` and `element` elements. The `complexType` element relies on `element` to provide the specific information. The attributes of this final child of `errorList` identify the features of this complex element. In this case, it is named `error`. The attribute `minOccurs`, not used in this example, has a default value of 1. Together with the `maxOccurs` attribute, it defines the cardinality of this element as one to many. Note, the value "`unbounded`" indicates no limit exists to the number of occurrences of this element. The most important attribute is `type`, which indicates where the definition of the element can be found. This is defined by the element type, `errorType`, and is prefaced with the namespace we are creating, `erl`.

   The complex element `errorType`, referenced by the element `errorList`, is defined next using the element `complexType`. The definition for the complex `errorType` element begins with a sequence of elements as defined by the element `sequence`. The `sequence` element is used to define the specific ordering of the elements it contains, and it defines three basic child elements: `number`, `message`, and `source`. The element `number` is defined as an integer. The elements `message` and `source` are defined as strings.

   The next two child elements, `module` and `lineNumber`, have two additional attributes. As shown in this example, schemas can specify the number of occurrences of its elements and attributes. Using the `minOccurs` attribute, you can indicate the minimum number of times an element can occur—either 0, meaning the element is optional, or 1, meaning it must occur at least once. A value of 1 is the default. Using `maxOccurs`, you can specify the maximum number of times the element can occur—either a 1, meaning it can occur one time at the most, or `unbounded`, meaning no limit exists to the number of times it can be used. The default, again, is 1. Here, both the `module` and `lineNumber` elements are defined as occurring 0 to 1 time each; in other words, they are optional elements.

Finally, an attribute is defined for the `errorType` element. This attribute begins with the `attribute` element, which has two attributes: `name` and `use`. The `name` attribute names the attribute and the `use` attribute specifies it's required. The attribute `use` can be one of five values: `default`, `fixed`, `optional`, `prohibited`, and `required`. `Default` means a default value is supplied if the attribute is missing in the XML document. `Fixed` means a value is always supplied for this attribute. `Optional` means the attribute isn't required, but it doesn't supply a default value. `Prohibited` means the XML is invalid if this attribute is used within the XML document. And `required` means the XML document isn't valid unless this attribute is specified.

Simple Types

Following the attribute declaration element, the `simpleType` element defines a user-defined type based on the schema datatype, `NMTOKEN`. Simple types are used to extend existing datatypes. In this case, we're refining `NMTOKEN`, which restricts values to valid XML names. As defined in Chapter 2, XML names must begin with a letter or an underscore, followed by letters, digits underscores, hyphens, and periods. The name cannot contain whitespace. While an XML name can contain a colon, it isn't wise to use a colon because colons are reserved for use with namespaces.

NOTE

We discuss schema datatypes in more detail later in this chapter.

In this case, the `severity` attribute is a `NMTOKEN`, which is further restricted to a small set of permitted values. The `NMTOKEN` datatype is restricted to these four possibilities using the `restriction` element. This element has one attribute, `base`, which specifies the base datatype being restricted. Within this element are four `enumeration` elements that specify the only permitted values: `info`, `warning`, `critical`, and `fatal`.

Crafting Meaningful Schemas

This is the entire schema, but is this really what we want to say? For the most part, the answer is yes, but not completely. Certainly, the last two elements—`module` and `lineNumber`—are optional, as we conclude from examining the sample XML in

Listing 3-1. Yet the definition spelled out by this schema says explicitly both module and lineNumber are optional. This means either module or lineNumber could be missing from an error element and this schema would still pronounce the XML as valid and correct. Do we really want a line number without the corresponding source file? And would it really make sense to identify the source file without also identifying the line number where the error occurred? What we want is both module and lineNumber to be grouped together as an optional sequence. To put it another way, we want to have an error element that will always exist in one of two ways: either it has both the module and lineNumber elements or it has neither. If an error element contains a module element, it must, therefore, be followed by a lineNumber element. And, if you must have a lineNumber element, it must be preceded by a module element.

This can be accomplished by modifying the previous definition of errorType, so it looks the definition shown in Listing 3-3.

Listing 3-3   *New Definition of* errorType

```
<xsd:complexType name="errorType">
    <xsd:sequence>
        <xsd:element name="number" type="xsd:integer"/>
        <xsd:element name="message" type="xsd:string"/>
        <xsd:element name="source" type="xsd:string"/>
        <xsd:sequence minOccurs="0">
            <xsd:element name="module" type="xsd:string"/>
            <xsd:element name="lineNumber" type="xsd:integer"/>
        </xsd:sequence>
    </xsd:sequence>
    <xsd:attribute name="severity" use="required">
        <xsd:simpleType>
            <xsd:restriction base="xsd:NMTOKEN">
                <xsd:enumeration value="info"/>
                <xsd:enumeration value="warning"/>
                <xsd:enumeration value="critical"/>
                <xsd:enumeration value="fatal"/>
            </xsd:restriction>
        </xsd:simpleType>
    </xsd:attribute>
</xsd:complexType>
```

Inside the original sequence is another sequence element. This second sequence is defined as being optional according to the minOccurs and maxOccurs attributes. For this reason, neither the module nor lineNumber elements require these attributes anymore. They are still both defined as strings but, now, they must both either be included or excluded from an `error` element. The schema does not validate XML that has one without the other. In addition, just as with the other `sequence` element, they must occur in the specified order.

Datatypes

An important aspect to schemas is its support for datatypes. Elements and their attributes can be datatyped to create type-safety validation. Datatypes can be standard primitives or user-defined within the schema. Table 3-1 lists the built-in primitive datatypes defined by the XML Schema specification.

`Derived` types are defined by building on existing datatypes, refining either primitive or other derived datatypes. The W3C specification has provided several built-in derived datatypes. The datatype from which a derived type is constructed

Datatype	Explanation
binary	A finite sequence of binary octets.
Boolean	The set of values either true or false.
decimal	Represents an arbitrary precision decimal value, which consists of digits separated by a decimal point, for example, 3.1415926.
double	Standard mathematical representation of real values corresponding to IEEE double-precision, 64-bit floating point values (IEEE 754-1985).
float	Standard mathematical representation of real values corresponding to IEEE single-precision 32-bit floating point values (IEEE 754-1985).
RecurringDuration	A duration of time (see timeDuration) with some particular frequency with a specific origin.
String	A finite sequence of characters conforming to ISO 10646.
timeDuration	A period of time consisting of the year, month, day, hour, minute, and seconds.
UriReference	A reference to a Uniform Resource Identifier.
ENTITY	Used to insert text or data in an XML document. Refer to the XML 1.0 specification for ENTITY.
ID	Used to specify a unique value for an element. Refer to the XML 1.0 specification for the attribute type ID.
IDREF	Used to refer to an ID attribute. Refer to the XML 1.0 specification for the attribute type IDREF.
NOTATION	Define named formats for unparsed entities.
QName	XML qualified name used in namespaces.

Table 3-1   *W3C Schema Primitive Datatypes*

Datatype	Basetype	Explanation
Byte	Short	Restricts the short datatype by setting maxInclusive to 127 and minInclusive to –128.
Date	timePeriod	Standard representation of a day, beginning at midnight and lasting until midnight of the following day.
Int	long	Restricts the long datatype by setting maxInclusive to 2147483647 and minInclusive to –2147483648.
integer	decimal	A finite sequence of digits without a decimal remainder.
Long	integer	Restricts the integer datatype by setting maxInclusive to 9223372036854775807 and minInclusive to –9223372036854775807.
negativeInteger	nonPositiveInteger	Restricts nonPositiveInteger by setting the maxInclusive to –1.
nonNegativeInteger	integer	Restricts integer by setting the minInclusive to 0.
nonPositiveInteger	integer	Restricts the integer datatype by setting maxInclusive to 0.
positiveInteger	nonNegativeInteger	Restricts nonNegativeInteger by setting the minInclusive to 1.
short	int	Restricts the int datatype by setting maxInclusive to 32767 and minInclusive to –32768.
Time	recurringDuration	Represents an instant of time that recurs every day and is based on ISO 8601. Restricts the recurringDuration datatype by setting its duration facet to P0Y (that is, zero), and its period facet to P1D (one day).
timePeriod	recurringDuration	A specific period of time with a given start and end time based on ISO 8601. Restricts recurringDuration by setting its period facet to P0Y (no recurrence).
ENTITIES	string	Refers to the XML 1.0 specification for ENTITIES.
IDREFS	string	Refers to the XML 1.0 specification for the attribute type IDREFs.
NCNAME	Name	Refers to the XML 1.0 specification for the noncolonized name.

Table 3-2   *W3C Built-in Derived Datatypes*

is called the `basetype`. Table 3-2 is a list of some built-in derived datatypes defined by the XML Schema specification.

TIP

Facets *are constraints applied to datatypes or simple types that define their use.*

Refining Elements and Attributes

XML Schemas offer a rich language to compose both simple and complex types. Often, these types form the basis of new types, which are either more sophisticated or limit them in some way. This extensibility is important because it enables developers to reuse and expand on existing definitions, rather than having to reinvent the wheel each time. This is natural and familiar to developers because it follows an object-oriented approach to developing types, providing a sort of inheritance.

In reality, though, XML Schemas provide refinement rather than inheritance. New types can be created by basing them on existing types, and then either expanding them with new child elements and attributes or by restricting them with specific rules.

The Base Attribute

To specify that one type extends another, we use the `base` attribute. Essentially, this pulls in the entire definition of the specified type. Anything that follows, such as new elements and attributes, refine the basetype, creating a new, expanded type, as shown in Listing 3-4.

Listing 3-4 *MySchema* **Example**

```
<xsd:schema targetNamespace="mySchema"
        xmlns:xsd="http://www.w3.org/2000/10/XMLSchema"
        xmlns:mySchema="mySchema" elementFormDefault="qualified">
    <xsd:complexType name="personType">
        <xsd:sequence>
            <xsd:element name="lastName">
                <xsd:simpleType>
                    <xsd:restriction base="xsd:string">
                        <xsd:length value="35"/>
                    </xsd:restriction>
                </xsd:simpleType>
            </xsd:element>
```

```xml
                <xsd:element name="firstName">
                    <xsd:simpleType>
                        <xsd:restriction base="xsd:string">
                            <xsd:length value="35"/>
                        </xsd:restriction>
                    </xsd:simpleType>
                </xsd:element>
                <xsd:element name="middleInitial" minOccurs="0">
                    <xsd:simpleType>
                        <xsd:restriction base="xsd:string">
                            <xsd:length value="1"/>
                        </xsd:restriction>
                    </xsd:simpleType>
                </xsd:element>
            </xsd:sequence>
        </xsd:complexType>
        <xsd:complexType name="employeeType">
            <xsd:complexContent>
                <xsd:extension base="mySchema:personType">
                    <xsd:sequence>
                        <xsd:element name="ssn">
                            <xsd:simpleType name="ssnType">
                                <xsd:restriction base="xsd:string">
                                    <xsd:length value="9"/>
                                    <xsd:pattern value="[0-9]"/>
                                </xsd:restriction>
                            </xsd:simpleType>
                        </xsd:element>
                        <xsd:element name="birthDate" type="xsd:date"/>
                    </xsd:sequence>
                </xsd:extension>
            </xsd:complexContent>
        </xsd:complexType>
</xsd:schema>
```

This schema defines two types: first, `personType`, and then `employeeType`. Rather than having to specify that an employee has a first, middle, and last name, we extend the `personType` by referencing it in our definition of `employeeType`. Thus, an element of type `employeeType` has a first, middle, and last name, but it also has a social security number and birth date.

The Four Element Content Types

Elements can contain one of four types of content: elements only; character data only; mixed, containing both elements and character data; or empty. The element model employeeType contains elements only. When defining a new complexType that will contain elements only, we use the complexContent element. If we define a new complexType that will contain character data only and no elements, we use the simpleContent element. Both complexContent and simpleContent can extend or restrict a base type. When using either of these elements, if no base type is specified, it is implied that the anyType is used. When we want to specify that an element will be mixed, containing both elements and character data, we assign the complexType attribute mixed a value of "true". By default, this attribute is "false". Normally, this type of content is not used as it often creates confusion. Finally, to specify that an element is empty, we do not define any element children or character data for the new type. Defining a complexType without any simpleContent or complexContent is shorthand for creating a new type that restricts the anyType to no child elements or character data. Of course, empty elements may still have attributes; they simply have no content.

The extension Element

The definition of employeeType in Listing 3-4 contains the child element, extension. This element has a required attribute of base, which specifies the base datatype we are extending. In this case, we are extending the personType complex type. The employeeType extends the personType to include a social security number (declared and defined locally) and a birthdate.

The restriction Element

In the example in Listing 3-4, we extend the definition of personType, so we used the extension element. We could restrict our definition of employeeType to exclude the middle initial and, thus, we would have specified restriction. For example:

```
<xsd:complexType name="restrictedEmployeeType">
    <xsd:complexContent>
        <xsd:restriction base="mySchema:employeeType">
            <xsd:sequence>
                <xsd:element name="middleInitial" minOccurs="0" maxOccurs="0"/>
```

```
        </xsd:sequence>
      </xsd:restriction>
    </xsd:complexContent>
</xsd:complexType>
```

Table 3-3 examines the way cardinality of child elements can be restricted.

Complex types that specify `extension` add new elements to an existing simple or complex type. In Listing 3-4, the `employeeType` extends the `personType`, adding to the existing first, middle, and last name elements, a social security number, a birth date, and an address.

Simple Types

Because complex types exist, simple types must also exist. *Simple* types are used to derive new datatypes and they are either a list or a restriction of some existing datatype. If a simple type is defined as a `list`, then it contains a series of atomic datatypes separated by whitespace. For example:

```
<xsd:simpleType name="stringListType">
    <xsd:list itemType="xsd:string"/>
</xsd:simpleType>
<xsd:element name="stringList" type="mySchema:stringListType"/>
```

Base Occurrences {minOccurs, maxOccurs}	Restricted Occurrences {minOccurs, maxOccurs}	Description
{0, 1}	{0, 0}	Removes an optional child element.
{0, unbounded}	{0, 0} or {0, n}	Eliminates a child element or specifies an upper limit.
{1, n}	{1, n-a}	Lowers the upper limit for a child element.
{1, unbounded}	{n, unbounded}, {n, m}	Specifies new upper and lower bounds for a child element.
{1, 1}		Cannot modify a required child element.

Table 3-3 *Restricting Cardinality of Child Elements for Complex Types*

would allow the following:

```
<?xml version="1.0" encoding="UTF-8"?>
<stringList
    xmlns="mySchema"
    xmlns:xsi="http://www.w3.org/2000/10/XMLSchema-instance"
    xsi:schemaLocation="mySchema C:\…\MySchema.xsd">
    item 1
    item 2
    item 3
</stringList>
```

NOTE

Atomic datatypes *are defined as having indivisible values.*

If, on the other hand, a simple type is defined as a `restriction`, then it limits the atomic datatype in some way. For example, to define a datatype for social security numbers, we might want to define a simple type that is a string of nine characters containing only digits. Pulling from the schema in Listing 3-4, this can be done by refining the base string datatype, and would look like this:

```
<xsd:simpleType name="ssnType">
    <xsd:restriction base="xsd:string">
        <xsd:length value="9"/>
        <xsd:pattern value="[0-9]"/>
    </xsd:restriction>
</xsd:simpleType>
```

This defines a `ssnType` as a simple type. The pattern facet contains two parts. The first element, `length`, limits the length of the string to 9. The second element, `pattern`, assigns the acceptable pattern as "`[0-9]`", restricting the string to the characters zero through nine. Thus, the following wouldn't be valid:

```
<?xml version="1.0" encoding="UTF-8"?>
<employee
    xmlns="mySchema"
```

```
    xmlns:xsi=http://www.w3.org/2000/10/XMLSchema-instance
    xsi:schemaLocation="mySchema C:\MySchema.xsd">
    <lastName/>
    <firstName/>
    <ssn>123a56789</ssn>
    <birthDate/>
</employee>
```

But this XML would be valid

```
<?xml version="1.0" encoding="UTF-8"?>
<employee
    xmlns="mySchema"
    xmlns:xsi="http://www.w3.org/2000/10/XMLSchema-instance"
    xsi:schemaLocation="mySchema C:\MySchema.xsd">
    <lastName/>
    <firstName/>
    <ssn>123456789</ssn>
    <birthDate/>
</employee>
```

We could make this look more like a social security number by defining the simple type this way:

```
<xsd:simpleType name="ssnType" base="xsd:string" derivedBy="restriction">
    <xsd:pattern value="[0-9]{3}-[0-9]{2}-[0-9]{4}"/>
</xsd:simpleType>
```

This simple type `ssnType` is now defined as three digits followed by a dash, two more digits and another dash, and then four more digits. Now, according to this definition, the following XML snippet would be considered invalid:

```
<ssn>123456789</ssn>
```

However, this snippet would parse correctly:

```
<ssn>123-45-6789</ssn>
```

Importing and Including Schemas

As you saw in the preceding sections, schemas are quite reusable and extensible, allowing new datatypes, attributes, and elements to be built from existing ones. In fact, this is one of the basic tenets of schemas, providing developers the ability to inherit, or more accurately refine, existing structure and to expand on this structure.

When constructing large vocabularies, however, developing one schema file can become difficult. Earlier in this chapter, you learned how namespaces are often broken down into smaller, modular pieces to facilitate a more manageable vocabulary. In reality, this applies more to schemas than to namespaces, because the former actually defines the elements and attributes in a vocabulary, while the latter are nothing more than imaginary boundaries used by parsers to reconcile otherwise nonunique names.

Including Schemas

Namespaces can be a bit confusing but, hopefully, understanding how they're used with schemas should clarify them a bit. Originally, namespaces were merely a tool to help parsers reconcile elements and attributes. But, when applied to schemas, namespaces can be used to group parts of a vocabulary into one namespace.

This can be accomplished with the schema element `include`. For this to work, the `targetNamespace` attributes used in each schema file must be the same. Then, several files can be included together to form one large schema namespace. For example, a schema could exist that defines `addressType`, as shown in Listing 3-5.

Listing 3-5   *Schema Defining* `addressType` *and Saved as Address.xsd*

```
<?xml version="1.0" encoding="UTF-8"?>
<xsd:schema
    targetNamespace="Employees"
    xmlns:xsd="http://www.w3.org/2000/10/XMLSchema"
    xmlns:emp="Employees">
    <xsd:complexType name="addressType" content="elementOnly">
        <xsd:sequence>
            <xsd:element name="streetAddressLineOne">
                <xsd:simpleType base="xsd:string">
                    <xsd:minLength value="1"/>
                    <xsd:maxLength value="35"/>
```

```
            </xsd:simpleType>
        </xsd:element>
        <xsd:element name="streetAddressLineTwo" minOccurs="0">
            <xsd:simpleType base="xsd:string">
                <xsd:maxLength value="35"/>
            </xsd:simpleType>
        </xsd:element>
        <xsd:element name="city">
            <xsd:simpleType base="xsd:string">
                <xsd:minLength value="1"/>
                <xsd:maxLength value="30"/>
            </xsd:simpleType>
        </xsd:element>
        <xsd:element name="state" type="xsd:integer"/>
        <xsd:element name="zipCode">
            <xsd:simpleType base="xsd:string">
                <xsd:length value="10"/>
            </xsd:simpleType>
        </xsd:element>
        <xsd:element name="zipCodeExtension">
            <xsd:simpleType base="xsd:string">
                <xsd:length value="4"/>
            </xsd:simpleType>
        </xsd:element>
        <xsd:element name="homePhoneNumber">
            <xsd:simpleType base="xsd:string">
                <xsd:minLength value="10"/>
                <xsd:maxLength value="20"/>
            </xsd:simpleType>
        </xsd:element>
        <xsd:element name="workPhoneNumber">
            <xsd:simpleType base="xsd:string">
                <xsd:minLength value="10"/>
                <xsd:maxLength value="20"/>
            </xsd:simpleType>
        </xsd:element>
    </xsd:sequence>
  </xsd:complexType>
</xsd:schema>
```

Next, modifying the schema from Listing 3-6, we could create the `person` schema:

Listing 3-6   *Schema Defining* `personType` *and Saved as Person.xsd*

```
<?xml version="1.0" encoding="UTF-8"?>
<xsd:schema
    xmlns:xsd="http://www.w3.org/2000/10/XMLSchema"
    targetNamespace="Employees"
    xmlns:emp="Employees">
    <xsd:include schemaLocation="Address.xsd"/>
    <xsd:simpleType name="ssnType" base="xsd:string" derivedBy="restriction">
        <xsd:pattern value="[0-9]{3}-[0-9]{2}-[0-9]{4}"/>
    </xsd:simpleType>
    <xsd:complexType name="personType">
        <xsd:sequence>
            <xsd:element name="lastName">
                <xsd:simpleType base="xsd:string">
                    <xsd:minLength value="1"/>
                    <xsd:maxLength value="35"/>
                </xsd:simpleType>
            </xsd:element>
            <xsd:element name="firstName">
                <xsd:simpleType base="xsd:string">
                    <xsd:maxLength value="35"/>
                </xsd:simpleType>
            </xsd:element>
            <xsd:element name="middleInitial" minOccurs="0">
                <xsd:simpleType base="xsd:string">
                    <xsd:maxLength value="1"/>
                </xsd:simpleType>
            </xsd:element>
        </xsd:sequence>
    </xsd:complexType>
    <xsd:complexType name="employeeType" base="emp:personType" derivedBy="extension">
        <xsd:sequence>
            <xsd:element name="ssn" type="emp:ssnType"/>
            <xsd:element name="birthDate" type="xsd:date"/>
            <xsd:element name="address" type="emp:addressType"/>
```

```
        </xsd:sequence>
    </xsd:complexType>
</xsd:schema>
```

TIP

The default format for the primitive datatype date is yyyy-mm-dd.

The schema in Listing 3-6 is saved as Person.xsd. Note, the second line, immediately after the `schema` element, is the `include` statement, which must follow the schema preamble and any `import` statements. To explain this another way, following the schema preamble, a schema may have zero or more `import` statements, followed by zero or more `include` statements. The `include` element has a mandatory attribute called `schemaLocation`. The parser uses this value to load the desired schema file.

Note, in both the `address` and `person` schemas previously listed, they both specify `Employees` as their `targetNamespace` value. Also, the `xmlns` attribute for both is also the same and uses the same prefix of `emp`. This is important because when they are assembled into one final schema—employee, in this case—the namespace for the entire vocabulary must be consistent. And, when they reference other types in the schemas, they prefix those types with `emp`. Listing 3-7 shows the `employee` schema.

Listing 3-7   *Schema for the Document Element* `employee` *Saved as Employee.xsd*

```xml
<?xml version="1.0" encoding="UTF-8"?>
<xsd:schema
    xmlns:xsd="http://www.w3.org/2000/10/XMLSchema"
    targetNamespace="Employees" xmlns:emp="Employees">
    <xsd:include schemaLocation="Person.xsd"/>
    <xsd:element name="employee" type="emp:employeeType"/>
</xsd:schema>
```

The schema in Listing 3-7 is simple and concise. It specifies only one `include` statement and one element. This schema doesn't need to include `address` here because the `person` schema does this already. The schema would actually generate an error if it tried to include that schema again. The `employee` element is quite basic, defining itself as `employeeType`, as defined in the namespace `emp`.

One of the better XML IDEs is XMLSpy. Among its many features is its capability to generate an XML Schema from an XML document. XMLSpy can also do the reverse and generate a skeletal XML file from an existing schema. Using this latter feature with the `employee` schema, we have the following:

```xml
<?xml version="1.0" encoding="UTF-8"?>
<employee
    xmlns="Employees"
    xmlns:xsi="http://www.w3.org/2000/10/XMLSchema-instance"
    xsi:schemaLocation="Employees C:\…\Employee.xsd">
    <lastName/>
    <firstName/>
    <ssn/>
    <birthDate/>
    <address>
        <streetAddressLineOne/>
        <city/>
        <state/>
        <zipCode/>
        <zipCodeExtension/>
        <homePhoneNumber/>
        <workPhoneNumber/>
    </address>
</employee>
```

NOTE

*XML skeletons, such as the one previously listed can be generated using tools like XMLSpy, found at **http://www.xmlspy.com**.*

Importing Schemas

Like inclusion, importing schemas builds a vocabulary from other, smaller schemas. Unlike inclusion, importing schemas uses more than one namespace. To import a schema, the syntax is similar to the include statement, but with two subtle differences:

```xml
<xsd:schema
    xmlns:xsd="http://www.w3.org/2000/10/XMLSchema"
    targetNamespace="mySchema"
    xmlns:mySchema="mySchema"
```

```
xmlns:other="otherSchema">
<xsd:import
    namespace="otherSchema"
    schemaLocation="C:\..\OtherSchema.xsd"/>
```

In the schema preamble, you must add an `xmlns` attribute that specifies the namespace for the schema you are importing, along with its namespace prefix. In this example, the namespace is `otherSchema` and the prefix is `other`. The `import` statement specifies the namespace of the schema being imported and, optionally, the location of the schema file. The namespace in the `import` statement must match the namespace specified in the schema preamble.

Unlike inclusion, where everything is treated as being part of one large schema, only the global elements and type definitions may be referenced from imported schemas. Local and anonymous types are unavailable. The difference between local and anonymous types, and the global elements and types that can be referenced from imported schemas, is the latter are direct descendants of the `schema` element.

In Listing 3-4, the `personType` definition is an example of a global type that could be referenced if it were imported into another schema. The `lastName`, `firstName`, and `middleInitial` local definitions would be unavailable, however.

Summary

This chapter focused on namespaces and XML Schemas. Namespaces by themselves can seem a bit arbitrary, but when used to specify a schema, they become quite useful. The following items summarize this chapter:

▶ Namespaces provide a way to group elements and attributes into one vocabulary using a unique name.

▶ Using the `xmlns` attribute, a namespace prefix is bound to a unique namespace name.

▶ Qualified names are created when an element or attribute is prefixed with the namespace prefix. Using qualified names eliminates ambiguity for parsers trying to reconcile elements or attributes with identical names.

▶ A namespace is considered the default namespace when it doesn't have a namespace prefix.

▶ XML Schemas offer developers a rich language to describe and define the structure, cardinality, datatypes, and overall content of their XML documents.

▶ Complex types define the content for each element. They can be derived from other simple and complex types. The new complex type either restricts or extends the `basetype` it refines.

▶ Simple types define new datatypes. They can be derived from primitive or other derived datatypes. They either list or restrict the `basetype`. Lists specify a sequence of the `basetype`, while a restriction applies additional rules.

▶ Schemas can be included together to form complete vocabularies using one namespace.

▶ Schemas can also be imported into other namespaces building new vocabularies.

The Document Object Model (DOM)

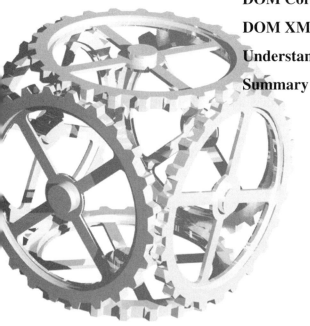

This chapter provides important information about the *Document Object Model* (*DOM*) that developers should understand to use the DOM effectively. Specifically, this chapter focuses on the DOM Level 2 Core and XML specifications as defined by a W3C Working Group. This isn't meant to be a complete reference and it doesn't describe all the attributes and methods. Instead, the focus is on providing information that describes how the interfaces fit together and how they're typically implemented.

One of the main features of this chapter is UML class diagrams, which show how interfaces in the Core and XML specifications are related. Some of the information shown by these diagrams helps explain why some attributes and operations with the same name have different implementations. In addition, developers who are familiar with the DOM may also be surprised by some of the information discussed in this chapter. For example, the MSXML parser hides the fact that an element cannot hold text or character data. In reality, elements contain Text nodes that actually hold the data and most processors hide this by extending the Element interface.

But this is only a sample of the information provided in this chapter. By understanding the DOM specifications, moving between different processor implementations is much easier. Also helpful is to understand the DOM when it comes to using processors that provide a rich set of extensions to the specifications. Developers who understand the structure and limitations can take better advantage of extended functionality. Future chapters in this book also have examples that use both the MSXML parser and the .NET System.xml classes, which represent two different implementations of the DOM specification.

DOM Introduction

The DOM is an *application programming interface* (*API*) defined by the *World Wide Web Consortium* (*W3C*) for XML and HTML documents. The W3C represents over 400 organizations responsible for producing common interfaces and industry standards for the *World Wide Web* (*WWW*). As a result, the DOM is an interface specification designed to work with any programming language. What's important to understand is that when we discuss documents, we're referring to structured data, not to physical files. In other words, the XML and HTML documents managed by the DOM needn't exist in a file format. These documents could be nothing more than strings loaded into a buffer in memory. Later in this section, we take a closer look at the object model and how to use it, but first a little history.

The DOM actually started as a common specification for managing HTML documents using JavaScript or Java programs in a browser. In fact, *Dynamic HTML*

(*DHTML*) was actually the baseline used as a starting point when the DOM Working Group was first organized. The initial purpose of the DOM was to provide a common programmatic interface for browsers to manipulate HTML elements as objects. As different organizations became involved, though, there were other applications, such as HTML and XML editors, which would benefit from this programming model. As a result, the DOM became a specification for managing XML and HTML documents. Another important concept to understand is this is a recommended specification and it is up to different vendors—like Microsoft and Sun—to provide implementations of this specification.

The W3C Working group that produced the DOM specification was careful to stay language-neutral. Nothing in the specification defines how any of these interfaces should be implemented. This is left up to the developers. Another goal of the working group was to make sure these interfaces were extensible. They expect developers to extend the functionality of the interfaces to support language-specific implementation requirements. Moreover, an interesting concept to note is this model provides the capability to manage documents using a simplified approach where everything is a node, or an *object-oriented* (*OO*) approach with the use of high-level interfaces. This will make more sense when we get into the specification descriptions but, essentially, everything is a node, the DOM only allows for richer OO constructs.

DOM Modules

The current DOM specification is referred to as a Level 2 specification, which can be divided into 14 separate modules. This represents a much more complete specification than what was found in the DOM Level 1 specifications. Two different levels of conformance also exist with these specifications, which are DOM Level 2 and DOM Level 2 module. To conform to DOM Level 2 specifications, the Core module needs to be implemented. If modules are implemented independent of the Core module, then they don't conform to DOM Level 2 specifications. This may be a little confusing, but the main point is the specification allows modules to be implemented independently. The following list shows all 14 modules found in the DOM Level 2 specification:

▶   Core

▶   XML

▶   HTML

▶   Views

▶   Style Sheets

- ► CSS
- ► CSS2
- ► Events
- ► User Interface Events
- ► Mouse Events
- ► Mutation Events
- ► HTML Events
- ► Range
- ► Traversal

The *Core interfaces* represent an object model for managing hierarchical structures, elements, and attributes. The XML module is limited to interfaces that used to be part of the DOM Level 1 Core extended interface specifications. Although we won't go into detail, it's interesting to note that the HTML interfaces extend Core functionality with HTML-specific operations while providing backward compatibility for DOM Level 0 implementations. DOM Level 0 implementations refer to functionality provided by Microsoft and Netscape for managing HTML documents. Because the primary focus of this book is XML, though, we only look at the interfaces defined in the DOM Level 2 Core and XML modules.

DOM Datatypes

Before getting into the DOM interfaces, we need to talk about datatypes defined as part of the specification. Only two types have been defined: DOMString and DOMTimeStamp. The DOMString was originally defined in the Level 1 specification using a typedef, which has been changed to a valuetype in Level 2. The DOMTimeStamp was introduced in the DOM Level 2 specification. Both of these datatypes are considered part of the Core module.

DOMString

As you know, one benefit of using XML and HTML documents is because they describe structured data by using human readable text, otherwise known as *strings*. The drawback is string definitions come in a wide range of sizes and types, depending on the language and platform. As a result, the W3C working group has defined a string type—called a DOMString—that supports international standards based on ISO-10646 definitions. Specifically, the character code set used is UCS-4 and the encoding type used is UTF-16. The actual definition of this string type is a sequence of 16-bit quantities, which can be described in IDL as follows:

```
valuetype sequence<unsigned short> DOMString;
```

This definition is used in the specifications, but it doesn't mean developers implementing the DOM interfaces need to provide a specific datatype called a `DOMString`. The only requirement is the actual datatype used to represent strings must confirm to the `DOMString` specification. In the Java Language bindings, this actually works out to a String object. In the *Standard Template Libraries* (*STL*), this would be a basic_string template that uses a w_char type. Finally, because case sensitivity between XML and HTML is inconsistent, any string comparisons are done on a character-code-by-character-code basis using 16-bit values.

DOMTimeStamp

This datatype was added for interoperability between different systems. The main purpose of the `DOMTimeStamp` is to define the size of a TimeStamp datatype using IDL specifications. The actual specification defines the `DOMTimeStamp` as follows:

```
typedef unsigned long long DOMTimeStamp
```

This shows a TimeStamp should be the size of a long. This may not be the same in all languages and platforms, but the IDL specification defines a *long* as holding 32 bits. For example, the ECMAScript language binds the `DOMTimeStamp` to a *date* type, which represents the same data size. As long as the language binding uses a datatype that holds 32-bit values, it will conform to specifications.

DOM Interface Specifications

The next three sections in this chapter focus on describing the DOM interface specifications for the Core and XML modules. This section provides detailed information on how the specifications are described. The next two sections provide in-depth information about interfaces in the Core and XML modules, respectively. Each of these sections starts with a diagram, which provides a high-level picture of the interfaces for the module being discussed. The diagram actually uses object-oriented modeling techniques to describe the interface relationships. Following the diagram, most of the interfaces in each module are described using a common interface language and plain text. The descriptions also contain implementation notes that provide helpful information for developers using these interfaces.

Modeling the Interface

Most references that describe DOM interfaces tend to focus on the interface definitions and not on the actual object model. They also describe how each of the interfaces interact with each other using text, but it's much more helpful to see a graphical representation. Within the past few years, the *Unified Modeling Language* (*UML*) has become a standard for object-oriented modeling. With UML models, we can describe the DOM interface relationships and the behavior of DOM objects with diagrams. This is powerful; a single diagram can be used to show a lot of information. In addition, diagrams are much easier to understand when describing these relationships and behavior. As a result, we use UML diagrams throughout this chapter and other chapters in this book. In addition, with the DOM interfaces in this chapter, we use static class diagrams because they provide a good static view of relationships between the different interfaces.

For the diagrams used in this chapter, the important UML notation to understand is the Generalization arrow. The *Generalization arrow* is an open arrowhead found on the end of lines connecting two interfaces together, which is used to indicate inheritance. The arrow points to the base interface that contains functionality a child interface is inheriting. The following illustration shows a base interface and a child interface that inherits functionality from the base interface:

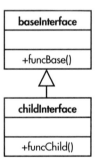

When looking at the two previous interfaces, you can see the Generalization arrow points to the baseInterface. In the previous example, the baseInterface has one method named funcBase and the childInterface has one method named funcChild. When the childInterface is actually instantiated, it exposes the funcBase method as one of its methods. In other words, the childInterface inherits functionality from the baseInterface. This means calling funcBase from an instance of childInterface is a valid operation. Remember, the child points to the base or parent using the Generalization arrow.

Describing the Interfaces

Even though we're using UML class diagrams, what's important to understand is the actual specification doesn't use classes or class diagrams at all. In fact, the actual specification only uses interface specifications, which are described using a common *Interface Definition Language* (*IDL*). The main goal of these specifications is to remain language- and implementation-neutral. In other words, they aren't imposing restrictions on how these interfaces are implemented. They could even be high-level wrappers around legacy applications that already manage XML and/or HTML documents. Also important to understand is that interfaces with attributes don't represent concrete objects with data. Instead, these attributes are typically implemented with `get()`/`set()` methods or a `get()` method for read-only attributes.

Instead of duplicating the W3C specifications here, the goal is to provide real-world information that can be used to work with DOM processors. Many different processors are available today. This isn't meant as a reference to specific implementations, although we do provide some implementation-specific information as an example of how different interfaces are actually used. The format used to describe each interface starts with a high-level description using plain-text and IDL definitions. Methods and/or attributes added or modified as part of the DOM Level 2 specification are shown using **bold** text in the IDL definitions. Any additional information about changes with DOM Level 2 will also be discussed. Following the description and definition, we look at implementation-specific details and implementation notes that provide useful information for developers.

DOM Core Module

Figure 4-1 is a static class diagram, which shows the DOM interfaces that are part of the Core specification. We look at the details of each interface later but, first, understanding the relationships helps, which is the reason for using a class diagram. What stands out first is that most of the classes inherit functionality from the Node class. In other words, most of the objects defined by the DOM have the same base functionality. Something else that stands out is both the document and element interfaces define a method with the same name—`getElementsByTagName`—that requires different implementations. When you understand the differences between

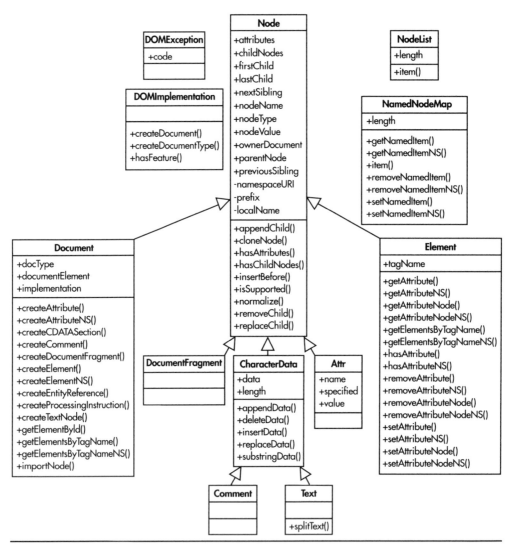

Figure 4-1   *Static class diagram—DOM Level 2 Core interfaces*

a document and an element, this makes sense. If you read the interface descriptions, however, this doesn't stand out as it does in a diagram. By now, you can see the power of diagrams, but we still need to use text when it comes to in-depth descriptions.

One of the biggest changes with the DOM Core interfaces is the support for XML namespaces. Chapter 5 provides much more detail on namespaces. For now, all you need to know is the DOM Level 2 specification supports namespaces. When looking through the diagram in Figure 4-1, along with the following descriptions, you see many of the methods have two implementations, such as getAttribute and getAttributeNS. The methods ending with NS are *namespace-aware* versions that should be used by namespace-aware applications. The other versions are referred to as *DOM Level 1 methods,* which support applications that aren't namespace-aware. In addition, according to the specifications, HTML-only implementations of the DOM aren't required to provide implementation of the namespace-aware methods.

NOTE

The use of newer namespace-aware methods and DOM Level 1 methods shouldn't be mixed in the same application.

DOMException

The main purpose of this interface is to provide a common object for handling exceptions. DOM exceptions should only be raised when circumstances prevent an operation from completing. As shown in the IDL definition in Listing 4-1, the DOM specification defines an interface with a single attribute. The definition also shows error constants defined outside the context of the DOMException interface. With the DOM Level 2 specification, five new error constants were also added.

Listing 4-1   *IDL Definition*

```
exception DOMException
{
  unsigned short    code;
};

// ExceptionCode
const unsigned short      INDEX_SIZE_ERR          = 1;
const unsigned short      DOMSTRING_SIZE_ERR      = 2;
const unsigned short      HIERARCHY_REQUEST_ERR   = 3;
const unsigned short      WRONG_DOCUMENT_ERR      = 4;
const unsigned short      INVALID_CHARACTER_ERR   = 5;
const unsigned short      NO_DATA_ALLOWED_ERR     = 6;
```

```
const unsigned short     NO_MODIFICATION_ALLOWED_ERR = 7;
const unsigned short     NOT_FOUND_ERR               = 8;
const unsigned short     NOT_SUPPORTED_ERR           = 9;
const unsigned short     INUSE_ATTRIBUTE_ERR         = 10;
const unsigned short     INVALID_STATE_ERR           = 11;
const unsigned short     SYNTAX_ERR                  = 12;
const unsigned short     INVALID_MODIFICATION_ERR    = 13;
const unsigned short     NAMESPACE_ERR               = 14;
const unsigned short     INVALID_ACCESS_ERR          = 15;
```

Implementation Notes

This interface was created to define exceptions that can be raised from various
methods and attributes in the DOM specification. When reading through the
actual W3C specifications, they identify methods and attributes that can raise
DOMExceptions. The actual implementation of this can vary a lot depending on
the platform. Some languages or platforms don't support the capability to raise an
error during execution. As a result, some implementations may return error codes
and others may use a separate interface that needs to be checked for errors. This
behavior is supported by the specification because the W3C committee realized
not all platforms or implementations suport the capability to raise exceptions.

The *Microsoft XML* (*MSXML*) parser is an example of an implementation that
doesn't support the capability to raise errors during execution. Instead, a new
interface was defined—called the IXMLDOMParseError—that is available through
the owner document. This interface doesn't derive from the DOMException
interface, but it does provide an error code attribute along with other attributes that
provide detailed error information. This implementation requires developers to
check the `Document.parseError` attribute, a Microsoft extension, to see if
errors were in the last operation. As you can see, this implementation is completely
different and doesn't even use the DOMException interface.

DOMImplementation

The W3C specification describes this interface as an interface that *provides a
number of methods for performing operations that are independent of any particular
instance of the document object model.* Currently, the interface specification defines
three methods. Two of the methods were added with the DOM Level 2 specification,
as shown in Listing 4-2.

Listing 4-2   *IDL Definition*

```
interface DOMImplementation
{
  boolean         hasFeature(in DOMString feature, in DOMString version);
  Document        createDocument(in DOMString namespaceURI,
                                 in DOMString qualifiedName,
                                 in DocumentType doctype);
  DocumentType    createDocumentType(in DOMString qualifiedName,
                                     in DOMString publicId,
                                     in DOMString systemId);
};
```

DOM Level 2 Changes

Previously, the DOM specification didn't define any operations for creating documents. This was left up to the implementer. With the DOM Level 2 specification, however, two new methods were added to support the creation of documents and `DocumentTypes`. This should help clear up much of the confusion about creating DOM documents. With DOM Level 1, different processors had to add this functionality, which tended to be different from one implementation to another. For instance, the Microsoft processor defines a `DOMDocument` object that can be created, and then loaded with XML. Another processor defined factory objects used to create the documents. When moving between different implementations, this was confusing and it took time to determine how to create a DOM document.

Implementation Notes

The `hasFeature` method can be used to determine if a particular module, or feature, is supported along with the specification level or version. With the Level 2 specification, the features a user can check for are modules, such as XML and HTML, which were listed previously. To determine the level supported, a user can also pass the level number in as a version. For example, the Level 2 specification would be checked using 2.0 for the version number. The following line of code shows a call checking to make sure the implementation supports XML Level 2 functionality:

```
bHasFeature = xmlDocument.implementation.hasFeature( "XML", "2.0" );
```

In this example. we access the implementation attribute of a Document object, which we discuss later. For now, knowing this attribute will return an instance of a `DOMImplementation` object is sufficient. If the processor supports Level 2 Core specifications—XML support—then `bHasFeature` will be true; otherwise, it will be false. With the Level 2 specification, passing in 1.0 also returns a true result because it's backwards-compatable with Level 1.

Node

One way to look at the *Node* interface is to view it as a datatype that can represent any data in a DOM document. When you think about it, a DOM document is nothing more than blocks of text grouped together in a structured format using tags. When implemented, a Node object can represent anything contained with an XML or HTML document. A Node object also defines behavior that supports the capability to group nodes into structured documents. We discuss this in more detail but, first, let's look at the IDL definition of the Node interface shown in Listing 4-3.

Listing 4-3   *IDL Definition*

```
interface Node
{
   // NodeType Constants
   const unsigned short      ELEMENT_NODE                 = 1;
   const unsigned short      ATTRIBUTE_NODE               = 2;
   const unsigned short      TEXT_NODE                    = 3;
   const unsigned short      CDATA_SECTION_NODE           = 4;
   const unsigned short      ENTITY_REFERENCE_NODE        = 5;
   const unsigned short      ENTITY_NODE                  = 6;
   const unsigned short      PROCESSING_INSTRUCTION_NODE  = 7;
   const unsigned short      COMMENT_NODE                 = 8;
   const unsigned short      DOCUMENT_NODE                = 9;
   const unsigned short      DOCUMENT_TYPE_NODE           = 10;
   const unsigned short      DOCUMENT_FRAGMENT_NODE       = 11;
   const unsigned short      NOTATION_NODE                = 12;

   readonly attribute  NamedNodeMap      attributes;
   readonly attribute  NodeList          childNodes;
   readonly attribute  Node              firstChild;
   readonly attribute  Node              lastChild;
   readonly attribute  DOMString         localName;
   readonly attribute  Node              nextSibling;
   readonly attribute  DOMString         namespaceURI;
   readonly attribute  DOMString         nodeName;
```

```
readonly attribute  unsigned short      nodeType;
         attribute  DOMString           nodeValue;
readonly attribute  Document            ownerDocument;
readonly attribute  Node                parentNode;
         attribute  DOMString           prefix;
readonly attribute  Node                previousSibling;

Node                appendChild(in Node newChild);
Node                cloneNode(in boolean deep);
boolean             hasAttributes();
boolean             hasChildNodes();
Node                insertBefore(in Node newChild, in Node refChild);
boolean             isSupported(in DOMString feature,
                                in DOMString version);
void                normalize();
Node                removeChild(in Node oldChild);
Node                replaceChild(in Node newChild, in Node oldChild);
};
```

DOM Level 2 Changes

Most of the changes to this interface focused on providing support for XML namespaces. The localName—namespaceURI—and prefix attributes are only valid with ELEMENT_NODE and ATTRIBUTE_NODE types that weren't created with DOM Level 1 methods, such as createElement. Remember, the DOM Level 1 methods are methods that don't end with NS. Three new methods were also added: hasAttributes, isSupported, and normalize. The hasAttributes method provdes a quick check to see if a node has attributes, which is currently only valid for ELEMENT NODES. The isSupported method implements the same functionality as found in the DOMImplementation hasFeature method. The normalize method was moved from the Element interface to the Node interface. This method combines adjacent TEXT NODES and removes EMPTY TEXT NODES on the full depth of the subtree under the current node.

Node Type

As discussed previously, the Node interface can be thought of as a datatype that contains and manages XML or HTML data. The constants defined in this specification are used to define the type of data a node is managing. The data in these documents can be anything you would find in XML and HTML documents such as tags, text, comments, or attributes. Table 4-1 lists the constants used to identify the Node type with a description of the data and behavior each Node type represents.

Constant	Description
ELEMENT_NODE	Elements represent the tags used to define blocks of data in a document. Elements can contain other nodes and elements but don't contain the actual text identified by the tags. This is the main Node type that developers use when manipulating documents. The important thing to understand about elements is they represent the actual tags and not the data identified by tags. Many implementations add methods to get and set text on an element. Under the covers, however, these methods use a TEXT NODE that is appended to the element. Elements are also the only Node type that contains attributes. Element attributes are found inside the opening tag in the form of name/value pairs separated by spaces.
ATTRIBUTE_NODE	This node is used to store attribute data. ATTRIBUTE NODES are found in the NamedNodeMap associated with the attributes property of an ELEMENT NODE. They are actually considered properties of an element, but they aren't children of the element and, thus, aren't considered part of the document tree. Because these are stand-alone entities, the parent and sibling attributes are null. In addition, because XML supports the capability to store entity references in an attribute the ATTRIBUTE NODE type supports the capability to reference TEXT or ENTITY REFERENCE NODES as children.
TEXT_NODE	A TEXT NODE is used to contain the actual text or data found between the Element tags. Understanding that most of the other Node types cannot hold the actual data is important; this is done with a TEXT NODE. The TEXT NODE also represents the leaf in a tree, which means they don't have any children.
CDATA_SECTION_NODE	A CDATA SECTION NODE is found with XML documents only and represents a block of text wrapped with a special tag that tells processors not to process the data found within the tags.
ENTITY_REFERENCE_ NODE	This is a Node type found only in objects that manage XML documents. This node is used to handle references to ENTITY NODES. Some XML processors may expand the reference when parsing the document, which means an ENTITY REFERENCE NODE may never be used in some implementations.
ENTITY_NODE	This is also a Node type that is only found in objects that handle XML documents. ENTITY NODES are used to handle special characters. They can even be used to link multiple XML documents together.

Table 4-1   *Node Types*

Constant	Description
PROCESSING_ INSTRUCTION_NODE	Processing Instructions are used with XML documents to keep processor-specific information with the XML text. For example, the text, `<?xml version="1.0"?>`, used to identify XML documents, is an example of a *Processing Instruction (PI)* that uses the reserved target of "xml." The question mark at the beginning and end of the instruction identify this as a PI.
COMMENT_NODE	This Node type represents the contents of a comment found between the `<!--` and `-->` tags in XML or HTML documents.
DOCUMENT_NODE	This is the Root node for the entire XML or HTML document. When processing XML or HTML documents, the DOCUMENT NODE represents the initial interface developers use.
DOCUMENT_TYPE_NODE	This Node type is used to hold document information. Currently, the W3C specification uses this to manage entities associated with the document. Future specifications will expand this functionality.
DOCUMENT_FRAGMENT_ NODE	The DOCUMENT FRAGMENT NODE represents a lightweight version of a document, which means it doesn't implement the functionality found in a Document object. The DOCUMENT FRAGMENT NODE is typically used to manage smaller blocks of text in a document.
NOTATION_NODE	This is another Node type only found with XML, which is used to represent a notation declared in the *Document Type Definition (DTD)*.

Table 4-1   *Node Types* (continued)

Attribute Values

Some of the attributes found in a Node object have different values, depending on the Node type, as defined in Table 4-1. When reading through the Node type descriptions, it's obvious different Node types have different implementation requirements. Because of this, attributes like the value and name are dependant on the Node type. Table 4-2 lists the values for three of the Node attributes affected by the Node type.

When you look through Table 4-2, you can see some of the different attribute values, based on Node type, which were described in Table 4-1. The one attribute that stands out is "attributes," which is only valid for ELEMENT NODE types. Probably the most important information this table provides is the knowledge that the actual value associated with a node can be different from one type to another. In most cases,

	Attributes	**nodeName**	**nodeValue**
Element	NamedNodeMap	tagName	Null
Attribute	Null	Name of attribute	Value of attribute
Text	Null	#text	Content of text node
CDATASection	Null	#cdata-section	Content of CDATA section
EntityReference	Null	Name of entity referenced	Null
Entity	Null	Entity name	Null
ProcessingInstruction	Null	Target	Entire content excluding the target
Comment	Null	#comment	Content of the comment
Document	Null	#document	Null
DocumentType	Null	Document-type name	Null
DocumentFragment	Null	#document-fragment	Null
Notation	Null	Notation name	Null

Table 4-2   *Possible Values for Attributes, nodeName, and nodeValue*

the nodeValue returns null. This is confusing to developers when they first use the DOM interfaces. In fact, when most people start working with the DOM, they expect an element's value to contain the actual text associated with the element. As seen in Table 4-2, they would get a null instead. In all implementations, an ELEMENT NODE contains a TEXT NODE that has the actual text value, if text is available. By understanding this behavior, developers can use different processors without many problems.

Implementation Notes

The main behavior that must be implemented for Node objects is the capability to manage relationships between all the nodes in a document. As a result, methods and attributes defined in the specification support the capability to navigate among parents, siblings, and children. Methods are also defined for inserting, removing, and appending children associated with the node. The Node interface also defines a method that can be used to create copies or clones of the node.

If a particular implementation decides to use a flat model instead of an OO model for the design, then the Node interface could be used for access to all the data in a document. In this type of implementation, you could have a Node structure that contains the relationship information and a set of methods that perform all the required operations. When using OO techniques in a design, the DOM specification supports high-level interfaces that provide specalized versions of the Node interface. These interfaces define attributes and methods for specific Node types and provide an object-based way of handling document data.

NodeList

The NodeList interface defines minimum attributes and methods needed to support ordered collections. This is a lightweight specification with a single attribute and a single method defined for interacting with a collection. The specification in Listing 4-4 shows the attribute and method:

Listing 4-4   *IDL Definition*

```
interface NodeList
{
  readonly attribute  unsigned long        length;

  Node                item(in unsigned long index);
};
```

Implementation Notes

This specification doesn't impose any implementation restrictions, but it does require the collection to maintain the order of nodes as they're found in the document. Most implementors extend this interface with methods related to the actual platform or language for handling collections. This minimal specification only supports the capability to enumerate through a collection of nodes. One interesting note is the DOM does require NodeLists to contain "live" collections, which means any changes to the underlying document are immediately reflected in the NodeList.

This is another interface developers use extensivly when they work with most DOM implementations. Because most of the nodes can contain zero-to-many subnodes as children, the methods used to extract nodes return a NodeList instead of a single Node object. The getElementsByTagName() method, shown in the Element and Document interfaces of Figure 4-1, is an example that returns a NodeList. Some implementations do provide extensions that enable users to retrieve a single node by name but, in most cases, users get a NodeList that contains nodes.

Most implementations return a NodeList with a length of zero if a requested node isn't found.

An example of an implementation that extends the NodeList specification is the *MSXML parsor,* which adds two additional methods: `nextNode()` and `reset()`. The `nextNode` method allows for easy iteration through the NodeList by returning the next node in the list. The `reset` method resets the iterator for additional loops through the list. The MSXML parsor also includes an _IEnum interface that supports the capability to use a For Each loop to iterate through the NodeList. The following code listing shows how to get a NodeList and iterate through that list in Visual Basic using the MSXML parsor.

```
Dim xmlChild As MSXML2.IXMLDOMElement
Dim xmlNodeList As MSXML2.IXMLDOMNodeList

Set xmlNodeList = xmlDoc.getAttributesByTagName( "Address" )
For Each xmlChild In xmlNodeList
   ... perform operation on Child
Next
```

NamedNodeMap

The NamedNodeMap is another interface designed to handle collections of Node objects. This interface is independent of NodeLists, even though it provides the same attribute and method found in a NodeList. As shown in the IDL definition in Listing 4-5, this specification also includes support to access the nodes in a collection by name.

Listing 4-5   *IDL Definition*

```
interface NamedNodeMap
{
  readonly attribute  unsigned long        length;

  Node      getNamedItem(in DOMString name);
  Node      setNamedItem(in Node arg);
  Node      removeNamedItem(in DOMString name);
  Node      item(in unsigned long index);
};
```

Implementation Notes

The only implementation requirements are a user must be able to access Nodes by name and by index with no restrictions on ordering. This is different from a NodeList, which does require the order is maintained. Also, as with the NodeList, a NamedNodeMap must be implemented as a "live" collection.

The `nodeName` attribute of a node is used as the key value for the collection. If you're adding a node with the same name as a previous node in the collection, the new node replaces the old one and the old node is then returned from the method call. Nodes that use a special name, such as #text shown in Table 4-2, cannot be stored in this collection because the names aren't unique. This behavior is by design. The W3C working group felt using the node name was preferrable to using aliases, which are more difficult to manage. Typically, NamedNodeMaps are used to manage collections of attribute nodes, which allow access to attributes by name.

Element

The *Element* interface represents a specialized version of a Node object. Specifically, the Element interface is designed to provide extended functionality for nodes with a nodeType of ELEMENT NODE. This is the main interface most developers use when working with documents using the DOM interfaces. As mentioned previously, one of the most important concepts to understand about elements is they represent the tags used to wrap data, not the actual text data. However, most processor implementations add functions that provide easy access to the text data contained within an element. The IDL definition in Listing 4-6 shows how an element is derived from a node and provides element-specific functionality.

Listing 4-6   *IDL Definition*

```
interface Element : Node
{
  readonly attribute  DOMString              tagName;

  DOMString      getAttribute(in DOMString name);
  DOMString      getAttributeNS(in DOMString namespaceURI,
                              in DOMString localName);
  Attr           getAttributeNode(in DOMString name);
  Attr           getAttributeNodeNS(in DOMString namespaceURI,
                                in DOMString localName);
```

```
NodeList        getElementsByTagName(in DOMString name);
NodeList        getElementsByTagNameNS(in DOMString namespaceURI,
                                       in DOMString localName);
boolean         hasAttribute(in DOMString name);
boolean         hasAttributeNS(in DOMString namespaceURI,
                               in DOMString localName);
void            removeAttribute(in DOMString name);
void            removeAttributeNS(in DOMString namespaceURI,
                                  in DOMString localName)
Attr            removeAttributeNode(in Attr oldAttr);
void            setAttribute(in DOMString name, in DOMString value);
void            setAttributeNS(in DOMString namespaceURI,
                               in DOMString qualifiedName,
                               in DOMString value);
Attr            setAttributeNode(in Attr newAttr);
Attr            setAttributeNodeNS(in Attr newAttr);
};
```

DOM Level 2 Changes

The only new functionality added was the `hasAttributes` method, which provides a quick check to see if an attribute exists. The `normalize` method included in this interface has been moved to the Node interface. All other changes to this interface focused on the new XML namespace support.

Implementation Notes

Most of the methods added to extend the Node behavior are focused on providing attribute support. These methods are defined so developers can get direct access to attribute nodes or values without having to go through a NamedNodeMap, as they would when using the attributes property defined in the Node interface.

We discussed that some processors, such as MXSML, hide the fact that Text nodes exist. Specifically, the `IXMLDOMElement` object that extends the Element interface defines an attribute named text, which is used to set and get text from the element. The following code listing shows an example of using the text attribute to add data to an element.

```
Dim xmlElement As MSXML2.IXMLDOMElement
Set xmlChild = xmlDoc.createElement("Name")
xmlChild.text = "John Doe"
```

You can see, this is quite easy to use and makes sense, but it can also cause trouble. The first time developers use a processor that doesn't implement this, they can get frustrated trying to determine how to add data. The following code listing shows the same operation as the previous example with a Java processor that doesn't implement a text wrapper.

```
IXMLDOMElement xmlChild;
Text xmlText;
xmlChild = (IXMLDOMElement)xmlDoc.createElement("Name");
xmlText = (Text)xmlDoc.createTextNode("John Doe");
xmlChild.appendChild(xmlText);
xmlChild.normalize
```

You can see this takes more work and isn't as intuative to use. In addition, notice the use of `normalize` on the `xmlChild` element. As previously described, this makes sure any Text subnodes are combined or removed if empty. When `normalize` is done, all the data should exist in the first (and only) Text subnode. In addition, because the DOM allows for multiple Text nodes at the same level, this resolves issues where some processors only persist the first one found when writing to disk. For this reason, `normalize` should be called before persisting an XML document when Text nodes are added this way.

We also previously discussed that the DOM interfaces allow for a simplified programming model using a Node object exclusivly or more OO-based models using additional interfaces like the element. Because of this design goal, several attributes and methods are found throughout the DOM specification that may have overloaded or specalized behavior. Because element is derived from node, it would make sense that the node's `nodeName` attribute would represent the tag name—and it does. But the W3C group also added a `tagName` attribute to the Element interface. In reality, both attributes always refer to the same value for Element objects.

Another example is the `getElementsByTagName` method, which can be found in different interface specifications, which aren't directly related to each other. When looking back at the diagram in Figure 4-1, you can see `getElementsByTagName` is declared in this interface and the Document interface. No direct relationship exists between these interfaces, however. They both extend the Node interface, but the Node interface doesn't declare this method. Instead, they represent completely different implementations that provide the same functionality and return the same result set. The only difference between implementations is the scope, which is limited to the element in this instance.

Document

The *Document* interface defines a specialized version of a Node object with a nodeType value of DOCUMENT NODE. As stated earlier, the document represents the Root node in a DOM document. In fact, many of the other Node types, such as element, text, and comment, must be created within the context of a document. What this means is these objects cannot exist unless they have an `ownerDocument` assigned. The main purpose of this extension is to provide definitions for creating the Node types that must have a document. The IDL definition in Listing 4-7 shows the extensions added to node functionality for document support.

Listing 4-7 *IDL Definition*

```
interface Document : Node
{
  readonly attribute  DocumentType        doctype;
  readonly attribute  DOMImplementation   implementation;
  readonly attribute  Element             documentElement;

  Attr                createAttribute(in DOMString name);
  Attr                createAttributeNS(in DOMString namespaceURI,
                                        in DOMString qualifiedName);
  Element             createElement(in DOMString tagName)
  Element             createElementNS(in DOMString namespaceURI,
                                      in DOMString qualifiedName);
  DocumentFragment    createDocumentFragment();
  Text                createTextNode(in DOMString data);
  Comment             createComment(in DOMString data);
  CDATASection        createCDATASection(in DOMString data)
  ProcessingInstruction  createProcessingInstruction(in DOMString target,
                                                      in DOMString data);
  EntityReference     createEntityReference(in DOMString name);
  Element             getElementById(in DOMString elementId);
  NodeList            getElementsByTagName(in DOMString tagname);
  NodeList            getElementsByTagNameNS(in DOMString namespaceURI,
                                             in DOMString localName);
  Node                importNode(in Node importedNode,
                                 in boolean deep);
};
```

DOM Level 2 Changes

Along with the namespace-specific versions of some methods, two additional methods were added to the Document specification: `getElementsById` and importNode. The `getElementById` returns an element with the ID passed in or null if the element doesn't exist. For this to work, an attribute must be defined as an ID attribute. The specification also doesn't support multiple elements with the same ID. The `importNode` method basically copies a node from one document into another. Specific rules define how this operation takes place, which are based on the type of node being imported. Before using this method, developers should review the DOM specifications to understand what happens with the imported node.

Implementation Notes

When implementing a method that manipulates a DOM document, the first object that must be created is the Document object. With DOM Level 1, the actual creation is vendor-specific; however, most implementations allow for the loading of physical files or string data. The MSXML parser also supports the capability to create an empty document, and then use the new Document object to create an element and assign it to the `documentElement` attribute. The Microsoft implementation defines this attribute as read/write, which is contrary to the specification previously shown. When assigning an element to the `documentElement` attribute, it's inserted into the Document's child list after any docType node. The following code listing shows how to create a DOM document using the Microsoft parser and the `documentElement` attribute:

```
Dim xmlDoc as New MSXML2.DOMDocument
xmlDoc.documentElement = xmlDoc.createElement( "Root" )
```

DOM Level 2 documents can be created using the DOMImplementation interface, which was discussed previously. Once a document has been created, the document is then used to create most of the other nodes to be inserted into the document.

One important concept to understand is most of the other Node types cannot exist independently of a Document object. They must be created within the context of a document. Because of this, the Document interface defines factory methods that can be used to create the other node types. When created, a node's `ownerDocument` attribute references the document that created it. If a node is removed from a document, its `ownerDocument` references the original document. When inserted into a new document, the `ownerDocument` is then reset to reference the new document. In addition, creating a node using the Document factory methods doesn't insert that node into the document. The node must be manually inserted using methods declared in the Node interface.

Most of the function definitions in this interface are geared toward creating these different types of Node objects that need a Document owner. The actual implementation of these methods creates specalized Node objects with the nodeType set to a value identified by the method name. For instance, the `createElement` method creates an Element object with the nodeType set to ELEMENT NODE. Note, these functions don't control the relationship of the nodes created. They only set the `ownerDocument`—the actual relationships are managed by the developer using Node interface methods to insert the new node.

Finally, this interface also defines the `getElementsByTagName` method independently from the Element interface where we saw it last. Remember, the interface specification shown in Figure 4-1 doesn't define this method in the Node interface, which means this method isn't related to the Element implementation. This is an example of the design paradigm that supports simplified and complex implementations. The behavior and results of this method are identical to the Element version. The only difference is this is designed to search the entire document.

DocumentFragment

The *DocumentFragment* is another node specialization with a nodeType value of DOCUMENT FRAGMENT NODE. Because a DocumentFragment is intended to act as a lightweight document, the interface doesn't define any additional methods or attributes. The IDL definition in Listing 4-8 shows an empty interface, which is derived from node.

Listing 4-8 *IDL Definition*

```
interface DocumentFragment : Node
{
};
```

Implementation Notes

The main purpose of this interface is to provide the capability to manage smaller subsections of a document as a block. An example implementation would include the process of pulling an Address element and all its children out of an XML document for an update. Once the Address element is updated, it can be inserted back into the main document with one method call. All the append/insert routines in the Node interface take a DocumentFragment and append/insert all the children and not the DOCUMENT FRAGMENT NODE. This is different from using an element to manage a block of data. When inserting an element into a document, the actual Element node, along with the children, is inserted.

The Document object could also provide the same functionality, but it represents a much more heavyweight object. No need occurs to instantiate an object with all the overhead a document has when only the Base node implementation is all we need. Finally, because this does allow for any type node at the root, it's possible to have DocumentFragments that aren't well formed. Adding a Text node as the only child of a DocumentFragment is an example of a document that isn't well formed. Because the actual Document interface doesn't allow this, it always creates well-formed XML.

Attr

The *Attr* interface defines a specialized version of a Node object with its nodeType set to ATTRIBUTE NODE. This interface is designed to manage attributes of an element. The IDL definition in Listing 4-9 shows only three attributes were added to support the extended functionality.

Listing 4-9   *IDL Definition*

```
interface Attr : Node
{
  readonly attribute  DOMString           name;
  readonly attribute  Element             ownerElement;
  readonly attribute  boolean             specified;
           attribute  DOMString           value;
};
```

DOM Level 2 Changes

The only change to this interface is the addition of a new attribute named ownerElement. This attribute returns the element that owns the attribute or it returns null if the attribute isn't used.

Implementation Notes

An Attr node is only used with elements, but they aren't directly related to Element objects. Instead, an element uses the attributes property of the Node interface to access a NamedNodeMap, which contains Attr objects. The Element interface does provide methods that can be used to interact directly with Attr nodes. Instead, the attributes property returns a NamedNodeMap. The MSXML parsor implementation extends the Element interface with methods that wrap the NamedNodeMap used to hold attributes. In other words, the MSXML parsor provides direct access to the attributes' NamedNodeMap.

When an attribute contains the default value that's defined in a DTD, the specified flag is then set to false. If the attribute contains a value from the original document or a user changes the value, then the specified flag is set to true. In all cases, the underlying implementation handles this flag. The only object attribute a user can modify is the value. In addition, because XML supports the capability to put entity references in an attribute, this node can also have children. These children can be TEXT or ENTITY REFERENCE NODES that contains entity references that aren't expanded.

CharacterData

The *CharacterData* interface extends the Node interface with methods and attributes for handling character data. This interface doesn't represent any of the valid DOM Node types, however. Instead, it's used as a base class for other Node types that need this functionality. Rather than define these methods and attributes in multiple interfaces, they are defined in this interface, and then inherited by other interfaces. The IDL definition in Listing 4-10 shows the attributes and methods defined by this interface.

Listing 4-10 *IDL Definition*

```
interface CharacterData : Node
{
          attribute DOMString            data;
  readonly attribute unsigned long       length;


  DOMString           substringData(in unsigned long offset,
                                    in unsigned long count);
  void                appendData(in DOMString arg)
  void                insertData(in unsigned long offset, in DOMString arg);
  void                deleteData(in unsigned long offset,
                                 in unsigned long count);
  void                replaceData(in unsigned long offset,
                                  in unsigned long count, in DOMString arg);
};
```

Implementation Notes

All the methods and attributes of this interface are designed to handle string data. The data attribute isn't allowed to have any length limits imposed by the implementation, however, the `DOMString` implementation may be unable to hold the entire data contents. If the data is too large for a `DOMString`, then the `substringData` method can be used to extract a range of data.

Be certain not to confuse this interface with the previously mentioned CDATASection. A CDATASection represents a valid DOM document type that contains character data, but it's implemented in a different interface named CDATASection. The CDATASection is one of the extended interfaces that's only found in XML documents.

Text

The *Text* interface defines a specialized version of a Node object with its nodeType set to TEXT NODE. This interface doesn't derive directly from the Node interface; instead, it extends CharacterData, which extends node. The main purpose of this interface is to handle the actual text—called character data in XML—of an Element or Attribute object. The IDL definition in Listing 4-11 shows one additional method that was added to handle character data.

Listing 4-11   *IDL Definition*

```
interface Text : CharacterData
{
  Text        splitText(in unsigned long offset);
};
```

Implementation Notes

When a document is first created, normally only one TEXT_NODE exists for each element that has character data. However, it's possible to add Text nodes or to split the TEXT NODE using the `splitText` method. If we do have multiple Text nodes associated with a single element, then it's possible only the first Text node will actually be persisted across editing sessions. The Node interface defines a method named `normalize`, which can be used to combine multiple Text nodes into a single Text node. The important thing to remember is this is the only Node type that holds the actual character data found in an XML document. The Element objects cannot hold or manage the character data associated with the element. Understanding this makes using the DOM much easier.

DOM XML Module

Figure 4-2 shows a UML static class diagram with all the XML interfaces shown. What should stand out is all these interfaces inherit functionality from the Node object, either directly or indirectly. In fact, all these interfaces just represent different Node types, described when the Node interface was discussed previously. Because all these Node types have already been described, we won't go into much more detail here. The main purpose of this section is to show how all the XML interfaces are related to the Node interface. The only interface that needs additional discussion is the DocumentType interface.

DocumentType

The *DocumentType* interface is used to manage a list of entities defined for a document. The Document interface, described previously, returns a `DocumentType` object from the `doctype` attribute. The only real functionality provided by this interface is the capability to list and look at entities and notations associated with the DTD for a document. Because unresolved issues still exist with DTDs and XML Schemas, DOM Level 2 doesn't support the capability to edit a `DocumentType`, as shown in Listing 4-12.

Listing 4-12   *IDL Definition*

```
interface DocumentType : Node {
  readonly attribute NamedNodeMap      entities;
  readonly attribute DOMString         internalSubset;
  readonly attribute DOMString         name;
  readonly attribute NamedNodeMap      notations;
  readonly attribute DOMString         publicId;
  readonly attribute DOMString         systemId;
}
```

Implementation Notes

Currently, a DOCUMENTTYPE NODE, otherwise known as the DTD node or DOCTYPE, can be created using the DOMImplementation interface methods. However, there is still no way to edit or modify a document's DTD. In addition, developers should be aware of the fact that when a DOCTYPE NODE is evaluated, any duplicate Entity references are discarded. Also interesting to note is the previously shown entities and notations attributes both return NamedNodeMaps

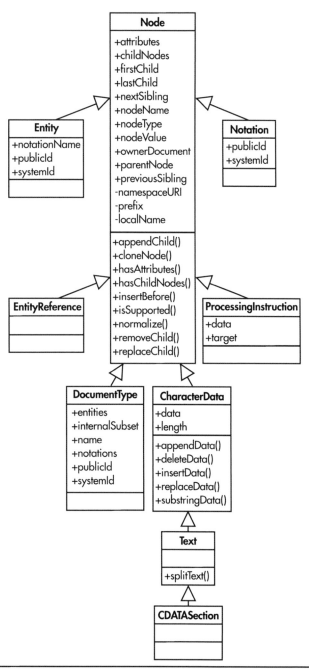

Figure 4-2   *Static class diagram—DOM Level 2 XML interfaces*

that contain ENTITY and NOTATION NODES. This allows for named access to the entities along with the capability to iterate over a collection of entities.

Understanding the Object Model

Now that we have a handle on the interface specification, it helps to understand how an object model is used to represent XML documents. XML itself is based on the *Standard Generalized Markup Language* (*SGML*), which has been around since 1986. Early programming interfaces designed to work with SGML were based on an abstract data model instead of an object model. With an abstract data model, programmers write methods or procedures to manipulate the data and produce the documents. This is a classic procedural-based approach, which is prone to errors when producing structured documents. With an object model, the data is encapsulated in objects and programmers use functions to manipulate the objects.

The reason procedural-based approaches are prone to errors is because developers are required to understand exactly how the DOM is structured. Typically, a procedural-based approach uses individual methods, or procedures, to perform functions such as opening and closing Element blocks, inserting PROCESSINGINSTRUCTION and DOCUMENTTYPE NODES in the correct place, adding a text node, and closing the main Document element. This means a developer needs to keep track of where they are in the hierarchy and to make sure they call the appropriate methods in exactly the right order. For instance, if a developer misses the method to close an opened Element block, that developer ends up with an invalid XML document.

By using objects, the data is protected, and the behavior of the objects define the structure, which means documents will always be structured correctly. With XML, the data contained in elements and the relationship between elements can be different from one document to another, but the actual structure of the elements never changes. In other words, the use of objects guarantees the elements will always have a closing tag. Specifications for the DOM object model also take this one step further and guarantee the documents will be well formed, but only if processors follow all specification rules. Independent of the DOM specification rules, several guidelines define a well-formed document, such as only one Root node is allowed and all nodes require an end tag. In reality, many of the processor implementations don't follow all the specification rules, which can result in documents that aren't well formed.

Before looking at the samples, we need to review the main relationships between objects that are instantiated using the DOM specifications. The Document object represents the entire XML document and provides the capability to create and access other objects. Element objects represent the tags only—they don't contain any of the text or character data. However, elements can contain any number of Child elements or TEXT_NODES. TEXT_NODES are the only objects that can hold text or character data for an element. A TEXT_NODE represents the leaf of a tree and doesn't support children.

The Contacts XML Document

To describe how objects are used to handle an XML document, we use a sample XML document that contains address information. Listing 4-13 shows an XML document named Contacts that contains an address book with two addresses. This is a sample of how the address data would be structured inside an XML document. Because this is only a sample document, we won't include a DTD, and the data in this document represents a minimum set. This is human-readable and organized in a way that groups the information into a hierarchical structure.

Listing 4-13 *XML Document*

```
<?xml version='1.0'?>
<AddressBook>
   <Address>
      <Name>Jane Doe</Name>
      <AddressLine>123 South Street</AddressLine>
      <AddressLine>Suite 400</AddressLine>
      <City>Anywhere</City>
      <State>US</State>
   </Address>
   <Address>
      <Name>John Hancock</Name>
      <AddressLine>321 North Street</AddressLine>
      <City>Anywhere</City>
      <State>US</State>
   </Address>
</AddressBook>
```

When you look at Listing 4-13, you can see the document contains a Root element named AddressBook, which contains two Address elements. The Address elements contain multiple elements to handle address data with two AddressLine elements in the first address and only one AddressLine element in the second address. This is representative of real addresses and supported well with XML documents.

If we were to write an application to handle the data shown in Figure 4-2, using abstract data methods, we would need to know how each of these Data elements is related. This could get pretty tricky with the `AddressLine` element. We would also have to write all the code to format the output, manage relationships, and manipulate the data in our application. This approach can be implemented with modular designs. While some would argue that a modular design would be simpler, in reality, this type of implementation is still procedural-based and prone to the same errors identified earlier. By using an OO approach, we wouldn't be responsible for writing code to manage the formatting and relationships. All of this is done by the objects.

The Contacts Object Model

Let's look at how we can take the data in Listing 4-13 and describe it using an OO approach. When using OO modeling techniques, you identify objects by using nouns that describe the concepts you are modeling. These concepts are captured and described during the analysis phase of an OO process. For this discussion, instead of using terms that are closer to real-world descriptions of an address, we describe this in terms of a document with elements and attributes. The reason for using these terms is to demonstrate how the structure in Listing 4-13 maps to the Document Object Model. With this in mind, the Contacts document shown in Listing 4-13 could have the following description:

> The Contacts XML is a document that contains address data. The address data is grouped into a hierarchical structure using identifiers or tags. These tags represent different elements of an address book, such as the book itself, addresses, and address attributes. The document itself contains one element. Some of the elements contain other elements, while some contain data only. All these elements along with the document have a name that's used for identification.

Now, if we continue with an OO analysis of this description, we can immediately identify two classes of objects: the document and element. Also obvious from the description, however, is that both a document and element have similar properties. They both have name attributes, and they both have relationships with other elements and with each other. This leads us to the conclusion that we can combine these common attributes into a base class with functionality that both the document and element classes can inherit. If we name this common base class a node, then we've described three of the objects found in the DOM.

The diagram in Figure 4-3 shows how the Contacts document would be described using an object model. As you can see, we have a Document object that contains a single `AddressBook` element. The `AddressBook` element contains several Address elements, which, in turn, contain `Name`, `AddressLine`, `City`, and `State` elements, and all of these contain TEXT NODES. The TEXT NODES in this example are all displayed with the actual text in bold. A definite parent/child/sibling relationship exists among all these objects. Some of the rules implemented with these objects aren't obvious when looking at the model, but they also define the relationships. For instance, an element can contain multiple elements and a Text node can only contain data. When generating the actual XML document, these rules and relationships guarantee that it will always be consistent and well formed.

By now, it should be obvious that the DOM is straightforward. In fact, the W3C working group that produced the specification was careful not to design a complex hierarchical object model. That may sound a little contradictive because we've been talking about how XML is used to describe hierarchical and structured data.

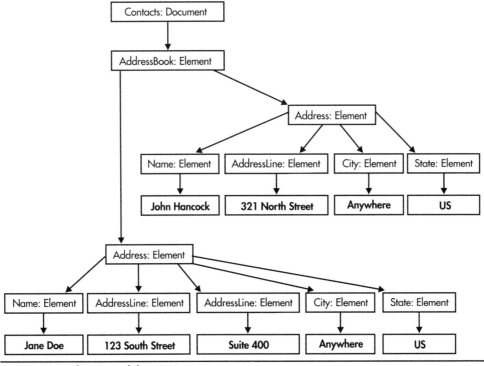

Figure 4-3   *Object model*

However, nothing in the object definitions requires hierarchical relationships, but they do support it. Instead, the document and all the elements are related to each other through the Node base class. The previously described Address Book could also be described with one element that contains all the address data in TEXT NODES. There are rules that define how the relationships can be formed, but nothing that forces a specific structure.

Summary

In this chapter, we've taken an in-depth look at the Document Object Model specifications defined by a W3C working group. This represents a common interface specification that can be used on multiple platforms and implemented in different programming languages. The main focus of this chapter was to provide information about the Level 2 Core specifications required for processing XML documents. Instead of describing all the attributes and methods included in the specification, there was a high-level description followed by implementation specifics. The goal was to provide information that developers can use when working with any DOM implementation.

One important concept we covered was that the first object created when working with DOM documents is the Document object. All other Node objects used hold the document data and must be created within the context of a Document object.

The following list summarizes this chapter:

▶ The DOM specification is language- and platform-neutral.

▶ One base interface called a *node* handles all the data in a DOM document.

▶ The Node object manages relationships between nodes based on the type of node.

▶ Attributes defined by the Node interface are dependent on the Node type.

▶ The Node object can be used exclusively for flat-model process-based implementations.

▶ The DOM specification provides several high-level interface specifications that derive from the node for object-oriented implementations.

▶ The DOCUMENT and DOCUMENTTYPE NODES are the only types that can be created independently.

▶ Most of the Node objects must be created within the context of a document.

▶ ELEMENT NODES only handle tag information and don't contain the actual text data.

- ► Elements are the only objects allowed to contain attribute information.

- ► Element attributes are stored in a NamedNodeMap and aren't directly related to the element.

- ► TEXT NODES, usually abstracted away by processor implementations, hold the actual text data.

- ► XML documents typically represent structured data with hierarchical relationships.

- ► The actual XML document is represented by a single DOM Document object. This object is also considered the Root node in a DOM implementation.

- ► The tags in an XML document map one-to-one with Element objects when loaded into a DOM processor.

Finally, there was a lot of information about the W3C specification, but we haven't even covered half the complete specification. We only looked at the interfaces found in the Core and XML modules. The Level 2 specification has 12 other modules. In addition, the specification covers other topics, like language bindings for Java and ECMA script languages, along with IDL definitions, production notes, and a glossary. The following URLs can be used to access the current DOM specifications:

```
http://www.w3.org/TR/DOM-Level-2-Core
http://www.w3.org/TR
```

The first URL references the Level 2 specifications. The second URL references the main page for W3C Technical Reports and Publications.

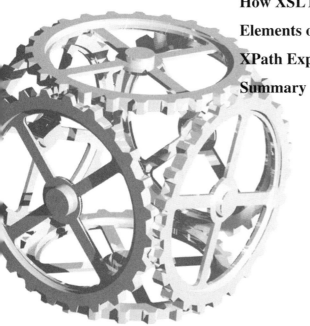

I n Chapter 2, we described XML as a metamarkup language. By itself, XML is fairly simple; it does nothing. But, in the last couple of chapters, we saw how parsers, *XML Schemas,* and the *Document Object Model* (*DOM*) offer tremendous functionality. You can use XML Schemas to add structure to your data, and then publish them for others to consume. You can use the DOM from within your applications to access and modify your XML. This chapter focuses on XSLT, which you can use to transform XML and produce output that can be displayed on the Web.

XSLT stands for *eXtensible Stylesheet Language Transformations.* The W3C describes XSLT as "a language for transforming XML documents into other XML documents." But XSLT can do more than that. Perhaps a better definition of XSLT requires a more generic slant: XSLT can transform the content and structure of an XML document into some other form.

While general and broad, this description hints at the power of XSLT. Another way to describe XSLT is to use an analogy: XSLT is to XML like SQL is to a database. Just as SQL can query and modify data, XSLT can query portions of an XML document and produce new content.

XSLT and XSL

XSLT is part of a much bigger family called *XSL* (*eXtensible Stylesheet Language*). XSL in its entirety represents two processes: tree transformation and formatting. XSLT focuses on tree transformation and can be used to process a source XML, producing a new XML document that can contain different nodes, different values, and different structures. The result tree, or *element and attribute tree,* may contain additional information like menus for Web applications. Or, the new tree could contain calculated values rather than the raw data. Or, maybe the tree has been reordered or filtered, creating a new, distinct tree.

The second process, formatting, is supported in XSL using the `fo` namespace, which stands for *formatting objects.* The `fo` namespace consists of elements and attributes to describe how the XML should be rendered. It's an extensive vocabulary that abstracts the process of displaying the content of the XML. The `fo` namespace provides the information necessary to present the XML, but leaves the actual rendering to the physical device. As described in Chapter 2, XML by itself separates content from presentation. The process of XSL formatting binds presentation to the XML content for specific rendering. This namespace is powerful, indeed, providing a rich language for producing high-quality output.

Saying that XSLT doesn't participate in the second process of XSL would be incorrect, however. On the contrary, XSLT can produce output that can be rendered.

One of the more popular uses of XSLT is to produce HTML so a source XML document can be viewed on the Web. XSLT can also produce plain text or even something as complex as a PDF file. Or, it can produce a document containing the formatting elements of the XSL `fo` namespace or other independent vocabulary, which can be used to render the XML directly.

But the `fo` namespace is more powerful than what is needed by standard browsers. This book is about building .NET Applications usable across the Web and, so, we focus on rendering XML as HTML. XSLT can accomplish this quite easily by itself or in conjunction with *Cascading Stylesheets* (*CSS* and *CSS2*). Thus, this chapter focuses on XSLT to produce HTML output.

XPath

When XSLT queries parts of an XML document, it makes use of another XML technology called *XPath*. XPath, like XML Schemas, the DOM, and XSLT, is a complex topic that could easily be the subject of an entire book. But, as we did with previous subject matters, we attempt to cover the essential details, providing a basis for the remaining chapters of this book. Therefore, we discuss XPath to the degree it's used by XSLT.

XPath was developed when the W3C realized significant overlap existed between the specification for selecting nodes using XSLT and the XPointer language. The W3C decided to create the XPath specification as the basis for both XSLT and XPointer.

The primary purpose of XPath is to select portions of an XML document using expressions to query for specific nodes within the document. But, it can also perform calculations, string manipulations, and evaluate expressions into boolean values.

How XSLT Works

XSLT documents are stored in stylesheets. The purpose of *stylesheets* is to transform XML. When a stylesheet transforms XML, a parser combines both the stylesheet and the XML to produce a new document. This document might be another XML document, or it could be HTML, or even plain text.

A good way to learn about XSLT is to jump in and look at some samples. Let's start with a simple one. The XML in Listing 5-1 contains information about the author Mark Twain and two of his book titles. The only new addition to this document is the Processing Instruction following the XML declaration. The Processing Instruction directs the parser to reference a stylesheet named

`Author.xsl`. The extension .xsl is standard for XSLT stylesheets. By including this instruction, however, the XML document won't parse correctly unless the parser can find and process the `Author.xsl` stylesheet.

Listing 5-1   *Simple XML Document*

```
<?xml version="1.0"?>
<?xml-stylesheet type="text/xsl" href="Author.xsl"?>
<author>
    <name>Mark Twain</name>
    <book>The Adventures of Huckleberry Finn</book>
    <book>Tom Sawyer</book>
</author>
```

Listing 5-2 contains the listing for the `Author.xsl` stylesheet.

Listing 5-2   *Simple XSLT Stylesheet*

```
<?xml version="1.0"?>
<xsl:stylesheet xmlns:xsl=" http://www.w3.org/1999/XSL/Transform">
    <xsl:template match="/">
        <html>
            <body>
                <xsl:apply-templates/>
            </body>
        </html>
    </xsl:template>
    <xsl:template match="author">
        <xsl:apply-templates/>
    </xsl:template>
    <xsl:template match="name">
        <H1>
            <xsl:value-of select="."/>
        </H1>
    </xsl:template>
    <xsl:template match="book">
        <li>
            <xsl:value-of select="."/>
        </li>
    </xsl:template>
</xsl:stylesheet>
```

Note how it looks just like XML, and it should. XSLT stylesheets are XML documents using the XSLT vocabulary.

When a parser transforms the XML in Listing 5-1, it loads the stylesheet in Listing 5-2 and produces the output in Listing 5-3.

Listing 5-3   *Stylesheet Output*

```
<html>
    <body>
        <H1>
            Mark Twain
        </H1>
        <li>The Adventures of Huckleberry Finn</li>
        <li>Tom Sawyer</li>
    </body>
</html>
```

Figure 5-1 shows the output viewed from a browser.

Let's examine the process the parser used to generate this output line-by-line. With both the XML document and the stylesheet loaded, it begins by examining the stylesheet. A stylesheet is composed of templates and each template tells the parser how to process XML. A template contains a pattern the parser uses to match against either the entire XML document or portions of the document. The parser applies the template to each portion of the XML that matches the pattern.

The stylesheet in Listing 5-2 begins with a standard template that almost all stylesheets use; it matches against the root of the XML document. The attribute `match` contains the value /. This is an XPath expression that says find the beginning of the XML document. In Listing 5-1, the beginning of the document is the first line

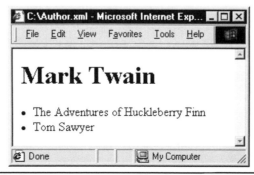

Figure 5-1   *Browser displaying XML processed by the stylesheet*

following the XML declaration. The parser applies the template, running through the XSLT statements it contains. The template begins by instructing the parser to emit several HTML tags. Note, because the default namespace is set to the HTML schema, these tags don't contain a namespace prefix.

NOTE

The XML declaration isn't a node and, thus, isn't accessible using XPath.

The output now contains an `<html>` tag followed by the `<body>` tag. The next line in the template is an XSLT `apply-templates` statement. When this statement appears without the `select` attribute specifying an element to match against, the parser tries to find the first template in the stylesheet that matches an element within the XML document, beginning with the current element or node. Because the parser is at the beginning of the XML document, it searches the XSLT for any templates that match against the children of the first line after the XML declaration. Because the `xml-stylesheet` Processing Instruction doesn't match any of the templates defined in the stylesheet, the parser skips over this line. Next, the parser comes to the third line of Listing 5-1, the root document element, `author`.

Here, the parser does find a template that matches and it begins to apply this template. This template contains `author` as its pattern and contains only one instruction: the `apply-templates` statement. This tells the parser to construct a list of nodes from the children of the `author` element. It processes these children by iterating through this list, applying the templates in the stylesheet that match against each node.

The parser finds a matching template for the first child element, `name`. It applies this template first by emitting an `<H1>` tag. Next, the parser encounters a `value-of` statement. This statement is equivalent to a `select` statement in SQL and tells the parser to pull out from the current node the value as specified in its `select` expression. Just like the `match` attribute for the `template` statement, the `select` attribute consists of an XPath expression. The simple expression "." refers to the value of the current element. Because the current element is `name`, the parser emits its content, `Mark Twain`. It follows this with a terminating `</H1>` tag and returns to the parent template.

The parser, having processed the `name` element and its associated template, moves to the next node in its list, the first `book` element. Once again, the parser finds a template that matches this element. The first instruction in this template is to emit the `<li>` HTML tag. Next, it contains a similar line to the one in the template for

the `name` element. The parser emits the contents of the current node, adding
`The Adventures of Huckleberry Finn` to the output. Finally, it adds
a terminating `</li>` tag.

This process is then repeated for the second `book` element. Another pair
of `<li>` and `</li>` tags are emitted, providing bookends for the second book
title, `Tom Sawyer`.

The entire list of children has now been processed for the `author` element and the
parser returns to the original template, continuing to process any remaining statements.
The parser emits a terminating `</body>` tag and finishes with the terminating
`</html>` tag. This is the end of the template and processing is complete.

The XSLT language is rich and powerful, therefore, no one right way exists
to create a particular stylesheet. We could get exactly the same result using the
stylesheet shown in Listing 5-4.

Listing 5-4   *Simple XSLT Stylesheet*

```
<?xml version="1.0"?>
<xsl:stylesheet
    xmlns:xsl="http://www.w3.org/1999/XSL/Transform"
    xmlns="http://www.w3.org/TR/html4"
    result-ns="">
    <xsl:template match="/">
        <html>
            <body>
                <H1>
                    <xsl:value-of select="author/name"/>
                </H1>
                <xsl:for-each select="author/book">
                    <li><xsl:value-of select="."/></li>
                </xsl:for-each>
            </body>
        </html>
    </xsl:template>
</xsl:stylesheet>
```

As you see in Listing 5-4, only one template is contained in this stylesheet.
The parser processes it much the same as it did the first stylesheet. Because there
are no `apply-template` instructions, it simply runs through each statement in
the template and stops.

The parser begins by emitting the three HTML tags: `<html>`, `<body>`, and `<H1>`. Then, it comes to a `value-of` statement with a different XPath expression than in the other stylesheet, `author/name`. For now, assume this means, "find the value of the `name` element that is the child of the `author` element." The / is used to provide a sense of hierarchy in XPath expressions: it finds a `name` element that matches this expression and emits Mark Twain. Then it adds the terminating `</H1>` tag to the output.

The next line in Listing 5-4 is the XSLT `for-each` statement. This is a standard looping command common to most programming languages, which instructs the parser to loop through all the element children matching against the value of the `select` attribute. In this case, the XPath expression specifies `author/book`, which means the parser loops through each `book` element that is the child of the `author` element. For each iteration through the loop, it emits a `<li>` tag, followed by the value of the node being processed, and a terminating `</li>` tag.

Once the loop iterates through all the `book` elements, it finishes by terminating the `<body>` and `<html>` tags, respectively. The parser has now applied this template in its entirety, and processing is complete. Despite the differences, both stylesheets yield exactly the same output.

Elements of Transformation

The XSLT language is an application of XML, which means it has its own well-defined vocabulary of elements and attributes. This section is devoted to defining the use of these elements and their attributes. `xsl` is the standard namespace prefix used for the XSLT namespace, so we also use it. And, while the elements are listed in alphabetical order, it's important to note the `stylesheet` element is the root element of the XSLT vocabulary and, thus, must be the first element in a stylesheet. In addition, all the child elements of the `stylesheet` element are referred to as *top-level* elements.

Not all the elements of XSLT are mentioned here. Instead, we focus on those elements used most often as a reference for examples later in this book. For a complete listing of the entire XSLT namespace, examine the specification at **http://www.w3.org/TR/xslt**.

xsl:apply-templates

The `apply-templates` element is used to apply a matching template, if one exists, to each child of the current node. Each child node is processed in turn, executing the appropriate template.

Attributes

Attribute	Usage	Value	Explanation
mode	Optional	QName	A name used to distinguish further which template to use for the list of nodes. A template must have a matching mode attribute to be considered for execution.
select	Optional	XPath expression	An expression used to select specific nodes. If omitted, all the children of the current node are selected.

NOTE

The datatype QName is a qualified name, which is either a simple NCName or an NCName with a namespace prefix.

Content

The `apply-templates` element may contain zero or more `sort` elements, and zero or more `with-param` elements.

Usage

The following snippet

```
<xsl:apply-templates select="//oranges">
    <xsl:sort select="price" data-type="number" order="ascending"/>
    <xsl:with-param name="nameOfFruit" select="string('Oranges')"/>
</xsl:apply-templates>
```

selects the list of nodes named `oranges`, and sorts the list based on the price child element in ascending order. For each node in the list, it passes to the matching template a value of `Oranges` to the template parameter `nameOfFruit`. Refer to the section of this chapter on the `template` element for a complete example.

xsl:attribute

The `attribute` element is used to add name/value attribute pairs to the output for the current element in the result tree. No other nodes can be added to this element in the result tree before these attribute nodes.

When XSLT is used to produce HTML output, this element is typically used to affect the values of style elements in the output. For example, the attribute element can display certain output text in different colors, depending on other values in the source XML document.

Attributes

Attribute	Usage	Value	Explanation
name	Mandatory	Qname	The name of the attribute to be generated by this statement.
namespace	Optional	URI	The namespace URI for the attribute being generated.

Content

The content of the `attribute` element contains the value of the attribute being generated. This value can be expressed simply as a textual value or by other XSLT elements that produce the value from the source XML.

Usage

For example, the following snippet of XSLT

```
<font>
    <xsl:attribute name="color">red</xsl:attribute>
    Hello World!
</font>
```

assigns the color red to the `<font>` element that surrounds the text `Hello World!`. The resulting HTML is

```
<font color="red">
    Hello World!
</font>
```

The value assigned by the attribute element can also be determined from the source XML. For example, the following snippet

```
<xsl:attribute name="color">
    <xsl:value-of select="textOutput/@desiredColor"/>
</xsl:attribute>
```

assigns the value of the `desiredColor` attribute of the `textOutput` element from the source XML to the `color` attribute of the `font` element, which is then emitted to the result tree. The `value-of` element, discussed later in this chapter, uses an XPath expression to select this value. The @ symbol identifies the node `desiredColor` as an attribute of the element `textOutput`. The / symbol is used by XPath to ascribe hierarchy to the expression.

xsl:call-template

The `call-template` element is used to invoke a named template, much like invoking a procedure call in a typical programming language like Microsoft Visual Basic and C++.

Attributes

Attribute	Usage	Value	Explanation
name	Mandatory	QName	The name of the template to be invoked.

Content

The content of the `call-template` element may contain zero or more `with-param` elements.

Usage

For example, the following snippet of XSLT

```
<xsl:call-template name="displayFruit">
    <xsl:with-param name="nameOfFruit" select="string('Apples')"/>
</xsl:call-template>
```

invokes the template named `displayFruit`, passing the parameter `nameOfFruit` a value of `Apples`. Refer to the section of this chapter on the `template` element for a complete example.

xsl:choose

The `choose` element is used to select different instructions for processing the source XML based on defined tests. This is similar to the `Select Case` statement in Microsoft Visual Basic and the `switch` statement in C/C++.

The choose element makes use of the when and otherwise XSLT elements to set up different execution paths based on results of predefined tests.

Attributes

This element doesn't have any attributes.

Content

The choose element may contain one or more when elements. And, optionally, it may contain one otherwise element, but it must be the last child.

Usage

Given the following source XML

```
<?xml version="1.0" encoding="UTF-8"?>
<?xml-stylesheet type="text/xsl" href="C:\Goldilocks.xsl"?>
<root>
    <porridge temperature="234"/>
    <porridge temperature="60"/>
    <porridge temperature="100"/>
</root>
```

the following stylesheet

```
<?xml version="1.0" encoding="UTF-8"?>
<xsl:stylesheet
    version="1.0"
    xmlns:xsl="http://www.w3.org/1999/XSL/Transform">
    <xsl:template match="/">
        <b>Porridge</b>
        <xsl:apply-templates/>
    </xsl:template>
    <xsl:template match="porridge">
        <p>Temperature <xsl:value-of select="@temperature"/>:
        <font>
        <xsl:choose>
            <xsl:when test="@temperature &gt; 150">
                <xsl:attribute name="color">red</xsl:attribute>
                Too Hot
            </xsl:when>
            <xsl:when test="@temperature &lt; 70">
                <xsl:attribute name="color">blue</xsl:attribute>
```

```
            Too Cold
        </xsl:when>
        <xsl:otherwise>
            <xsl:attribute name="color">green</xsl:attribute>
            Just Right
        </xsl:otherwise>
        </xsl:choose>
        </font>
        </p>
    </xsl:template>
</xsl:stylesheet>
```

produces the following HTML:

```
<b>Porridge</b>
<p>Temperature 234:
    <font color="red">Too Hot</font>
</p>
<p>Temperature 60:
    <font color="blue">Too Cold</font>
</p>
<p>Temperature 100:
    <font color="green">Just Right</font>
</p>
```

When you walk through this example, you see the template matching the `porridge` elements contains a `choose` element, which contains two `when` elements and an `otherwise` element. The two `when` elements test the value of the temperature attribute of the current node. If the value of the attribute is greater than `150`, then two instructions are executed: the `attribute` element assigns the `font` element's `color` attribute to a value of `red`, and the text `Too Hot` is written to the output. If the value is less than `70`, then the `font` element's `color` attribute is set to `blue`, and the text `Too Cold` is sent to the output. If the value doesn't fall into either category, then the `otherwise` element is executed, which sets the `font` element's `color` attribute to `green`, and emits the text `Just Right`.

xsl:decimal-format

The `decimal-format` element is a top-level element used to control the way the XPath `format-number()` function formats numbers into strings. This element neither affects the way the `number` and `value-of` elements format numbers for output nor the XPath `string()` function.

Attributes

Attribute	Usage	Value	Explanation
decimal-separator	Optional	character	Specifies the character used to separate the integral whole number from its fractional counterpart. The default is ".".
digit	Optional	character	Specifies the character used to indicate digits in the format pattern. The default is #.
grouping-separator	Optional	character	Specifies the character used to separate numbers exceeding thousands, millions, and so forth. The default is ,.
infinity	Optional	string	Specifies the string that represents a value of infinity. The default is Infinity.
minus-sign	Optional	character	Specifies the character used to indicate negative numbers. The default is -.
name	Optional	QName	Binds a name to this decimal format. If omitted, this format becomes the default.
NaN	Optional	string	Specifies the string used to represent a nonnumerical value, NaN, or "not-a-number." The default is NaN.
pattern-separator	Optional	character	Specifies the character used to separate the pattern used for positive values from the pattern used for negative numbers. The default is ;.
percent	Optional	character	Specifies the character used to represent the percent sign. The default is %.
per-mille	Optional	character	Specifies the character used to represent the per-mille sign or the sign used to represent the percentage of thousandths. The default is the Unicode character #x2030, ‰.
zero-digit	Optional	character	Specifies the character used in the format pattern to indicate leading zeroes. The default is 0.

Content

The `decimal-format` element is an empty element, containing no other content or child elements.

Usage

Here's an example of using this element in a stylesheet:

```
<xsl:decimal-format
    name="american-standard"
    decimal-separator="."
    grouping-separator=","/>
```

Later in the same stylesheet, the following line

```
<xsl:value-of
    select="format-number(345343.456, '#,##0.00', 'american-standard')"/>
```

would yield this output

```
345,346.46
```

while this line

```
<xsl:value-of
    select="format-number(3.456, '#,##0.00', 'american-standard')"/>
```

would yield this output

```
3.46
```

xsl:for-each

The `for-each` element provides looping functionality similar to the standard for-loops found in programming languages like Microsoft Visual Basic and C++. This instruction is often used when the source XML is highly consistent. When the source is not so coherent, the `template` element can be used as an alternative.

Attributes

Attribute	Usage	Value	Explanation
select	Mandatory	XPath Expression	Selects the set of nodes to be processed by the for-each element.

Content

The for-each element may contain zero or more sort elements, followed by output elements.

Usage

Here's an example of using this element in a stylesheet:

```
<xsl:for-each select="//oranges">
    <xsl:sort select="price" order="ascending" data-type="number"/>
    Price: <xsl:value-of select="price"/>
</xsl:for-each>
```

This sample generates a list of nodes containing all the oranges elements from the source XML. This list is sorted by the child element price. Then the parser iterates through each node in the list emitting the value of each price element.

xsl:if

The if element provides if-then functionality, similar to if-then clauses found in programming languages like Microsoft Visual Basic and C++. However, unlike these languages, XSLT doesn't provide an else clause.

Attributes

Attribute	Usage	Value	Explanation
Test	Mandatory	XPath Expression	Provides the Boolean expression to be tested.

Content

The if element may contain a set of output elements.

Usage

Here's an example of using this element in a stylesheet:

```
<font>
    <xsl:if test="porridge[@temperature > 150]">
        <xsl:attribute name="color">red</xsl:attribute>Too Hot
    </xsl:if>
</font>
```

This sample is similar to the example for the choose element but, unlike that example, there aren't any alternative paths. Either the expression proves to be true and the output is generated, or it's skipped altogether.

xsl:import

The `import` element is a top-level element that must come before any other children of the `stylesheet` element. It's used to import one stylesheet into another. However, the rules and definitions of the importing stylesheet take on a higher precedence than those of the stylesheet being imported.

Attributes

Attribute	Usage	Value	Explanation
href	Mandatory	URI	Contains the URI reference to the stylesheet being imported.

Content

The `decimal-format` element is an empty element, containing no other content or child elements.

Usage

```
<xsl:stylesheet
    version="1.0"
    xmlns:xsl="http://www.w3.org/1999/XSL/Transform">
    <xsl:import href="C:\…\AnotherStylesheet.xsl"/>
</xsl:stylesheet>
```

xsl:include

The `include` element is a top-level element used to include one stylesheet into another. Unlike the `import` element, the rules and definitions of the included stylesheet take on the same precedence as those of the including stylesheet.

Attributes

Attribute	Usage	Value	Explanation
href	Mandatory	URI	Contains the URI reference to the stylesheet being included.

Content

The `decimal-format` element is an empty element, containing no other content or child elements.

Usage

```
<xsl:stylesheet
    version="1.0"
    xmlns:xsl="http://www.w3.org/1999/XSL/Transform">
    <xsl:include href="C:\…\AnotherStylesheet.xsl"/>
</xsl:stylesheet>
```

xsl:otherwise

The `otherwise` element is used within a `choose` element, much like a final `else` or `default` statement in modern programming languages. If none of the test conditions in any of the other `when` elements are satisfied, then the instructions in the `otherwise` element are executed by default.

Attributes

The `otherwise` element has no attributes.

Content

This element may contain output elements.

Usage

Refer to the section of this chapter on the `choose` element for an example on how the `otherwise` element is used.

xsl:output

The `output` element is a top-level element used to control the format of the output generated by the stylesheet. This element is used during the second stage of processing, when the result tree from the first stage is written to an output stream or file.

Attributes

Attribute	Usage	Value	Explanation
cdata-section-elements	Optional	Whitespace separated list of QNames	Lists the elements whose textual content is to be output as CDATA sections.
doctype-public	Optional	string	Specifies the public identifier used in the document type declaration (if any) in the output.
doctype-system	Optional	string	Specifies the system identifier used in the document type declaration (if any) in the output.
encoding	Optional	string	Specifies the character encoding used to encode sequences of characters.
indent	Optional	"yes" | "no"	Determines whether the output should be indented to highlight its hierarchical structure.
media-type	Optional	string	Binds a media-type to the output, typically MIME.

Content

The `decimal-format` element is an empty element, containing no other content or child elements.

Usage

```
<xsl:output method="xml" version="1.0" encoding="UTF-8" indent="yes"/>
```

xsl:param

The `param` element can be used either as a top-level element to create a global parameter or within a `template` element to define a local parameter. If used as a child of a `template` element, then it must be the first child element.

Attributes

Attribute	Usage	Value	Explanation
name	Mandatory	QName	Assigns a name to the parameter.
select	Optional	XPath Expression	Assigns a default value for the parameter. When used within a `template`, the caller can assign a different value, overriding this default value.

Content

If the `select` attribute is supplied, this element is empty. Otherwise, this element may contain elements that define a default value for the parameter.

Usage

This snippet

```
<xsl:param name="nameOfFruit" select="NameOfFruit"/>
```

defines a parameter named `nameOfFruit` and provides a default value of `NameOfFruit`.

xsl:preserve-space

The `preserve-space` element is a top-level element used to control the way whitespace is handled (see `strip-space`).

Attributes

Attribute	Usage	Value	Explanation
elements	Mandatory	NameTest	Lists the elements whose whitespace-only text nodes are to be preserved during processing.

Content

The `decimal-format` element is an empty element, containing no other content or child elements.

Usage

This element instructs the parser to maintain whitespace-only text nodes occurring as children of the elements specified in the `elements` attribute. So, the following

```
<xsl:preserve-space elements="apples oranges"/>
```

preserves whitespace-only text nodes for the elements `apples` and `oranges`.

xsl:stylesheet

The root element for XSLT is `stylesheet`; therefore, it must be the first element of every XSLT document.

Attributes

Attribute	Usage	Value	Explanation
extension-element-prefixes	Optional	NCNames	Lists the namespaces used by this stylesheet that provide extension elements and extension functions.
exclude-result-prefixes	Optional	NCNames	Lists the namespaces not to be copied into the result tree.
id	Optional	Name	Used to identify a stylesheet so it can be referenced by another XML document.
version	Mandatory	Number	Identifies the version of XSLT used by the stylesheet.

Content

The stylesheet element can contain several types of child elements, referred to as *top-level* elements. Of these, we delve into the following elements:

Child Element	Description
attribute-set	Used to define a named set of attribute name/value pairs, which can be applied to an output element. Uses the attribute element to create the sets of attributes. Refer to the XSLT specification, section 7.1.4, for more information.
decimal-format	Specifies the characters and symbols used by the format-number() function to convert numbers into strings.
import	Used for importing other stylesheets.
include	Used for including other stylesheets.
key	Defines a named key for use with the XPath function key(), allowing a stylesheet to index nodes and their values. Refer to the XSLT specification, section 12.2, for more information.
namespace-alias	Aliases a namespace in the stylesheet, mapping it to another namespace used in the output. Refer to the XSLT specification, section 7.1.1, for more information.
output	Defines the output of the resulting file during the second stage of transformation.
param	Defines a global parameter (or local parameter when used inside the template element) in a stylesheet and assigns it a default value. This is different from the variable element because templates can be called passing in a value for the param element.
preserve-space	Defines the way whitespace is preserved in the result tree.
strip-space	Defines the way spaces are stripped out of the source XML.
template	Defines rules for producing output against some specified matching portion of the source XML.
variable	Defines a global variable (or local variable when used inside the template element) in a stylesheet and assigns it a value.

Usage

The following snippet

```
<xsl:stylesheet
    version="1.0"
    xmlns:xsl="http://www.w3.org/1999/XSL/Transform">
```

demonstrates the most common usage of this statement, specifying the version and the schema namespace for the XSL vocabulary.

xsl:template

The `template` element is a top-level element and is essential for any meaningful stylesheet. The `template` element is used to define how portions of an XML document should be transformed. Essentially, transformation begins with this element.

Attributes

Attribute	Usage	Value	Explanation
match	Optional	XPath Expression	Used to generate a list of nodes to be processed by this template. If this attribute isn't present, then there must be a `name` attribute.
mode	Optional	QName	The mode of the template. When `apply-templates` is used to process a list of nodes, only those templates with a matching mode are invoked.
Name	Optional	QName	The name of this template. If this attribute is missing, then a `match` attribute must exist.
Priority	Optional	Number	A number used to prioritize which template should be invoked when more than one template matches a given node.

Content

Child Element	Description
Param	When used within a template, defines a local parameter. Templates can be called passing in a value for the `param` element.

The rest of the content of the `template` element are the instructions for generating the result tree.

Usage

As an example, say you have an XML document that contains information about some fruit purchased recently. The document contains the type of fruit, its place of origin, where it was purchased, the quantity, and the price of the purchase. For example, the XML in Listing 5-5 is processed using the stylesheet shown in Listing 5-6:

Listing 5-5 *Apples and Oranges XML Document*

```
<?xml version="1.0" encoding="UTF-8"?>
<?xml-stylesheet type="text/xsl" href="C:\…\ApplesOranges.xsl"?>
<root>
    <apples>
        <origin>California</origin>
        <quantity>1000</quantity>
        <price>35</price>
    </apples>
    <oranges>
        <origin>California</origin>
        <quantity>2000</quantity>
        <price>22</price>
    </oranges>
    <oranges>
        <origin>Florida</origin>
        <quantity>1500</quantity>
        <price>21</price>
    </oranges>
    <apples>
        <origin>Florida</origin>
        <quantity>1200</quantity>
        <price>26</price>
    </apples>
</root>
```

Listing 5-6 *Apples and Oranges Stylesheet*

```
<?xml version="1.0" encoding="UTF-8"?>
<xsl:stylesheet
    version="1.0"
    xmlns:xsl="http://www.w3.org/1999/XSL/Transform">
    <xsl:template match="/">
        <html>
```

```
      <body>
      <xsl:apply-templates select="//apples">
          <xsl:sort select="price" data-type="number" order="ascending"/>
      </xsl:apply-templates>
      <xsl:apply-templates select="//oranges">
          <xsl:sort select="price" data-type="number" order="ascending"/>
      </xsl:apply-templates>
      </body>
      </html>
   </xsl:template>
   <xsl:template match="apples">
      <xsl:call-template name="displayFruit">
          <xsl:with-param name="nameOfFruit" select="string('Apples')"/>
      </xsl:call-template>
   </xsl:template>
   <xsl:template match="oranges">
      <xsl:call-template name="displayFruit">
          <xsl:with-param name="nameOfFruit" select="string('Oranges')"/>
      </xsl:call-template>
   </xsl:template>
   <xsl:template name="displayFruit">
      <xsl:param name="nameOfFruit" select="NameOfFruit"/>
          <p>
              <b><xsl:value-of select="$nameOfFruit"/>:</b>
              <ul><li>Origin: <xsl:value-of select="origin"/></li></ul>
              <ul><li>Quantity: <xsl:value-of select="quantity"/></li></ul>
              <ul><li>Price: <xsl:value-of select="price"/></li></ul>
          </p>
   </xsl:template>
</xsl:stylesheet>
```

The stylesheet in Listing 5-6 demonstrates the way many of the XSLT elements we have discussed can be used. The main purpose of this stylesheet is to group like fruit together, and then to sort them in ascending order by price. This is akin to the GROUP BY and ORDER BY statements in SQL.

As usual, the stylesheet begins with a template element that uses the pattern / to match against the first line of the XML document. The first instruction of this template is to apply any and all templates against the list of elements matching the name apples.

In addition, before the list of nodes is passed off to any matching templates, the list is sorted using the sort element. The select attribute indicates which element or attribute to sort on, in this case, the `price` element. The `data-type` attribute, with a value of `number`, instructs the parser that the value being sorted is a number. And the `order` attribute, set to `ascending`, says to sort in ascending order. So now, you've accomplished an `ORDER BY` SQL instruction. The sorted list is passed to any and all matching templates.

One template's `match` attribute contains the pattern `apples`. Therefore, this template is used for the entire sorted list. Despite how the XML document was organized, XSLT is clearly restructuring the result tree to have the list of elements named `apples` come first. Essentially, this is a `GROUP BY` statement with `apples` as the first token in the list.

The instructions inside this template call another template by the name of `displayFruit`, passing it a value of `Apples` for the parameter `nameOfFruit`. The `displayFruit` template now produces the actual output. It begins by emitting two HTML tags: `<p>` and `<b>`. Then, using the `value-of` element, it writes to the output the value of the parameter `nameOfFruit`, which, in this case is `Apples`. After terminating with a `</b>` tag, the template emits `<ul>` and `<li>` tags to create a bulleted, indented line of text, beginning with `Origin:`. It uses a `value-of` element to select the value of the `origin` child element of the current `apple` element. The template terminates the line with the `</li>` and `</ul>` tags. It does the same thing for the `quantity` and `price` child elements, using the `value-of` element to write their respective values to the output, bracketed them with the `<ul><li>` and `</li></ul>` HTML tags, and the text `Quantity:` and `Price:`. The template finishes with a terminating `</p>` tag. It does this for each `apples` element in the sorted list of nodes.

Once this template has run its course, it yields to the prior template, which has also completed all its instructions. So now focus is returned to the original template. There, the next instruction to be executed looks just like the first one, except it operates on all the `oranges` elements.

Again, the list of nodes is sorted by the `price` element, but this list is passed to the template with the `match` attribute set to `oranges`. This results in a result tree with the `oranges` elements grouped after the `apples` elements. Just as the template did for the `apples` elements, this template calls the `displayFruit` template, passing the `nameOfFruit` parameter a value of `Oranges`.

The `displayFruit` template executes just as it did before, but now on the list of `oranges` elements, which have been sorted in ascending order by `price`. First, it emits a `<p>` tag. Then the template surrounds the parameter value of `Oranges` with

<b> and </b> tags. And, then, it creates three bulleted, indented lines containing the values of the `origin`, `quantity`, and `price` elements, respectively.

Once the template has done this for each node in the list, execution is ultimately returned to the original template and processing is complete. This stylesheet produces the output in Listing 5-7:

Listing 5-7   *Apples and Oranges Output*

```
<html>
    <body>
        <p>
            <b>Apples:</b>
            <ul><li>Origin: Florida</li></ul>
            <ul><li>Quantity: 1200</li></ul>
            <ul><li>Price: 26</li></ul>
        </p>
        <p>
            <b>Apples:</b>
            <ul><li>Origin: California</li></ul>
            <ul><li>Quantity: 1000</li></ul>
            <ul><li>Price: 35</li></ul>
        </p>
        <p>
            <b>Oranges:</b>
            <ul><li>Origin: Florida</li></ul>
            <ul><li>Quantity: 1500</li></ul>
            <ul><li>Price: 21</li></ul>
        </p>
        <p>
            <b>Oranges:</b>
            <ul><li>Origin: California</li></ul>
            <ul><li>Quantity: 2000</li></ul>
            <ul><li>Price: 22</li></ul>
        </p>
    </body>
</html>
```

And Figure 5-2 shows how the HTML from Listing 5-7 is displayed in a browser.

Figure 5-2 *Browser view of apples and oranges*

xsl:value-of

The `value-of` element is used to send a value from the specified element or attribute to the result tree.

Attributes

Attribute	Usage	Value	Explanation
disable-output-escaping	Optional	"yes" | "no"	A value of yes instructs the parser to allow special characters such as < to be output rather than using the XML escape form <. The default value is no.
select	Mandatory	XPath Expression	Selects the value to be sent to the output.

Content

The element is always empty.

Usage

The following snippet

```
<xsl:value-of select="origin"/>
```

selects the value of the origin element for output.

xsl:variable

The variable element can be used either as a top-level element to create a global variable or within a template element to define a local variable.

Attributes

Attribute	Usage	Value	Explanation
name	Mandatory	QName	Assigns a name to the variable.
Select	Optional	XPath Expression	Assigns an initial value for the variable. If this is omitted, then the contents of this element define the value of the variable.

Content

If the `select` attribute is supplied, this element is empty. Otherwise, the contents of this element are used to define the value of the variable.

Usage

The following snippet

```
<xsl:variable name="anotherVariable">
    <xsl:value-of select="fruit/price"/>
</xsl:variable>
```

creates a variable named `anotherVariable`, and assigns it the value of the `price` element. The XPath expression used in the `select` attribute finds the value of the price element by examining the current element and selecting the first `fruit` child element. From there, it then finds the first `price` child element.

xsl:when

The `when` element is used within a `choose` element body to evaluate a particular condition. If the condition tests true, then the output instructions it contains are executed.

Attributes

Attribute	Usage	Value	Explanation
Test	Mandatory	XPath Expression	Defines the test expression that resolves to a Boolean value.

Content

The `when` element contains output elements.

Usage

Refer to the `choose` element for an example of how this element is used.

xsl:with-param

The `with-param` element is used within either the `apply-templates` or `call-template` element to set the value of local parameters used inside a template.

Attributes

Attribute	Usage	Value	Explanation
Name	Mandatory	QName	The name of the parameter that will be assigned a value.
Select	Optional	XPath Expression	Assigns the value for the parameter.

Content

If the `select` attribute is supplied, this element should be empty. Otherwise, the body contains the value to be assigned to the parameter.

Usage

The following snippet

```
<xsl:call-template name="displayFruit">
    <xsl:with-param name="nameOfFruit" select="string('Apples')"/>
</xsl:call-template>
```

calls the `displayFruit` template, first passing the template's `nameOfFruit` parameter a value of `Apples`.

XPath Expressions

In describing the XSLT elements, we used examples containing XPath expressions to select values for output, to calculate results, and to test conditions. XPath allows XSLT to navigate the source XML quickly using a string that describes the navigation path. It also provides functions that act on nodes to generate values or test whether a particular condition is true.

As with XSLT, an example is the best way to begin understanding how XPath expressions work within a stylesheet. The following XML is similar to the apples and oranges example in Listing 5-5 used to describe the `template` element. In Listing 5-8, though, the XML contains only `apples` elements:

Listing 5-8   *Just Apples XML Document*

```
<?xml version="1.0" encoding="UTF-8"?>
<?xml-stylesheet type="text/xsl" href="C:\…\JustApples.xsl"?>
<root>
```

```
    <apples>
        <origin>California</origin>
        <quantity>1000</quantity>
        <price>35</price>
    </apples>
    <apples>
        <origin>Florida</origin>
        <quantity>600</quantity>
        <price>24</price>
    </apples>
    <apples>
        <origin>Florida</origin>
        <quantity>1000</quantity>
        <price>30</price>
    </apples>
    <apples>
        <origin>California</origin>
        <quantity>400</quantity>
        <price>20</price>
    </apples>
    <apples>
        <origin>California</origin>
        <quantity>100</quantity>
        <price>28</price>
    </apples>
    <apples>
        <origin>Florida</origin>
        <quantity>1200</quantity>
        <price>26</price>
    </apples>
</root>
```

The stylesheet in Listing 5-9 operates on this XML, trying to calculate certain values for those `apples` elements originating from the same state:

Listing 5-9 *Just Apples Stylesheet*

```
<?xml version="1.0" encoding="UTF-8"?>
<xsl:stylesheet
```

```
    version="1.0"
    xmlns:xsl="http://www.w3.org/1999/XSL/Transform">
    <xsl:template match="/">
        <html>
        <body>
        <xsl:variable
            name="origins"
            select="//origin[not(. = preceding::origin)]"/>
        <xsl:for-each select="$origins">
            <xsl:variable
                name="sameOrigin"
                select="//apples[origin = current()]"/>
            <p>
                <b><xsl:value-of select="."/></b>
                <ul><li>
                    Quantity:
                    <xsl:value-of select="sum($sameOrigin/quantity)"/>
                </li></ul>
                <xsl:apply-templates select="$sameOrigin">
                    <xsl:sort select="price" order="ascending"/>
                </xsl:apply-templates>
            </p>
        </xsl:for-each>
        </body>
        </html>
    </xsl:template>
    <xsl:template match="apples">
        <xsl:if test="position() = last()">
            <ul><li>Max: <xsl:value-of select="current()/price"/></li></ul>
        </xsl:if>
        <xsl:if test="position() = 1">
            <ul><li>Min: <xsl:value-of select="current()/price"/></li></ul>
        </xsl:if>
    </xsl:template>
</xsl:stylesheet>
```

When the XML in Listing 5-8 is combined with the stylesheet in Listing 5-9, the HTML in Listing 5-10 is generated.

Listing 5-10   *Just Apples Output*

```
<html>
    <body>
        <p>
            <b>California</b>
            <ul><li>Quantity: 1500</li></ul>
            <ul><li>Min: 20</li></ul>
            <ul><li>Max: 35</li></ul>
        </p>
        <p>
            <b>Florida</b>
            <ul><li>Quantity: 2800</li></ul>
            <ul><li>Min: 24</li></ul>
            <ul><li>Max: 30</li></ul>
        </p>
    </body>
</html>
```

And Figure 5-3 shows how the HTML from Listing 5-10 is displayed in a browser.

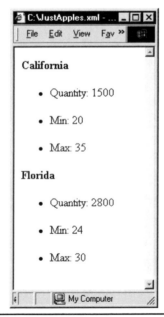

Figure 5-3   *Browser view of just apples*

Let's walk though this example, line by line. The stylesheet in Listing 5-9 begins, as usual, with a template that matches against the beginning of the source XML using the expression /. This special character, /, can be used in several ways to denote hierarchy within an XML document and to navigate up or down the XML node tree. Table 5-1 details several different ways it can be used.

NOTE

An axis is a direction of navigation through the XML tree from a starting point. This is discussed later in this chapter.

Back to the stylesheet in Listing 5-9, the first line in the template creates a variable named `origins`. It assigns this variable a value based on the XPath expression

Expression	Meaning
/	Matches the first node of the source XML, including any comments or Processing Instructions, excluding the XML declaration.
//apples	The `AbrreviatedAbsoluteLocationPath` expression, //, indicates the expression begins at the document root element. It selects all the `apples` elements in the document.
//apples[@type='red']	Finds all the `apples` elements in the document with an attribute named `type` having a value of `red`. The @ symbol is used to indicate the search continues along the attribute axis.
//oranges[origin='Florida']	Finds all the `oranges` elements in the document whose child element `origin` contains the value `Florida`.
.//origin	Selects all the `origin` elements that are children of the current node context.
//*/*	Selects all elements in the document that have an element as a parent. Basically, this selects all elements in the document, except those that are the immediate children of the root node. The * matches against any element.
//*	Selects all the elements in the document, including the root document element.

Table 5-1   *XPath Hierarchy*

`//origin[not(. = preceding::origin)]`. The part of this expression containing the instruction `preceding::` is used to search along the sibling axis, selecting all preceding siblings of the type `origin`. The `.` is used to select the value of the current `origin` element. The entire expression translates to: select all the `origin` elements in the document whose values do not equal any of the values of the preceding siblings. Essentially, it selects the set of all `origin` elements whose values are distinct. When applied against the XML in Listing 5-8, it selects the first `origin` element that contains the value of `California` and the first `origin` element that has a value of `Florida`.

The second line is a `for-each` element that loops through all the nodes in the variable `origins`. Note the use of `$` to indicate the value of the variable `origins`. In this example, the variable `origins` contains two `origin` nodes: one containing the value of `Florida` and one containing the value of `California`.

The first line in this loop creates a variable named `sameOrigin`. This variable is assigned all the `apples` elements in the document whose child element `origin` has the same value as the value of the current node. Because this is the first time through the loop, the value of the `origin` element is `California`. The net effect is that the `sameOrigin` variable is assigned all the `apples` elements in the document whose child element `origin` has a value of `California`. This is an excellent way to group elements together based on a particular value.

The next line emits a `<p>` tag followed by the value of the current node, which, in this case is `California`, bracketed by `<b>` and `</b>` tags.

Next, a sum is calculated and emitted, surrounded by `<ul><li>` and `</li></ul>` tags, respectively. The sum is generated by using the `sum()` XPath function. It adds together the values of all the `quantity` child elements in the `sameOrigin` variable. Because the `sameOrigin` variable contains only those `apples` elements whose `origin` value equals `California`, this emits the sum of all the apples originating in California. In this case, the value is `1500`.

The next instruction in the template is an `apply-templates` element. The `select` attribute is assigned the value of the `sameOrigin` variable, which is a list of `apples` elements. The template that matches against `apples` elements is then invoked. Because the `apply-templates` element contains a `sort` element, the list of `apples` elements is passed to this new template sorted by the `price` element in ascending order. This template contains two `if` elements; the same thing could also be achieved using the `choose` element. In any case, the first `if` element tests whether the current element is the last element in the list. The `position()` method returns the numeric position of the current node within the list of nodes passed to the template. The `last()` function essentially returns the number of nodes in this list. The first time through, this is obviously false.

The second `if` element tests whether the current node is the first element in the list by comparing the value returned by the `position()` method to the number 1. Of course, the first time through, this tests true, so the element's body is executed. The instructions contained with the element output the following: `<ul><li>` tags, the string `Min:`, the value of the current node's `price` element using the `current()` method to return the current node, and then, finally, the tags `</li></ul>`.

When this template processes the last node in the list, the first `if` element evaluates to true. At this point, the following output is generated: `<ul><li>` tags, the string `Max:`, the value of the current node's `price` element, again, using the `current()` method to return the current node, and then, finally, the terminating tags `</li></ul>`.

At this point, execution is returned to the calling template. It emits a terminating `</p>` tag, and then loops to the next element in the variable `origins` list of nodes. The second, and last, element in that list is the first `apples` element that was found containing an `origin` element with a value of `Florida`. The previous process is then repeated, generating a list of all the `apples` elements that originated in Florida. The sum of quantities is calculated, equaling `2800` in this case. And then, the minimum and maximum prices are determined for this list in the same manner as the list of `California` nodes. The final output appears as shown previously in Figure 5-3.

Expressions

XPath expressions provide XSLT with the power to select nodes based on particular criteria. For example, it offers a way to select only those nodes that satisfy certain constraints or test true against some comparison. The expressions are evaluated and a list of nodes is returned. If no nodes meet the criteria, then the list is empty.

Comparisons like equality, nonequality, less-than, and greater-than relationships are typical examples of expressions. Referencing other portions of the source tree is also possible. Table 5-1 showed some common examples of selecting specific branches using the `AbsoluteLocationPath` and `AbbreviatedAbsoluteLocationPath` expressions.

Another common expression is the `AbbreviatedStep` defined by two symbols: `.`—which evaluates to the current context node and `..`—which refers to the parent of the context node. For example, this line from the end of the stylesheet in Listing 5-9

```
<xsl:value-of select="current()/price"/>
```

could be written like this

```
<xsl:value-of select="./price"/>
```

and still yield exactly the same result.

Search Axes

In the example shown in Listing 5-9, some of the XPath expressions used a search axis to assemble the proper list of nodes. A *search axis* is a way of looking at the nodes in an XML tree in one specific direction. For example, the `ancestor` axis narrows the search to contain only the lineage of nodes from the document root down to the parent of the current node. It ignores all siblings, focusing instead on the parent node, the grandparent node, and so on all the way back to the beginning. For example, let's examine what happens when the XML document in Listing 5-11 is processed by the XSLT stylesheet in Listing 5-12.

Listing 5-11   *Ancestor.xml*

```
<?xml version="1.0" encoding="UTF-8"?>
<?xml-stylesheet type="text/xsl" href="C:\Ancestor.xsl"?>
<root>
    <streetAddress value="123 Main Street">
        <city value="San Francisco">
            <state value="CA">
                <zipCode value="12345">
                    <company>ACME Corp</company>
                </zipCode>
            </state>
        </city>
    </streetAddress>
</root>
```

Listing 5-12   *Ancestor Stylesheet*

```
<?xml version="1.0" encoding="UTF-8"?>
<xsl:stylesheet
    version="1.0"
    xmlns:xsl="http://www.w3.org/1999/XSL/Transform">
```

```
    <xsl:output
        method="xml" version="1.0" encoding="UTF-8" indent="yes"/>
    <xsl:template match="/">
    <html>
        <body>
            <xsl:apply-templates select="//company"/>
        </body>
    </html>
    </xsl:template>
    <xsl:template match="company">
        <h1><xsl:value-of select="//company"/></h1>
        <h2>Address:</h2>
        <h3>
            <xsl:apply-templates select="ancestor::*/@value"/>
        </h3>
    </xsl:template>
    <xsl:template match="@value">
        <xsl:value-of select="."/>
        <xsl:choose>
            <xsl:when test="position() &lt; (last() - 1)">, </xsl:when>
            <xsl:when test="position() &lt; last()">&#32;</xsl:when>
        </xsl:choose>
    </xsl:template>
</xsl:stylesheet>
```

Although the XML document in Listing 5-11 may not represent the ideal way to structure the data, it demonstrates how the `ancestor` axis operates. Applying the stylesheet to the XML in Listing 5-11 generates the following output:

```
<?xml version="1.0" encoding="UTF-8"?>
<html>
    <body>
        <h1>ACME Corp</h1>
        <h2>Address:</h2>
        <h3>123 Main Street, San Francisco, CA 12345</h3>
    </body>
</html>
```

As you can see, the `ancestor` axis generated a list of nodes from the top of the document down to the parent of the current node.

NOTE

An XPath axis operates on the XML nodes in the order they appear in the XML document, ignoring any sorting applied to the nodes. In other words, if a template employs an XPath axis, and the template's list of nodes was previously sorted by an `xsl:sort` *statement, the results may be different than expected, as the axis will ignore the sort order of the nodes and recognize their physical ordering instead.*

Table 5-2 lists some of the more common axes used in XPath. For a complete list, refer to the XPath specification, section 2.2, rule 6. The reference, "current context node," in the axis descriptions identifies the starting node for the search axis.

Axis	Meaning
`ancestor`	Compiles a list of nodes consisting of the parent node, the grandparent node, and so on up to the document root, ignoring siblings of any kind.
`ancestor-or-self`	This is the same as the `ancestor` axis, but also includes the current context node.
`@	attribute`	This returns the list of attributes for the context node.
`descendant`	Compiles a list of node children and their children of the original context node, recursively. The sequence of nodes is in the order they appear in the document.
`descendant-or-self`	This is the same as the `descendant` axis, but also includes the current context node.
`following`	Returns the list of nodes that appear after the current context node, excluding ancestors. It won't contain any attribute or namespace nodes (namespace nodes are those nodes prefixed by a namespace).
`following-sibling`	This axis returns the list of sibling nodes that come after the current context node, which have the same parent node as the context node.
`preceding`	Returns the list of nodes that appear before the current context node, excluding ancestors. The sequence of nodes is in reverse document order. It won't contain any attribute or namespace nodes.
`preceding-sibling`	Compiles a list of sibling nodes that come before the current context node and share the same parent node as the context node. They appear in reverse document order.

Table 5-2   *Common XPath Axes*

An axis is specified within an XPath expression by prefixing the node with the axis name and a double colon `: :`. The exception to this rule is the attribute axis. When using the abbreviated form of the attribute axis, `@`, the double-colon prefix isn't used.

Functions

Functions play an important role in XPath, providing the capability to convert strings to numbers and numbers to strings, and to calculate new values from existing values. Functions offer XSLT the processing power to transform the source XML content into something new.

For example, the `string()` function evaluates to a string representation of the given value. The function `number()` converts strings into numbers. And the `format-number()` function formats a number given a specific format. This format can further be defined using the `decimal-format` element described earlier in this chapter. The following use of the `format-number()` function

```
<xsl:value-of select="format-number(4567.89, '$#,##0.00')"/>
```

converts the given number into this:

```
$4,567.89
```

Other numeric functions, such as `sum()` and `count()` can calculate totals on a given node set. The `sum()` function adds up the values within the node set, while the `count()` function operates on a given list of nodes and returns the total number of nodes within the set.

More popular functions like `position()` and `last()` return numeric values about the current set of nodes within a particular context. The `position()` function returns the position of the current context node as it relates to the entire set of nodes. The `last()` function returns the numeric position of the last node in the list. Listing 5-9 uses these functions to determine if the current node the template is operating on is either the first node or the last node in the list.

Summary

This chapter has shown that XSLT is a rich programming language derived from XML and provides developers with the power to query portions of the source XML and transform it into a desired output form. XSLT has a number of elements defined in its schema to offer developers with all the tools to generate both new XML documents and dynamic presentation.

XSLT relies on XPath to query and modify portions of a source XML document. XPath uses expressions to select portions of the source XML tree. These expressions can include searches along specific axes. Each axis type prunes the source XML in a particular fashion so the transformation processes only select nodes in the tree. For example, the ancestor axis selects only those nodes that form the direct path from the root node of the document all the way down to the current node's parent—all siblings are ignored. The descendant axis, on the other hand, selects all the current node's children, and their children, and so on, recursively. In addition, XPath provides functions to perform calculations, conversions, and comparisons.

In most of the code examples used in this book, we use XSLT and XPath to generate HTML from XML for consumption by client browsers. This isn't the only purpose of XSLT by far, but it does make transforming pure data content into pure presentation content easy. For a complete reference on XSLT and XPath, read the specifications at the W3C Web site, **http://www.w3.org**.

Taking Advantage of Structured Data

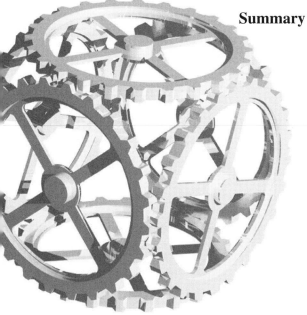

I n this chapter, we look at how developers can take advantage of structured XML data in their applications. We start by reviewing the definition of structure and applying it to two well-known types of data structure: relational and hierarchical. Next, an example component along with Web pages is developed to provide benchmark information. Specifically, we show performance differences between using ADO Recordsets or XML to pass data. During the development of this example, we use the C# language and show how .NET components can be exposed as COM+ configured components. This information should be useful to any developers who want to integrate legacy platforms with .NET using DCOM interfaces. The last section of this chapter examines stateless architectures and discusses how XML also provides a great benefit in this area of design.

Understanding Structured Data

The term "structure" has several different meanings but, in general, it describes how something is put together. When you talk about the structure of a building, you're talking about how that building was constructed. In software, the way different pieces of an application fit together can be considered a *structure.* Another way to approach this is to think of structure as a way to define how different elements are arranged in a composition. In a building, those elements are construction materials. In software applications, those elements can be binary files and objects. The concept of structure can be applied to many different things, including data. With regard to structured data, we're describing how different elements of data are put together to represent a grouping of information. Two common data structure terms developers are familiar with are *relational* and *hierarchical,* which represent different ways data can be arranged.

Seeing examples can help you to understand the differences between relational and hierarchical structure. In this chapter, we start building the foundation for managing and viewing employee contact information. The fictitious company in this example represents a consulting firm, but the structure can be applied to any type of business that has multiple projects and offices. The concepts discussed in this chapter come from real-world implementations and there's also some useful information about system design. Finally, to keep the scope within reasonable boundaries, we're only interested in phone numbers and the relationship among employees, managers, projects, and offices.

The following list describes business rules that must be considered when designing the database structure for our application:

- An Employee can be assigned to multiple projects.

- Projects can have multiple Employees assigned, but only one Project Manager.

- Each Employee is assigned to a single Office and Manager.

- The Employee's Manager isn't the same as the Project Manager.

- The Manager's office isn't required to be the same as the Employee's office.

- An Office can have more than one Manager.

- A single Manager can be associated with multiple Projects and Employees.

When examining these rules, it's apparent we need a many-to-many relationship between Employees and Projects. We also need a way to assign an Office and a Manager—independent of each other—to each Employee. These relationships are fairly complicated and best described in a database schema diagram. As a result, the first step in designing our application is to define a database schema, which represents the relational structures, as previously described. Next, we discuss different viewpoints of the data and describe ways to structure this data in a hierarchical structure. Once you have a good handle on the data, the rest of this chapter describes different ways to take advantage of XML's capability to handle structured data.

Relational Structure

Most developers today have been exposed to relational databases and the way data is typically arranged in these databases. *Relational data* represents a structure where different groups of data are associated with each other through a common link. In a database, the row in a table represents a group of data and the relationships are managed using primary and foreign keys. These tables and keys represent the actual structure of the data in a relational database. Figure 6-1 shows an *Entity Relationship* (*ER*) diagram that describes the data and relationships for our employee contact example. This diagram represents the way data is structured relationally and supports the business rules discussed previously.

As you can see, the diagram in Figure 6-1 shows several different types of relationships, such as one-to-one, one-to-many, and zero-to-many. The notation we use to describe these relationships is called *crow's foot*. The connection that looks like a crow's foot represents many and the single-line connection represents one. For instance, the relationship between Employee and Manager shows a one on the Employee side and a many on the Manager side. This represents a one-to-many relationship, where an employee can have many manager entries, but a manager can only have one employee entry. In other words, an employee can be a manager on

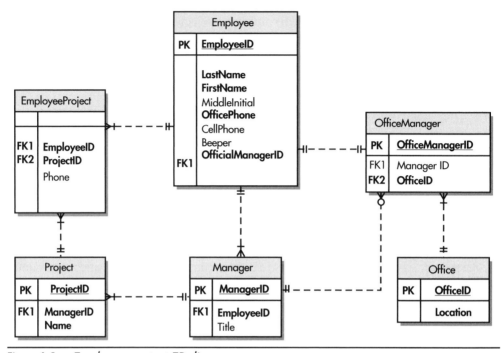

Figure 6-1 *Employee contact ER diagram*

different projects or offices, but a manager represents a single employee. The connector that describes the relationship belongs on the related table.

The diagram in Figure 6-1 also shows many-to-many relationships with the use of additional tables called *join* tables. The EmployeeProject table represents a join table used to implement a many-to-many relationship between employees and projects. An employee is connected to many EmployeeProject entries and a project is also connected to many EmployeeProject entries. By following the connection of an employee through this table to a project we can see that an employee can be connected to many projects. The same holds true when we follow the connection of a project through this table to the employee.

The following table lists all the database tables shown in Figure 6-1 with a description of each table and the relationships supported.

Table	Description	Relationships
Employee	This table contains individual contact information for each Employee in the company.	The OfficeManagerID represents a one-to-one relationship with the OfficeManager table.
Project	This table contains Project information, such as the name and Manager for each Project.	The ManagerID represents a one-to-many relationship with the Manager table. A single Manager can be associated with multiple Projects.
EmployeeProject	This is a many-to-many join table that links the Employee table with the Project table. This table also contains an entry for a contact phone number that's unique for each Employee/Project relationship.	This relationship allows for multiple Projects per Employee and multiple Employees per Project.
Manager	This table contains information about each Manager.	An Employee can hold many management positions while a Manager represents one Employee.
Office	This table contains Office-specific information, such as the Location.	An OfficeManager is associated with only one Office, but an Office can have many Managers.
OfficeManager	This is another join table that links an Employee with their Manager and their Office independent of each other.	The ManagerID is linked to the Manager table with a zero-to-many relationship. This allows for the entry of top-level Managers. The OfficeID is linked to the Office table with a one-to-many relationship. This means a single Office can be related to multiple OfficeManager Entries.

As you can see, the ER diagram in Figure 6-1 does a good job of describing the relational structures graphically. These structures are well suited for relational databases where most operations are *set* based, but they're not always useful in an application. *Applications* typically need to restructure the data to support object-oriented or procedural-based operations. These new structures can be object-based or hierarchical, depending on the implementation. In addition, many object-based solutions used to manage data are often designed with a hierarchical structure.

Hierarchical Structure

A *hierarchical* data structure is based on ranking different elements of data, one above the other, using parent/child/sibling relationships. This might sound a lot like relational structures but, in reality, a hierarchical structure isn't suited for defining all the relationships found in relational structures. We examine exactly what that means in the following paragraphs but, first, let's look at an example of hierarchical structure.

The *Folders* tree on the left side of Windows Explorer is a common example of a hierarchical structure. When you look at the following screenshot, there's a top-level parent named Desktop, with five children named My Documents, My Computer, My Network Places, Recycle Bin, and Internet Explorer. Desktop has five child nodes. Its first child is My Documents, which, in turn, has child nodes of My Pictures and Visual Studio Projects. My Pictures and Visual Studio Projects are called *siblings* because they share the same parent: My Documents. In this example, you can see how folders are ranked one above the other with the Desktop folder at the highest ranking.

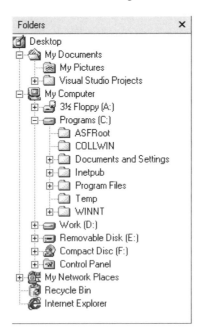

Earlier, we stated that a hierarchical structure isn't suitable for all types of relationships. One example of this is the many-to-many relationship between Employees and Projects discussed previously. In a relational structure, Figure 6-1, this is handled by using link elements that join the two data sets together. With this many-to-many relationship, Employees are linked to a list of Projects they belong to and the projects are linked to the Employees in that Project. Attempts at representing this in a hierarchical structure would end up creating a continuously expanding tree where an Employee is the parent of a Project that is the parent of an Employee that is the parent of a Project, and so forth. To create a hierarchical structure, we would need to take different viewpoints of the data, which is exactly how applications restructure relational data.

When building applications to manipulate data, developers typically use a form-based design that takes a specific viewpoint. The actual structure of objects or data used by the form would be based on the viewpoint taken. For example, if an application took an Employee-centric view of the data, then a hierarchical data structure would include Projects as children under Employees, but then stop at that level, so there's no need to include Employees assigned to each Project. The reverse would be a Project-centric view where each Project would have Employees as children and stop at that level; including the Projects assigned to each Employee wouldn't be necessary. Because XML documents represent hierarchical data structures, you can see how XML would be useful in these types of applications.

Because hierarchical structures are relational in nature, converting between relational and hierarchical data is easy, as long as viewpoints are used. The following XML listing shows an Employee-centric view of hierarchical data from a database using the relational structure defined in Figure 6-1.

```
<Employee EmployeeID='10'>
   <LastName>...</LastName>
   <FirstName>...</FirstName>
   <OfficePhone>...</OfficePhone>
   <Project ProjectID='1'>
      <Manager ManagerID='1' EmployeeID='2'>
         <Name>...</Name>
         <Title>...</Title>
      </Manager>
      <Name>...</Name>
      <Phone>...</Phone>
   </Project>
   <Manager ManagerID='1' EmployeeID='2'>
      <Name>...</Name>
      <Title>...</Title>
   </Manager>
   <Office OfficeID='1'>
      <Location>...</Location>
   </Office>
</Employee>
```

As you can see, the previous data structure contains most of the elements found in Figure 6-1, but not all the relationships. In fact, some of the data is merged to provide a DataSet suitable for use in an application. Now, let's look at a Project-centric view of the same data.

```
<Project ProjectID='1'>
   <Name>...</Name>
   <Employee EmployeeID='10' IsManager='false'>
      <LastName>...</LastName>
      <FirstName>...</FirstName>
      <OfficePhone>...</OfficePhone>
      <ProjectPhone>...</ProjectPhone>
   </Employee>
   <Employee EmployeeID='2' IsManager='true'>
      <LastName>...</LastName>
      <FirstName>...</FirstName>
      <OfficePhone>...</OfficePhone>
      <ProjectPhone>...</ProjectPhone>
   </Employee>
</Project>
```

Again, you can see most of the data elements are captured, but the structure is different. In this example, we also modified one of the data elements, changing `Phone` in the `EmployeeProject` table to `ProjectPhone` and placing it under `Employee`, which is appropriate for this viewpoint. Another difference that stands out is the addition of an attribute, IsManager, which uses data found in the Project table that isn't included as part of this data set. Later chapters in this book examine some of the new features in ADO.NET and SQL 2000 that handle most of these XML translations automatically. This chapter focuses on doing the translations by hand, however, to get a lower-level look at the mapping between relational and hierarchical XML data.

At this point, most developers who are familiar with ADO might be thinking they could do the same thing with Recordsets. ADO even supports hierarchical Recordsets, which let you create a single query that returns all the necessary data, structured appropriately for an application. In all honesty, this is exactly what you should use when accessing a database directly, from either an application or a middle-tier component. However, when it comes to moving data across machine and network boundaries, ADO Recordsets aren't the best choice. Even though Recordset objects use a custom marshaler that moves data into the remote proxy, many operations, such as applying filters, still reach back across to the server. The data and metadata is also marshaled to the client using many individual variables, which has a significant impact on performance. With the use of XML, structured data can be passed across to remote clients as a single unit, completely separated from the server, which is much faster. Because XML is so much more efficient, Microsoft has even added XML streaming features to ADO.NET, which is discussed in Chapter 12.

So far, we stated that the hierarchical structure of XML data is ideal for use in most applications. Within an application, however, you would use objects to manipulate the data instead of directly accessing the XML. We also stated that XML is a great solution for passing data across network boundaries. By using XML, we can convert the data into a string, and then send that string across the boundary instead of passing objects. Another benefit of using XML is the capability to pass the structure of the data along with the data. However, even with this information, it probably still isn't clear exactly when you should and should not pass XML data. You wouldn't want to design all interfaces to pass everything as XML and you wouldn't want to use objects for everything.

TIP

The key to using XML as a method for passing data comes with understanding where a design crosses network and process boundaries.

Using Structured XML Data

As you can imagine, many different uses exist for XML data within an application. Many applications today use XML to store configuration information instead of putting it in the registry or an INI file. .NET uses XML for deployment descriptors and Web configuration files. Applications are also taking advantage of XML to pass data between different components, which is the main focus of this discussion.

As mentioned earlier, understanding when XML is appropriate for passing data is important. For instance, it wouldn't make a lot of sense to convert the data from an object into XML, pass that data to a different object, and then re-create the original object when both objects are running in the same process space. Instead, passing a reference of the object, which is then accessed directly from the other object, is much more efficient. If these objects were running in separate processes or on different machines, however, this would be inefficient and sometimes impossible to accomplish.

In most cases, it's easy to determine when network and process boundaries are crossed. In other cases it can be much more subtle. For instance, COM objects can be hosted in a DLL or Executable. When hosted in an Executable, the object runs in a separate process space, while the DLL object will run in the same process space as the caller. Unless the developers using this component know how it's hosted, they might not know if it's running in-process or out-of-process.

Developers and architects need to understand where the network and process boundaries are. Most of the decisions made during design determine these boundaries, but configuration changes can also have an effect on where they are. Rather than get into a lengthy discussion of system architectures, we focus on three different implementations of Web pages using COM components. As we dig deeper into .NET throughout this book, you can see a big difference exists between COM components and .NET managed components. However, COM is still valid and it provides a better-known design model for this discussion. In addition, as pointed out earlier, an ADO Recordset is designed to handle data and even includes a custom marshaler for remote data access, which makes it a good example for this discussion.

Building the Server Interface

Because all the previously mentioned configurations use the same server components, we start by creating a C# Library component to be exposed as a COM+ configured component. Even though the .NET Framework doesn't directly create COM components, it does support the use of COM and, with a little work, creating COM interfaces from .NET components is possible. Several reasons exist for using COM in this example, however, the main reason is to provide comparisons between using objects to pass data across network and process boundaries versus passing XML data in a string or stream. Most of the driving force behind SOAP and Web services focuses on the flexibility and interoperability of using XML in this manner. Another reason for using COM was to demonstrate how to build COM+ configured components using C# and the .NET Framework.

NOTE

When using the term "interface" in these discussions, we aren't referring to the type of class in .NET called an Interface. Instead, we're referring to the method interface used by client applications when accessing our components.

For the first phase of this example, we start with an interface named *Contacts,* which exposes methods used to retrieve a list of Employees as either an ADO Recordset object or XML data in a string. The component demonstrates how to reference and use a COM component, and an ADO Recordset, as well as how to take advantage of the `System.XML` interfaces. In addition, instead of using Visual Basic or VC++, the interface is developed using the C# language, which is new to Visual Studio.NET. With all the descriptions out of the way, it's time to start looking at the project. The complete project is also available with Chapter 6 examples on the McGraw-Hill/ Osborne Web site at **www.osborne.com** in the Downloads section. Navigate to the Examples\Chapter6 directory for this book.

As mentioned previously, the example application was developed using Visual Studio.NET. The project created for this example is a Visual C# Class Library project named "CompanyInfo". This project contains two main classes: Contacts and EmployeeList. The Contacts class defines the external interface for COM and the EmployeeList is an object that handles employee lists.

Contacts Class

The declaration of the Contacts class uses attributes to define the COM-specific details. For this example, we use a `Guid` and `Transaction` attribute. The following code snippet shows the class declaration.

```
using System;
using System.Runtime.InteropServices;
using System.EnterpriseServices;
using ADODB26;

namespace CompanyInfo
{
    /// <summary>
    /// COM Class used to implement the Contacts interface.
    /// </summary>
    [Guid("0F68977E-5291-411d-8F18-66475AC1FE15")]
    [Transaction(TransactionOption.NotSupported)]
    public class Contacts : ServicedComponent
    {          interface code...
    }
```

The `Guid` attribute is available in the `System.Runtime.InteropServices` namespace and it enables us to assign a unique GUID to the COM class. The GUID can be generated using the Create GUID tool available in Visual Studio. The `Transaction` attribute is available in the `System.EnterpriseServices` namespace and is used to set the COM+ transaction setting to `NotSupported`. Many more attributes are in both the `InteropServices` and `EnterpriseServices`, but these are the only two we need for this example. The last important piece of information in the previous code listing is that Contacts derives from `ServicedComponent`. This is available in the `EnterpriseServices` namespace and is required to install this component into a COM+ application.

This is only one way to define a managed class that can be accessed by COM interfaces. If this class were only accessed by local components running on the same server as the managed component, then we wouldn't need to use the `EnterpriseServices`. We could also declare this class without the use of the `InteropServices` and the `Guid` attribute. This configuration was chosen, however, for specific reasons. The `Guid` attribute enables us to define GUIDs for the class, which translates to the COM CLSID used in the registry. If we don't assign a GUID, then the `EnterpriseServices` will create a new one every time the component is compiled. The `EnterpriseServices` are required to register the interface with the COM+ Services Manager, which enables us to export a proxy of the interface to external servers. We'll get into more specifics as we discuss how to configure, build, and register the components.

EmployeeList Class

The *EmployeeList* class is a data object that wraps an ADO Recordset object. When created, it initializes a connection string to access the database and instantiates the Recordset object. There's one method to open the Recordset and others to return the Recordset or the data as XML in a string. This object is used by the Contacts interface to retrieve the data. Because we're returning an ADO Recordset, we need an assembly reference for that object before we can compile it.

TIP

When using COM objects within a C# class, you might encounter locking problems with Apartment Threaded COM components. An earlier version of this application used the MSXML Parser instead of System.Xml. When testing that version under load with multiple threads accessing the interface, the application would lock up. By switching to a FreeThreaded version of the MSXML parser, the locking issue was resolved.

One of the major differences with .NET components is they use an *assembly,* which contains information about the interfaces, version, resources, and relationships defined for that component. Chapter 9 provides more in-depth information about assemblies, which is an important concept to understand when it comes to .NET applications. The assembly is considered a single unit, but can be associated with several files. Typically, assembly information is embedded directly into the binary file produced during compilation. As mentioned, part of the assembly information includes references to other assemblies and COM objects. COM objects themselves are referenced through the use of assemblies, which describe the information about the object needed by other .NET components. This assembly information is easy to create when using the Visual Studio.NET development environment.

Creating Assemblies for COM Components

Although we needn't create an assembly for the ADO component, this is easy to do and might be necessary, especially if you want a specific version. The Add Reference dialog box available from the References context menu lets the developer select a COM reference. This creates an assembly for you that enables access to the component from within the managed class. The only problem is this wouldn't let our `Contacts` class access the component because we need to create a strong name for the `Contacts` assembly. This might seem a little confusing, but it's not too bad. A strong name is used to guarantee the assembly has a unique name, which is required when registering an assembly with COM. One of the rules with strong names is any assembly that uses strong names cannot access another assembly that doesn't use strong names.

NOTE

A Context menu is accessed by right-clicking an item typically displayed in a tree view. When referencing a context menu, we use the name shown in the tree. For instance; the References context menu is found on the References node of the CompanyInfo project tree in the Solution view.

Strong names can be created using a utility provided with the .NET Framework. This utility program is located in the FrameworkSDK\Bin directory, which isn't defined in the path environment variable. If you use the Command Prompt link available on the Visual Studio.NET Tools menu, however, it automatically sets the environment variables for you. The following code listing shows how to create a strong name for use in an assembly:

```
sn -k ADODBKey.snk
```

The −k switch tells the strong name (`sn`) utility to generate a key file that can be used in the assembly. This file should be generated in the directory that will be used to build the assembly file in the next step. This key file can be referenced using assembly attributes in a project and it can be used with the Type Library Import tool used to create assemblies for COM components.

Included with the .NET Software Development Kit is another utility called *TlbImp,* which takes type library information from a COM object and creates an assembly file. Visual Studio.NET already comes with an assembly we can use for the ADO objects. If you don't have one or you want to target a specific version, however, this is easy to do. The following code listing demonstrates how to create an assembly and make it available to VS.NET projects. You should use the Command Prompt link mentioned previously and you might need to modify the destination directory to reference the current .NET framework version installed on your computer.

```
cd \Program Files\Common Files\System\ado
TlbImp msado26.tlb /keyfile:ADODBKey.snk /out:ADODB26.dll
regasm ADODB26.dll
gacutil /i ADODB26.dll
copy ADODB26.dll c:\WINNT\Microsoft.NET\Framework\v1.0.3705
```

As you can see, it doesn't take too much work to create an assembly for a COM object. For this example, we decided to target the 2.6 version of ADO instead of the current version available in Visual Studio. The `TlbImp` utility uses the key file created earlier to create an assembly named ADODB26.dll. This assembly is then registered for use by COM components with the `regasm` utility and finally added to the *Global Assembly Cache* (*GAC*), which also requires a strong name, using the `gacutil` utility. The component needs to be registered in the GAC, so it can be shared by multiple applications without copying the assembly to the application directories. Finally, we need to copy the assembly into the Framework directory, so we can reference it from Visual Studio. The following screenshot shows the References explorer, accessed from the References context menu described earlier, with the new assembly highlighted:

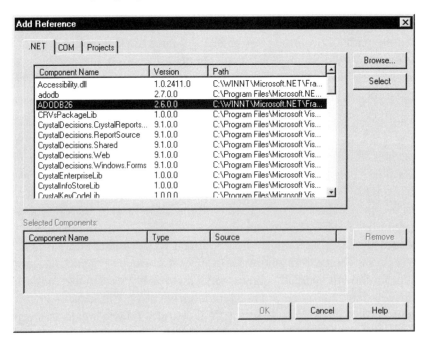

You should also notice the adodb assembly on the line directly above our ADODB26 reference. This is the current version that's preregistered by the Visual Studio development environment. If you didn't want to create the 2.6 specific version, you can use this assembly and change the ADODB26 references in code to ADODB.

Compiling and Testing the Components

Now that the assembly is created and added as a reference, we can finish compiling the first example. Again, all the source code can be found on the McGraw-Hill/Osborne Web site, which means we aren't going to show all the code here. Instead, this is focused more on the configuration and steps required to build COM+ components using C# and the .NET Framework. Before attempting to build and register the component, we need to create a strong name key for our component. Using the same syntax described previously, we'll create a key named `"ContactsKey.snk"` and copy it into the CompanyInfo directory. This key is then referenced in assembly attributes found in the `Assembly.cs` class.

Figure 6-2 shows the Project Properties dialog box, which is accessed by the CompanyInfo context menu. The two fields we're interested in are the Output Path and Register for COM Interop settings. Instead of using separate Debug and Release directories for the output, which is the default, it's easier to manage compiling both

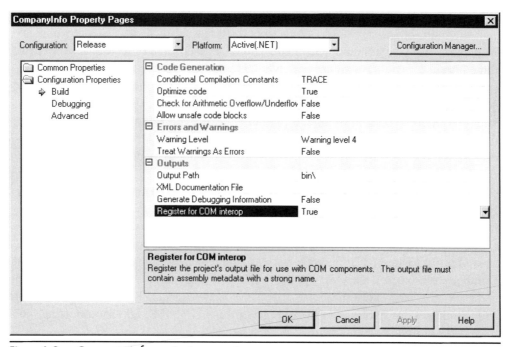

Figure 6-2   *CompanyInfo project properties*

to a single directory when registering this as a COM+ component. As a result, the Output path is set to bin\ for both Debug and Release builds. Next, we need to set a flag that tells the compiler to register the component as accessible to COM. This is the alternative to using the `regasm` utility discussed previously. Notice the Register for COM Interop field is highlighted. The following description discuses the requirement for strong names.

The next step in preparing the project for compile is to add the assembly attributes we'll need for COM. The following code listing shows the four entries added to `AssemblyInfo.cs` to build the assembly for this component:

```
[assembly: AssemblyKeyFile("..\\..\\ContactsKey.snk")]
[assembly: ApplicationName("CompanyApp")]
[assembly: ApplicationID("7B8507AC-03C4-417a-9486-1A887CC201EE")]
[assembly: ApplicationActivation(ActivationOption.Server)]
```

The first line references the strong name key file created earlier. This reference needs to use a relative path back to the project root directory because the intermediate object files are built into separate obj/Debug and obj/Release directories. This attribute is included in the Visual Studio generated file with a description of its use. The next three lines are attributes that are only available in the `EnterpriseServices` namespace. The `ApplicationName` defines the COM+ application name to be used and the `ApplicationID` defines a globally unique ID to be used. Both of these aren't required—you can use one or the other—however, finding the application by name in Component Services Manager is much easier, while early bound components can use the ID. The last line sets the COM+ application activation setting to Server instead of the default, which is Library.

We're finally ready to build the component. This can be accomplished by selecting build from the CompanyInfo context menu or using the Build menu in Visual Studio. Once the CompanyInfo component is compiled, it can be accessed locally by any COM component or by another .NET-managed component. For testing purposes, a second project named "CompanyTest" was added to the same solution that holds the CompanyInfo project. This test application has a single form with a command button and a text box used to test the `CompanyInfo` classes. Once all the testing is complete and the classes are stable, it's time to register this in a COM+ application using the `regsvcs` utility.

The following code listing shows the syntax used to register this component:

```
regsvcs CompanyInfo.dll
```

Once we run this utility, a new COM+ application will be created, which is shown in the following screenshot.

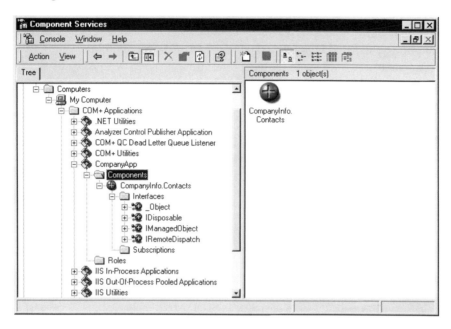

Now that the component is built and registered, we need to build some test ASP pages to use it. As mentioned previously, the component exposes two methods: `getEmployeesRec` and `GetEmployeesXml`. As the names indicate, the first method returns a list of employees in a Recordset and the second method returns the same data as XML in a string. To test these methods, and then perform benchmark comparisons, we need to build two ASP pages: one that uses the Recordset and another that uses XML.

Building the Web Pages

The purpose of this chapter is to demonstrate advantages of using structured data—namely XML structured data—in distributed applications. To demonstrate the advantages, we decided to compare the use of ADO Recordsets versus XML data across network and process boundaries. The first step, Building the Server Interface, is complete and we have an interface that returns a list of Employees either in a Recordset or as XML data. The next step is to build a set of ASP pages that use the

EmployeeList data returned from the CompanyInfo.Contacts interface. The two pages we create are EmployeesRec.asp and EmployeesXml.asp, not very imaginative, but the names are descriptive, so no problem should occur determining which page handles which datatype. The solution also includes two additional files— CompanyScripts.asp and Employees.xslt—which are described later. Both of these pages produce exactly the same table, shown in Figure 6-3, with a list of Employees. The database also contains 80 Employees, all of which are returned in this example, but aren't shown.

EmployeesRec ASP

The first page we look at is EmployeesRec.asp, which is a standard ASP page that uses a Recordset object. The reason we use a standard ASP page for this project instead of ASP.NET is so we can deploy these pages to other platforms that don't have .NET installed. Listing 6-1 shows the code from EmployeesRec.asp, which is a mix of server-side script and HTML. In this example, the server-side script is

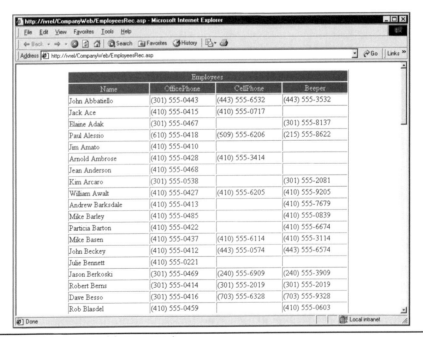

Figure 6-3 *Employees Table in a Web page*

included inline with the HTML using the percent sign syntax, `<% . . . %>`. The rest
of the file contains standard HTML code used to generate a table.

Listing 6-1 *EmployeesRec.asp*

```
<%@ Language=VBScript  EnableSessionState=False%>
<!-- #Include File="CompanyScripts.asp" -->
<%
' Initialize the Contacts object and get a list of employees
' into an ADO Recordset object
Set objContacts = Server.CreateObject( "CompanyInfo.Contacts" )
Set rsData = objContacts.getEmployeesRec
%>
<html>
<head></head>
<body>
<table align="center" cellspacing=1 width="75%" border=1>
   <tr bgcolor=teal>
      <td align="center" colspan="4">
         <font color="white">Employees</font></td>
   </tr>
   <tr bgcolor=teal>
      <td align="center"><font color="white">Name</font></td>
      <td align="center"><font color="white">OfficePhone</font></td>
      <td align="center"><font color="white">CellPhone</font></td>
      <td align="center"><font color="white">Beeper</font></td>
   </tr>
<%
' start a loop
Dim strLine
while rsData.EOF = false
%>
   <tr bgcolor=white>
      <td><%=rsData.Fields.Item("FirstName") + " " +
          rsData.Fields.Item("LastName")%></td>
      <td><%=FormatPhone(rsData.Fields.Item("OfficePhone"))%></td>
      <td><%=FormatPhone(rsData.Fields.Item("CellPhone"))%></td>
      <td><%=FormatPhone(rsData.Fields.Item("Beeper"))%></td>
```

```
    </tr>
<%
    rsData.MoveNext
wend
%>
</table>
</body>
</html>
```

Starting at the top of EmployeesRec.asp, we include another ASP file named CompanyScripts.asp, which contains VBScript utility methods. The first section of server-side script code instantiates the `CompanyInfo.Contacts` objects, and then retrieves the Employee List into a Recordset object named `rsData`. The first section of HTML code defines a table with two header rows for the table and column headings. Next, a server-side script block is opened inline and a `while` loop is started against the Recordset, which was retrieved at the beginning of the page. Inside the loop, HTML and script code are mixed to retrieve values from the Recordset and format them correctly. Once all the rows are displayed, the table is closed and the HTML body is closed. The end result is the table displayed in Figure 6-3. This is a simple example, but it does access five fields from 80 records, which represents 400 data elements used to populate this table. That doesn't include the fields we aren't accessing and the metadata that's also part of an ADO Recordset. This is significant when it comes to passing this data across network and process boundaries.

When looking at the code in Listing 6-1, where the Recordset data is accessed, a method named "`FormatPhone`" is used to format the phone numbers. This is one of the VBScript functions, shown in the following code, which was included with the CompanyScripts.asp file. The actual Phone number data is stored as digits without any formatting information in the database. Formatting is left up to the presentation layer.

```
' function used to format the Phone numbers
function FormatPhone( strRaw )
   dim strPhone
   if Len(strRaw) = 10 then
      strPhone = "(" + Left( strRaw, 3 ) + ") "
      strPhone = strPhone + Mid( strRaw, 4, 3 ) + "-"
      strPhone = strPHone + Right( strRaw, 4 )
      FormatPhone = strPhone
   else
      if strRaw <> "" then
         FormatPhone = strRaw
      else
         FormatPhone = " "
```

```
      end if
   end if
end function
```

EmployeesXml ASP

Listing 6-2 shows the code found in the EmployeesXml.asp file, which uses XML data instead of a Recordset object. One of the most significant differences is this code doesn't contain any HTML. All the HTML code can be found in the XSLT stylesheet, which we'll review later. This page only contains server-side script, which is used to parse and transform the XML into HTML using an XSLT stylesheet. The actual stylesheet is cached in the ASP Application object using an XSLTemplate object.

Listing 6-2   *EmployeesXml.asp*

```
<%@ Language=VBScript  EnableSessionState=False%>
<!-- #Include File="CompanyScripts.asp" -->
<%
   ' Initialize the XML Source object
   Set objSource = Server.CreateObject( "MSXML2.DOMDocument" )
   objSource.async = false

   ' Initialize our Contacts Interface and load the XML
   Set objContacts = Server.CreateObject( "CompanyInfo.Contacts" )
   if objSource.loadXML( objContacts.getEmployeesXml ) = true then
      ' First check the Application cache... passing True allows
      ' updating of the cached template
      CheckCache "Employees", False

      ' create the processor and do the transform
      Set objProc = Application("Employees").createProcessor()
      objProc.input = objSource
      objProc.output = Response
      objProc.transform
   else
      ' write out the error
      Response.Write source.parseError.reason & " Line:" &
                     source.parseError.line
   end if
%>
```

As with EmployeesRec, this page also includes the CompanyScripts.asp file, which includes a VBScript method used to help with caching. The first section of code shows the creation of an XML DOM Document used to parse the XML data returned from the Contacts Interface. Next, the `CompanyInfo.Contacts` object is created using the same method, as shown in Listing 6-1. Once the object is instantiated, the `getEmployeesXml` method is called to pass XML data into the `LoadXml` method of the DOM Document. If the parse operation is successful, we can then transform the XML data with the XSL stylesheet.

Before getting into the actual transform, taking a closer look at the method used to cache the stylesheet can help. The MSXML2 Type Library includes an object named "`XSLTemplate`" that can be used to cache XSL stylesheets in the `ASP Application` object. Instead of loading and parsing the XSL stylesheet every time we need to perform a transform, it stays loaded in memory using a thread-safe template cache. This represents a significant improvement in performance when it comes to using XSL for HTML generation. The following code listing shows the `CheckCache` method included in the CompanyScripts.asp file.

```
' method to check the cache
sub CheckCache( strName, bForce )
   ' is this a new app instance or are we forcing an update?
   If IsEmpty(Application(strName)) or bForce = True Then
      ' create the template and a FREE Threaded DOM Document
      Set objTemplate = Server.CreateObject("MSXML2.XSLTemplate")
      Set objStyle = Server.CreateObject("MSXML2.FreeThreadedDOMDocument30")
      objStyle.async = false
      objStyle.ValidateOnParse = false

      ' Load the stylesheet using the name passed in
      if objStyle.load( Server.MapPath( strName + ".xslt")) = true then
         objTemplate.stylesheet = objStyle
         Set Application(strName) = objTemplate
      else
         ' write out any errors
         Response.Write objStyle.parseError.reason & " Line:" &
                        objStyle.parseError.line
      end if
   End If
end sub
```

This is a common method that's called after the XML is loaded to make sure the XSL stylesheet is cached in the `Application` object. The second parameter allows for updates to the cache if the XSL file has been changed. When looking at the code, you can see that, first, an `XSLTemplate` object is created and stored in the `Application` object. This is a FreeThreaded component that won't cause threading problems with the ASP Application object. Next, a FreeThreaded version of a DOM document is created and loaded with the XSL stylesheet. Note, the

`ValidateOnParse` flag is set to false. This is required because the stylesheet uses a DTD to define Entity references, which we look at later. Once the stylesheet is loaded, it's associated with the `XSLTemplate` by assigning it to the Template's stylesheet property.

The next step in processing `EmployeesXml.asp`, Listing 6-2, is to create a template processor and transform the XML into HTML. The *Template processor* is a lightweight component that provides access to the stylesheet cached in the `XSLTemplate` object. Its main purpose is to hold the working set during transformation. Once the processor is created, its source and output parameters are set to the `XML Document` and `Response` objects, respectively. By assigning the `Response` object to the output parameter of the processor, any output is sent directly to the client through the `Response` stream, which is much faster than using `Response.Write`. The actual XSL stylesheet used to perform the transform is similar in content to the `EmployeesRec` code shown in Listing 6-1.

Employees XSLT Stylesheet

The code listing in Listing 6-3 shows the two templates used to generate HTML from the XML data. You can see the HTML code used to generate the table is identical to the HTML code shown in Listing 6-1. The template used to handle Employee data is also similar to the block of code shown in Listing 6-1, which handles each row of data inside the loop. By comparing the following XSL with code found in the `EmployeesRec.asp` file, you can see how similar they are. The biggest difference between the two, however, is by using XSL. Generation of the HTML is accomplished without reaching into objects that may have been created in a different process or machine. All the objects we used to generate the HTML were created in the same process space as the ASP Application.

Listing 6-3   *XSLT Templates Used to Generate HTML*

```
<!--This handles the root template in the document-->
<xsl:template match="/">
   <table align="center" cellspacing="1" width="75%" border="1">
      <tr bgcolor="teal">
         <td align="center" colspan="4">
            <font color="white">Employees</font></td>
      </tr>
      <tr bgcolor="teal">
         <td align="center"><font color="white">Name</font></td>
         <td align="center"><font color="white">OfficePhone</font></td>
         <td align="center"><font color="white">CellPhone</font></td>
         <td align="center"><font color="white">Beeper</font></td>
```

```
      </tr>
      <xsl:apply-templates select="Employees/Employee" />
   </table>
</xsl:template>

<!--Handles each employee Node found in the XML-->
<xsl:template match='Employee'>
   <tr bgcolor="white">
      <td><xsl:value-of select="FirstName"/> 
         <xsl:value-of select="LastName"/></td>
      <td><xsl:value-of
select="rda:FormatPhone(string(OfficePhone))"/></td>
      <td><xsl:value-of
select="rda:FormatPhone(string(CellPhone))"/></td>
      <td><xsl:value-of select="rda:FormatPhone(string(Beeper))"/></td>
   </tr>
</xsl:template>
```

There are a couple of interesting points to discuss with the code shown in Listing 6-3. In the Employee template block, a nonbreaking space is used to separate `FirstName` from `LastName`. This is inserted as an Entity Reference, but XML doesn't support this reference; it's only used by HTML documents. What we did was insert a DTD into the prolog of this stylesheet, as shown in the following, that defines the `nbsp` entity. This was also the reason we had to turn off `ValidateOnParse` when the stylesheet was loaded into a DOM document. If validation is enabled, this DTD entry causes an error because it's looking for the XML root element, which isn't part of this file.

```
<?xml version="1.0" encoding="UTF-8" ?>
<!DOCTYPE xsl:stylesheet [
<!ENTITY nbsp " ">
]>
<xsl:stylesheet xmlns:xsl="http://www.w3.org/1999/XSL/Transform"
                xmlns:msxsl="urn:schemas-microsoft-com:xslt"
                xmlns:rda="http://www.rdacustomsoftware.com/Script"
                version="1.0">
```

Also shown in the previous code listing is the stylesheet declaration used for this file. Notice several namespaces are defined, which is required to insert script blocks into the XSLT code. The `msxsl` namespace is used for Microsoft-specific tags and the `rda` namespace is used for application-specific tags. When looking at the Employee template in Listing 6-3, you can see the calls to `FormatPhone` are all prefixed with the `rda` namespace. In this case, we aren't using VBScript from the ASP to format phone numbers. Instead, a JScript block is inserted into the XSLT code, as the following code shows, which is executed on the server when the XML is transformed.

```
<!--Formats a Phone number for display-->
<msxsl:script language="JScript" implements-prefix="rda">
function FormatPhone( strRaw ) {
   if( strRaw.length == 10 ) {
      strPhone = "(" + strRaw.substr( 0, 3 ) + ") ";
      strPhone += strRaw.substr( 3, 3 ) + "-";
      strPhone += strRaw.substr( 6, 4 );
      return strPhone;
   }
   else if( strRaw.length != 0 ) {
      return strRaw;
   }
   else {
      return " ";
   }
}
</msxsl:script>
```

When you look at the previous code listing, you can see the `msxsl` namespace was used to identify this script block. The reason for a different namespace is that script processing is an extension added by Microsoft and isn't defined as part of the XSLT specifications. Using a different namespace for tags that aren't part of the specification is recommended and supported by the specification. The application-specific namespace is used to identify entities defined as part of the application.

Now that the ASP pages are created, the next step is to define configurations to be used to test Web pages. You can configure Web sites in many different ways and the most appropriate configuration must be determined on a case-by-case basis. The configuration used depends on the content and/or application being deployed as a Web site. The next section looks at three common configurations used with Web sites today.

Configuring the Web Sites

When you design a Web site, one of the most critical aspects to the architecture is understanding the configuration of the Web, application, and database servers to be deployed. If the configuration isn't understood, then components designed for use by the Web site can cause significant performance and scalability issues. (Scalability is discussed in detail later in this chapter.) For now, what's important to understand is a good design can perform badly if the configuration isn't considered in the design.

For this discussion, we focus on three different configurations. The first configuration is named *Web Content* and it represents a site that serves read-only content with no security requirements. The next configuration is called *Web Application,* which represents a Web site that implements a business application that requires security and uses business components. In the Web Application configuration, the business components are located on the same machine as the Web server. The final configuration is named *Web Distributed Application* and represents a Web site that uses business components distributed across different application servers. All these configurations represent Windows DNA designs, which is appropriate for comparing the difference between COM objects and XML. The following descriptions provide more detail on each of these configurations.

Web Content

Web Content represents a straightforward Web site that retrieves data from a data source and displays it to users. Security is nonexistent or minimal, which means the site doesn't take advantage of Security Roles or the COM+ Security Context. The business components used to retrieve data are loaded in a COM+ Library application to take advantage of its object management capabilities. This type of configuration would be used with Web sites that provide content for the general public, such as news reports and items of interest. Typically, these sites have a high volume of traffic and must be designed with performance in mind.

The distinguishing features of this configuration include the following:

▶ Business components are deployed on the same machine as the Web server.

▶ Business components are installed in a COM+ Library application for performance, which means they're running in the same process space as IIS.

Web Application

Web Application represents a business application deployed as a Web site. Many businesses are converting legacy client/server applications into intranet Web applications because of the ease of deployment and maintainability. Businesses are also starting to build complex business applications that are used by clients from the Internet. With this type of application, the security requirements are more restrictive and should take advantage of security roles and the security context information. Transactional requirements for handling data may also exist, which could use the *Distributed Transaction Coordinator* (*DTC*). Typically, this type of application should be configured to use business components in a COM+ Server application.

You should use Server applications instead of Library applications with this type of design for many different reasons. One of the biggest reasons is the security and transaction context information isn't available if it's deployed to a Library Package on a Windows NT4 platform. Windows 2000 has improved the context support, which means it's available with Library applications in COM+. Other reasons exist for using Server applications, however, such as process isolation, load balancing, and, in some cases, security isolation. By running the components in a separate process, there's less chance that an exception can cause problems with a Web site running on the same machine. With a large application, sometimes it's beneficial to split the processing load among multiple processors, which can be accomplished with Server applications. Finally, in some cases, a specific identity is required to access a resource. With a Server application, you can assign a specific identity to the components running within that application.

The distinguishing features of this configuration include the following:

▶ Business components are deployed on the same machine as the Web server.

▶ Business components are installed in a COM+ Server application for isolation, DCOM support, and context information on a Windows NT4 platform.

▶ Business components run in a separate process space from the Web components.

Web Distributed Application

This represents a distributed business application deployed as a Web site. With this type of design, the business components are located on a separate physical machine from the Web server. This separate machine is typically called an *Application server,* which is used to isolate business processing from other processing requirements. Many different reasons occur for using this type of design. With most Web site configurations, the Web servers are deployed in a section of the network called the *Demilitarized Zone (DMZ)*, which has limited access to the business's private network. In some cases, business components used by the Web site need access to network resources that aren't available in the DMZ. Another example would be a Web site that takes advantage of existing business components already deployed on a different machine.

The distinguishing features of this configuration include the following:

▶ Business components are deployed on a different machine from the Web server.

▶ Business components are installed in a COM+ Server application for DCOM support.

▶ Business components are running on a completely different machine from the Web components.

Now that we've defined different configurations, the next step is to run some benchmark tests against these configurations. As some people would say, this is where the rubber hits the road. We find out if XML is a better solution or if somebody made a big mistake. All kidding aside, you should see that XML does provide a major benefit, as long as it's used appropriately.

Benchmarking the Configurations

Because these are Web Applications, the Microsoft Web Application Stress tool is used to perform the benchmark testing. This is a free tool that can be found at **http://webtool.rte.microsoft.com**. The Microsoft Web Application Stress tool is easy to set up and use, and it records scripts from browser activity and allows for manual editing of the scripts. This tool can also be configured to use multiple threads and users to simulate a heavy concurrent load on the Web site.

Figure 6-4 shows two different physical configurations used to perform the benchmark testing. As you can see from the diagram, two different servers are

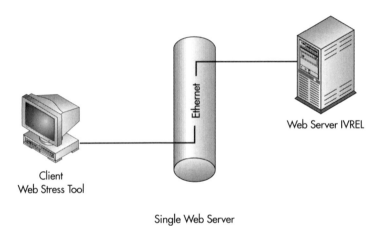

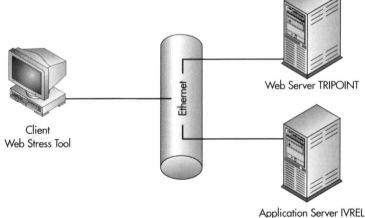

Figure 6-4   *Physical test configurations*

used: one named "IVREL" and the other named "TRIPOINT". The *IVREL* server is a Windows 2000 Server with the .NET SDK and Visual Studio.NET installed. This is where the `CompanyInfo.Contacts` component is physically installed. When testing the two logical configurations that use a single server, this machine is also configured as a Web server with the ASP and XSLT files installed. The second machine, the *TRIPOINT* server, is a Windows 2000 server installation configured with a Web server that doesn't have the .NET SDK or Visual Studio.NET installed. When testing the Distributed Application configuration, this machine is used as a Web server that accesses the `CompanyInfo.Contacts` object using DCOM. The IVREL server becomes an Application server that hosts the `Contacts` object in a COM+ Server application.

To access the components through DCOM, the CompanyApp package we installed in COM+ is first exported as an application proxy, shown in the following illustration, which creates an installation program. To create the application proxy, right-click on the COM+ application in the Component Services manager and select Export from the context menu. This installation program can be used on clients to register the interfaces and configure the DCOM registry settings.

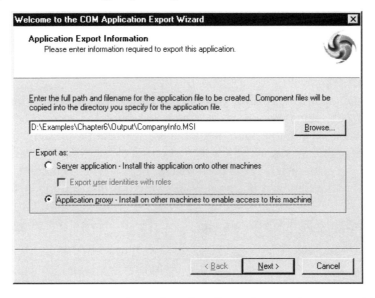

Once the components are registered on the client, they can be accessed in the same fashion as if they were installed on the same machine. With DCOM objects, the *Service Control Manager* (*SCM*) is used to interact with the server where the components are installed. Briefly, the SCM creates a proxy using information found in the registry, and then it calls the server where the component is installed, telling the server to create an instance and pass back a reference. The SCM then hooks the proxy to the reference, allowing access to the instance of the component on the server through the proxy. This is a quick description, but the important thing to understand is the actual object instance is still on the server; the client only has a proxy reference to it.

Now that everything is configured and ready to go, it's time to start running the benchmark tests. Two different types of benchmark tests should be performed: one checked performance with a single thread and another tested performance under load. Both types use the same configurations and ASP pages, and both run all the tests for one minute. The configuration that checked for performance under load uses ten threads running continuously, which is sufficient for our purposes. Our main interest is in showing differences between the use of ADO Recordsets and XML data.

Table 6-1 shows the first set of results with a Single thread. Four different pieces of information were captured for the benchmark tests. The first column shows the configuration, described previously, and the datatype or ASP page used. The second column, labeled Hits, shows the number of page hits returned during the test period. The more hits, the better it performed. The next two, TTFB and TTLB, both show an average time taken to retrieve data per request, starting from the beginning of the request. The first one shows the time taken to get the *First Byte* (*FB*) of data, while the second one shows the time taken to get the *Last Byte* (*LB*). Both these numbers help show how responsive the system is under different test conditions. The last column contains the number of requests handled per second. Higher numbers indicate better performance.

When you examine the results, you can see a Recordset performs much better when it runs in the same process space, which makes a lot of sense. The XML data didn't do quite as well in this configuration, but it still didn't do badly. Moving on to the next set of numbers, you can see the Recordset did perform badly. In fact, with the Recordset, a great difference in performance occurs when running in a Library application versus a Server application. When you look at the numbers for XML,

Configuration—Datatype	Hits	TTFB	TTLB	Requests/Sec
Web Content—Recordset	547	103.98	107.78	9.12
Web Content—XML	510	106.62	115.51	8.49
Web Application—Recordset	51	1161.80	1165.67	0.85
Web Application—XML	475	115.28	124.21	7.91
Web Distributed App—Recordset	13	4410.08	4414.23	0.22
Web Distributed App—XML	378	147.63	156.65	6.29

Table 6-1   *Benchmark with Single Thread*

nowhere near the difference in performance exists. Little change occurred. Again, the final set of numbers shows a big loss of performance with the Recordset object when used across network boundaries. And, once again, the XML data performance stayed consistent with little degradation.

This first benchmark test shows two significant findings. First, there's no doubt a Recordset will perform well when everything is running in the same process space. This can be dangerous, however. If the configuration is changed to use a Server Application or a separate application server, the performance is dramatically affected. Second, although the XML data didn't perform as well when accessed in the same process, it greatly outperformed the Recordset in all other configurations. In addition, the XML data performance was consistent across all configurations.

Table 6-2 shows the results obtained when the Stress tool was configured to use ten threads. This forced a higher load on the server and tested each configuration's capability to handle concurrent requests.

Once again, the Recordset outperformed XML data when running in the same process space, but not by much. In addition, the Recordset performance degraded rapidly when crossing network and process boundaries. One positive note is the Recordset did handle the additional load without a problem. In fact, the Recordset improved slightly when tested under 100 threads. Nevertheless, what's even better is the XML data performed in a consistent manner and out-performed an in-process recordset when used in a distributed design. The performance numbers between Table 6-1 and Table 6-2 are consistent in the XML configurations with the exception of improved performance under load. This is extremely encouraging news to software architects. They can be confident that XML can handle configuration changes without the drastic variances in performance you would get with objects.

Some developers might be suspicious of the fact that application performance improved under load. If you look at the numbers closely you can see the individual call performance decreased under load, which is indicated by the *Time To First Byte*

Configuration—Datatype	Hits	TTFB	TTLB	Requests/Sec
Web Content—Recordset	636	928.84	933.32	10.59
Web Content—XML	600	972.15	984.85	9.99
Web Application—Recordset	43	13207.47	13212.37	0.72
Web Application—XML	548	1068.52	1081.60	9.12
Web Distributed App—Recordset	20	23606.85	23616.75	0.33
Web Distributed App—XML	762	758.63	774.60	12.68

Table 6-2   *Benchmark Test with Ten Threads*

(*TTFB*) numbers. Without a load these numbers are low, which means the response back to the client was faster than the response time under load. However, the COM+ executive was able to handle the extra load by handling the requests with multiple threads. This multithreading capability allowed the overall performance to improve when the application was under load. Now, we really didn't put a major stress on this application. There would have been a point where the load was too much for the system, which is the point that you start adding additional hardware to handle the load.

With the benchmark information shown in Tables 6-1 and 6-2, there's no doubt the XML implementations did hold up when the rubber hit the road. This is good news, which means we can use XML in our applications with confidence. You still need to be careful not to go overboard when using XML, however. For instance, it wouldn't be appropriate to convert a 100-megabyte file of delimited data into XML to load it into a database. Bulk copy programs exist that do a much better job with this type of data. When it comes to handling smaller data sets typically used by applications and Web pages, however, XML really holds up. XML data can also be used for more than returning data from a database. It can also be used to implement stateless architectures.

Stateless Architectures

A *stateless architecture* represents a system designed with multiple layers that interact with each other through stateless interfaces. A *stateless interface* represents one or more function calls into a component that does not have any prior information associated the caller. Within the past several years, stateless architectures have become a hot topic because they can handle a high volume of activity.

With the explosive growth of the Internet, systems developed to support Internet-based applications and content needed to handle a large number of concurrent users. The capability for an application to handle this high-volume load is called its *scalability*. In other words, when we talk about an application's scalability, we're referring to its capability to grow from handling a small concurrent load to handling a high concurrent load. A system can scale in two different ways: increasing server resources, such as memory and processors, is called *scaling up*, while spreading the work across multiple servers is called *scaling out*.

Scaling Up and Out

When we talk about *scaling up,* we're referring to a system or application's capability to take advantage of additional resources on a single server. These resources include multiple *Central Processing Units* (*CPUs*), additional memory, encryption accelerators, and other resources that can be added to a server to improve performance. Most of the development platforms in use today produce applications capable of taking advantage of these resources. Developers need to be aware of some issues, however, especially concerning multiprocessor equipment. With earlier versions of the Microsoft XML parser, performance decreased when deployed on a machine that had more than two processors. The standard compiler used by MFC and Visual Basic applications, as recent as Visual Studio 6.0, has a known issue with memory management on multiprocessor machines. Because this is beyond the scope of this book, we don't go into further detail, but you can see that designing a system to scale up takes additional consideration.

When it comes to *scaling out,* we're referring to the capability of a system or application to handle more users by adding additional servers. What this means is a bank of servers are used to handle requests. In some configurations, a user is directed to the same server during a single session. With many configurations, however, each call from a user is directed to the first available server, which could be the same one or a different one. In most Web site deployments, the middle-tier components that handle Web requests are installed on the same server. In other cases, the middle-tier components may be deployed to separate application servers to improve Web performance. n-tier business applications also use application servers with middle-tier components. In all these configurations, different performance and distribution issues must be considered to scale out successfully. This is where stateless architectures implemented using structured XML data provide benefit.

Review of State

For the purpose of this discussion, we define *state* as nothing more than data or information used to process requests. As mentioned in Chapter 1, a stateless architecture doesn't mean we won't have any state information. Some type of state always exists. It only means state information is managed differently based on operational boundaries. Different types of state also exist, differentiated primarily by the lifetime of the data that represents the state. *Persistent State* is typically database records or files with the longest lifetime. *Application State* is available only during the life of an application. *Session State,* specific to Web applications, is only available during the current session. *Instance State* is only available during the instance of an object. Finally, *Context State* is only available during the life of a method call. When discussing stateless architectures, the two main types of state we're interested in are Instance and Context.

Instance State

Instance State is the data associated with a specific instance of an object that's been created and initialized. Another way to think of it is the value of each attribute or variable in an object is also considered Instance State. In typical object-oriented designs, the attributes of an object are set and retrieved through one or more calls to getter and setter methods. Calls are then made to methods to implement the object's functionality. In all cases, this requires more than one call to the component. What this means is, once a component is created, it must be able to maintain its state information until the client finishes and releases the component. This works fine in most cases, but if the component were to be accessed across a completely stateless interface, this does not work.

Another way to think about instance state is to consider objects that require instance state as statefull objects. The instance data is tied to the lifetime of the object and represents the state of the object. When making multiple calls to a statefull object, or one that has instance state, the caller often depends on that object maintaining state from the previous call. With a stateless object, or one that doesn't maintain instance state, the caller doesn't expect any state from a previous call.

One example of a completely stateless interface is the `ADODB.DataSpace` component. This component represents an interface that allows access to remote business components across network boundaries using HTTP. When a business component is accessed using the `DataSpace` object, every call to the business component represents a call to a brand new instance of that component. If we were trying to access a standard business component with attributes and operations, the attributes would be reset on every call.

Another example of deployments that demonstrate the same behavior is components installed in a COM+ Application, which uses `SetComplete`, `SetAbort`, or the `Auto Complete` feature. In all these cases, the actual component is deactivated and released to free up resources. This is a common design for transactional components and is also used with nontransactional components to minimize resource use. As with the DataSpace interface, each call accesses a brand new instance of the component that doesn't contain any instance information from a previous call.

Context State

Context State is the solution to problems with Instance State when components are accessed across completely stateless interfaces. Instead of initializing an object's attributes before invoking methods, the attribute data is passed in with the call. This attribute data is called *Context Data,* which fits because it defines the context of the method call. A major benefit of using this type of state information is all the data needed to perform an operation is sent in one call. When accessing components across network and process boundaries this can be significant, as shown in the previous benchmark testing.

With this in mind, XML should obviously be the perfect candidate for Context State. Not only can we send in a large amount of state information, we can also send complex hierarchical structure information. For developers, XML is one technology that's made designing and implementing stateless architectures much easier. For example, several years ago developers were encouraged to use the ADO Recordset and the RDS DataSpace objects for stateless designs. You can imagine the frustration over performance and complexity these designs imparted on team members. With XML in place, the design is much easier to implement and much more robust when deployed. When using XML to pass Context State, we're creating stateless components, which we review in the next section.

Stateless Components

We established that even in a stateless design, state information still exists. So, what exactly does it mean when someone is designing a stateless architecture or building stateless components? Probably the best description of a *stateless component* is one that doesn't have any instance state available. A *stateless architecture* is a design that uses stateless components for an interface. As previously mentioned, other cases exist where a new instance of an object is created for every call, which also requires a stateless design. Along with using components or interfaces that might not support instance state, scalability requirements would be another reason to implement a stateless design.

Typically, stateless components are controllers or processors that use the parameters passed in to instantiate other components that perform the actual work. These other components are usually more *object-oriented* (*OO*) in design, but it isn't uncommon to mix process-based and OO-based components in a stateless design. The two main reasons for implementing a stateless design are transaction isolation and scalability. Most applications that need to scale also have high performance requirements, which is the main reason for a mix of process and OO-based components in this type of design.

By streamlining some operations into process-based functionality, we use less resources and perform fewer operations in the middle tier. That equates to faster response times to the user and a capability to scale up. In other words, the capability to handle more requests as resources are added is considered scalability. As you add additional resources, usually hardware, the design that uses fewer resources will also handle a higher number of requests than a traditional OO-based design. This is the reason we can state that a mixed design, which uses fewer resources, will scale better on the middle tier.

The Contacts interface used to return the Employee list is an example of a stateless interface that uses a process-based component. This interface will also be expanded in future chapters to add more components that use a traditional OO-based design. For now, let's examine the actual code inside the Contacts interface methods, which the following shows.

```
/// <summary>
/// Opens an EmployeeList and returns the data in a Recordset
/// </summary>
public ADODB26.Recordset getEmployeesRec()
{
   EmployeeList eData = new EmployeeList();
   if( eData.Open() == true )
   {
      return eData.getRecordset();
   }
   return null;
}


/// <summary>
/// Opens an EmployeeList and returns the data as XML in a String
/// </summary>
public String getEmployeesXml()
{
   EmployeeList eData = new EmployeeList();
   if( eData.Open() == true )
   {
      return eData.toXML();
   }
   return "<Error>Unable to open dataset</Error>";
}
```

You can see no real work is performed in either of the previously shown methods. Both of them create an `EmployeeList` object, open the object, and then use an accessor method to get the data. In reality, the `EmployeeList` object is a wrapper around an ADO Recordset, which provides access to the opened Recordset or returns it as XML data. Because we're pulling data straight out of a database for display on a Web page, no need exists to enforce strict type checking. As a result, we convert the Recordset directly into XML and return that to the client. Traditionally, OO designs would populate objects with data from the database, and then convert these objects as needed. The extra step of converting the data into objects for read purposes isn't useful and wastes processing time. When data is coming the other way, however, such as with an update operation, traditional OO components should be used when necessary.

At this point, we've only focused on stateless interface design. As we get into the next chapter on the *Simple Object Access Protocol* (*SOAP*), we look at alternate ways to access and manipulate this same data. Later chapters combine these approaches to produce .NET components that take advantage of Web services and SOAP. These methods also use traditional OO-based objects to perform business rule checking and update operations. The SOAP interface depends heavily on XML and is also the foundation for stateless Web service interfaces discussed in Chapter 8.

Summary

This chapter provided in-depth information about the advantages of using structured XML data across network and system boundaries, as well as within stateless architectures. We began by reviewing the definition of structure and applying it to two well-known types of data structure. Next, an example was developed that provided benchmark information on performance differences between using objects or XML to pass data. During the development of the example, we got a look at the C# language and saw how .NET components can be exposed as COM+ configured components. The benchmark numbers also showed XML is much better when crossing process and network boundaries, but the ADO Recordset typically outperformed XML when everything was in process. Finally, we spent some time examining stateless design and discussing how XML provides benefit to stateless architectures.

The following points summarize the chapter:

▶ Structure describes how something is put together.

▶ Two well-known types of data structure are relational and hierarchical.

▶ Hierarchical structure cannot show the same type of relationships as relational structure can.

▶ Many applications use data structured in a hierarchical fashion.

▶ XML is the perfect choice for handling structured data that needs to be passed across network and process boundaries.

▶ COM objects can be used and returned from .NET components.

▶ .NET components can be configured to run in a COM+ application.

▶ ADO Recordsets outperform XML *only* when used in-process. XML implementations outperform Recordsets in all other configurations.

▶ XML can also be used to implement stateless architectures.

▶ Using structured XML data to pass context state is often an excellent way to implement stateless business components.

Simple Object Access Protocol (SOAP)

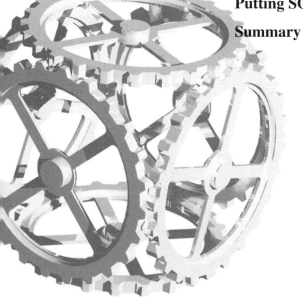

This chapter provides an in-depth look at the Simple Object Access Protocol (SOAP) 1.1 specifications. Instead of simply regurgitating the specifications, this chapter approaches them from a slightly different angle. In addition, all the actual schema definitions that make up the SOAP encoding, serialization, and message rules are examined. We start with a high-level overview of messages, jump straight into the encoding and serialization rules, followed by an in-depth look at message rules. Even within the discussion on encoding and serialization, there's a high-level discussion of serialization, followed by encoding, and then an in-depth look at serialization. This approach was used to minimize the need to reread different sections, making it easier to grasp the specifications completely in a shorter time. At the end of the chapter, we discuss a sample application that uses SOAP services in an ASP page to handle requests from an HTML client.

What Is SOAP?

Most people tend to think of SOAP as nothing more than a protocol for Remote Procedure Calls (RPC) over Hypertext Transfer Protocol (HTTP). However, this is only one implementation of *SOAP,* which is defined as a lightweight protocol for passing structured and typed data between two peers using XML. The specification doesn't require the use of HTTP or even a request/response type of conversation. Instead, SOAP can be used with any protocol that supports the transmission of XML data from a sender to a receiver. In fact, both Microsoft and IBM have implemented SOAP messages over SMTP, which means SOAP messages can be routed through e-mail servers.

The bottom line is SOAP is nothing more than a lightweight messaging protocol, which can be used to send messages between peers. The main goals of SOAP are focused on providing a common way to package message data and define encoding rules used to serialize and deserialize the data during transmission. Another goal is to provide a model that can be used to implement RPC operations using SOAP. All these goals are considered "orthogonal" in the specification, which means they are independent, but related. For example: A SOAP message should define encoding rules, but these rules needn't be the same rules defined in the specification.

The Message Exchange Model

Even though SOAP is basically a one-way protocol, it can be used to transmit XML data using any type of conversation supported by the transport protocol used. This means SOAP can be used for one-way, multicast, or request/response operations as long as the transport protocol supports them. These different operations are referred to as "message exchange models" in the SOAP specification. The patterns are actually implemented by combining SOAP messages. For example: The request/ response model is implemented with two SOAP messages: one that carries the request and one that carries the response.

Another important concept to understand with SOAP is it's intended to be transmitted along a message path from the sender to the receiver. This message path can pass through multiple stops before reaching the final receiver. This allows for processing of the message at one or more stops along the way. The actual implementation of transmitting the data across the message path is again based on the transport protocol used.

One good analogy to use with SOAP is to think of it in terms of an interoffice message. Most people are familiar with the concept of interoffice envelopes, which are used to send information between people or groups in an organization. On the front of the envelope are a series of lines, used to enter sender and receiver information, such as the department and name. When the receiver gets the message, that person crosses their name off the list on the envelope. The next step is based on information found on the envelope or in the message. If the message was one way, it stops there, and the envelope can be reused for another message. If the sender needs a response, then the receiver reverses the sender and receiver information on the envelope's next line and sends it back. The message could also be intended for multiple people, in which case the receiver passes it on to the next person on the list.

We mentioned previously that one of the goals of SOAP is to define how messages are packaged for transmission. The name of the XML element used to package the SOAP data is actually called the *SOAP envelope.* Inside the envelope, we can find header information and the actual message data. This is explored in more detail when we look at the SOAP envelope later in this chapter. However, the main point here is the SOAP message contains the information used to control its movement along the message path. This information is independent of the actual transport protocol used to transmit the SOAP message, which is similar to the way interoffice mail is handled.

HTTP Bindings

Another set of goals the SOAP team wanted to accomplish was to provide information on how to bind SOAP with a transport protocol. Because SOAP was primarily developed to support distributed services over the Internet, they chose the HTTP protocol. Two different bindings have been defined in the specification: one for standard HTTP and one for the HTTP Extension Framework. For this discussion, we only look at the standard HTTP implementation. Information about the HTTP

Extension Framework can be found in the SOAP specifications. Also important to understand is the SOAP specification doesn't override HTTP semantics. Instead, the binding of SOAP over HTTP maps to existing HTTP semantics.

Few requirements exist when using SOAP over HTTP. The main restriction is this: a SOAP message can only be sent using POST operations. For both an HTTP Request and Response, the Content-Type of the document must be set to "text/xml." This is important to remember because, if the content type isn't set correctly, the data could be transformed into a format that isn't readable by XML parsers. For instance, if the type was set to "text/html," invalid HTML characters would be converted to escape sequences that a parser couldn't use. The specific requirements for a request or response are detailed in the following paragraphs.

HTTP Request

The HTTP Request is required to have at least one header field with the name "SOAPAction." This field is mandatory and contains a URI that's used to indicate the intent of the SOAP message. The specification also allows for more than one SOAPAction field to support multiple intentions. No restrictions are imposed on the format of the URI that's used. In addition, the SOAPAction field isn't meant to replace the HTTP Request-URI, which typically maps to a FORM's action field. However, if the SOAPAction is initialized with an empty string, this means the intent can be found in the Request-URI. If the field doesn't contain any value, this means no indication of intent exists.

NOTE

A URI is a unique name recognized by the processing application that identifies a particular resource. URIs include Uniform Resource Locators (URLs) and Uniform Resource Name (URN).

The SOAPAction field is a little confusing and there's been a lot of discussion about how to use it on news servers. The field can be used in a variety of different ways. The following list shows some examples:

- ► SOAP HTTP Servers can use the SOAPAction field to route the message to different receivers.

- ► Firewalls or other servers can use the SOAPAction field to filter the SOAP message.

- ► Messaging implementations can use the SOAPAction field to indicate the message being sent.

- ► RPC implementations can use the SOAPAction field to identify the method name.

As you can see, this field can be used in many different ways. Currently, with RPC implementations, the SOAPAction field usually contains a namespace with the method name appended. The following code listing shows an HTTP Request header that's used to transmit a SOAP message.

```
POST /Pattern HTTP/1.1
Content-Type: text/xml; charset="utf-8"
Content-Length: nnnn
SOAPAction: "urn:rdacustomsoftware-com:Employee.GetEmployees"
```

HTTP Response

The response header returned from an HTTP SOAP request doesn't return anything different than a normal HTTP response, however, restrictions exist on the status codes. For any successful receipt and processing of an HTTP SOAP message, the status code returned should be in the $2xx$ range. If errors occurred—system or application—then the status code returned must be 500, "Internal Server Error." If a status code of 500 is returned, then the SOAP message must also contain a SOAP Fault element. The SOAP Fault is discussed in more detail later in this chapter.

RPC over SOAP

We already discussed the fact that SOAP supports the capability to implement Remote Procedure Calls (RPC). By taking advantage of the SOAP binding over HTTP, a request and response model supports the capability to invoke a method, and then to return the response. The actual implementation in SOAP is straightforward with few rules. The following is a description of the rules for implementing RPC in SOAP when using the SOAP encoding rules:

▶ The method is represented as a structure in the SOAP message. The structure, of course, is XML, and the element that represents the method must have the same name as the method. In addition, the element's datatype must match the datatype defined for the return value.

▶ Each parameter in the method is represented as a child element that's named after the parameter and defines the same datatype as the parameter. The parameter elements must follow the same order as the parameters in the method.

▶ Responses are structured the same way a method call is structured. The name of the response element isn't specified, but the standard implementation is to append "Response" to the method name.

▶ If the response returns a value, then the first child element contains the value. As with the response name, no specifications exist on what this element should be named, but the datatype must match the type defined for the method's return value. You can use one of the SOAP defined elements we discuss later, you could name it Response, or you could name it anything else.

▶ Any `out` or `in/out` parameters are also returned in the response structure following the "Response" element. These parameter elements must be named the same as the method parameter with the datatype also matching. And, as with the method call, these return parameters must maintain the same order as the original method.

▶ If errors are in the method invocation, then the SOAP Fault element must be returned. We discuss SOAP Faults in more detail later in this chapter.

As you can see, these rules are easy to follow and make RPC over SOAP easy to understand and implement. However, the previous description was also based on the use of SOAP encoding rules, which we examine shortly, and different encoding rules might be used. In addition, nothing in the specifications prohibits the use of different rules. Regardless of the rules used, RPC is still supported and the SOAP RPC rules are still valid. Instead of elements containing data, however, attributes may contain the data. In other words, the actual SOAP RPC specification is more generic than the previously provided description.

SOAP Is More Than RPC

Because HTTP is a request/response protocol, it is also an ideal candidate for demonstrating RPC implementations using SOAP. Unfortunately, this one implementation has been the primary focus of most discussions on SOAP. SOAP was meant to provide a lightweight protocol for sending structured and typed data using XML. Instead of using method names and parameters, a SOAP message could be sent a server that routes it to multiple receivers in an organization. In addition, one of the changes between the SOAP 1.0 and 1.1 specifications was to move the HTTP binding information to the bottom of the document to take the focus off HTTP. By now, it should be obvious that SOAP is much more than an RPC protocol over HTTP.

SOAP Encoding

Encoding rules are used to describe how data should be formatted for a particular operation. One example is the character encoding rules identified by the UTF-8 value typically used for XML and HTML. This set of rules defines how characters are represented using binary numbers a computer can understand. The operation of converting a character from the letter *A* to a value of 0x41 is considered encoding the character. Converting the value of 0x41 back to a letter *A* is called *decoding*. The operation of encoding data, transporting that data from one location to another, and then decoding it is also called *serialization*.

NOTE

For this discussion, binary data is considered encoded data. Character data is the human-readable, decoded, format found in XML documents.

The XML encoding rules handle the conversion of character data to and from binary data. In addition, programming languages that use XML have different binary representations of the data contained in the document. Numbers are an example of datatypes that can have a wide range of binary representations. On some systems, an integer is a 16-bit value while, on other systems, it may be a 32-bit value. In XML, the data is always represented as character data, which means an integer needs to be converted into character data when it's included in an XML document. If the system that converts the XML character data back into binary data assumes the number is an integer, a corruption of data can occur. For example, if a 32-bit system sends the number 48,000 to a 16-bit system, the resulting conversion to an integer will be incorrect because the maximum positive value a 16-bit integer can hold is 32,767. What we need is something that describes what an integer is, so systems know how to convert it from binary data to character data and back again, which is where the SOAP encoding rules apply.

Understanding Serialization

Before we get into the SOAP encoding rules, it helps to get a solid understanding of what happens when data is serialized using SOAP. We previously mentioned the operation of encoding, sending, and then decoding data is referred to as serialization. This makes sense in the context of sending messages; however, another definition is "serialization is the process of writing or reading an object to or from a storage medium." With SOAP, the objects are datatypes and the storage medium is an XML document. When the XML document is serialized, you can think of the document as an object and the storage medium for the document can be memory or file based.

With a SOAP message, several translations occur when data is sent from one system to another. Figure 7-1 shows the flow of an integer from a C++ application to a Java application. In the top-left corner is the C++ code that defines an integer and

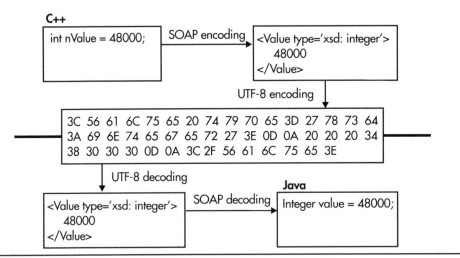

Figure 7-1 Serialization

assigns it the value of 48000. Next, SOAP encoding rules are applied to the integer and we end up with an XML element that has a type of integer. The XML document is then encoded with UTF-8 encoding rules and transmitted to the receiver as binary data. Once it reaches the receiver, the binary data is decoded using UTF-8 rules to convert the data back into character data. Finally, the XML character data is decoded using SOAP rules to create a Java integer with the value of 48000. This is an example of a simple datatype. SOAP also defines rules that handle much more complex datatypes.

The SOAP specification also defines a comprehensive set of rules for serialization, which defines how the application data should be handled. These serialization rules aren't the same as encoding rules, which are also found in the specification. Encoding rules define how the data should be converted from binary form to text and back again. Serialization rules define how the XML data should be structured for SOAP messages, which represents a restriction on how XML is used. Normally, data can be carried in XML as an attribute or as element content. The SOAP serialization rules only allow for data to be carried as element content.

Before we get into the serialization rules, several things are associated with encoding rules that you need to understand first. This is one area that makes the actual SOAP specifications somewhat confusing. The serialization rules are presented before the encoding rules, which means you need to read through everything several times before it makes sense. Instead of repeating that here, we look at the encoding rules next, and then follow up with the serialization rules.

Encoding Rules

The SOAP encoding rules are based on XML Schema specifications, which were discussed in Chapter 3. These specifications cover everything from simple datatypes, such as integers, to complex datatypes, such as structures with nested structures. However, some restrictions and extensions exist to the XML Schema defined in the SOAP specifications. When using SOAP encoding, any restrictions defined in the SOAP specification take precedence over the XML Schema specifications. In addition, it isn't mandatory for an implementation to use the SOAP encoding rules. Nothing is stopping a company from defining its own encoding rules for SOAP implementations. To ensure compatibility with a wide audience, however, the use of SOAP encoding rules are encouraged.

NOTE

When discussing the SOAP encoding rules, two terms are used throughout the specifications, which the reader needs to understand: accessor and value. Accessor is the reference used to access application data in a message. With SOAP, the element names are typically used as accessors. Value is the actual application data being encoded.

The SOAP encoding rules are contained in a W3C Schema that uses the following namespace declaration:

```
xmlns:SOAP-ENC='http://schemas.xmlsoap.org/soap/encoding/'
```

The URL identified in this namespace also represents the physical location where the schema can be found. These rules are based on W3C Schema specifications with additional attributes, elements, and datatypes designed to support the previously mentioned SOAP serialization rules. The majority of elements defined in the schema is based on simple xsd:type definitions with additional attributes added. For instance, the SOAP encoding rules define an element named SOAP-ENC:string based on the `xsd:string` type.

The specification also identifies two different types of elements that can be used in SOAP messages. The first type is called an *independent element,* which is defined as a top-level element. Independent elements can be a named element or one of the SOAP defined elements with an `id` used to access the element. The second type of element is called an *embedded element,* which are all other elements not at the top level. At this point the need to distinguish formally between independent and embedded elements may not be obvious, but this will make more sense as we discuss the encoding and serialization rules. As mentioned earlier, the encoding rules define elements and datatypes designed to support serialization. The next step is to examine some of these datatypes and describe how the SOAP elements are defined.

Common Attributes

One of the first definitions in the SOAP encoding schema is an attribute group named `commonAttributes`, shown in Listing 7-1. This group is used to add common attributes to all the elements defined in the schema. These common attributes are used to provide multireference access to elements in a SOAP message. An element can be defined with an `id` and then referenced from other elements. In addition, elements can reference other elements in the same schema or elements defined in an external source, using the `href` attribute. Finally, by adding the `anyAttribute` definition, it is valid to include attributes from other namespaces to SOAP defined elements without violating the schema.

Listing 7-1   *Common Attributes Defined*

```
<attributeGroup name='commonAttributes'>
  <attribute name='id' type='ID'/>
  <attribute name='href' type='uriReference'/>
  <anyAttribute namespace='##other'/>
</attributeGroup>

<element name='string' type='tns:string'/>
<complexType name='string' base='string' content='textOnly'>
  <attributeGroup ref='tns:commonAttributes'/>
</complexType>
```

Listing 7-1 also shows the element definition for a string type that includes the `commonAttributes` group in the type definition. The result is a SOAP string type that can be identified using the `id` attribute. This same element could also reference another element by using the `href` attribute. One rule when using the `href` attribute is the element shouldn't contain data, but no schema definitions enforce this rule. Finally, other attributes can be added to this element, which is done with arrays and the SOAP-ENC:position attribute, discussed later in this chapter.

The string type shown in Listing 7-1 is only one example of a definition that includes common attributes. All the simple types found in the W3C Schema specification—along with the majority of SOAP datatypes—have also been defined as elements with a `commonAttributes` group. Understanding how these attributes are used is important in understanding the encoding and serialization rules. Listing 7-2 shows several XML snippets that use the SOAP defined elements and common attributes. The first line in Listing 7-2 defines the namespace SOAP-ENC, which references the SOAP schema. Throughout the rest of this chapter, we assume SOAP-ENC is always defined this way. The next block of code shows schema definitions for three different elements. And, finally, the last two blocks of XML data show different ways to include the data in a SOAP message.

Listing 7-2   *Using Common Attributes*

```
xmlns:SOAP-ENC="http://schemas.xmlsoap.org/soap/encoding/"

<element name="EmployeeFirstName" type="SOAP-ENC:string />
<element name="LastName" type="SOAP-ENC:string />
<element name="EmployeeLastName" type="SOAP-ENC:string />

<SOAP-ENC:string id="FirstName">John</SOAP-ENC:string>
<EmployeeFirstName href="#FirstName" />

<LastName id="LastName">Doe</LastName>
<EmployeeLastName href="#LastName" />
```

The next-to-last group of XML data in Listing 7-2 shows the use of a SOAP defined element as an independent element with an `id` of "FirstName". As mentioned previously, an element in a SOAP message can be named or it can use the predefined SOAP elements based on SOAP datatypes. When using one of the SOAP elements, you also need to use the `id` attribute to access the element when processing the message. Remember, the SOAP string datatype, shown in Listing 7-1, is defined with the `commonAttributes` attribute group. The second element, EmployeeFirstName, is defined as a SOAP string that uses the `href` attribute to reference the first element.

The last group of XML data in Listing 7-2 shows the use of a named element defined as a SOAP string. This element is also assigned an `id` of LastName. The second element, EmployeeLastName, was also defined as a SOAP string that uses the `href` attribute to access the LastName element. This implementation isn't much different from the first implementation. The only difference is this: LastName was defined as part of the message's schema, while SOAP-ENC:string is defined as part of the SOAP schema.

Compound Datatypes

The SOAP encoding schema also defines two compound types for handling structured data named Struct and Array. The *Struct* datatype is used to handle data where the values are accessed by name. This also means the accessor names must be unique within a Struct. The *Array* datatype is used to handle data where the values are accessed by ordinal position within a sequence. The Array datatype also supports the capability to handle partial arrays and sparse arrays. In addition, the SOAP specifications support generic structured data similar to Structs and Arrays, but they don't use the SOAP compound types as a base.

SOAP-ENC:Struct

Listing 7-3 shows the definition of a Struct from the SOAP encoding schema. The first line defines an element named Struct based on the Struct complexType, which is defined in the same schema. The next block of XML data is a model group used to define a sequence of elements that can have any name. The last block of XML data is used to define the actual Struct datatype. This definition includes the Struct group with a `maxOccurs` of one, along with the `commonAttributes` attribute group that's included in most SOAP datatypes. The only constraint for a Struct datatype is it can contain multiple elements, but each element name must be unique.

NOTE

The use of tns as a namespace for types in the code samples represents the target Namespace of the schema being defined. For example, the use of "tns:Employee" refers to a datatype named Employee defined in the same schema.

Listing 7-3   *SOAP-ENC:Struct*

```
<element name='Struct' type='tns:Struct'/>
<group name='Struct'>
  <any minOccurs='0' maxOccurs='*'/>
</group>
<complexType name='Struct'>
  <group ref='Struct' minOccurs='0' maxOccurs='1'/>
  <attributeGroup ref='tns:commonAttributes'/>
</complexType>
```

Listing 7-4 shows two different schema definitions that can be used to describe an Employee structure with two elements. Both of these definitions represent the same encoding rules, however, the first one is much more condensed. By using the SOAP-ENC:Struct datatype, no need exists to include the sequence declaration and reference attributes. These definitions also support the capability to define structures with an `id` attribute, which can then be included in other structures with `href` attributes. The last definition in Listing 7-4 shows a generic XML structure that contains an element of type Employee and another element of type SOAP-ENC:Struct.

Listing 7-4   *Defining Structures*

```
<element name='Employee' type='tns:Employee' />
<complexType name='Employee' base='SOAP-ENC:Struct'>
  <element name='FirstName' type='string' />
  <element name='LastName' type='string' />
</complexType>

<element name='Employee' base='tns:Employee'>
<complexType name='Employee'>
  <sequence minOccurs='0' maxOccurs='1'>
    <element name='FirstName' type='string' />
    <element name='LastName' type='string' />
  </sequence>
  <attribute name='href' type='uriReference'/>
  <attribute name='id' type='ID'/>
  <anyAttribute namespace='##other'/>
</complexType>

<complexType name='EmployeeDetails'>
  <element name='Employee' type='tns:Employee'/>
  <element name='Manager' type='SOAP-ENC:Struct'/>
</complexType>
```

Now that you have a good handle on how structures should be defined, let's put it to use. Listing 7-5 shows three blocks of data that could be found in a SOAP message. The first block is an independent element that uses the SOAP-ENC:Struct element with an `id` of `Manager-1`. The second block of data is another independent element that contains EmployeeDetails information and conforms to the schema definition in Listing 7-4. Because the Employee element is based on the Employee type, it also contains the First and Last name elements. The Manager element was defined as a SOAP-ENC:Struct and it uses the `href` attribute to reference the first block, which contains the actual manager data. The last block of data is another EmployeeDetails block with different employee information, but the same manager. By taking advantage of references in SOAP messages, the amount of duplicate data sent between peers can be minimized.

Listing 7-5 *Using Structured Data*

```
<SOAP-ENC:Struct id="Manager-1">
  <FirstName>John</FirstName>
  <LastName>Hancock</LastName>
  <Title>Project Manager</Title>
</SOAP-ENC:Struct>

<e:EmployeeDetails xmlns:e="Employee-URI" >
  <Employee>
    <FirstName>Jane</FirstName>
    <LastName>Doe</LastName>
  </Employee>
  <Manager href="#Manager-1" />
</e:EmployeeDetails>

<e:EmployeeDetails xmlns:e="Employee-URI" >
  <Employee>
    <FirstName>Jack</FirstName>
    <LastName>Quick</LastName>
  </Employee>
  <Manager href="#Manager-1" />
</e:EmployeeDetails>
```

SOAP-ENC:Array

Once we begin moving from Structs to Arrays, things become more complicated. The Array datatype is designed to handle large amounts of data. It wouldn't make sense to use a Struct for multiple rows of data returned from a database. Instead, arrays of Structs or arrays of simple datatypes are more suited to handle these types of datasets. In addition, because arrays can handle large datasets, they need to provide flexible ways to manage that data. As with anything that must be flexible or generic, the complexity of implementation gets more difficult as flexibility is increased.

The Array datatype definition shown in Listing 7-6 is much more complex than the Struct definition shown in Listing 7-3. The first block of data shows a datatype definition used for array position attributes. The second set of data defines several attributes and an attribute group named *arrayAttributes* that uses these attributes.

This attribute group is included in the Array datatype definition, which makes the `arrayType` attribute mandatory for Arrays. The `arrayType` attribute is used to define the type and size of an array, while the `offset` attribute is designed to support the transmission of partial arrays. The third block of data defines an attribute and an attribute group used to identify array elements by position and to support the capability to transmit sparse arrays. The arrayMemberAttributes group isn't actually added to any datatype definitions. Instead, the attribute is used when needed, which is supported by the `anyAttributes` definition found in the commonAttributes group. The final block of data is the actual SOAP-ENC:Array definition, which is similar to the Struct definition with the addition of the arrayAttributes attribute group.

Listing 7-6   *SOAP-ENC:Array*

```
<simpleType name='arrayCoordinate' base='string'/>

<attribute name='arrayType' type='string'/>
<attribute name='offset' type='tns:arrayCoordinate'/>
<attributeGroup name='arrayAttributes'>
  <attribute ref='tns:arrayType' minOccurs='1' />
  <attribute ref='tns:offset'/>
</attributeGroup>

<attribute name='position' type='tns:arrayCoordinate'/>
<attributeGroup name='arrayMemberAttributes'>
  <attribute ref='tns:position'/>
</attributeGroup>

<element name='Array' type='tns:Array'/>
<group name='Array'>
  <any minOccurs='0' maxOccurs='*'/>
</group>
<complexType name='Array' content='elementOnly'>
  <group ref='Array' minOccurs='0' maxOccurs='1'/>
  <attributeGroup ref='tns:arrayAttributes'/>
  <attributeGroup ref='tns:commonAttributes'/>
</complexType>
```

As you can see, the Array datatype provides support to handle sets of data, while the Struct datatype is designed for individual structures of data. Although this isn't a goal, one reason for defining a structure like this is to provide the capability to transmit subsets of data. Most presentation components or applications have a limit on the amount of data they can handle. If you tried sending a data set with 10,000 records to a browser, the performance would be bad and some browser versions would crash with this much data. Typically, data sets that contain rows of data from a table are structured like an array. By using the Array datatype, it's possible to send only a block of 100 rows, which represents a partial array. In addition, you could send a few selected rows spread throughout a data set, which represents a sparse array. Finally, the SOAP specification also allows for multidimensional arrays and arrays within arrays.

Listing 7-7 shows several schema definitions that use the SOAP Array datatype. As you can see, the definitions are similar to the Struct type, but the implementation is different. The first definition shows a single-dimension array that contains Employee elements. The second is also a single-dimension array, but this one is defined as allowing any element name and type within the array. The last definition is a multidimensional array that contains the two arrays defined previously. Remember what we said about flexibility adding complexity: the real complexity with the Array datatype comes in the variety of different ways arrays can be implemented.

Listing 7-7 *Defining Arrays*

```
<element name='Employees' type='tns:Employees'/>
<complexType name='Employees' base='SOAP-ENC:Array' >
  <element name='Employee' type='tns:Employee'/>
</complexType>

<element name='Projects' type='tns:Projects'/>
<complexType name='Projects' base='SOAP-ENC:Array' >
  <any type='ur-type' />
</complexType>

<complexType name='CompanyInfo' base='SOAP-ENC:Array >
  <element name='Employees' type='tns:Employees' />
  <element name='Projects' type='tns:Projects' />
</complexType>
```

Listing 7-8 shows several different ways to describe single-dimension arrays within SOAP messages. The first example uses the Array datatype defined in the SOAP-encoding schema. The `arrayType` attribute is used to identify the type and number of elements in the array with the number located inside square brackets. For example, the first line in Listing 7-8 shows `arrayType='xsd:string[2]'`, which means the array type is xsd:string and has two elements. Also possible is to use an empty array size value, also known as the *asize value,* when the number of elements is unknown. The element names are arbitrary and can be anything, which is consistent with the Array type declaration in Listing 7-6.

Listing 7-8   *Single-Dimension Arrays*

```
<SOAP-ENC:Array SOAP-ENC:arrayType='xsd:string[2]' >
  <Item>StringOne</Item>
  <Item>StringTwo</Item>
</SOAP-ENC:Array>

<SOAP-ENC:Array SOAP-ENC:arrayType='xsd:ur-type[3]' >
  <Item xsi:type='xsd:int'>123</Item>
  <Item xsi:type='xsd:long'>654321</Item>
  <Item xsi:type='xsd:String'>StringData</Item>
</SOAP-ENC:Array>

<Projects id='Projects-1' SOAP-ENC:arrayType='xsd:ur-type[2]' >
  <xsd:int>123</xsd:int>
  <SOAP-ENC:String'>StringData</SOAP-ENC:String>
</SOAP-ENC:Array>

<Employees id='Employees-1' SOAP-ENC:arrayType='tns:Employee[2]' >
  <Employee>
    <FirstName>Jane</FirstName>
    <LastName>Doe</LastName>
  </Employee>
  <Employee>
    <FirstName>Jack</FirstName>
    <LastName>Quick</LastName>
  </Employee>
</Employees>
```

The second and third examples in Listing 7-8 show the use of an xsd:ur-type, which can represent any datatype. When the arrayType is defined as an xsd:ur-type, the elements must identify the type of data they contain by using xsi:type definitions or the actual type definition as the element name. The xsd:ur-type examples in Listing 7-8 show both ways that are valid for defining the element type. The second xsd:ur-type example also uses the Projects element defined in Listing 7-7.

The final example in Listing 7-8 shows an array of Employees also defined in Listing 7-7. Note, the `arrayType` is still required to indicate the type of elements included in the array. This means the original definition of Employees could have left out the element definition; however, by defining the element in the schema, the Employees array only supports Employee elements.

The next section of XML code, shown in Listing 7-9, represents two different types of multidimensional arrays. The first is a two-dimensional array of strings: the first size attribute represents rows and the second represents columns. The specification also allows for multiple dimensions and arrays within arrays. For example, the `arrayType` could have been defined as `'xsd:string[2,3,2]'`, which would indicate each column has two items.

Listing 7-9   *Multidimension Arrays*

```
<SOAP-ENC:Array SOAP-ENC:arrayType='xsd:string[2,3]'>
  <Item>Row1Col1</Item>
  <Item>Row1Col2</Item>
  <Item>Row1Col3</Item>
  <Item>Row2Col1</Item>
  <Item>Row2Col2</Item>
  <Item>Row2Col3</Item>
</SOAP-ENC:Array>

<CompanyInfo SOAP-ENC:arrayType='xsd:ur-type[][2]'>
  <Employees href='#Employees-1'/>
  <Projects href='#Projects-1'/>
</CompanyInfo>
```

The second block of XML data in Listing 7-9 shows an array that contains multiple arrays. This example uses the Employees and Projects elements populated in Listing 7-8 and defined in Listing 7-7. When an array is contained within a second array, its dimensions are listed first. In this example, the size of both Employees and Projects are unknown, which is indicated by the use of an empty setting. If the inner arrays were also multidimensional, the definition might look something like `'xsd:ur-type[,][2]'`, which identifies them as multidimensional arrays of unknown size. The example in Listing 7-9 also uses an array type of `xsd:ur-type`, which is a super type that includes all other types. If the innermost elements were all defined as the same simple type, such as an int or string, then that type would be used in the `arrayType`.

NOTE

SOAP Array indexes are zero-based, which means the first element in an array of five elements would be at position zero and the last element would be at position four.

The last set of XML data, shown in Listing 7-10, represents partially transmitted and sparse arrays. The first block of data defines an array of six strings with an offset value of four. This indicates only the data starting at position four in the array will be transmitted. Because arrays are zero-based, position four represents the second to last, or the fifth element out of six. As a result, only the last two elements are transmitted.

Listing 7-10   *Partially Transmitted and Sparse Arrays*

```
<SOAP-ENC:Array SOAP-ENC:arrayType='xsd:string[6]'
                SOAP-ENC:offset='[4]'>
  <Item>String Five</Item>
  <Item>String Six</Item>
</SOAP-ENC:Array>

<SOAP-ENC:Array SOAP-ENC:arrayType='xsd:string[,][6]'>
  <SOAP-ENC:Array href='#Array-5' SOAP-ENC:position='[4]'/>
</SOAP-ENC:Array>

<SOAP-ENC:Array id='Array-5' SOAP-ENC:arrayType='xsd:string[8,8]'>
  <Item SOAP-ENC:position='[1,5]'>Row2Col6</Item>
  <Item SOAP-ENC:position='[2,6]'>Row3Col7</Item>
  <Item SOAP-ENC:position='[3,7]'>Row4Col8</Item>
</SOAP-ENC:Array>
```

The last two blocks of data in Listing 7-10 represent sparse arrays. The first is a multidimensional array that contains multidimensional arrays of strings. In this example, only one of the outermost elements are included, which is the fifth element at array position four. This element contains a reference to the multidimensional array of strings that actually contains the data. The inner array could also have been added by using an `arrayType` instead of an `href` and inserting the subelements directly under the outermost element.

The innermost element in our multidimensional array is defined as another multidimensional array of strings, which is the last block of data in Listing 7-10. In this example, we only transmit three of the elements from the array. The `position` attribute uses the same syntax as dimension size attributes to define the index of a specific element in the array.

Serialization Rules

We're back to serialization again, and, we hope by now it makes sense why these weren't discussed before encoding rules and the SOAP datatypes. To be honest, some of the serialization rules were already discussed, specifically when arrays were covered. In addition, before looking into the encoding rules, we discussed what serialization is and how it works. With the encoding rules, we saw how different datatypes are defined and referenced within SOAP. The serialization rules further define how SOAP data must be structured when using the SOAP-encoding rules.

   The following list is a summary of the serialization rules found in the SOAP 1.1 specifications:

▶ All values are represented as element content.

▶ Multireference values must be defined as independent elements. Single-reference values can be independent or embedded.

▶ All elements that contain values must have a type definition by using either `xsi:type` attributes, schema-defined attributes, or elements. The datatype can also be defined by reference with array definitions.

▶ Multireference values must be identified with an `id` attribute defined as an ID type and accessible through the use of `href` attributes defined as uri-reference types. If an `href` attribute is used, then the element isn't expected to have content.

▶ Two types of data exist: simple and compound. *Simple datatypes* are defined as elements that don't contain subelements. *Compound datatypes* are defined as elements that contain subelements.

▶ Arrays can be multidimensional and they can contain single-reference or multireference values.

▶ All arrays must define an `arrayType` attribute, which has both type and size components, with the following type and dimension information.

   ▶ The type must be the same as the element type or a supertype of all elements in the array. If the array is multidimensional, then the type must represent the innermost element.

   ▶ The size component of the `arrayType` attribute should contain the sizes of all arrays, starting with the outermost array on the left.

► If an array contains other arrays, then the contained array's size attribute should be included in the arrayType definition to the left of the outer array's size attribute. For example, an array of strings may define the following arrayType: `'SOAP-ENC:arrayType='xsd:string[6]'`. However, if the array contained arrays of strings, the definition would be different: `'SOAP-ENC:arrayType='xsd:string[][6]'`.

► If a size isn't defined, then the size is unknown. However, size is still determined by examining the data.

► SOAP arrays can use an `offset` attribute to transmit partial arrays.

► Array member elements can use a `position` attribute to include specific elements in a transmission.

As you can see, these rules are based on the use of the datatypes and constructs defined by the SOAP encoding rules. By using these rules along with the SOAP encoding rules, interfaces are much more available to a larger audience. Remember this about the SOAP specifications we touched on at the beginning of this chapter: Each of the specification parts are orthogonal to each other, which means implementations aren't required to use SOAP encoding and serialization rules to be compliant with SOAP specifications. Once again, however, following standards makes more sense than inventing your own set of rules.

One possible reason for developing your own set of rules would be for internal business applications with unique data or transport constraints. For instance, large data sets perform badly when the structure is element-based instead of attribute-based. A company that handles a lot of large data sets internally could define an encoding scheme that defines attribute accessors instead of element accessors. The only drawback is the SOAP servers that process these messages must know how to handle the datatypes. This isn't difficult to do. XML is easy to use, but the consumers of the SOAP interface would be limited.

If you're familiar with the SOAP specifications, you might have noticed we haven't discussed the actual structure of SOAP messages in detail yet. We did cover the message structure at a high level, but left the details for later. The specifications start with the structure of SOAP messages, and then get into the encoding rules. The only problem is when you first read through the message specifications a lot doesn't make sense. However, we've now gone through the majority of encoding and serialization rules found in the specification. Now, it's finally time to look at the details of how SOAP messages are actually structured.

SOAP Messages

The interoffice message analogy used at the beginning of this chapter is a close representation of SOAP messages. Each SOAP message is contained in an element named *Envelope.* Inside the envelope, the message can include an element named *Header,* which carries additional information about the message. The message data is found in an element named *Body,* which, if included, follows the Header. The only thing that doesn't fit the analogy is an element named *Fault.* This element is added to the Body element if an error occurs when processing a SOAP request.

We've already gone through an in-depth look at the rules and structures associated with the schema for handling SOAP data. In this section, we examine the schema for handling SOAP messages. This schema can be considered an Envelope schema that uses the following namespace definition:

```
xmlns:SOAP-ENV='http://schemas.xmlsoap.org/soap/envelope/'
```

Similar to the namespace for SOAP Encoding rules, the URL in this namespace can be used to access the actual schema definition. Before getting into the Envelope, Header, and Body definitions, several global definitions are in the schema that we should consider.

Specifically, three global attributes, shown in Listing 7-11, are defined in the SOAP-ENV namespace. Both the `mustUnderstand` and `actor` attributes are meant to be used only by elements within the Header. The specification defines them at a global level, so they can be used by elements within the Header element. The Header element itself doesn't reference these attributes. We discuss their use in more detail when we discuss the Header element.

Listing 7-11   *Envelope Schema Globals*

```
<attribute name='mustUnderstand' default='0'>
  <simpleType base='boolean'>
    <pattern value='0|1'/>
  </simpleType>
</attribute>

<attribute name='actor' type='uri-reference'/>

<simpleType name='encodingStyle' base='uri-reference' derivedBy='list' />
<attributeGroup name='encodingStyle'>
  <attribute name='encodingStyle' type='tns:encodingStyle'/>
</attributeGroup>
```

The `encodingStyle` attribute, shown in Listing 7-11, is used to define the encoding rules that should be used. This attribute can be used on any element and applies to all children of that element unless a child defines a new `encodingStyle`. Normally, this would be set to the SOAP encoding namespace as the following shows.

```
SOAP-ENV:encodingStyle='http://schemas.xmlsoap.org/soap/encoding/'
```

Earlier, we discussed the possibility that a company might want to define its own set of encoding rules. If a company has its own encoding rules, then the `encodingStyle` attribute should reference that set of rules.

The `encodingStyle` attribute isn't meant to define schema locations, which seems a little confusing when all the samples use URLs. Instead, this is treated as a reference name the SOAP server can use to determine how to process the message. In addition, the SOAP specifications don't define a default set of rules, which means a SOAP engine parsing the message would use its own default rules, which would normally be the SOAP encoding rules. This attribute can also contain multiple URI references and it can be defined with an empty value. If the attribute is defined as an empty value, then all encoding style claims from preceding definitions are turned off.

Throughout all the previous descriptions we used message specific schemas to define the message data. But we haven't discussed how that schema data is actually accessed to validate the structures. At first, the `encodingStyle` attribute looked like a good candidate for defining schema location. But, as discussed previously, this is only used as a reference name. The truth is, a variety of ways exist in which schema data can be accessed.

The most common method for accessing schema data is to use a URL in the namespace definition that references the actual schema location. The SOAP specifications also support the W3C Schema specifications and the use of an `xsi:schemaLocation` attribute, which is described in Chapter 3. In all cases, the schema specification states the validating parser should first look for an embedded schema or one that's loaded in a schema repository before attempting to access external resources. The following guidelines describe how the SOAP parser should look for the schema:

1. If the schema information is embedded in the XML data, then use that.

2. Attempt to locate the schema, either in the document or in a local repository using the schemaLocation URI.

3. Attempt to locate the schema, either in the document or in a local repository using the namespace URI.

4. Attempt to locate the schema in an external resource using the namespace URI.

5. Attempt to locate the schema in an external resource using the schemaLocation URI.

6. The last ditch effort is to attempt to locate a schema using only the namespace name.

The previous list also represents the order of priority to be used when looking for a schema. With Web services, discussed in Chapter 8, the schema data is typically located in a local schema repository. One important aspect to note is this: if a schema cannot be located locally, the namespace URI takes precedence over the schemaLocation URI when attempting to locate an external resource.

SOAP Envelope

Listing 7-12 shows the schema definition of a SOAP envelope. As you can see, this isn't at all complex. References exist to the Header and Body elements, along with support to handle any additional elements or attributes. Important to note is the Header element has a `minOccurs` of zero, while the Body element has a `minOccurs` of one. In other words, the Header element is optional, but the Body element is required. One thing not defined in the schema, which is a SOAP rule, is any additional attributes or elements must be namespace-qualified. Other rules undefined in the schema are these: the Header element must be an immediate child of the Envelope if present, and the Body element must immediately follow the Header. If a Header element isn't used, then the Body element must be the immediate child.

Listing 7-12   *SOAP Envelope*

```
<element name="Envelope" type="tns:Envelope"/>
<complexType name='Envelope'>
  <element ref='tns:Header' minOccurs='0'/>
  <element ref='tns:Body' minOccurs='1'/>
  <any minOccurs='0' maxOccurs='*'/>
  <anyAttribute/>
</complexType>

<SOAP-ENV:Envelope
    xmlns:SOAP-ENV='http://schemas.xmlsoap.org/soap/envelope/'>
  . . .
</SOAP-ENV:Envelope>
```

Another important rule to remember is the SOAP envelope must be the top-level element in the XML document that contains the message. In addition, the XML document must not contain Document Type Definitions (DTDs) or processing instructions. Other than this, SOAP messages follow standard guidelines for XML documents, with the addition of XML Schema and XML Linking Language support.

Listing 7-12 also has an XML snippet that shows the definition of a SOAP envelope element. As mentioned previously, the namespace is defined as SOAP-ENV and uses a URI that references the schema. This is also the only method currently available for versioning the Envelope schema. When new schemas are defined, then this namespace URI will be updated with a different reference. This new reference represents a new version and is a standard way of versioning schemas. The W3C Schema specification already has several different versions: the 1999 version, `http://www.w3.org/1999/XMLSchema`, and the 2001 version, `http://www.w3.org/2001/XMLSchema`, are examples. The only change is in the year, but they represent two different versions.

SOAP Header

The *SOAP Header* is used to hold additional information about a message without affecting the message. As mentioned previously, if the Header is included, it must be an immediate child of the SOAP envelope element. Listing 7-13 shows the schema definition of a Header element. As you can see, no specific elements or attributes are defined for it. The definition does support the capability to add any element or attribute, however. And, as with the envelope, the SOAP rules specify that any elements or attributes added to this element must be namespace qualified.

Listing 7-13   *SOAP Header*

```
<element name="Header" type="tns:Header"/>
<complexType name='Header'>
  <any minOccurs='0' maxOccurs='*'/>
  <anyAttribute/>
</complexType>
```

As you can guess, the SOAP Header can be used in many different ways. The following is a short list of some different uses:

▶   The SOAP Header can contain authentication information, such as a user name and password or a session key.

▶ It can contain transaction information, such as a transaction key used to group database operations.

▶ Different sections of the SOAP message can be identified for a specific server.

▶ It can be used to implement a multicast transmission, where the header contains information about the next receiver of the message.

▶ It can contain state information carried between requests.

These are only a few different implementations that give you an idea of how powerful headers are.

When a SOAP server encounters a header in the SOAP message, it's required to look at the Header and determine if any actions are required and what those actions are. The Header itself doesn't contain data; instead, the Header information is placed in subelements called Header elements. The SOAP Header may also contain multiple Header elements. To help a server determine if it should process a Header element, the two global attributes—`actor` and `mustUnderstand`—are used. These attributes are only valid on Header elements, which are immediate children of the Header.

actor Attribute

At the beginning of this chapter, we said a message travels along a message path from a sender to a receiver. This path could include multiple intermediate servers that handle a message along the way. The `actor` attribute is used on a Header element to indicate who should handle the information. If a server determines it should handle a Header element, then it must remove that element from the SOAP message. The server can add a new Header element before passing it on to the next server.

If a Header element doesn't contain an `actor` attribute, this indicates the final recipient of the message is the actor. However, this doesn't mean the final recipient must process or understand the Header element.

mustUnderstand Attribute

This attribute is used on Header elements to indicate if the receiver of that element must understand the element. As shown in Listing 7-11, this is a Boolean attribute that can only contain a value of 0 or 1. If the value is 0, this indicates the recipient isn't required to understand the Header element. If the value is 1, the receiver is required to understand the message.

If the `mustUnderstand` attribute isn't used, the default value is 0. In other words, if the attribute isn't used, then the receiver isn't required to understand the Header element.

SOAP Body

This is where the actual message data is added to a SOAP message and, like the Header, the Body element doesn't contain any data itself. Instead the Body element can contain multiple child elements, which are called *body entries.* Each body entry must be encoded as an independent element with `id` and `href` attributes. The body entry elements must also be namespace qualified, and they can contain an `encodingRules` attribute. The body entries don't contain `actor` and `mustUnderstand` attributes like the Header element. Instead, all body entries are meant for the final receiver of the message. In addition, the final receiver must be able to understand and process the message.

Although no direct relationship exists between Header elements and Body elements, a Body element is equivalent to a Header element with the default `actor` and a `mustUnderstand` value of 1. In other words, if a Header element doesn't define an `actor` and defines a `mustUnderstand` value of 1, then it must be processed with the body entries. This could be used to force authentication or transactions associated with the body entries.

RPC Method Call

Listing 7-14 shows a SOAP message that represents an RPC method named "GetDetails," which contains a single parameter named "EmployeeID." This is a valid SOAP message and is used in the sample program discussed at the end of this chapter. As we discussed, the top element is named *Envelope* and is namespace qualified with the SOAP-ENV namespace. The Envelope element also contains the `encodingStyle` attribute, which is then applied to all child elements.

Listing 7-14   *SOAP Body with Method Call*

```
<SOAP-ENV:Envelope

     SOAP-ENV:encodingStyle='http://schemas.xmlsoap.org/soap/encoding/'
     xmlns:SOAP-ENV='http://schemas.xmlsoap.org/soap/envelope/'>
  <SOAP-ENV:Body>
    <rda:GetDetails xmlns:rda='urn:rdacustomsoftware-com:Employee'>
      <EmployeeID>14</EmployeeID>
    </rda:GetDetails>
  </SOAP-ENV:Body>
</SOAP-ENV:Envelope>
```

The first immediate child element of the Envelope in Listing 7-14 is the SOAP Body. The Body contains one entry named "GetDetails," which is namespace qualified with the `rda` namespace. This is the RPC method element described previously. In addition, the GetDetails element contains the one RPC parameter element previously described. This message represents a method call sent to the SOAP server using an HTTP request.

RPC Method Response

The result of the GetDetails call is shown in Listing 7-15. This example is an actual response from the SOAP server in the sample application for this chapter. The response uses more of the SOAP attributes than we've discussed in this chapter. For example, the Envelope defines both SOAP namespaces and the xsi namespace used by W3C Schema specifications. The response entry in the Body uses the xsi namespace and `schemaLocation` attribute to identify the location of the rda schema. The Projects element is defined as a SOAP:Array in the schema and this example shows the use of the arrayType attribute.

Listing 7-15   *SOAP Body with Method Response*

```
<SOAP-ENV:Envelope
      SOAP-ENV:encodingStyle=http://schemas.xmlsoap.org/soap/encoding/
      xmlns:xsi=http://www.w3.org/2000/10/XMLSchema-instance
      xmlns:SOAP-ENV=http://schemas.xmlsoap.org/soap/envelope/
      xmlns:SOAP-ENC="http://schemas.xmlsoap.org/soap/encoding/" >
  <SOAP-ENV:Body>
    <rda:GetDetailsResponse
         xsi:schemaLocation="urn:rdacustomsoftware-com:Employee
         http://localhost/Chapter7Web/Employee.xsd"
         xmlns:rda="urn:rdacustomsoftware-com:Employee" >
      <Employee>
        <EmployeeID>11</EmployeeID>
        <LastName>Barley</LastName>
        <FirstName>Mike</FirstName>
        <MiddleInitial>C</MiddleInitial>
        <OfficePhone>4105550485</OfficePhone>
        <CellPhone/>
        <Beeper>4105550839</Beeper>
      </Employee>
      <Manager>
        <LastName>Arcaro</LastName>
        <FirstName>Kim</FirstName>
```

```
      <Title>Office Manager</Title>
    </Manager>
    <Projects SOAP-ENC:arrayType="rda:Project[2]" >
      <Project>
        <ProjectID>3</ProjectID>
        <Name>November Banking</Name>
      </Project>
      <Project>
        <ProjectID>5</ProjectID>
        <Name>Zulu Market</Name>
      </Project>
    </Projects>
  </rda:GetDetailsResponse>
 </SOAP-ENV:Body>
</SOAP-ENV:Envelope>
```

One other point about the example in Listing 7-15 is this: the response contains a result set with mixed data structures, which represents the power of RPC over SOAP or, more precisely, the power of XML. By using XML, we can send structured data across loosely coupled binary interfaces without the dependency problems caused by tight coupling. However, this loose coupling also makes sending incorrect data structures easy on a request or response. Web services, discussed in Chapter 8, implements tighter coupling through service contracts. But application errors can still occur in any method call. As a result, the SOAP specifications also include an element meant to handle error information named *SOAP Fault.*

SOAP Fault

As previously mentioned, this element is designed to handle errors in SOAP messages. There must only be one Fault element in a SOAP message and it must be contained in the SOAP Body. In addition, if a SOAP Fault has been added, then the Body shouldn't contain any other entries. Listing 7-16 shows the schema definition for a SOAP Fault found in the Envelope schema. The schema defines four elements to contain the error information: *faultcode, faultstring, faultactor,* and *detail.* Both the faultactor and detail elements are optional.

Listing 7-16   *SOAP Fault Schema*

```
<complexType name='Fault' final='extension'>
  <element name='faultcode' type='qname'/>
  <element name='faultstring' type='string'/>
```

```
    <element name='faultactor' type='uri-reference' minOccurs='0'/>
    <element name='detail' type='tns:detail' minOccurs='0'/>
</complexType>

<complexType name='detail'>
    <any minOccurs='0' maxOccurs='*'/>
    <anyAttribute/>
</complexType>
```

Both the faultcode and faultstring are required elements and must be used to describe the error. In addition, the faultcode must be a namespace qualified value that can be used for processing. The faultstring should describe the error and shouldn't be used for processing. Listing 7-17 shows an example of a Fault response in the sample program. This is generated by the *SoapMessageObject,* which is included in the Microsoft SOAP Toolkit version 2.0.

Listing 7-17 *SOAP Fault Example*

```
<SOAP-ENV:Envelope
       xmlns:SOAP-ENV="http://schemas.xmlsoap.org/soap/envelope/" >
  <SOAP-ENV:Body>
    <SOAP-ENV:Fault>
      <faultcode>SOAP-ENV:Client</faultcode>
      <faultstring>Invalid Method Name: GetFault</faultstring>
      <detail/>
    </SOAP-ENV:Fault>
  </SOAP-ENV:Body>
</SOAP-ENV:Envelope>
```

The SOAP specifications have also defined four fault codes to be used with SOAP Fault entries. The specification also states these fault codes are required when describing faults defined in the specification. As you see, these codes are generic and are meant to be extended. The way you extend the code is by adding a more specific code separated from the generic code using (.)dot notation. For example, the sample in Listing 7-17 shows a generic code of `SOAP-ENV:Client`. A more specific code is `SOAP-ENV:Client.Employee`. Table 7-1 lists the four fault codes that are defined.

As mentioned previously, the faultactor and detail elements are both optional. In addition, they're meant for two different sections of a SOAP message. The faultactor is intended for errors with handling a Header element and indicates the actor that

SOAP Fault Codes	Description
VersionMismatch	This is used if an invalid namespace was used.
MustUnderstand	This is returned if the target server is unable to process a header element marked with a `mustUnderstand` of 1.
Client	This is an indication the client sent invalid information. This could be a badly formed request or constraints from a header causing the server not to accept the message.
Server	This indicates an error with processing the message. This could be a system error or anything else that keeps the server from completing the request.

Table 7-1   *SOAP Fault Codes*

encountered the fault. Normally, a fault in the body wouldn't include this attribute, but it could be set to the receiver of the body. The detail element is meant to handle detailed information from an error with body entries. The detail element also works in a similar manner as Header and Body elements. It only contains subelements, which are called detail elements and must be included if an error is in the body. The SOAP specification also states that the detail elements must not contain any information about Header errors.

Putting SOAP to Use

We've gone through the SOAP specifications in detail, and now it's time to see how SOAP is really used. Right now, many different vendors and developers are producing SOAP applications. One of the biggest must be the .NET initiative from Microsoft. Although buried deep under the covers, the Web service and Remoting methods used in .NET take advantage of the SOAP protocol. These interfaces can still use other types of transport protocols. However, SOAP is the default protocol for Web services at all times, as well as for remote calls—called Remoting in .NET—when the calls cross machine and process boundaries.

Chapter 8 looks at Web services and discusses more of the .NET implementation in detail. At this point, we focused on SOAP outside the context of Web services and .NET. The reason for understanding SOAP at this level is many applications and platforms will need to integrate with Web services and .NET using only the SOAP message protocol. In reality, a big mix of technologies is going to be in use over the foreseeable future. SOAP makes it easy for all of those technologies to work together. For example: An HTML page on a Web site running on NT 4.0 using older technologies might need to use data from a Web service running on a .NET platform. In contrast, a .NET application may need to access information from an older system running on an IIS 4.0 platform. In addition, either of these platforms could interact with a Web service running on a Java platform. All of this is possible today, and we have developed an application that demonstrates how it can be accomplished.

Sample Application

The sample application can be downloaded from the Downloads section of the McGraw-Hill/Osborne Web site: **www.osborne.com**. This contains an HTML page that uses XML data islands to interact with an ASP page, which uses objects from the Microsoft SOAP toolkit version 2.0. The example also takes advantage of XML for SQL Server and uses XML templates to invoke queries against the database. XML template queries are explained in more detail in Chapter 11. Interesting to note, however, is the queries also use XSL templates, described in Chapter 3, to convert the query into a SOAP response.

Once you download the sample application, it should be expanded into a separate directory while maintaining the directory structure. A backed-up SQL Server database named Employee.bak is included; it should be restored to an existing SQL Server installation. This is the same database used in other examples, so restoring this database a second time isn't necessary if that has already been done. The HTML page is designed to be stand-alone and can run from any location with an IE 5.0 browser installed. The ASP page and XML templates must be running on a system that has IIS 5.0, SQL Server 2000 and the SOAP toolkit from Microsoft. Detailed information about setup and configuration is in the readme file.

The application itself is an Employee directory that can be used to return detailed information about each employee. The top of the page contains buttons to get the list of employees, get details, and get a Fault element. The bottom of the page contains the actual SOAP request and SOAP response messages that are sent back and forth. These messages were used to generate some of the sample code shown earlier.

When using the application, the employee list must be retrieved first before attempting to get details. The GetDetails call is also invoked if a user's name is double-clicked in the list displayed. As mentioned before, the HTML page can be run from any location. The only modification is to change the URLs in the JavaScript used to access server resources from "localhost" to the name of the server that contains the Web site. By working with this sample and looking at the code examples, you should get a good understanding of how SOAP works.

Summary

This chapter provided detailed information on the SOAP message protocol, along with examples on using SOAP. We began with a high-level view of SOAP messages, and then jumped into the SOAP encoding and serialization rules. While discussing serialization, we also started at a high level, and then provided more detail after getting a good understanding of the encoding rules. Once the low-level rules were discussed, we moved on to details of the actual SOAP message. We also discussed the use of SOAP in various implementations and provided a sample application that uses SOAP in HTML pages and ASP.

The following list covers the main topics discussed:

▶   SOAP message overview with a discussion of HTTP binding and RPC over SOAP

▶   SOAP encoding rules and datatype definitions

▶   In-depth look at SOAP schemas that define the encoding rules

▶   SOAP serialization rules along with an explanation of how serialization works

▶   Examples that only use the SOAP message protocol

Understanding Web Services

IN THIS CHAPTER:

What Is a Web Service?

Designing Web Services

Building Web Services

Universal Discovery, Description, and Integration (UDDI)

Summary

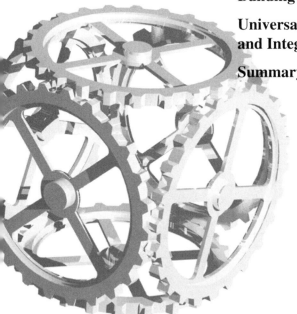

This chapter starts by describing what a Web service is and how to use Web services in applications. We discuss how to design Web service interfaces and when it's appropriate to use Web services in a design. The discussion on design techniques focuses on distributed design and the difference between application-based interfaces and object-based interfaces. We also examine an actual Web service design implemented on an internal business application. After examining the design techniques, we build a Web service using the same data and information discussed in Chapters 6 and 7.

While building the Web service, you have a chance to look at some of the features available with Visual Studio.NET that make it easy to build, deploy, and access Web services. The main focus of this chapter is Web service design. Much more detailed information about building Web services with .NET can be found in Chapter 14. Some of the .NET features you look at in this chapter are DataSets and how to use them to describe Web service interfaces. In addition, you examine the framework support for generating test harnesses and *Web Service Description Language* (*WSDL*) files. We also review the integration with UDDI and the capability to locate and insert external Web service references into an application. Finally, on the subject of UDDI, you learn what UDDI is, and how businesses and individuals can take advantage of UDDI to register and locate services.

What Is a Web Service?

What is a Web service? is a question that probably has many developers confused right now. Most of the descriptions and examples found online or in articles focus on using a Web service like an object. When described as an object interface, it sounds like Web services replace COM or J2EE, which is incorrect. In fact, Web services are meant to provide an interface into applications built using today's object-based platforms like .NET, COM, and J2EE. The key difference is a Web service is an application interface, not an object interface. In addition, Web services are targeted for distributed applications, where a loosely coupled interface is preferred over tightly coupled object interfaces.

To understand Web service, we still need to look at the technical description, so let's start with that. Next, we discuss real-world descriptions of Web services and where they fit into application development. Most of the discussions in this chapter focus on implementing Web services using HTTP and SOAP, but it's important to understand you aren't limited to these protocols. In fact, a Web service can be anything that's accessible via the World Wide Web.

The Technical Description

A Web service is described as programmable application logic accessible via standard Web protocols. This definition shows up in almost every discussion of Web services, but what exactly does it mean? If you're familiar with COM, then you might have noticed this definition sounds a little familiar. In fact, COM automation objects are described as programmable objects. A *programmable object* can be described as an instantiation of a class that can be manipulated in your application by calling member functions. The controls used in a Visual Basic application or data access components like *ActiveX Data Objects* (*ADO*) are considered programmable objects. A Web service takes this concept farther by allowing programmatic access to other applications through the use of standard Web interfaces.

The problem with COM objects, or any other programmable object, is they tend to be difficult to use in a distributed environment. The programmatic interfaces are based on *Remote Procedure Call* (*RPC*) specifications that are platform-specific. Several high-level interfaces exist, such as DCOM and CORBA, that sit on top of the RPC layers to make implementation easier. For these interfaces to work, however, a client needs to know where the object is located and how to communicate with that object. In other words, if the object uses DCOM, the client must communicate using DCOM. In addition, security and configuration can cause further restrictions on the use of programmable objects in a distributed environment.

With a Web service, you don't have the same platform limitations because they're based on standard protocols available to many platforms. The RPC layer is implemented using common Web-based protocols already in use today. The high-level interface layer that sits on top of the Web protocols can be based on XML Schemas, which are also widely supported. As you can see, the use of standard protocols makes it much easier to deploy and access Web services, but understanding that a Web service isn't recommended for all types of interfaces is important.

A Web service should only be used when unknown clients exist or when the use of standard Web protocols is preferable to using low-level RPC interfaces. With distributed or client/server designs, in a controlled environment, the use of DCOM, CORBA, or binary over TCP/IP would be the preferred choice because they perform much better than Web service. The important term here is a *controlled environment,* which means you must have control over both the server and client. We examine this in more detail when discussing the COM+ Web service design, but one interesting thing to note is the reason most companies began using Web-based applications was to alleviate the need to install or configure application-specific data on client machines, which rules out most RPC implementations.

So far we've established that a Web service is a piece of application logic that can be used by other applications in a distributed environment. We also stated that a Web service is based on open standards. In most cases, these standards are HTTP and XML, however, it's possible for a Web to be implemented using other Web-based protocols and data structures. *Hypertext Transfer Protocol* (*HTTP*) is a transport protocol, supported by most platforms, which represents the RPC layer of a Web service. *eXtensible Markup Language* (*XML*), also supported by most platforms, is used to define the structure of the interface between remote clients and Web service applications.

The Real Description

Although the definition of a Web service is pretty straightforward, it's still unclear when Web services should be used and how you would use them in an application. This is a controversial subject: some developers try to replace business objects with Web services, while others believe they're only useful as high-level interfaces between two businesses. A middle ground exists between the two that makes more sense and helps resolve many issues with distributed applications. The best approach to Web services is to think of them as an interface into systems that need to be accessed using Web-based protocols.

These system interfaces should also be high-level interfaces that provide application services, rather than low-level interfaces into application objects. The difference between the two has to do with the amount of communication between components and the need to maintain state using these interfaces. Traditional low-level object interfaces require initialization method calls to perform operations and additional method calls to access the attributes or data. This type of interface doesn't work well in a distributed environment where objects are spread across machine and network boundaries. Instead, for distributed applications, the system interface should seek to minimize the required number of method calls. Ideally, most operations should only take one call that returns all the required data.

As mentioned previously, a Web service isn't only an interface between two businesses. Web service can be used to provide interfaces between applications in a company along with components in an n-tier distributed design. Things like credit-card processing or Yellow Page services represent implementations that make sense in a *Business-to-Business* (*B2B*) interface. Employee lookup and management services can be used between different applications in a company. These same interfaces can be used in a single application to distribute the business components across different servers. All these are valid implementations that represent high-level interfaces into applications.

Later in this chapter, you take an in-depth look at designing Web services, and then you build a Web service based on the employee examples discussed in Chapters 6 and 7. You see how the employee information could be used in a B2B interface, between applications in a company, and within a single application. While reading Chapters 6 and 7 prior to this one isn't necessary, the information they contain provides the foundation for the information discussed in this chapter. Chapter 6 focuses on structured data and how XML resolves issues with distributed design. Chapter 7 examines *Simple Object Access Protocol* (*SOAP*) and looks quickly at how it can be used in a distributed design with the SOAP Toolkit. The employee Web services we discuss in this chapter will be developed using Visual Studio.NET.

Web Service Platforms

Another aspect about Web services that should be clarified right away is that these aren't unique to the Windows.NET platform. This should be obvious because Web services are based on open standards, however, most of the recent discussions about Web services have centered around .NET. The .NET platform makes building and using Web services much easier than ever before, but Web service designs have been around for a long time. In addition, Web service designs can be implemented using any development platform that supports Web-based protocols. In fact, many of the major J2EE application vendors are starting to add support for Web services into their application servers.

To be honest, the concept of Web services has been around for a while, but it wasn't called Web services. If you developed a Java Applet that runs in a client browser, and then reaches back to a Java Servlet to perform operations, you've developed a Web service. Another example includes remote scripting in ASP, which uses client-side script to access methods in ASP pages running on the server. These are both examples of Web service designs that have been in use on different platforms long before .NET was introduced. Even though they were based on open Web standards, however, they tended to be proprietary in implementation.

With early Web service designs, developers had no way to build a client that accessed a server interface without having intimate knowledge of the server implementation. A Java Applet can access an ASP page or use client-side script in a browser to access a Java Servlet, but the implementation might not always work. The actual data returned might not be structured in a format the client can handle and the client would need to know exactly what that format was. The only way to find out was either to develop the server application or have access to information about the format used. The current phase of Web service design resolves these issues with the use of standards-based data structures, interface descriptions, and discovery services.

Defining the Standards

Microsoft is currently teamed with other major venders like IBM and Ariba to define standards for Web services. These standards include specifications like SOAP and WSDL, which is an XML Schema that defines how Web service interfaces are described. The standards also include a Yellow Pages type registry of available services called the *Universal Discovery, Description, and Integration* (*UDDI*) Service, which is a Web service itself. These standards help make Web services available to a much wider audience and help facilitate a distributed services model where companies provide common services that can be used by any application that needs them.

Along with defining these standards, all three companies have provided different implementations based on the standards. Microsoft has developed a SOAP Toolkit that includes utilities to generate WSDL files automatically. The Microsoft .NET Framework also provides utilities to generate WSDL files, just by sending an HTML query to a Web service. Chapter 14 provides more in-depth information on developing Web services with Visual Studio.NET. In this chapter, we use Visual Studio.NET, but the focus is on the design and implementation of Web services. Finally, all three of these venders have also implemented UDDI registries that companies can use to register their services. As a result, we will look at UDDI and examine how it can be used to register and locate Web services. We will also look at the integration of UDDI into the Visual Studio.NET development environment.

Designing Web Services

By now, it should be obvious that a Web service is best implemented as an interface for a distributed application. As discussed previously, these applications can be distributed within a company or around the world. With this in mind, let's start with a discussion on design techniques for building distributed applications, followed by an example of a distributed design that uses Web services. Once you have a good handle on these design techniques, we'll explore how to implement and use Web service interfaces.

Distributed Design

Distributed applications are complicated and difficult to build. In fact, a large majority of distributed application projects end up going over budget, getting canceled, or failing outright. The main reason for this has to do with the complexity of integrating the different components that make up the complete application. Several different factors add to this complexity, such as the type of RPC interface used and the boundaries that method calls have to cross. These boundary layers can be different threads within a single process, different processes on a single machine, or several machines connected in a network. Understanding these boundaries and the way data moves across these boundaries is critical to the successful implementation of a distributed design, which was demonstrated in Chapter 6.

NOTE

Throughout this discussion on design, we'll use the terms "client" and "server." These aren't the client applications and server applications found in a client/server design. Instead, the client is only the object that's making a call to another object, which becomes the server.

We have two basic types of interfaces between components: tightly coupled interfaces and loosely coupled interfaces. With a *tightly coupled interface,* the client must have information about all the parameters and parameter types of the server method before it can be compiled. With a *loosely coupled interface,* the client doesn't need this information until it's running and makes the call to the server. Web services represent a loosely coupled interface where the client isn't required to have specific knowledge about the server interface until it's ready to make the call. In fact, Web services are considered *self-describing interfaces,* which is about as loosely coupled as you can get.

Understanding where to use the different types of interfaces in a design is important when it comes to distributed applications. If you have a server component that's accessed by clients from different machines on a network, tightly coupled interfaces can cause many problems when it comes to development and deployment. On the other hand, if all your components are running in the same process space, and they use Web services to communicate, you end up with major performance problems. An ideal design approach is to use tight coupling within the same process space, and then move toward looser coupling when crossing process or network boundaries.

This still doesn't mean you should use Web services for all loosely coupled interfaces. In fact, different degrees of loose coupling can be used in a design. The interfaces can be defined to take only a string parameter and return a string as the result. This same approach can be used with ADO Recordsets or .NET DataSets. In these cases, the client needs to know the interface is a string or a Recordset and must couple to that interface. However, the actual parameters used in the implementation can be encapsulated in those datatypes. For instance, with the string type, you can pass multiple parameters in a comma delimited string or, even better, in an XML structure passed as a string. You can package up data into a single datatype in many different ways and pass those parameters into an interface. This type of packaging is still considered loose coupling and represents a way to implement chunky method calls.

Breakdown of a COM+ Web Service Design

So far, we've talked about interface coupling in distributed designs with some indication of where different types of interfaces belong, but not enough to see how it all fits together. Figure 8-1 shows an actual Web service design implemented with COM+ technologies on a Microsoft platform. The application that used this design was a form-based Web Application with over 140 Web pages and interfaces with several external systems. The application was deployed internally and only available to internal systems within the company. Some of the Web service interfaces in this application are also used by other groups in this company to get application data from us.

This design in Figure 8-1 represents one possible way to implement Web services within an organization. On the browser, you could count on having *Internet Explorer* (*IE*) version 5.01 or higher, but weren't allowed to install any additional components. Because of this restriction, we could only rely on the use of standard HTTP protocols, available with IE, to interact with the server. Because Web service interfaces are based on HTTP, we could take advantage of them in this design. As you can imagine, this is still quite complex. It works, but it must rely on many different factors. When you learn about building Web services with .NET in Chapter 14, you'll appreciate how easy it is to implement distributed designs with .NET.

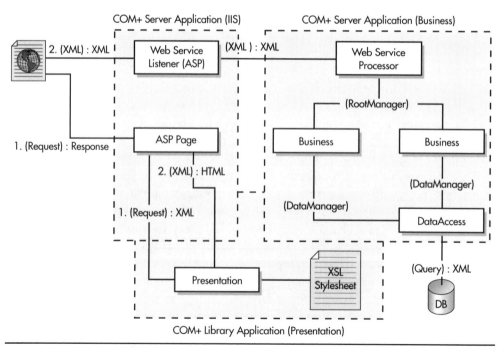

Figure 8-1   *COM+ Web service design*

This could have been done without the use of Web services, where all the content is generated on the server, but that means every action against the server requires a complete reload of the content in the browser. With the use of Web services, you can take advantage of XML support built into IE and make calls to the middle tier using the XMLHTTP protocol. You can also take advantage of XML data islands in the browser to bind the data with HTML elements. Furthermore, because Web services were used, other applications within the organization could interact with your business layer without using your presentation layer. The shaded areas in Figure 8-1, with dashed lines around them, represent different COM+ packages that make up the overall implementation. Starting with the presentation tier, we'll look at each major tier in the design.

Presentation Tier

The *presentation tier* represents all the components used to generate a display with which users can interact. The components of a presentation tier aren't necessarily located in the same physical location. With the design shown in Figure 8-1, the browser page (far left), ASP page, Presentation component, and XSL stylesheet are all part of the presentation tier.

Starting from the left in Figure 8-1, the browser makes a call into an ASP page, installed in an IIS COM+ application, to get the initial data for the page. The call between the browser and the IIS application crosses network boundaries and is done with HTTP protocols. Once inside the IIS application, calls are made into a presentation component that converts the Request object, instantiated by IIS, into XML data. Because the presentation component is installed in a COM+ Library application, it will run within the same process space as the IIS application. In addition, because the ASP page and presentation component are all in the same process and part of the same development effort, no problems occur with using tight coupling and objects.

The presentation component handles all the navigation and initial generation of HTML for the application. This is done by first generating XML that contains information about the page, data passed in on the QueryString or HTTP Form, and SiteMap information, which describes the page layout. This XML is then transformed into HTML with the use of an XSL stylesheet. Next, the HTML is sent back to the browser where it's displayed. So far, we haven't interacted with the business tier to perform any business operations. In other words, a complete separation exists between the presentation tier and the business tier. One thing to remember is, even though we might be calling components on the same server as the business tier, they're still considered part of the presentation tier.

Business Tier

As with the presentation tier, the *business tier* isn't limited to components running on the same physical machine. With the example shown in Figure 8-1, the Web Listener is part of the business tier. In addition, all the components in the top-right gray box of Figure 8-1 are part of the business tier. These components include a Processor object, Business objects, and Data objects. The processor uses a *Façade design,* which means it's a single entry point that hides the actual entry point into the underlying objects. This Façade object knows how to handle requests from the presentation tier and what business components to use. The data components in this design provide an abstraction layer between the business components and the data services tier. These components are still part of the business tier.

When the Web Application needs to perform business operations, it makes a call into the business tier through the use of a Web service listener. The listener is instantiated as an ASP page that lives in the IIS application process space. The interaction between the browser and ASP page uses standard HTTP protocols. The Web service listener then instantiates a Web service processor that's part of the business tier and passes the XML request as string data. Once the business tier has processed the request, it returns the data in an XML string format back to the Web service listener, which then sends it back to the browser as an HTTP response.

The business objects in this design are all packaged into a separate COM+ Server application, which represents a process boundary between the presentation and business component. As a result, we don't want to implement tight coupling or pass objects between these layers. To accomplish this, the business layer uses a Façade object, which is the Web service processor shown in Figure 8-1. As mentioned previously, this processor object exposes an interface that takes XML as a string input and returns XML as a string. Inside the processor, it instantiates a *RootManager object,* which is nothing more than a wrapper that provides operations on the XML data structure we're using. The RootManager is then used to interact with the XML and determine what actions need to be performed.

The RootManager object is then passed into business components that perform business operations based on parameters included in the XML passed into the Façade. In this design, the interface is still somewhat loosely coupled; it only expects the single object reference. Coupling still exists, though. Both sides need to know about the RootManager object. Also, within the business components, they can instantiate and use other objects, not shown, that do have tightly coupled interfaces. This design decision is unique to distributed Web Applications where a majority of the requests only retrieve data. Instead of instantiating a bunch of tightly coupled business objects and converting them into XML, it's much more efficient to encapsulate data-centric objects with business objects that perform operations on the data. By passing objects, you also get a performance advantage of direct access to the XML loaded in an object, instead of constantly converting it into objects and back into strings for each business action that must be performed.

The next step is to encapsulate the actual data requests into a DataManager object and pass that object into data access components. In reality, the DataManager is encapsulated by the RootManager and has direct access to the XML object the RootManager encapsulates. The only difference is the DataManager exposes additional methods used to perform data access operations against the data services tier. The important thing to understand here is the data access components are still part of the business tier. They are deployed within the same COM+ application, or process space, and they use tighter coupling than you would with an interface that crosses process and network boundaries.

When the data access component completes its call to the data services tier, it returns control to the business component. The business component can then call additional data access components or return control to the processor. The processor can call additional business components or, if the action is complete, return the result to the Web service listener as XML string data. Finally, the Web service listener passes that data back to the browser where it's processed.

Data Services Tier

The *data services tier* represents all the components associated with a database engine. This includes stored procedures, views, database schema, and even the XML interfaces provided by newer versions of the SQL Server OLE DB provider by Microsoft. Some of these new XML interfaces include *mapping schemas,* which is an XML Schema that maps database fields to XML elements, and *XML templates,* which is a template-based way to define XML interactions with SQL Server. In addition, SQL Server supports new keywords that can be used to return the query results as XML, instead of a Recordset.

In this design, we used SQL Server 2000 for the data services tier because it supports the use of XML in queries and stored procedures. The interface layer between the business tier and the data services tier represents another layer that crosses process boundaries and, in most cases, network boundaries. This interface is handled by low-level data access protocols, such as OLE DB, which, in turn, use low-level RPC interfaces, such as TCP/IP and Named Pipes. For this design, the query can be accomplished through XML mapping schemas or stored procedures. In all cases, the data is returned in an XML format, which is then added to the XML encapsulated by the DataManager.

Putting It Together

Now that we've walked you through all the layers of the design shown in Figure 8-1, let's go back through it from start to finish and see how it all fits together.

▶ The browser requests content from an ASP page, crossing network and process boundaries. This interface uses HTTP, which passes string data across these boundaries.

▶ The ASP object interacts with a presentation component to handle initialization of the XML and to generate HTML that's returned to the browser. The interfaces between the ASP page and presentation component are tightly coupled because they both operate in the same process space.

▶ The browser calls back into a Web service listener, which then calls a Web service processor in the business tier. The interface layer between the browser and the listener is HTTP. The interface between the Web service listener and processor is loosely coupled with the use of XML passed as a string. In other words, the data is passed through the Web Listener directly to the Web processor without transformation.

▶ Within the business tier, the XML is encapsulated in objects, and then manipulated by business and data components to perform the action requested. All these interfaces are in the same process space, which means tighter coupling can be used and objects can be passed around by reference.

▶ Interaction with the data services tier uses low-level interfaces that require tighter coupling, but are designed for performance. The data services tier returns XML back to the business tier, which is then encapsulated and manipulated.

▶ When the business tier is done, the XML is returned to the browser through the Web Listener where it's displayed or processed.

As you can see, the Web service requests represent loosely coupled interfaces that take advantage of standard protocols and data structures. The processor that handles the request represents a *chunky* interface, which represents an interface where multiple operations are packaged into one call. The business component interfaces are more tightly coupled to take advantage of the performance benefit with everything running in the same process space.

Several key concepts also stand out in this design. The presentation and business tiers are completely separated. This approach allows for rapid development of an application because no coupling dependencies occur between the presentation and business tier. Because a Web service interface was used for the business tier, no client dependencies or installation requirements exist, other than the use of IE 5.01 or greater. The Web service interface can also be used by any other group within the organization to perform business actions. Finally, and most important, the interface into the business tier uses chunky method calls that represent an application-based interface versus an object-based interface.

Although the design in Figure 8-1 shows one way to use Web services within an organization, you can use and take advantage of Web services in many other ways. Also, because this design is meant for a closed environment, it doesn't take advantage of protocols and services like SOAP, WSDL, and UDDI, which would make it available to a much wider audience. However, this is still a Web service design that takes advantage of loose coupling and standard protocols. We hope this example gives you an idea of how to design Web service interfaces. The next step is to look at how you can build a Web service accessed by a much wider audience.

Building Web Services

In Chapters 6 and 7, we developed applications that interfaced with Employee data and returned either a list of employees or detail information for a specific employee. Chapter 6 focused on XML structure and performance advantages of using XML across network and process boundaries. In Chapter 7, we focused on the SOAP protocol and how to use it when making requests to interfaces that support SOAP. In fact, we built a Web service using the SOAP Toolkit that interacted directly with a data services tier using XML template support in SQL Server 2000. In this chapter, we continue with the same application but, instead of using the SOAP Toolkit and direct calls to SQL Server, we build a Web service application using Visual Studio.NET.

The application developed for this chapter will be deployed as a public Web service that exposes a directory of employees at our fictitious consulting company. Because this is a publicly exposed Web service, we'll take advantage of standard protocols like SOAP and WSDL, and discuss how a UDDI directory can be used to register and locate this Web service. This application uses the same design concepts discussed previously, but it's meant for a much wider audience, which fits the implementation most people think of with Web services.

By using Visual Studio.NET, the Web service application is much easier to build than the one described in Figure 8-1. The .NET Framework takes care of all the plumbing for you, so you don't need to know anything about SOAP or WSDL to build and deploy this application. The only extra work involved is registering this with a UDDI registry because that requires the use of a separate software development kit (SDK). As mentioned previously, the design of the application is similar to the one discussed in Figure 8-1, however, we use DataSet objects instead of custom objects to manipulate the XML. The new DataSet object that's part of ADO.NET provides a wrapper to XML data and is automatically converted into XML when passed across HTTP boundaries.

Acme Employee Directory Design

Figure 8-2 shows a new diagram that represents the design pattern used for our .NET-based design. As you can see, this is similar to the design used by the COM+ implementation, without the presentation component. At this point, we're focused on the Web service, which is why the presentation layer only includes the Web service file and an HTML page. Chapters 15 and 16 discuss .NET presentation components in much more detail. Interesting to note is the Web service still uses a listener and a processor. In this case, the listener is the .asmx file deployed to the Web site and the processor is the .asmx.cs or code behind the file that runs within the *Common Language Runtime (CLR)* engine.

Inside the business tier, you still have business and data access objects that pass a DataSet object around, instead of the RootManager. As mentioned previously, the DataSet is passed as XML when it's sent across HTTP but, within the business tier,

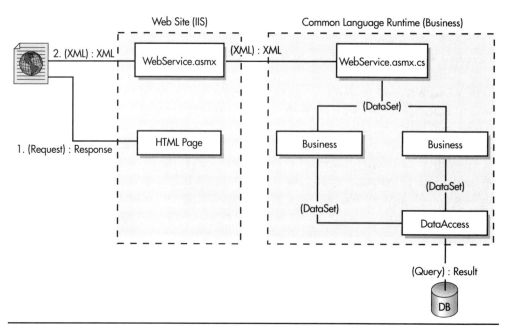

Figure 8-2   *.NET Web service design*

the DataSet is passed as an object reference, which is much more efficient. By using a DataSet in the interface, any client that understands XML can use the returned data. You can also take advantage of having the XML converted back into a DataSet if the client is .NET, which means the client wouldn't need to deal with XML at all. The cool thing about all this is you needn't worry about the boundary layers as much anymore. The .NET Framework can automatically handle the conversion of objects for you, while still providing the capability for developers to control what objects are passed.

Figure 8-3 shows a class diagram of the objects that you will develop for this application. When you look at this diagram, it might not make sense as to why there's a separate business class, bcEmployee, because it has the same methods as the Web service. This design is meant to be implemented with multiple business objects accessed by only a few Web services. In most implementations, a single Web service would be used to call multiple business components. Because this is a small example application, however, you only have the one business class. In addition, with a

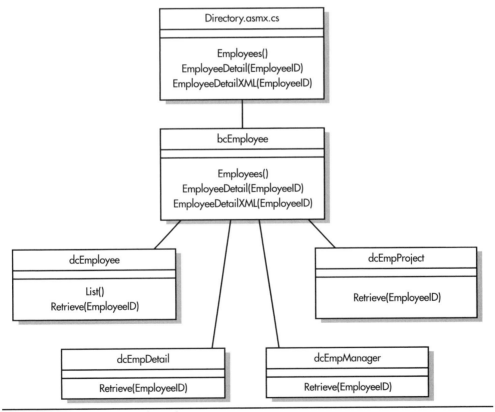

Figure 8-3   *Web service class diagram*

complete application, your data access components would also provide additional methods, such as Update and Delete.

The important information to get from the diagram in Figure 8-3 is the three different methods exposed by your Web service and the main objects used to implement the design pattern, shown in Figure 8-2. The reason two different methods are used to get employee details is to demonstrate the use of table-based data and XML-based data in our DataSets. With table-based data, you're making queries against tables and loading the results into the DataSet. With XML-based data, we're getting an XML result from SQL Server and loading that into the DataSet. The first approach enables you to return detailed schema information with less effort. The second approach only makes one call into the Data Services layer, but requires more work in the middle tier to convert it into a structured DataSet.

Building the Application

The first step to building the application is to start up Visual Studio and create a new Web service application. As with other examples for this book, you can find all the sample code discussed in this chapter on the McGraw-Hill/Osborne Web site located at **http://osborne.com** in the Downloads section of the site. For this example, we'll choose C# as the development language. The application should be named AcmeDirectory and will be deployed to the inetpub\wwwroot\AcmeDirectory directory by default. Once the application is started, the next step is to rename the Web service file to Directory.asmx. Next, you need to add the classes shown in the previous diagram and start to work on the implementation. Before you begin to implement the methods, we need to accomplished a few other tasks first.

Data Services

Before starting work on the middle-tier components, we need to work on the data services tier. Because this application builds on the existing Employee database used in other samples, we needn't build that from scratch. The data services tier does need to be installed in a SQL Server database, however, because our application takes advantage of XML support in SQL Server and uses the SqlDataAdapters in the implementation. A sample database is included with the chapter examples if it hasn't already been installed. Also, included with the sample code for this application are several SQL script files that contain the stored procedures used by this application. These stored procedures should be loaded into SQL Server, which can be done with Query Analyzer.

Most of these stored procedures are straightforward, but we do have one that will be different for anyone who hasn't used the XML support in SQL Server. This stored procedure is named uspEmployeeDetailsXML and it uses the FOR XML EXPLICIT directive in SQL Server to generate an XML result set, instead of returning standard rowset-based results. When you look through the script file for this stored procedure, the query is quite complicated. Four different queries are combined with a UNION statement, and then converted into XML. The following listing shows the XML structure that will be returned from this query.

```
<EmployeeDetailDS>
    <Employee employeeID=''>
        <LastName/>
        <FirstName/>
        <MiddleInitial/>
        <OfficePhone/>
        <CellPhone/>
        <Beeper/>
    </Employee>
    <Manager>
        <LastName/>
        <FirstName/>
        <Title/>
    </Manager>
    <Project>
        <Name/>
    </Project>
</EmployeeDetailDS>
```

XDR-Based DataSets

Once you have the stored procedures installed in the database, you need to generate the DataSets that will be returned from this application. This requires a little extra effort that might be unnecessary, but it enables you to expose XSD schemas that clients can use to get information about the DataSet structures that will be returned. Without the XSD files, the clients would need to get this information from the DataSet that's returned, instead of getting it before they make the call. Also, by creating DataSets in Visual Studio, you get the added benefit of strongly typed DataSets that can be accessed like standard objects, instead of using index variables.

It's quite easy to generate these files with Visual Studio.NET. The first step is to create a connection to your database using the Server Explorer, which is shown in Figure 8-4. When creating the connection, choose the Employee database and use a password to access the database, instead of a trusted connection, unless you also want to set up all the security for this. Once you have a database connection in place, you're ready to start adding the DataSets, which are XSD files bound to code files. To add a new XSD file, you need to select *Add New Item* from the project menu. When the dialog box is displayed, select DataSet from the list of items that can be added, and then type in the name of the new DataSet. For this application, you have two DataSets: `EmployeesDS` and `EmployeeDetailDS`.

Once the DataSets have been added, the actual schema information can be generated by dropping database objects from the connection shown in Figure 8-4 into the designer window for each DataSet. The designer for the XSD file type supports a DataSet view and an XML view. You can use the DataSet view to drop tables, columns, views, and even stored procedures into the designer window. The information is converted to an XML Schema that can be further modified in the XML view. Figure 8-5 shows the DataSet view for the DetailDataSet XSD file and Listing 8-1 shows the XML generated.

Listing 8-1   *DetailDataSet Schema*

```xml
<?xml version="1.0" encoding="utf-8" ?>
<xsd:schema id="DetailDataSet"
    targetNamespace="http://www.AcmeConsulting.com/EmployeeDetailDS.xsd"
    elementFormDefault="qualified"
    xmlns="http://www.AcmeConsulting.com/EmployeeDetailDS.xsd"
    xmlns:xsd="http://www.w3.org/2001/XMLSchema"
    xmlns:msdata="urn:schemas-microsoft-com:xml-msdata">
  <xsd:element name="EmployeeDetailDS" msdata:IsDataSet="true">
    <xsd:complexType>
      <xsd:choice maxOccurs="unbounded">
        <xsd:element name="Employee">
          <xsd:complexType>
            <xsd:sequence>
              <xsd:element name="EmployeeID" type="xsd:int" />
              <xsd:element name="LastName" type="xsd:string" />
              <xsd:element name="FirstName" type="xsd:string" />
              <xsd:element name="MiddleInitial" type="xsd:string"
                                               minOccurs="0" />
              <xsd:element name="CellPhone" type="xsd:string"
                                               minOccurs="0" />
              <xsd:element name="Beeper" type="xsd:string"
                                               minOccurs="0" />
            </xsd:sequence>
          </xsd:complexType>
        </xsd:element>
        <xsd:element name="Manager">
          <xsd:complexType>
            <xsd:sequence>
              <xsd:element name="LastName" type="xsd:string" />
              <xsd:element name="FirstName" type="xsd:string" />
              <xsd:element name="Title" type="xsd:string"
                                       minOccurs="0" />
```

```
                </xsd:sequence>
            </xsd:complexType>
        </xsd:element>
        <xsd:element name="Project">
            <xsd:complexType>
                <xsd:sequence>
                    <xsd:element name="Name" type="xsd:string" />
                </xsd:sequence>
            </xsd:complexType>
        </xsd:element>
        </xsd:choice>
    </xsd:complexType>
    <xsd:unique name="EmployeeDetailDSKey1" msdata:PrimaryKey="true">
        <xsd:selector xpath=".//Employee" />
        <xsd:field xpath="EmployeeID" />
    </xsd:unique>
  </xsd:element>
</xsd:schema>
```

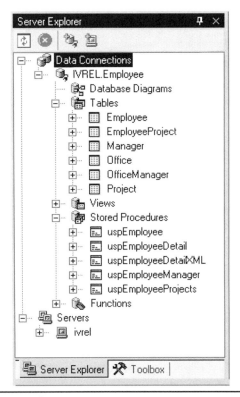

Figure 8-4   *Database connection*

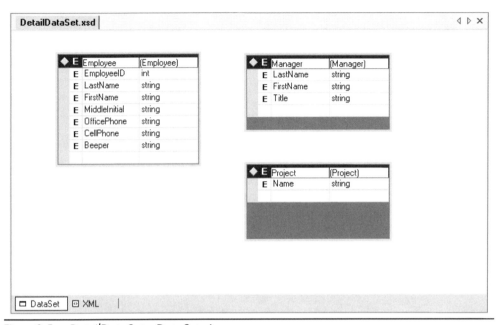

Figure 8-5   *DetailDataSet—DataSet view*

Most of the schema information shown in Listing 8-1 was automatically generated by dropping the tables on to the designer window. The only changes made were to remove fields that wouldn't be returned in the actual result sets. The other DataSet (XSD) file was generated in the same manner as this one. By creating DataSets in this manner, the compiler automatically generates a bound DataSet object for this schema. You can now use these schema references as actual DataSet objects, instead of instantiating a DataSet object, and then reading in the XSD schema information. In addition, by returning these DataSets from the Web service interfaces, the .NET Framework code used to generate WSDL files automatically will also include references to these schema files.

Listing 8-2 shows the Web service code and Listing 8-3 shows the business service code used to retrieve employee details from the application. Both these methods use the DataSet shown in Figure 8-5 and Listing 8-1. The data access components called from the middle tier use SqlDataAdapters to invoke the queries against the database, and then fill the DataSet passed into the constructor with the data retrieved from the database. As you can see, a lot of code isn't involved in building this application. All the hard work of filling the DataSets with data and converting them is handled by .NET. As a developer, you only need to focus on the application and not the plumbing, which is how a good framework should be designed.

Listing 8-2 *Web Service Function*

```
//
// Web service method used to return employee details. This returns
// three separate tables in a single data set
//
[WebMethod]
public EmployeeDetailDS EmployeeDetail( int EmployeeID )
{
    bcEmployee EmpBusiness = new bcEmployee();
    return EmpBusiness.EmployeeDetail( EmployeeID );
}
```

Listing 8-3 *Business Service Function*

```
// get employee details from three different sources
public EmployeeDetailDS EmployeeDetail( int EmployeeID )
{
    // initialize a DataSet
    EmployeeDetailDS DetailDS = new EmployeeDetailDS();

    // get the EmployeeData
    dcEmployee oEmp = new dcEmployee();
    oEmp.Retrieve( DetailDS, EmployeeID );

    // get the Manager data
    dcEmpManager oMgr = new dcEmpManager();
    oMgr.Retrieve( DetailDS, EmployeeID );

    // get the project data
    dcEmpProject oPrj = new dcEmpProject();
    oPrj.Retrieve( DetailDS, EmployeeID );

    // return the result
    return DetailDS;
}
```

Observations

DataSets are easy to use, but some limitations exist. When using a stored procedure with multiple SELECT statements, the first one uses the table name from the Fill method, but each additional table also uses that name with a number appended. For instance, if you have three tables in the result and passed the name Table into the Fill method, the first one would be named Table, while the second and third would be Table1 and Table2, respectively. There is a method on the Data Adapter, however, that can be used to modify these default names.

```
SqlDataAdaptor daDetails = New SqlDataAdapter();
'... initialize the Data Adapter

' fix table mappings
daDetails.TableMappings.Add( "Table", "Employee" );
daDetails.TableMappings.Add( "Table1", "Manager" );
daDetails.TableMappings.Add( "Table2", "Project" );

' invoke the command and fill the DataSet
DataSet dsDetails = New DataSet();
daDetails.Fill( daDetails, "Table" );
```

When the fill operation is complete the dsDetails DataSet will contain three tables with the correct names.

Returning XML from a stored procedure has other limitations that you should be aware of. When using stored procedures with FOR XML directives, the data is loaded into the DataSet as an HTML-encoded string. You can get this data into a structured DataSet, but this means using a DOM parser and decoding the XML before attempting to load it into the parser. The code in dcEmpDetail.Retrieve() demonstrates how to load this type of result into a structured DataSet.

As a general rule, our tendency is to minimize the number of resources used in a Web Application design on the middle tier. This includes reducing the number of database connections and objects used to process a request. What we found is this: DataSets are geared more toward table-based operations with flat structures. As discussed previously, these tables can come from a SELECT statement against a table or view along with tables returned from stored procedures, but it's difficult to pull a hierarchical XML result set from the database in a single call. This can be done, but it takes a little extra work.

Examining the Results

Once the application is built, you can take advantage of .NET Framework support to examine what the SOAP interface looks like, along with the WSDL file that describes the interfaces. With the new Visual Studio.NET development environment, testing and debugging has improved and it's still a familiar environment for anyone used to Visual Studio. When you press the Run command in Visual Studio, a browser is automatically launched and navigated to the Web service file. When this file loads, the .NET Framework automatically generates a test harness for the Web service. Figure 8-6 shows a browser with the first page of the test harness created. This page provides two types of links: one to get the WSDL file, or Service Description, and another to test the interface for each method in the Web service.

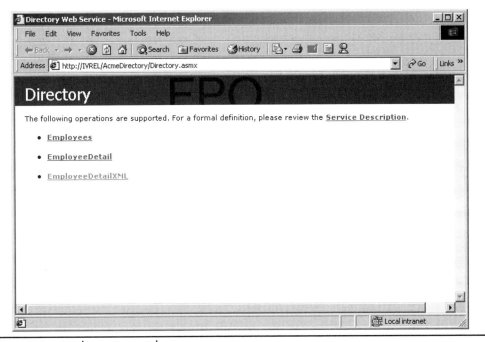

Figure 8-6   *Web service test harness*

Testing the Interface

The following screen shows the top of the page displayed when the EmployeeDetail link is accessed. From looking at this illustration, you can see the framework created an input box based on what it saw in the schema. When a value is entered, and the Invoke button is pressed, the Web service is called and the result is then displayed in a browser.

Figure 8-7 shows the same browser window scrolled down to two sections that describe the SOAP messages that will be sent and received. The first section shows the SOAP request and the next section shows the response. The display also shows parameters that should be passed in and the result expected. If you read Chapter 7, this structure should look familiar because it's based on the RPC binding for HTML, described in the specifications for SOAP. In this case, the request is `EmployeeDetail` and it takes an `EmployeeID` parameter, which is an integer. The `EmployeeDetailResponse` returns a DataSet as an `EmployeeDetailResult`. These descriptions parallel the interface definitions in our Web service and adhere to the SOAP specifications previously mentioned.

Not shown in Figure 8-7 are two additional HTTP-based interfaces that are also implemented by the framework. One is a GET-based method, where the `EmployeeID`

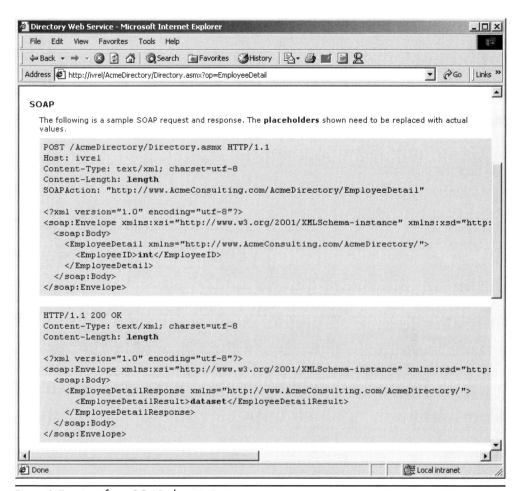

Figure 8-7   *Interface SOAP description*

is passed in on the Query string. The other is a POST operation where the `EmployeeID` is passed in as a Form variable. The test harness uses the GET method to test the application methods. If you look at Figure 8-7, you can see the browser address has our asmx file loaded with a QueryString command of `op=EmployeeDetail`. Figure 8-8 shows the result of entering an `EmployeeID` of 11 in the input box and pressing Invoke. As you can see, the `EmployeeID` is passed into the Web service on the QueryString.

The screenshot in Figure 8-8 only shows the result from the query to the database, which is located after schema information in the result. Not shown in Figure 8-8 is the schema specification for the result, which matches the schema description shown previously in Listing 8-1. As you can see from this screenshot, we have an `EmployeeDetailDS` element that contains `Employee`, `Manager`, and `Project` elements. These elements also use the namespace defined in the `EmployeeDetailDS`, which was discussed previously. Figure 8-9 shows the WSDL file generated when you press the Service Description link, as shown in Figure 8-6.

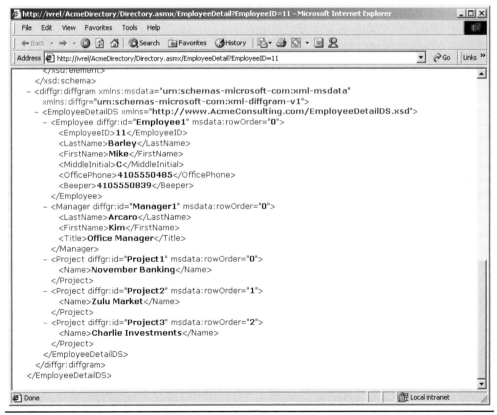

Figure 8-8   *Web service result*

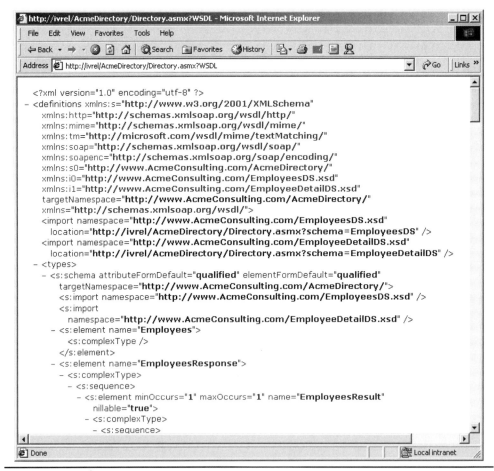

Figure 8-9   *Web Service Description Language (WSDL)*

If you look at the browser address box shown in Figure 8-9, you can see the link navigated to the same Web service file and passed WSDL in on the QueryString. This tells the framework you're requesting the Web Service Description, which then generates and returns the WSDL file automatically. Instead of having to use a different link for this information, users can easily get the information directly from the same link they have for the actual Web service. When looking at the data returned in the Service Description, you can also see references to our EmployeesDS and EmployeeDetailDS schema files. These references enable clients to download the actual schemas used to describe the DataSets that will be returned from the interface. If the client isn't a .NET client, they can use this information to access the different elements in the DataSet result, which was shown in Figure 8-8.

Web Service Description Language (WSDL)

We've already mentioned the WSDL specification often throughout this chapter, but what exactly is it used for? The answer is straightforward: this file contains a schema that describes the interface for a Web service. In our example program, we have one Web service with three methods. The WSDL file, generated by the framework, shows all three interfaces, along with the three different operations, SOAP, HTTPGET and HTTPPOST, that are available. This file is quite large, so we'll break it down into a couple of sections that focus on the SOAP descriptions. Listing 8-4 shows a section from the WSDL file that describes the datatypes to be used for the Employees and EmployeeDetail methods.

Listing 8-4   *WSDL Types Element*

```
<types>
<s:schema attributeFormDefault="qualified" elementFormDefault="qualified"
        targetNamespace="http://www.AcmeConsulting.com/AcmeDirectory/">
<s:import namespace="http://www.AcmeConsulting.com/EmployeesDS.xsd" />
<s:import namespace="http://www.AcmeConsulting.com/EmployeeDetailDS.xsd"/>
<s:element name="Employees">
  <s:complexType />
</s:element>
<s:element name="EmployeesResponse">
  <s:complexType>
    <s:sequence>
      <s:element minOccurs="1" maxOccurs="1" name="EmployeesResult"
                                        nillable="true">
        <s:complexType>
          <s:sequence>
          <s:any namespace="http://www.AcmeConsulting.com/EmployeesDS.xsd"/>
          </s:sequence>
        </s:complexType>
      </s:element>
    </s:sequence>
  </s:complexType>
</s:element>
<s:element name="EmployeeDetail">
  <s:complexType>
    <s:sequence>
      <s:element minOccurs="1" maxOccurs="1" name="EmployeeID"
                                        type="s:int" />
```

```
      </s:sequence>
    </s:complexType>
</s:element>
<s:element name="EmployeeDetailResponse">
  <s:complexType>
    <s:sequence>
      <s:element minOccurs="1" maxOccurs="1" name="EmployeeDetailResult"
                                    nillable="true">
        <s:complexType>
          <s:sequence>
            <s:any namespace=
                 "http://www.AcmeConsulting.com/EmployeeDetailDS.xsd" />
          </s:sequence>
        </s:complexType>
      </s:element>
    </s:sequence>
  </s:complexType>
</s:element>
</types>
```

When looking through Listing 8-4, you can see the datatypes are described using XSD-schema syntax. Four different elements are defined in this listing: `Employees`, `EmployeesResult`, `EmployeeDetail`, and `EmployeeDetailResult`. These elements match the elements that describe the different requests used to pass data to the Web service and get a result back. The `Employees` element doesn't contain any other elements because no parameters are passed in on the request. The `EmployeesResponse` element contains a namespace reference to the EmployeesDS schema, which is the data that will be returned from this method. The `EmployeeDetail` element contains another element named `EmployeeID`, which is the parameter passed into the method call. The last element, `EmployeeDetailResponse`, contains a namespace reference to the EmployeeDetailDS schema, which is the data returned from this method.

Listing 8-5 shows the bindings used to interact with the Web service using SOAP. When looking through the listing, two operations are defined, `Employees` and `EmployeeDetail`. The third method in our interface, EmployeeDetailXML, wasn't included because it's the same as EmployeeDetail. All these operations define a `soapAction` that matches the method name, along with input and output sections that use the `soap:body`, which is consistent with SOAP specifications. An interesting point is the `style` element indicates these interfaces are document-based versus RPC-based, but Figure 8-7 shows a SOAP structure that's RPC-based.

The difference is in actual implementation versus description. Even though the description shows parameters are passed in and parameters are returned, when invoked, the actual result is an XML document, shown in Figure 8-8.

Listing 8-5 *WSDL Binding Element*

```
<binding name="DirectorySoap" type="s0:DirectorySoap">
  <soap:binding transport="http://schemas.xmlsoap.org/soap/http"
                style="document" />
  <operation name="Employees">
    <soap:operation soapAction=
          "http://www.AcmeConsulting.com/AcmeDirectory/Employees"
          style="document" />
    <input>
      <soap:body use="literal" />
    </input>
    <output>
      <soap:body use="literal" />
    </output>
  </operation>
  <operation name="EmployeeDetail">
    <soap:operation soapAction=
          "http://www.AcmeConsulting.com/AcmeDirectory/EmployeeDetail"
          style="document" />
    <input>
      <soap:body use="literal" />
    </input>
    <output>
      <soap:body use="literal" />
    </output>
  </operation>
</binding>
```

By putting the datatypes shown in Listing 8-4 together with the binding information in Listing 8-5, you have enough information to make calls into your Web service. Much more information is in the WSDL file, but the sections looked at give you the main information needed. This information, combined with the schema information referenced in the namespace, is enough to build a client application against the Web service.

HTML Client Application

The sample code for this chapter also contains an HTML file that can be used to test the Web service interface using the information gathered from the WSDL file and schema descriptions. This test page is the same one used in Chapter 7 with little modification. In Chapter 7, you were making calls into an ASP page that used the SOAP Toolkit. In this chapter, you're making calls into a .NET Web service. In both cases, you use SOAP to make requests against a Web service. And, once again, the Web services expose application-based interfaces that return blocks of data, instead of single parameters.

Figure 8-10 shows a screenshot of the test application with the list of employees loaded and a set of detailed information for one employee loaded. Below the test

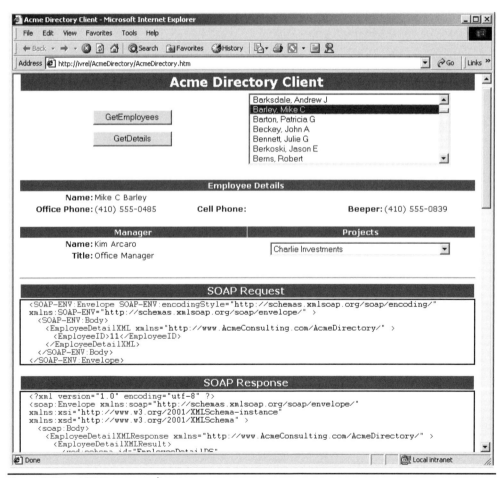

Figure 8-10   *HTML test application*

data are the SOAP request message sent and the SOAP response received. The entire SOAP response isn't shown, but it's exactly the same data shown in Figure 8-8 and the schema is the same one discussed in Listing 8-1. The important thing to note is this isn't a .NET client. Instead, it's a generic HTML page that can be displayed in an IE 5.01+ browser that uses XMLHTTP to talk to the Web service.

HTML Client-Side Script

As mentioned previously, the test HTML page uses client-side script to interact with the Web service. Listing 8-6 shows a snippet of code used to request the list of employees and Listing 8-7 shows a common method used to invoke the request. When looking at Listing 8-6, the first operation is to call the common method `sendRequest` and pass it the name of an XML data island that contains the SOAP message and the `soapAction` you're accessing. In this case, the `soapAction` is `http://www.AcmeConsulting.com/AcmeDirectory/Employees`, which was shown in the SOAP binding information in Listing 8-5. The result is an XML document that can be accessed using DOM support in IE 5.01+. As you can see, we're extracting the list of employees and adding the name information into a select box.

Listing 8-6   *Client-Side Javascript*

```
var xmlResp = sendRequest( xmlGetEmployees,
            "http://www.AcmeConsulting.com/AcmeDirectory/Employees" );
   // Get the employee nodes and walk through them
   var xmlEmployees = xmlResp.selectNodes("//Employee");
   for( var nIdx=0; nIdx < xmlEmployees.length; nIdx++ )
   {
      // get the name
      var xmlDoc = xmlEmployees[nIdx];
      var strName = " " +
                    getText( xmlDoc, "LastName") + ", " +
                    getText( xmlDoc, "FirstName") + " " +
                    getText( xmlDoc, "MiddleInitial");

      // add it to the list
      var oOption = document.createElement("option");
      oOption.text = strName;
      oOption.value = getText( xmlDoc, "EmployeeID");
      selEmployees.add(oOption);
   }
```

Listing 8-7   *Client-Side Function*

```
function sendRequest( xmlDoc, strAction )
{
   // Display the SOAP Request
   divRequest.innerHTML =
             xmlDoc.transformNode(xmlStylesheet.documentElement);

   // Create a request object and initialize it
   var req = new ActiveXObject("Microsoft.XMLHTTP");
   req.open( "POST", strServer + "Directory.asmx", false);
   req.setRequestHeader("Content-Type", "text/xml; charset='UTF-8'");
   req.setRequestHeader("SOAPAction", strAction);

   // Send the SOAP Request
   req.send(xmlDoc.xml);

   // Display the SOAP Response
   var responseDOM = req.responseXML;
   divResponse.innerHTML =
             responseDOM.transformNode(xmlStylesheet.documentElement);
   // Return the response
   return responseDOM;
}
```

The function in Listing 8-7 is used by both our methods to invoke the actual Web service request. The first line of code uses a stylesheet loaded in an XML data island to display the SOAP request to be sent. The next section of code uses the XMLHTTP object to POST the SOAP request to the Web service. Notice the content type is set to `text/xml` and the `SOAPAction` is set to the action passed in from the code in Listing 8-6. After the request is sent, the XML response is loaded into an XML DOM object and displayed using the same stylesheet as the request. Finally, the DOM object is returned to the calling function where it's processed.

Universal Discovery, Description, and Integration (UDDI)

UDDI is a directory service that business and individuals can use to register and look for Web services. This directory service works basically like the Yellow Pages, where users can search for available Web services and get information about those services. Currently, Microsoft, Ariba, and IBM provide UDDI directories that are available to use. To round out this discussion on Web services, we need to introduce UDDI and describe how it's used, but we won't go into much detail. A number of white papers are available that provide in-depth details, but with the use of SDKs provided by Microsoft and other companies, it isn't necessary to get too deep into the specifications to use UDDI.

As mentioned, Microsoft provides an SDK that can be used with Visual Studio 6.0, which also includes a class library for Visual Studio.NET. The SDK interfaces make it easy to register and look for Web services. In addition, the Visual Studio.NET development environment provides a dialog box that can be used to search for and add external Web references to an application. This dialog box is accessed by selecting Add Web Reference on the Project menu. Figure 8-11 shows a screenshot of the Add Web Reference dialog box with two Web services displayed that are available from Continental Airlines. When you click one of these Web services, the WSDL file is retrieved and a button is enabled at the bottom to add this service to your application. When the Web service is added, Visual Studio.NET generates classes that can be used to interact with the Web service. This makes adding external Web services to any .NET application easy to do.

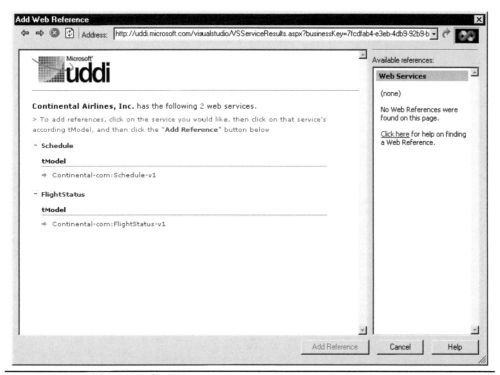

Figure 8-11 *Add Web Reference*

Finding and Accessing a Web Service

Even though .NET makes it easy to build and use Web services, understanding how the interaction works among Web service clients, UDDI, and Web services can still help (we'll only provide a general understanding here). Figure 8-12 is a diagram that shows the flow of messages among a client, UDDI, and a Web service. The first set of messages is a request to UDDI to locate a Web service.

Several messages are involved in getting information from a UDDI registry. UDDI is, itself, a Web service that provides drill-down methods for locating information. The first step is to search for a company. The next step is to get details about that company. The third, and last, step is to get details about the services provided by that company. In addition, if you're looking for specific information, you can bypass the drill-down set of requests and go directly to the information you want.

The next set of messages shown in Figure 8-12 is a request to the Web service to get the Web service description. With .NET applications, this is a matter of accessing the Web service and passing WSDL on the QueryString. Figure 8-12 shows the request to get the WSDL for our sample application. The Continental Airlines Web service, shown in Figure 8-11, is also a .NET application that uses the same method for accessing the WSDL file. For other Web service applications, the UDDI information would contain a link to the actual WSDL file itself.

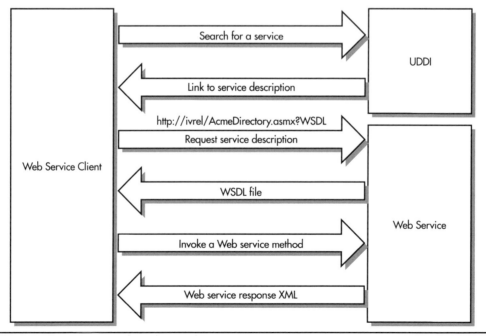

Figure 8-12 *Discover, describe, and interact*

The final set of messages shown in Figure 8-12 is the actual interaction with the Web service itself. This would be the point where the Web service client invokes the SOAP request and gets a SOAP response back from the client.

Finally, understand that UDDI isn't only for Web services. Any business can register itself with UDDI and provide a description of its business with a phone number used as contact information. Businesses can also publish other types of Web service operations, such as HTML pages used to get information about the company. In other words, UDDI is like a Yellow Pages directory that anyone can use to get a wide variety of information about any kind of available service.

Summary

This chapter focused on describing Web services, providing information on how to design Web services applications, as well as in-depth information on how to build Web services using Visual Studio.NET. During the design discussion, we said Web service interfaces should be application-based and not object-based. We also demonstrated what an application-based interface is with our sample application. Along with discussing design, we looked at an actual Web service design that was used for an internal business application.

While building our test application, we discussed other components available with .NET, such as DataSets and DataAdapters. In addition, we looked at the .NET Framework support with the capability to generate a test harness automatically, along with WSDL files used to describe the Web services. We rounded out the chapter with a sample Web service client application, a discussion of UDDI, and how Web service clients can discover and interact with Web services.

The following list summarizes the information covered in this chapter:

- ▶ Web services are programmable interfaces.

- ▶ Web service interfaces should be application-based and not object-based.

- ▶ Web services can be implemented in a variety of ways on different platforms.

- ▶ A Web service design is a distributed design.

- ▶ Web services shouldn't be used for every system interface. Web services should only be used when you have a wide range of client applications that need to access Server applications through HTTP.

- ▶ Web services can be used in an application in many different ways.

- ▶ Visual Studio.NET makes building, deploying, and accessing Web services easy.

► .NET supports the capability to convert objects, such as a DataSet, automatically into XML when passing it across HTTP.

► The .NET Framework provides built-in functionality to generate test harnesses and WSDL files for a Web service.

► Web service description files are used to get detailed information about Web services.

► UDDI makes Web services available to a wide variety of clients.

.NET Framework

OBJECTIVES

▶ Explore the CLR and how it manages code throughout the lifecycle of an application.

▶ Learn about the Common Type System and its key role within the .NET Framework.

▶ Examine characteristics that can be applied to classes and class members, and learn how classes are organized in namespaces.

▶ Learn how to take advantage of XML support in SQL Server by exploring FOR XML, OPENXML, Schema mapping, and XML Templates.

▶ Explore how ADO.NET fits in the .NET Framework, and use Managed Providers to interact with the disconnected portion of ADO.NET.

▶ Explore ADO.NET classes and use them in developing distributed applications.

Common Language Runtime (CLR)

IN THIS CHAPTER:

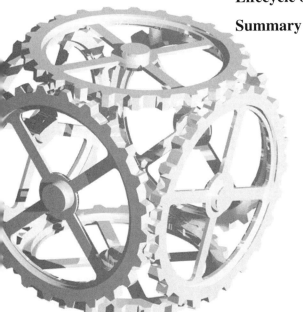

This chapter starts with a look at where the Common Language Runtime (CLR) fits into the .NET Framework with a high-level look at some of the run-time services provided. Next, we dig under the covers to examine the structure of .NET executable files and learn how the Runtime Engine loads and executes these files. During this examination of the .NET CLR, different topics are covered, such as run-time hosts, assemblies, assembly binding, and security. Security topics include a discussion of the different types of security available and how they're implemented by the Runtime Engine.

The last section in this chapter examines the lifecycle of an application from development to deployment to execution. During the development phase, we use some of the .NET tools to examine files and different sections of code discussed earlier in the chapter. During the deployment stage, we look at different types of tools that can be used during the deployment phase. Finally, during the execution stage, we examine the different steps the Runtime Engine takes to load, compile, and execute MSIL code.

When finished with this chapter, developers will have a solid understanding of how the CLR loads, executes, and manages application code. Some aspects of the CLR aren't discussed in detail, however, because of the scope and complexity involved with those areas. Specifically, we only discuss exception handling, garbage collection, and thread management at a high level. Most of the information, needed by developers to understand what these services are, is provided. To gain more in-depth knowledge, developers can refer to the documentation available with MSDN or the Visual Studio.NET development environment.

Inside the .NET Framework

Before digging into the internals of the CLR, we need to step back and see where it fits into .NET and the *.NET Framework,* which is a common framework used by all .NET applications. Figure 9-1 shows a diagram of the .NET Framework in relation to development languages, tools, and the operating system (OS). The .NET Framework in this diagram is surrounded by a dashed bold line. As you can see, it consists of two main sections: the framework classes and the CLR. In this chapter, we focus on the CLR and the role it plays in managing the execution of .NET applications. In Chapter 10, we dig into the framework classes and the Common Type System, which is the glue that ties everything together.

When discussing .NET, it's important to understand the .NET Framework is only one aspect of the overall big picture. .NET is much more than a new programming

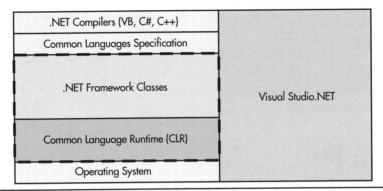

Figure 9-1   *The .NET Framework*

language and a Runtime Engine: .NET represents a new distributed platform that includes clients, servers, and services. The .NET Framework does represent a foundation for .NET applications, however, and the CLR represents the heart of that framework. As a Runtime Execution Engine, the CLR converts .NET code into system code, and then manages that code while it's running. The CLR also interacts with other .NET clients, servers, and services to provide an integrated environment for all these components to coexist without conflict.

System Integration

The relationship between the CLR and Visual Studio.NET, shown in Figure 9-1, indicates that CLR interacts with other .NET applications. This interaction is used by the CLR to implement services, such as security and side-by-side deployment. These services represent cases where the CLR reaches into external applications to get information. In addition, the interaction isn't limited to applications. The CLR can interact with .NET servers, as well as other .NET services.

The following list shows some of the features implemented by the CLR:

► Manages the execution of code

► Object-oriented design with strong type safety

► Provides memory management and garbage collection

► Supports cross-language integration

► Portable to different OSs

The CLR can manage code and provide the interoperability described, through the use of a *Common Type System* (*CTS*) and a *Common Language Specification* (*CLS*). When applications are developed using a CTS, the Runtime Engine inside the CLR is able to identify and manage those objects. In addition, by supporting standards defined in the CLS and using common types, components can be extended by different languages and managed by the CLR. As you can guess, the CTS is the key to how all the different components can interoperate.

Common Type System

Chapter 10 discusses the CTS in detail, however, getting a higher level of understanding of the common types before we move on can help you. The .NET Framework supports two types of variables: value types and reference types. A *value type* represents data that can be accessed directly with a variable. These are typically primitive types, such as integers or characters. A *reference type* represents an address, or reference, to the data stored in a variable. Access to a reference type is considered indirect because the system first gets the address, and then uses that address to access the data. When value types are managed by the .NET Runtime Engine, they're converted into reference types through a process called "Boxing," which is also discussed in Chapter 10.

One of the key distinctions between value types and reference types is that value types are allocated on the stack and automatically destroyed when they fall out of scope. Reference types are always allocated on the heap. When a value type is boxed, it means a wrapper reference type is allocated on the heap and the value of the value type is copied into it. So, all reference types are allocated on the heap and all value types are allocated on the stack.

All reference types in .NET are derived from `System.Object`, which means they all provide the same basic operations. The Runtime Engine uses these base operations to manage the lifetime and execution of objects. In addition, the .NET Framework provides several other base types, such as `Array` and `ValueType`, which derive from `System.Object` and expose additional operations used by the Runtime Engine to manage these types. When developing applications with languages that target the CLR, these base classes are used automatically. In other words, no need exists to derive directly from `System.Object` or `System.ValueType`, and the specifications don't support that. Instead, the language compiler is responsible for ensuring that the components all inherit the proper functionality needed by the Runtime Engine.

TIP

All objects in .NET are derived from `System.Object`, which provides basic operations used by the Runtime Engine.

Run-Time Services

As previously mentioned, the CLR provides several run-time services. One of those services is a just-in-time (JIT) compiler that converts intermediate code into system code. This compiler is typically called by the Runtime Engine as each method is called, however, code can also be precompiled to native code during deployment. While an application is running, the CLR manages the allocation of memory for objects and releases those objects when they're no longer needed. By managing object references and the memory they use, common programming mistakes are reduced and memory leaks are eliminated. In addition, the CLR manages threading for applications and provides support for asynchronous operations.

Other services provided by the Runtime Engine include exception handling, type-safety, and security. Exception handling in .NET is robust and mandatory, you can't develop .NET-managed components without supporting exception handling. This doesn't mean you must implement exception handlers. The framework provides one by default. But this does mean all errors will be trapped by the Runtime Engine and handled accordingly. This does not mean, however, that you shouldn't implement exception handlers, as the default behavior is typically not desirable. Type safety is directly related to the CTS and the fact that all objects derive from `System.Object`. Because the Runtime engine has direct access to type information, it can prevent occurrences such as invalid cast operations and buffer overruns. Security is an integral component of the CLR with support for code inspection, security policies, integration with security providers, and encryption services.

To take advantage of the run-time services provided, a compiler needs to generate code that will target the CLR. This means the code must support the common language specifications and all types must be supported by the CTS. When developing code that's designed to run inside the CLR, that code is called *managed code*. Currently, Visual Studio.NET provides several different languages, such as C#, C++, and VB.NET that generate managed code. In addition, with the C++ compiler, developers have the option of creating unmanaged code, which won't execute within the CLR.

NOTE

Code that's targeted to run in the CLR is called managed code. Anytime we refer to code or an application as "managed," we're talking about something that runs inside the Runtime Engine.

Targeting the CLR

The first step in building components to run within the CLR is to choose a development language that supports the CLS. As mentioned previously, Microsoft currently provides compilers for Visual Basic, C++, C#, Java, and JScript that will generate managed code. In addition, academia and other language vendors are providing CLS-compliant compilers for languages such as APL, COBOL, Eiffel, Fortran, Haskell, ML, Perl, Python, RPG, Scheme, and Smalltalk. All these compilers will generate intermediate code, which is called Microsoft Intermediate Language (MSIL). During run-time execution or when deployed, this MSIL code is converted into OS-specific or *native* code by the CLR.

One thing to remember is not all of these languages are completely equal. While it will be possible to create an object in Visual Basic and extend that object in C#, limitations exist in most languages that restrict some operations. For instance, the Visual Basic language doesn't support any operators that can be used to manipulate bits in a value like the shift operators in C++ and C#.

The only language designed from the ground up to support the CLS is C#. Visual Basic.NET is an upgrade to Visual Basic 6.0, with new keywords added to support the CLS. Many other changes were also done in Visual Basic to make it compatible with the common language specifications. The C++ language was updated to support the CLR with the use of language extensions. With the C++ language, you can build applications that generate native code and managed (MSIL) code in the same application.

Choosing the actual development language is somewhat of a religious battle for most developers. The factors used to make a decision are based on experience and comfort level with the different languages involved. On the other hand, there are some very significant factors that need to be considered. VB.NET is designed to handle Rapid Application Development (RAD) of small applications. The VB.NET development environment actually compiles the code as you type, which can cause major problems with large applications. In fact, with a recent Web project developed in VB.NET, we had to break the project into several small sub-projects because the development environment became difficult to use. It took several minutes to switch between screens and several seconds of delay after each line of code. The C# language, however, is designed for enterprise development and will handle large application development without the overhead found in VB.NET.

TIP

VB.NET is designed to support the rapid development of small applications. The VB.NET development environment does not handle large enterprise applications very well. On the other hand, C# and the C# development environment is designed to support large enterprise applications.

Regardless of the target application, most Visual Basic developers will probably migrate toward VB.NET initially, but once C# gains major acceptance, it will probably be the language of choice. The reason for this statement is because VB.NET is different from older versions of Visual Basic. Trying to remember all the differences in VB.NET is more difficult than learning a new language. In addition, because VB.NET doesn't support all the language features available in C#, an occasional necessity will occur to develop components using C#. What we've found is this: as developers become more familiar with the ease of development and power available in C#, they find themselves migrating to it as their language of choice.

Regardless of which language you choose to use, all of them support the generation of MSIL code, discussed previously, and *metadata,* which is used to describe the references, types, and data used by the code. This metadata information includes the version numbers, security policies, and other information used to identify a reference uniquely, such as *strong names,* which are used to uniquely identify the assembly. The Runtime Engine uses the metadata to find resources, instantiate classes, manage memory, manage object references, enforce security, and maintain run-time boundaries around the code. The MSIL code and metadata information generated are all inserted into the binary .dll and .exe files, which are the end result of compiling .NET components.

Developing .NET Applications

Over the past ten years, the development of Windows applications has evolved from building single stand-alone applications to building distributed applications that can seamlessly share functionality with each other. Figure 9-2 shows that evolution process, starting with stand-alone applications and ending with .NET assemblies running in an application domain. With stand-alone applications, little, if any, communication between applications occurred. The Windows OS provided different ways to share data, but this was difficult and tended to couple two applications together tightly.

The next evolution was COM, shown in the middle of Figure 9-2, which provided a major breakthrough in distributed application development. With COM, accessing functionality from other components is much easier, but this requires an intermediate language that provides a common layer between the different components. This layer forces data to go through several different translations to move between the different layers. In addition, COM applications make heavy use of registration entries to store configuration and location information, which makes them fragile. In other words, breaking an existing COM application is easy by modifying the registry or moving a component.

With .NET, the COM restrictions are gone. Different components can access each other directly without the additional layer. This is accomplished through the use of a CTS, discussed previously, on which components in .NET are built. In addition, all the configuration information is stored directly in the files instead of in the registry,

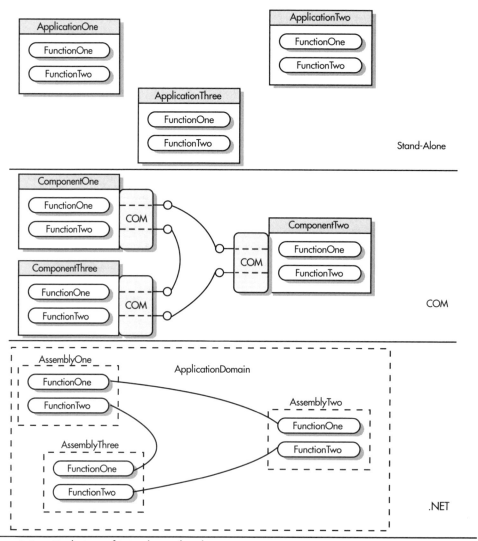

Figure 9-2   *Evolution of Windows development*

which eliminates the registry and deployment issues associated with COM. The bottom section in Figure 9-2 shows how the components in .NET are grouped and how one function can directly access another function in a different component. With .NET, these components are called *assemblies* and the boundary around all the components that make up an application is called an *application domain.* Before getting into the details of assemblies and application domains, it helps to start with the information contained in .NET executable files.

Run-Time Executables

The binary .dll and .exe files generated when compiling .NET code are called *Portable Executable* (*PE*) files in the Windows OS. These files use a standard header, called a *PE Header,* which the OS recognizes and uses to create a new process and start executing code. We get into more detail about the PE Header in the section "Developing the Application" but, for now, all you need to know is the .NET compilers will insert this header into compiled components. Figure 9-3 shows the PE Header along with two other sections that contain the code and data found in the PE file.

The first section shown in Figure 9-3 is the PE Header discussed previously. When the Windows OS sees this header section in a file, it uses the information to find the entry point and start execution of the code. The original design of the PE Header was meant to be extensible and Microsoft has extended it for .NET. The extension added was a *Common Language Interface* (*CLI*) header that contains information about the run-time version to use and the entry point into the application. When a .NET-aware host loads this executable, it will look for the CLI Header entry. If it finds that entry, it uses the information there to make some checks and start executing code.

The next section in Figure 9-3 contains the MSIL code generated from the language-specific code we write as developers. This code is normally compiled into native code during run-time execution, but it can also be compiled ahead of time. The MSIL code is *pseudocode,* which uses tokens to access information in the metadata. As mentioned previously, all the different .NET languages produce this MSIL code when compiling an application. That doesn't mean they'll all generate exactly the same code, however. Instead, each compiler generates MSIL, based on the actual structure in the language and any optimizations applied.

The last section in Figure 9-3, metadata, is the key that ties everything together. Remember, everything in .NET is based on a CTS. Even the classes we create in our applications are part of that CTS. The metadata contains tables that hold information about all the types and members in an application. Chapter 10 discusses members in more detail but, for now, all you need to know is a *member* can represent the functions and attributes of a class. In addition to tables, the metadata also contains blocks of

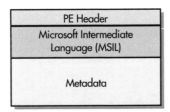

Figure 9-3   *.NET Executable internals*

data, known as *heap data,* that contain all the strings, GUIDs, and binary (blob) data used by the application. This includes the names of all types and members in the system.

The way information in the metadata tables is accessed is through the use of tokens. A *token* is a 4-byte number that represents the table and row where the information can be found. The top byte references the table and the bottom three bytes indicate the row. These tokens are used by the MSIL code and within the metadata to reference types and members stored in the tables. The heap data is also accessed through the use of tokens. These tokens are calculated based on the heap section and position in that section. For instance, if the *User Strings* section is assigned a value of 7, and one of the strings starts at position 1C inside the block, the token for that string would be 7000001C.

At this point, you know that executables targeting the CLR contain a PE Header, MSIL code, and metadata, but how does the code execute? In addition, you know the PE Header contains an entry point to start executing code, but that doesn't help explain how the CLR gets involved. The key to this is understanding what a run-time host is and how it loads the Runtime Engine.

Run-Time Hosts

A *run-time host* is a separate application that loads the Runtime Engine, and then executes the code found in your application. The official definition is that a run-time host loads the Runtime into a process, creates the application domains within the process, and loads and executes user code within those application domains. *Application domains* are discussed in the upcoming section "Application Domains," but first you need to understand what a host is. How does executing your application cause a run-time host to load the CLR? To be honest, this is something that seems a little like magic at first, but when you understand it, everything makes sense.

In every OS is a program, usually called a *shell,* which is an application that loads and executes other applications. With the Win32 OS, this shell application is the one that loads the PE file you want to execute, reads the PE Header, and starts execution of the code. When you install the Component Update as part of the Visual Studio.NET installation, you're replacing the existing Win32 shell with one that contains a run-time host for executing .NET applications. Newer OSs like Windows XP will be shipped with a shell program that already contains the run-time host, which means they're ready to execute .NET applications right out of the box.

Application Domains

As previously mentioned, the run-time host is responsible for creating an application domain, and then executing the user code in that domain. With standard Win32 applications, each application runs in a separate process and a process can contain multiple threads. The process boundary between applications was a hard wall: applications couldn't directly share data and an error in one application wouldn't affect the other. With the CLR, a new boundary layer, called an application domain, separates each application. The *application domain* represents a hard wall around the application. Data can't be directly shared across that wall and errors in one won't affect the other. The difference is this: a single process can contain multiple application domains.

This doesn't mean all .NET applications are loaded into the same process space. Most windows applications will run in their own process space, as they always have but, in other cases, multiple application domains make sense, like inside a browser or a Web server. What typically happens with a Windows shell application is the *Shell* run-time host is loaded into a new process, just like any other windows application, and that host then creates an application domain. When you dig under the covers, you'll find a couple application domains are created, but the overall effect is that each Windows application will execute in its own process.

Currently, the .NET Framework ships with three different types of run-time hosts, which are described in Table 9-1. You see that with the ASP.NET and Microsoft Internet Explorer hosts a possibility exists that multiple application domains will be created in the same process space. With ASP.NET, when the protection setting is set to Low, one run-time host is in the main IIS process, when it's set to Medium, a separate process handles multiple Web Applications, and when the setting is on High, each Web Application gets its own process space. With Internet Explorer, only one process space is there: the browser. In this case, all the application domains are created in the same process.

So far, we've focused on a single file and how that file is executed. We haven't discussed how that file gets access to other .NET resources or how it would be handled if the file were a .dll and not an .exe. With .NET, a .dll file isn't the same as a traditional .dll you would find in the System32 directory. With a traditional .dll file, an application uses Windows API functions to load the component in memory and start executing code. With .NET, the Runtime Engine is responsible for loading all external resources and making sure the user code can access that resource.

Manifest

The CLR can load all the resources and tie everything together through the use of metadata and tokens, which we described previously. But the CLR still needs something to identify what all the resources are, what versions to use, and how to implement security. Another piece of information in the metadata we haven't

Run-Time Host	Description
Shell	Win32 shell application that loads and executes Windows applications. This is the run-time host used to load and execute .NET Windows applications.
ASP.NET	This is a host that sits on top of IIS. When .NET Web Applications are accessed through IIS, this host is responsible for loading the CLR and executing the code. Each Web site will receive its own application domain, but the process they run in is controlled by the Application Protection settings.
Microsoft Internet Explorer	This run-time host is part of the Internet Explorer (IE) browser application. With .NET, it's possible to load and execute browser-based controls. The run-time host takes advantage of IE extensions and uses MIME filters to recognize the .NET code and load the CLR. Each Web application will receive its own application domain by default.

Table 9-1 *Run-Time Hosts*

discussed yet is something called the manifest. With .NET, each component or application is called an assembly. An assembly can be a single .dll or .exe file and it can also be multiple files. All assemblies are required to have a *manifest,* which is a table containing information about external resources, along with local resources used by the component.

Assemblies

Assemblies are considered the "building blocks" of .NET applications. Each *assembly* represents a logical unit of code, which could be a stand-alone .exe or a .dll used by other assemblies. As previously mentioned, each assembly has a manifest that contains information about the assembly. Along with the reference information already discussed, the manifest contains a version number and it can also contain security requirements, strong names, activation information, and other custom attributes added by the user code. When external resources are included in the manifest, they're included as assemblies with their version information and other attributes.

NOTE

An assembly is a logical unit of code that represents a complete application or component. Any time the word "assembly" is used, you can think of it as being the .NET analog of an .exe or .dll found in pre-.NET applications.

The code shown in Listing 9-1 is a partial manifest for an assembly named MyApplication. The application shown in this code listing uses the mscorlib, which is the Runtime Engine, and System assemblies. Each of the external resources have a public key token and a version number. The *public key token* represents a unique key used to reference assemblies with a strong name, which includes any assembly loaded in the Global Assembly Cache (GAC). The *GAC* is a common location where assemblies can be installed and shared by other assemblies, similar to the System32 directory in Windows. Following the external assembly references is the main assembly reference for MyApplication. The module's assembly contains the standard version attribute, a hash algorithm setting, and a list of custom attributes. The custom attributes are set in the user code, either in a separate file or as attributes in one of the code files.

Listing 9-1 *Assembly Manifest*

```
.assembly extern mscorlib
{
  .publickeytoken = (B7 7A 5C 56 19 34 E0 89 )
  .ver 1:0:3300:0
}
.assembly extern System
{
  .publickeytoken = (B7 7A 5C 56 19 34 E0 89 )
  .ver 1:0:3300:0
}
.assembly MyApplication
{
  .custom instance void
    [mscorlib]System.Reflection.AssemblyDescriptionAttribute::.ctor(string)
    = ( 01 00 00 00 00 )
  .custom instance void
    [mscorlib]System.Runtime.InteropServices.GuidAttribute::.ctor(string)
    = ( 01 00 24 31 41 39 31 43 35 33 43 2D 45 39 33 32 2D 34 32 34 45 2D
        42 34 42 43 2D 36 43 32 45 45 46 34 43 34 34 32 42 00 00 )
  .custom instance void
    [mscorlib]System.CLSCompliantAttribute::.ctor(bool)
    = (01 00 01 00 00)
  .custom instance void
    [mscorlib]System.Reflection.AssemblyCompanyAttribute::.ctor(string)
    = ( 01 00 00 00 00 )
  .custom instance void
    [mscorlib]System.Reflection.AssemblyTitleAttribute::.ctor(string)
    = ( 01 00 00 00 00 )
```

```
.custom instance void
    [mscorlib]System.Reflection.AssemblyTrademarkAttribute::.ctor(string)
    = ( 01 00 00 00 00 )
.custom instance void
    [mscorlib]System.Reflection.AssemblyCopyrightAttribute::.ctor(string)
    = ( 01 00 00 00 00 )
.custom instance void
    [mscorlib]System.Reflection.AssemblyProductAttribute::.ctor(string)
    = ( 01 00 00 00 00 )
.hash algorithm 0x00008004
.ver 1:0:002:23603
}
.module MyApplication.exe
// MVID: {AEAA8861-7D48-41D2-B1CF-A91FBD251C55}
.imagebase 0x11000000
.subsystem 0x00000002
.file alignment 4096
.corflags 0x00000001
```

Below the assembly references in Listing 9-1 are additional settings used by the Runtime Engine. The `module` setting contains the name or names of the module(s) that makes up this assembly. The `subsystem` setting is used to indicate what type of application this is. In this example, shown in Listing 9-1, the subsystem value is 2, which indicates this is a Windows Form application. If the value were 3, it would indicate this was a Windows Console application. The following illustration shows where this manifest information fits in the file and shows what a Single-File assembly contains.

Single-File Assembly

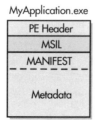

MyApplication.exe

| PE Header |
| MSIL |
| MANIFEST |
| Metadata |

The majority of assemblies you develop will probably be Single-File because this is the default method used to generate assemblies in .NET. You can, however, create a Multi-File assembly, where several files represent a single assembly. Figure 9-4 shows an example of what a Multi-File assembly might look like. Notice only one of

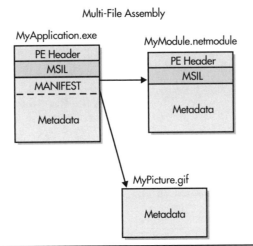

Figure 9-4   *Multifile assembly*

the files contains the manifest. This is a restriction in .NET, an assembly can only contain one manifest. In addition, notice the extension on MyModule is `.netmodule`, which we'll discuss shortly. The other file in Figure 9-4 is a resource file named MyPicture.gif. Resources typically are loaded directly into the metadata as binary (blob) data, however, it's possible to keep this data in a separate file, and then include it in the assembly as a reference.

   In some cases, when you develop applications, you might have a section of code that's fairly large, but not used often. As a result, you might not want to load that code into memory every time your application is executed. One of the options available when compiling code with a .NET compiler is to choose a target type named *module.* When the target type is *module,* it will generate a file that doesn't contain manifest information with an extension of `.netmodule`, illustrated with the MyModule file shown in Figure 9-4. This file can be included in other assemblies through the use of a keyword named `addmodule`. By generating a separate module and creating a Multi-File assembly, application performance can improve because the modules and resources are only loaded when they're referenced in the application.

Binding to an Assembly

The process of locating and loading the different assemblies found in a manifest is referred to as *assembly binding.* Typically, the Runtime Engine is responsible for binding assemblies, but it's also possible to load an assembly dynamically using the

Reflection classes in .NET. You can even create new assemblies in code using reflection, and then dynamically load that assembly into the Runtime Engine. This is a fairly complex operation and something that most applications won't use. Instead, most applications will be single-file assemblies that reference other assemblies located in the same directory or in the GAC.

The following list shows the high-level steps the Runtime Engine uses to locate and bind an assembly:

1. The Runtime Engine will look in different configuration files for information on where to find an assembly.

2. Currently loaded assemblies will be searched to see if the assembly is already loaded.

3. The GAC is searched for all assemblies with a public key token.

4. File directories are probed to look for the assembly.

Configuration Files

The Runtime Engine uses three different configuration files to locate assemblies. The first configuration file is the one associated with the application: these have the same name as the application, with an extension of .config. For instance, the MyApplication config file would be named "MyApplication.exe.config". The second configuration file is called a *publisher policy* file, which can be distributed with an assembly when it's upgraded. The third configuration file is a global configuration file, called "machine.config," found in the CONFIG directory under the .NET Framework directory installed on your machine.

All these configuration files start out as XML files with elements that can be used to identify where an assembly is located. In the case of publisher policy configuration files, the configuration is compiled into its own assembly and installed in the GAC. As a result, these policies have an effect on all applications that use the shared component. As mentioned previously, the publisher policy files are usually installed during an update to the shared component. This file contains information about the new assembly and can indicate that a new version should be used, instead of the version referenced in the manifest. The application configuration file can override the publisher policy file with the use of Safe mode. To use Safe mode, the following element is used in the configuration file: `<publisherPolicy apply="yes|no" />`. When searching through configuration files, the Runtime Engine uses the order we used previously: application.config, publisher policy, and machine.config.

In practice, most applications won't use the configuration files to specify the physical location. Configuration files are typically used to hold application-specific information and normally aren't used to define where an assembly is located. If that information is found, however, it will be the only place the Runtime Engine looks. In other words, if the configuration files contain information about the location of an assembly and the Runtime Engine can't find that assembly, the binding will fail and the assembly-binding process will stop.

Loaded Assemblies

If the configuration information does not indicate a specific location to use, the run time will look at loaded assemblies next. Instead of trying to search other places for an assembly, it's much faster simply to reference what is already loaded. This can cause problems if you aren't careful with the names given to assemblies. For example, assume you performed the following steps:

1. You create an assembly named "MyUtilities", and then reference that in another assembly named "AppOne". Both of the AppOne-specific assemblies are located in a directory named "AppOne".

2. You create a new utility assembly named "MyUtilities", and then reference that from another assembly named "AppTwo". Both of these assemblies are located in a directory named "AppTwo".

3. You add the AppOne assembly as an external reference to the AppTwo assembly, and you then update the AppTwo configuration file with information to locate the AppOne assembly in the appropriate directory.

Both of the application assemblies reference another assembly named "MyUtilities". The AppTwo assembly is able to locate the AppOne assembly through the use of configuration information. Neither of these assemblies contain information about where to locate the MyUtilities assembly. The problem happens when AppTwo is loaded into a Runtime Engine and the engine starts the process of binding the assemblies. If the AppOne reference is processed after the MyUtilities reference, the Runtime Engine will use the MyUtilities assembly from AppTwo, instead of the assembly referenced by AppOne. This happens because none of the configuration files indicate where to find MyUtilities. As a result, when the Runtime Engine loads the assemblies referenced by AppOne, it sees that it already has an assembly named MyUtilities loaded and uses that reference.

If you know that all you need to do with .NET is make sure all assemblies are installed in the same directory, this might not seem right. Why didn't the AppOne assembly use the assembly in its directory by default? The answer has to do with the order of steps used to bind assemblies. The last place the Runtime Engine looks for an assembly is the directory. With the example previously described, the wrong assembly is used because the Runtime Engine will look for loaded assemblies before it will look in a directory. It's possible, however, to avoid this issue by using strong names, which is required for any assembly stored in the GAC.

Global Assembly Cache (GAC)

The GAC is used to hold assemblies that are shared by other assemblies, such as all the .NET Framework assemblies. To install an assembly in the GAC, it must have a strong name. Strong names can be created using a utility provided with the .NET Framework. This utility program is located in the FrameworkSDK\Bin directory, which isn't defined in the path environment variable. If you use the Command Prompt link available on the Visual Studio.NET Tools menu, however, it automatically sets the environment variables for you. The following code listing shows how to create a strong name for use in an assembly:

```
sn -k MyAssemblyKey.snk
```

The `-k` switch tells the strong name (`sn`) utility to generate a key file that can be used in the assembly. This file should be generated in the directory that will be used to build the assembly. This key file can be referenced using assembly attributes in a project and it can be used with command-line switches used to compile an assembly.

Once the strong name key is generated and the assembly is compiled using the strong name, another utility in the .NET Framework SDK can be used to install the assembly in the GAC. The following code listing shows how MyAssembly.exe would be loaded into the GAC:

```
gacutil -i MyAssembly.exe
```

Attempting to register an assembly in the GAC without a strong name will fail. Once the assembly is registered, it can then be referenced by any other assembly that needs the functionality. When one assembly references another from the GAC, the `extern` assembly reference will contain a public key token.

Now this might sound a lot like adding DLL files to System32, with all the associated "DLL Hell" issues that go along with that. The GAC, however, is different and doesn't suffer from the same issues. You can install multiple assemblies with the same name, but with different version numbers, in the GAC, side-by-side. The strong name generated for an assembly also takes into account the version number, so each version of the same component will have a different strong name. As a result, two different assemblies can reference different versions of an assembly in the GAC without conflict. In fact, one assembly can reference one version of a component in the GAC, along with another assembly that references a different version of the same shared assembly, referenced by the initial assembly. Okay, that was definitely a mouthful, but the bottom line is this: within one application, multiple versions of the same assembly can be loaded and used.

Probing File Directories

The last step the Runtime Engine takes to locate and bind an assembly is to probe directories looking for the assembly. This step starts by looking in the config files to see if a `<codebase>` element is defined. If this element is defined, then the Runtime Engine uses that to probe the directory looking for a file with the same name as the assembly. Like the GAC, when using the code-base element, all assemblies stored at that location must use a strong name. When the Runtime Engine attempts to load the assembly, it checks the name, version, public key, and culture to make sure the assembly is valid. If the assembly can't be found and a code base is defined, the Runtime Engine will stop processing and the binding will fail.

If no code base is defined, the Runtime Engine will start looking through directories to find the assembly. Four different pieces of information are used to perform this probing:

▶ The assembly name

▶ The directory where the application is being executed, known as the application base

▶ The culture attribute, if used, found in the assembly

▶ The Private binpath—a setting named *binpath*—that can be found in a configuration file or added to the application domain through a method

Most of this is pretty straightforward, but the culture might be something fairly new. With .NET, the concept of supporting multiple languages is built in to the overall architecture. The culture setting is used to indicate what culture should be applied to different elements, such as the language used along with the date and numeric formats. For instance, in the United States, the Culture setting would be en-US, which indicates the English—United States culture should be used.

When applied to applications, developers usually need to create different versions of the application to support different cultures. When the culture is set for an application, the assembly is installed in a subdirectory that uses the culture for a name. By using this method, you might have a base directory with multiple subdirectories, each containing a culture-specific version of the assembly.

With this information in mind, let's take the following settings and examine the path the Runtime Engine will use to look for the application.

```
Assembly Name:      MyApplication.exe
Application Base:    d:\dev\application
Culture:             en-US
binpath:             bin

d:\dev\application\en-US\MyApplication.exe
d:\dev\application\en-US\MyApplication\MyApplication.exe
d:\dev\application\bin\en-US\MyApplication.exe
d:\dev\application\bin\en-US\MyApplication\MyApplication.exe
```

Finally, the Runtime Engine uses one last piece of information in an attempt to locate and bind an assembly. This information has to do with the current binding context and is related to using the `Assembly.LoadFrom()` method. This method enables you to load an assembly into an application domain by giving it a path or URL to look for that assembly. If an assembly loaded this way references another assembly, then the Runtime Engine will use the path information from the `LoadFrom` method to locate the second assembly.

Security

Security is another element built in to the .NET Framework architecture and integral to targeting the CLR when building applications. This is a large and complex topic, so we can't possibly get into any real depth in this section. We will, however, look at some of the key concepts involved and see how the Runtime Engine applies the different checks. With .NET security, it's possible to restrict access based on the identity of a piece of code or the identity of a specific user. These two types of checks are called *code access security* and *role-based security,* respectively. Before you learn about the differences between the two, Table 9-2 lists some of the important concepts developers need to understand.

Two other terms are associated with security that will come up when reading through the .NET security specifications: declarative security checks and imperative security checks. The *declarative security checks* are performed by adding attributes to the code. These attributes are stored in the metadata and used by the Runtime Engine to implement permission checks. Different types of declarative checks can be performed and they can be applied to different levels of code. *Imperative security*

Security Concept	Description
Authentication	This is the process of validating the identity of a user through the use of credentials. The authority used to validate the credentials can be windows-based, custom, or third party.
Authorization	This deals with determining if a user or piece of code is allowed to perform an operation or access a specific section of code.
Permissions	These are objects the .NET security architecture uses to implement security. The permission objects are used for both code-access and role-based security. The Runtime Engine initializes several different permission objects, based on the type of application and the operation being performed. For instance, if an application requires authentication, a `PrincipalPermission` object is created and initialized during startup, with information about what permissions the authenticated user has.
Principal	This represents the identity of the user currently authenticated. .NET has several different types of principals, which are based on the type of authentication used, such as Windows or Custom.
Security Policy	This is a set of rules, set by system administrators, used to assign permissions to code. The security policy can be configured through a tool available in the .NET Framework. The Runtime Engine uses information about the code to determine what set of policies apply. This information is called *evidence* and the process of checking these permissions is called *evidence-based security*.
Type Safety	This has to do with being able to access memory locations in an application and isn't focused on the programmatic-type safety associated with the common type system. What this really deals with is making sure boundaries around different entities aren't violated. For instance, one object isn't allowed to access a private member of another object. In addition, code in one application domain isn't allowed to access code in another.

Table 9-2 *Key Security Concepts*

checks are programmatic checks, where a developer calls methods to check specifically for permissions. Both declarative and imperative checks are used for code-access security, as well as role-based security.

Code-Access Security

Code-access security is based on validating that a particular piece of code has appropriate security permissions to execute. Every .NET application is validated using a security policy as part of the managed execution process. Bypassing this security check within an application isn't possible, but an application can control how permissions are applied against other applications that access its functionality. Figure 9-5 shows a screenshot of a Microsoft Management Console snap-in provided with the .NET Framework, named "mscorcfg.msc". This utility application is used to configure the CLR, which includes configuring the security policies. The snap-in can be found in the .NET Framework directory, instead of the Framework SDK directory. The common path for this directory is [WINNT]/Microsoft.NET/Framework/ v1.0.[xxxx]/. The actual name of the Windows directory or version number can be different from one machine to another.

The screenshot in Figure 9-5 shows the run-time security policy tree expanded and the main page for run-time security displayed on the right. The run-time policy is divided into three main policy levels: Enterprise, Machine, and User. The *Enterprise level* is meant for all code in a network where a distributed configuration file is used.

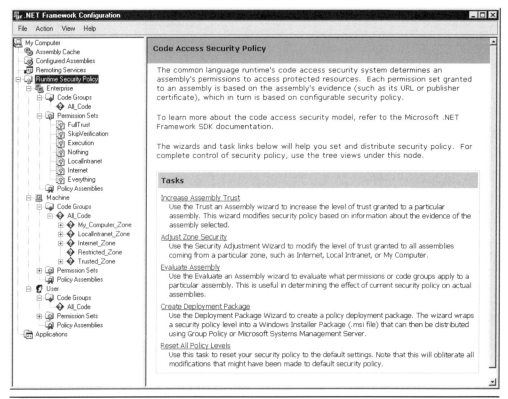

Figure 9-5   *.NET Framework configuration*

This policy can only be modified by enterprise or domain administrators. The *Machine level* is used to set permissions for code running on a specific computer. Administrators are the only users who can modify these settings. The *User level* is used to set permissions on user code. These permissions can be modified by an administrator or a user. One final level—the Application Domain policy—isn't shown in the configuration tool. These policy settings are configured through code running in the CLR and are used to manage permissions at the application domain level.

When an assembly is loaded, the Runtime Engine checks permissions for the code, starting at the lowest policy level. If the code has rights to execute at that level, a check is performed at the next level up. Each level is checked until reaching the top level, which is the Enterprise level. Attributes can also be added to the code that tells the Runtime Engine to check the call stack and make sure every user in the call stack has access to the section marked by the attribute. With code-access checks, the declarative attributes can be applied to Assembly, Class, and Member levels. If a permission check fails anytime during the call-access checks, a security exception is thrown.

An assembly can also be configured to request specific permissions through the use of attributes. Nothing requires you to request permissions, but this can make handling security violations easier. If you request a specific set of permissions, administrators can use a tool—named pview—to examine those permissions and configure a policy for your application. One aspect to requesting permissions is you must also include exception handlers to trap security exceptions. Permissions can also be refused. If you know areas exist in your application where a potential risk for unwanted behavior exists, you can refuse specific permissions to mitigate the risk.

When the .NET Framework is installed on a machine for the first time, a default set of policies is implemented, which are shown in Figure 9-5. All the permission sets shown under the Enterprise level are the same for Machine and User levels. These permission sets handle most of the basic restrictions that need to be applied. In addition, new permission sets can be added with different restrictions. Notice the Enterprise and User levels only have one code group named "*All_Code*". This is a base group applied to all code as the CLR loads assemblies. By default, this group is given *FullTrust* rights, which means the code has full access to all resources at that level. The Machine-level code group settings in Figure 9-5 are different, however. Additional groups have been added under *All_Code* that apply different restrictions. These groups are associated with the different zones available to Web Applications running in IE to restrict access to machine resources.

Knowing administrators have this level of control over what the code is allowed to access on a machine is significant. With non-managed code, such as an ActiveX control, administrators will tend to restrict their installation because of the potential for damage from these applications. Because .NET managed code always goes through these code-access checks, administrators can allow the installation of .NET applications with a high-level of confidence that they won't cause damage. As developers, we've had to limit the use of browser-based controls, which makes building dynamic user interfaces on a Web page difficult. With .NET, you can finally develop rich user interfaces for Web Applications with the expectation that administrators will allow it because of the code-access checks. In the section "Lifecycle of an Application," you learn about the actual lifecycle of an application and see exactly when these code-access checks are applied.

Role-Based Security

Role-based security is based on assigning roles to principals, and then restricting access to different sections of code by checking the current principal's role. Remember, a *principal* is defined as the user who is currently authenticated. Unlike the code-access checks, role-based checks don't support walking the call stack to check permissions on all users in the call chain. Instead, it will only check the principal associated with the current thread handling the request. Understanding why the thread identity is used gets pretty deep into Windows security, so we won't go there. All you need to understand is this: only the current principal is checked. The main object used to perform role-based security is the `PrincipalPermission` object.

The `PrincipalPermission` object can be initialized by the Runtime Engine when using Windows authentication or it can be initialized by user code when using custom authentication. When using declarative role-based security, the Runtime Engine is responsible for making the checks and throwing exceptions. When using imperative role-based security, the user code is responsible for making the checks and throwing appropriate exceptions. The most common place to use role-based security is with Web Applications, but it can be used in any type of .NET server or client application. In addition, role-based security will use Windows security groups when configured to use Windows authentication and impersonation.

Listing 9-2 gives an example that uses Windows security for authentication, and then uses imperative role-based security checks to make sure a user belongs to a specific role. The first section of code is a partial listing of the web.config file, which can be found at the root level of all Web Applications. Listing 9-2 shows the three main elements we're interested in when configuring windows authentication. To use Windows identities and perform authorization checks, the `authentication` element should be set to Windows. It could also be set to Forms, Passport, or None if you aren't using Windows authentication.

Listing 9-2   *Role-Based Security Check*

```
"Web.config"
<configuration>
  <system.web>
    <authentication mode="Windows" />
    <identity impersonate="true"/>
    <authorization>
      <deny users="?" />
      <allow roles="IVREL\MyAdmins,IVREL\MyUsers,"/>
    </authorization>
  </system.web>
</configuration>

"MyApplication.vb"
Dim myPrincipal as WindowsPrincipal
AppDomain.CurrentDomain.SetPrincipalPolicy(PrincipalPolicy.WindowsPrincipal)
myPrincipal = CType(Thread.CurrentPrincipal, WindowsPrincipal)
If myPrincipal.IsInRole("IVREL\MyAdmins") = True Then
    ... code
End If
```

To use role-based security with Windows identities, the `identity` element should be set to `impersonate="true"`, which sets the identity of threads in the application to the current principal. The last section in Listing 9-2 contains subelements used to restrict access based on users and roles. In this example, we're denying access to all anonymous users and allowing access to the roles listed. Notice the roles are all qualified with the machine name where the security group is located.

The Visual Basic code at the bottom of Listing 9-2 demonstrates how to implement imperative-based security checks. For these checks, we're using a `WindowsPrincipal` object, which is declared on the first line. The next line calls `SetPrincipalPolicy` on the current application domain. This is required to instantiate a `PrincipalPermission` object and initialize it with the security groups to which the current principal belongs. The third line is used to initialize the `WindowsPrincipal` object with the current principal. Once you have the principal object initialized, you can use that to perform role-based checks. The principal object also contains information, such as the user name, associated with the current principal.

Security involves much more than the limited amount of information covered in the past few pages. This information, however, does cover the basics and gives you a starting point for implementing security in applications. The main concepts that should stand out are that code access and role-based security are both based on the same security framework. Security can be implemented by the Runtime Engine using declarations and it can also be implemented in user code with imperative checks. Using both declarative and imperative security is even possible in the same application. Finally, all code managed by the Runtime Engine is required to pass code-access checks to execute.

Lifecycle of an Application

Now that you've examined all the different aspects to developing applications that target the CLR, let's walk through the process of developing, deploying, and executing a sample application. As you walk through the process of building your application, you'll use some of the tools available with the .NET Framework to examine different parts of the process. The sample application you'll build is going to be a simple console application that displays "Hello VS.NET!" in a command window. The reason for using a simple example is this enables us to dig deeper into things like the MSIL code, without adding too much complexity.

Developing the Application

As mentioned previously, the first step is selecting the development language to use. This is an important step. You want to make sure you choose a language that supports the functionality required. Even though you can mix different languages in the development of an application, this usually isn't a good idea. While most languages are similar and they all generate MSIL code, the syntax between the languages can be different and, often, it isn't possible to find developers able to support multiple languages. For developing new applications in Visual Studio.NET, the optimal language choice is C# because this language was designed from the ground up for .NET. As a result, C# is the language we'll choose for this example.

The example code will be available online at: **http://osborne.com** in the Downloads section of the McGraw-Hill/Osborne Web site; however, it will probably be more helpful to walk through this example and build the code as you go.

We're ready to start building code. The first step is to launch Microsoft Visual Studio .NET (VS.NET) from the program menus. If this is the first time you've started VS.NET, it will display a page that can be used to customize the development environment. At this point, let's leave the defaults intact. On the left-hand side, you should see a menu with the selection Getting Started on the top. Select that menu item, and then you should see the Start Page with links available to open an existing project or to start a new one. If you've already configured VS.NET, it will normally start with this page displayed, unless you modified the configuration to use a different start-up action. If you don't see the Start Page, you can also use the File menu at the top to start a new project.

The following steps describe how to create our new application:

1. Select the New Project link from the Start Page or use the File | New | Project menu selections to display the dialog box shown here.

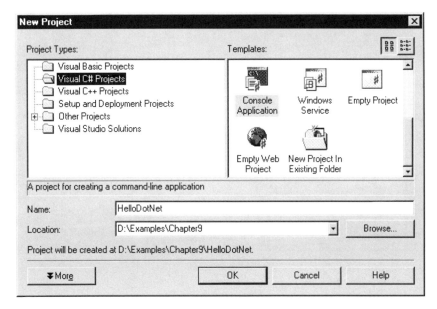

2. Select Visual C# Projects from the list of project types in the top-left window.

3. Choose Console Application in the Templates window on the right.

4. Select the Browse button at the bottom to choose the directory where you want to install the project. In this example, we're installing this project in the following directory: `D:\Examples\Chapter9`.

5. Enter the name of the application in the Name field above the Location field that was set with the project directory we just chose. The name for this sample application is `HelloDotNet`.

6. Once all the settings are updated in the dialog box, select OK to create the new application.

We now have a new project named "`HelloDotNet`", which is shown in Figure 9-6. Before adding any code to this new project, let's look at some of the files automatically

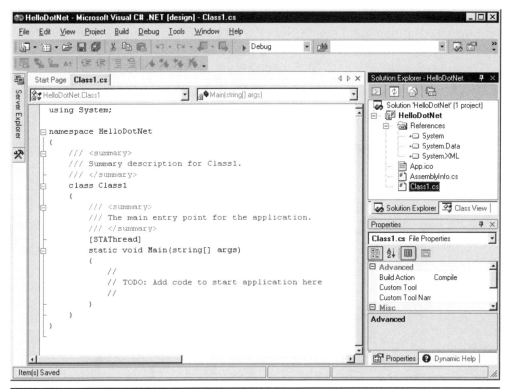

Figure 9-6   *New project*

generated for us. If you look at the Solution Explorer in the top right-hand corner of Figure 9-6, you can see we have a solution named `HelloDotNet` with one project that has the same name. Under this project, we have a References folder, with several references added, and the following three files: App.ico, AssemblyInfo.cs, and Class1.cs. All of this was automatically generated by VS.NET when we created the application.

In addition to the creation of files, VS.NET also generates the initial code we need to get started, which is shown in the Edit window in Figure 9-6. Because this is a console application, it requires the declaration of a method named "`Main`", which is the entry point for this application. For our example, most of the coding is already done. All you need to do is add the following line of code inside the `Main` function below the `TODO` comment.

```
Console.Write("\nHello .NET!\n");
```

This will write the text "Hello .NET!" out to the console window, which is the window associated with a command prompt in Windows. The \n characters added to the string are equivalent to vbCrLf in Visual Basic, which is used to insert a linefeed into the output. Once the line of code is added, select Build Solution or Build HelloDotNet from the Build menu to build the application.

We're done with development! One line of code later, we have a Windows console application that writes text out to the console window. Now, we have to admit this isn't very useful, however, it should help illustrate how easily you can develop .NET applications. Before moving on to deployment and the execution of this application, let's look at the files produced. Figure 9-7 shows the screenshot of a Framework SDK tool, named Ildasm, which is used to disassemble MSIL code. To run this tool, navigate to the Program Files/Microsoft Visual Studio.NET/ FrameworkSDK/Bin directory and execute Ildasm.exe. Once the program is launched, you can load our HelloDotNet application by selecting File | Open and navigating to the Bin/Debug directory under the HelloDotNet project and selecting HelloDotNet.exe.

The Ildasm tool, shown in Figure 9-7 can be used to examine more than the MSIL code generated. It can also be used to view metatdata. In fact, the first item shown under the project is the MANIFEST, which is metadata that lists the assemblies used by this application. Listing 9-3 shows the manifest information for our application, which is similar to the previous Listing 9-1. In this example, we only have two assembly references: the Runtime Engine and HelloDotNet. Inside the HelloDotNet assembly, we have custom attributes along with an attribute used by Visual Studio

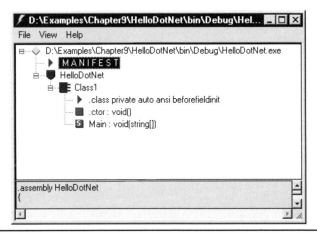

Figure 9-7 *Ildasm tool*

for debugging. In addition, the subsystem attribute is set to 3, which, if you remember, is used to indicate this is a console application.

Listing 9-3 *HelloDotNet Manifest*

```
.assembly extern mscorlib
{
  .publickeytoken = (B7 7A 5C 56 19 34 E0 89 )
  .ver 1:0:3300:0
}
.assembly HelloDotNet
{
  .custom instance void
      [mscorlib]System.Reflection.AssemblyCopyrightAttribute::.ctor(string)
      = ( 01 00 00 00 00 )
  .custom instance void
      [mscorlib]System.Reflection.AssemblyKeyFileAttribute::.ctor(string)
      = ( 01 00 00 00 00 )
  .custom instance void
      [mscorlib]System.Reflection.AssemblyDelaySignAttribute::.ctor(bool)
      = ( 01 00 00 00 00 )
  .custom instance void
      [mscorlib]System.Reflection.AssemblyTrademarkAttribute::.ctor(string)
      = ( 01 00 00 00 00 )
  .custom instance void
      [mscorlib]System.Reflection.AssemblyKeyNameAttribute::.ctor(string)
      = ( 01 00 00 00 00 )
  .custom instance void
      [mscorlib]System.Reflection.AssemblyProductAttribute::.ctor(string)
      = ( 01 00 00 00 00 )
  .custom instance void
      [mscorlib]System.Reflection.AssemblyCompanyAttribute::.ctor(string)
      = ( 01 00 00 00 00 )
  .custom instance void
   [mscorlib]System.Reflection.AssemblyConfigurationAttribute::.ctor(string)
      = ( 01 00 00 00 00 )
  .custom instance void
     [mscorlib]System.Reflection.AssemblyDescriptionAttribute::.ctor(string)
      = ( 01 00 00 00 00 )
  .custom instance void
      [mscorlib]System.Reflection.AssemblyTitleAttribute::.ctor(string)
      = ( 01 00 00 00 00 )
  // --- The following custom attribute is added automatically,
  //     do not uncomment -------
```

```
  //.custom instance void
  //    [mscorlib]System.Diagnostics.DebuggableAttribute::.ctor(bool, bool)
  //    = ( 01 00 01 01 00 00 )
  .hash algorithm 0x00008004
  .ver 1:0:764:30840
}
.module HelloDotNet.exe
// MVID: {DF43F7F9-F05C-4981-ABC7-0EA3F22EBB42}
.imagebase 0x00400000
.subsystem 0x00000003
.file alignment 512
.corflags 0x00000001
```

The one question you probably still have is where did the custom attributes shown in Listing 9-3 come from? These attributes are set in the AssemblyInfo.cs file generated when we created the project. Listing 9-4 shows a partial listing of the code found in the AssemblyInfo file. With C#, attributes are enclosed in square brackets, [ ] and the `assembly:` keyword tells the compiler these are assembly attributes.

Listing 9-4   *AssemblyInfo.cs*

```
using System.Reflection;
using System.Runtime.CompilerServices;

//
// General Information about an assembly is controlled through the following
// set of attributes. Change these attribute values to modify the
// information associated with an assembly.
//
[assembly: AssemblyTitle("")]
[assembly: AssemblyDescription("")]
[assembly: AssemblyConfiguration("")]
[assembly: AssemblyCompany("")]
[assembly: AssemblyProduct("")]
[assembly: AssemblyCopyright("")]
[assembly: AssemblyTrademark("")]
[assembly: AssemblyCulture("")]
```

When looking through the attributes added in Listing 9-4, you can see they match the `custom` attributes added to the assembly in Listing 9-3. For instance, the following attribute in Listing 9-4

```
[assembly: AssemblyTitle("")]
```

is associated with the following custom attribute in the assembly section of the manifest shown in Listing 9-3:

```
.custom instance void
    [mscorlib]System.Reflection.AssemblyTitleAttribute:.ctor(string)
```

The only difference is `Attribute` was appended to the name. These entries both represent the same thing, however.

Along with the capability to examine the manifest, the Ildasm tool also enables you to dump all the MSIL and metadata code out to a text file or view MSIL code on the individual functions. Listing 9-5 shows the MSIL code generated for the `Main` function. The MSIL code is quite easy to read. Simply by looking at the commands in the listing, you can tell it loads a string, calls a function, and then returns.

Listing 9-5   *MSIL Code*

```
.method private hidebysig static void  Main(string[] args) cil managed
{
  .entrypoint
  .custom instance void [mscorlib]System.STAThreadAttribute::.ctor()
      = ( 01 0 00 00 )
  // Code size       11 (0xb)
  .maxstack  1
  IL_0000:  ldstr      "\nHello .NET!\n"
  IL_0005:  call       void [mscorlib]System.Console::Write(string)
  IL_000a:  ret
} // end of method Class1::Main
```

Two attributes in Listing 9-5 should be singled out: the `entrypoint` attribute and the `custom` attribute. The `entrypoint` attribute was added by the compiler because it knows the `Main` function is an entry point. The Runtime Engine requires all executable applications to contain an entry point. You won't find one of these on a library assembly, though, because they're always referenced by other assemblies. A reference to the entry point is added to the CLI Header section of the PE Header, which the Runtime Engine uses to start execution of the application. The `custom` attribute is used to represent the `[STAThread]` attribute, which was assigned to the `Main` function in Figure 9-6.

One thing that appears to be missing— the tokens we discussed previously. By default, the Ildasm tool doesn't display the tokens. This tool is meant to be a textual representation of the code and the metadata. As a result, the token information doesn't provide much information. You can, however, view this information by selecting View Tokens from the View menu. The View menu in the Ildasm tool has many different settings that you can use to filter what's displayed.

Deploying the Application

Now that you have your application built, it's time to deploy it. To be honest, this is one of the easiest tasks with .NET applications, which is contrary to COM applications. As mentioned previously, the application could be installed in the GAC, but most applications are installed into their own directory. Several different tools can also be used during deployment, which administrators can use to validate an application or precompile an application during deployment. In addition, VS.NET provides several setup and deployment projects that can be used to create installation applications.

As mentioned previously, any application deployed to the GAC must have a strong name. Once you create the strong name, you can install it using the gacutil application, discussed previously. As a general rule, however, most applications shouldn't be installed in the GAC. The only time you would install an application or library in the GAC is if it will be used by many other applications. Even then, installing an assembly in the GAC isn't necessary because each application only needs to include a reference to the assembly in its application. One benefit of the GAC is the capability to install multiple versions side-by-side without causing any conflicts. The main point here is you need to think carefully before adding anything to the GAC.

The most common scenario for deployment is to copy all the required files into a directory. That's all there is to deployment—there's nothing to register. All the application information is contained in the metadata and the configuration files are located in the same directory. As discussed previously, an administrator could deploy components to different directories, and then use config settings to indicate where they are, but this is the exception and not typical. Because all the components are deployed together, no issue usually exists with version updates. If components are distributed and config files are used to indicate locations, however, an issue might occur. This is where an application developer would use a publisher policy config file to resolve any version issues.

One of the many tools installed with the .NET SDK is a tool named *PEVerify*, which was designed as a deployment tool for administrators to use to verify the .NET PE files are valid. Remember, a PE file is a Portable Executable, which the Windows OS, and run-time shell recognize as executable files. To run PEVerify, open the Command prompt that's available in the Microsoft Visual Studio .NET | Visual Studio .NET Tools menu. From the command prompt, navigate to the

Bin/Debug directory where our HelloDotNet.exe file is located and execute the following command:

```
PEVerify HelloDotNet.exe
```

The following screen shows the command prompt with the `PEVerify` command executed. The default action is to verify both the MSIL code and metadata, however, several different command-line switches can be used to control different actions performed. To get a list of available commands, execute `PEVerify` by itself or with the `-?` switch. When PEVerify runs, it implements all the code-access checks defined for the application. The output shows the classes and methods in `HelloDotNet` were valid.

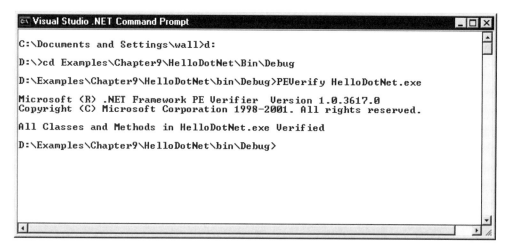

Another tool that can be used during deployment is a precompiler named *NGen*, which produces machine-specific code from MSIL code. This generated code is inserted into the GAC as a *Native Image* and then mapped to the MSIL code in the application assembly. Normally, you'd want to let the JIT compiler used by the Runtime Engine compile the MSIL code as needed. The reason for this is, even though precompiled applications might start faster, they tend to run slightly slower because of the mapping required between the MSIL code and the precompiled native code. The JIT compiler and the Runtime Engine are designed for performance but, in some cases, it might be necessary to load an application as fast as possible. In these cases, using the NGen tool during deployment would be appropriate.

The following screen shows the command prompt after the NGen tool was run against our `HelloDotNet` application, and then running the application. Notice the output from NGen displays the program name, version, culture, and public key token, all of which are standard attributes used by the GAC. In addition, notice the public key token is set to null, which indicates we don't have a strong name. The interesting part about all of this, however, is the precompiled native code is added to the GAC by the NGen tool. But how can that be true? We've stated previously that all assemblies in the GAC require a strong name. The difference is the native code is added to the GAC with the Type set to Native Images, which is handled differently from other GAC entries and doesn't require a strong name. Instead, these entries are used by the Runtime Engine to execute code that was precompiled.

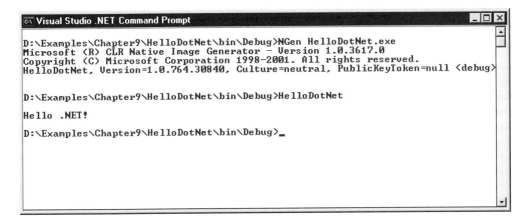

Executing the Application

The actual execution of this application is straightforward. We need to open a command prompt, navigate to a directory that contains the application, and then execute it. The output isn't spectacular either. We get an empty line, a line with Hello .NET! followed by another empty line. The part we're interested in, though, is what happens behind the scenes to execute this application. We already know the Windows shell application contains a Runtime Engine that recognizes information in the PE Header, creates an application domain, and starts executing code. The actual execution of this code goes through several different steps to perform code checks, verify the code, and then compile it to native code before executing it.

Figure 9-8 shows a flow diagram that describes the process involved with checking, compiling, and executing the code. This process starts with a PE file that contains MSIL code and metadata, and is shown on the top left as a circle. The first step in executing the code is to load the assembly using an assembly loader. Once the assembly is loaded, the code-access checks are performed using evidence from

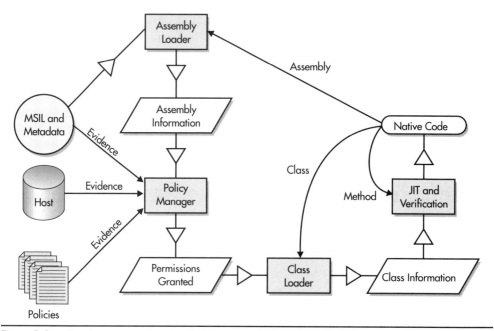

Figure 9-8   *Runtime execution process*

different sources. After the code-access checks are done, the class that contains the entry point is loaded using the class loader. From there, the specific entry point method—usually Main or WinMain—is compiled using the JIT compiler, and then executed. During the JIT step, code is also verified to make sure it's type safe.

Figure 9-8 also shows what happens as new assemblies, classes, and methods are handled during the execution of an application. As code executes, the entry point method calls other methods to perform operations. As each new method is called, the Runtime Engine branches to the appropriate step, based on currently loaded code. If the assembly a method belongs to hasn't been loaded, the Runtime Engine will branch to the assembly loader. The same thing happens if an assembly is loaded, but the specific class that contains the new method hasn't been loaded. The Runtime Engine will branch to the class loader before compiling the method. Finally, if both the assembly and class are already loaded, the Runtime Engine will branch only to the JIT compiler to generate native code and execute the method.

The main information to get from this process is that assemblies and classes aren't loaded until referenced. In addition, each method is compiled when accessed, not when the class or assembly is loaded. Once a class has been compiled, the Runtime Engine will use the compiled version for each subsequent call to the same method.

The overall result is an application that loads code only when needed and reuses compiled code for fast performance.

Along with loading code and compiling methods, the CLR performs many other run-time services while the code is executing. We discussed some of those services earlier in this chapter. Some of the more significant services to learn about are exception handling, thread management, and garbage collection. We've already discussed exception handling throughout this chapter. The main thing to remember is exception support is mandatory and implemented by the Runtime Engine. With *thread management,* the Runtime Engine provides commands and attributes that can be used to create and manage threads in the application. The actual discussion of using threads is beyond the scope of this chapter, however, many good examples are included with VS.NET.

Garbage collection is another topic that won't be discussed in detail. Instead, the main thing you need to understand as a developer is the Runtime Engine will manage the destruction of resources that are no longer used. We're no longer required to free memory allocations or release objects when finished with them. This doesn't apply to external resources, such as database connections, which we allocated during execution. These resources must be cleaned up or released manually within the code.

Summary

We started this chapter by looking at the .NET Framework and examining how the CLR is used to manage code during execution. To build applications that target the CLR, you need to use a compiler that generates PE Header information that a .NET Runtime Engine can recognize, along with MSIL code and metadata. Once the PE file is compiled, run-time hosts are used to load and execute the .NET application. Assemblies are used to define application boundaries along with version, culture, and strong-name information associated with an application. You also learned what metadata is, and how MSIL and metadata are tied together with the use of tokens. Some of the tools available in the .NET Framework SDK were examined and used to look at code or perform operations.

The last section walked through the development, deployment, and execution of an application that runs in the CLR. As part of the deployment discussion, you learned deployment is easy and flexible. You also learned how to preverify and precompile MSIL code. And, you learned how the Runtime Engine loads assemblies and classes during execution, and when the Runtime Engine compiles methods into native code. Some of the other services such as thread management, exception handling, and garbage collection were briefly discussed.

The following list highlights some of the topics discussed:

- ▶ Role of the CLR in the .NET Framework
- ▶ Run-time services available
- ▶ Run-time hosts
- ▶ Portable Executable files
- ▶ MSIL code and metadata
- ▶ Definition of assemblies
- ▶ Binding assemblies
- ▶ Security
- ▶ Application deployment
- ▶ Run-time execution of application code
- ▶ Tools available to view code and perform operations

.NET Framework
Classes

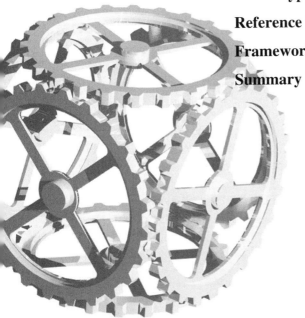

In this chapter you learn how classes are organized within the .NET Framework and learn about the Common Type System (CTS). The *CTS* is a fundamental concept in .NET, which defines how types are declared, used, and managed. You examine the different types of data, such as value types and reference types, that are defined by the CTS. In addition, you look at the rules used to control how different types are managed and how objects in .NET interact. In the last section, you take a quick pass through most of the namespaces found in the .NET Framework and learn how they're grouped.

Inside the .NET Framework

In Chapter 9, we focused on the Common Language Runtime (CLR) and how it fits into the .NET Framework. We also discussed how the framework is divided into two major sections: the CLR and the .NET Framework classes. Figure 10-1 shows the same .NET Framework diagram used in Chapter 9, with additional detail on the Framework classes. The *Framework* classes are typically grouped into Base classes, Data classes (ADO.NET and XML), ASP.NET classes, and Windows Forms classes. These groupings help break the Framework classes into main functionality groups and aren't meant to show relationships or dependencies. In reality, the .NET Framework classes shown in Figure 10-1 are only a sub-set of the programming interfaces developers use to write .NET applications.

NOTE

The term "Interface" can lead to some confusion. Specifically, the .NET Framework provides a reference type similar to a class that's called an Interface. However, most technical discussions describe functions used to access a component as the interface to that component. Throughout this chapter, anytime we reference the .NET Interface type, we'll use italics. Any other discussion that uses the term "interface" is talking about the functions exposed by a component.

When reading through all the technical articles that discuss the .NET Framework classes, you'll find they're discussing a programming interface for developers. This programming interface provides the capability to access databases, interoperate with other applications, access system resources, design graphical interfaces, and much more. Before .NET and the .NET Framework, developers relied on a variety of different components and programming interfaces to access this functionality. In addition, each programming language had its own representation of common datatypes. In contrast, the programming model for .NET is based on an object-oriented structure,

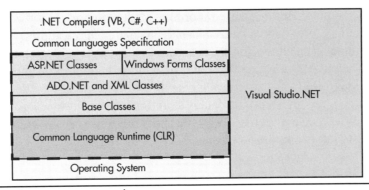

Figure 10-1 *The .NET Framework*

which itself is based on a CTS. This CTS supports the capability to share components between languages and provides a common framework for developing applications using different programming languages.

Common Type System

The Common Type System (CTS) is ultimately the foundation for .NET Framework classes and the foundation of .NET programming. In other words, everything in the .NET Framework is based on the use of a CTS. Understanding this concept is key to understanding how the .NET Framework is put together. In addition, with a solid grasp of the CTS, developers will have a much better understanding of how to develop .NET applications in any language they choose.

With .NET, two different type classifications are found in the CTS: value types and reference types. Computer programs store the data they use while running in the memory of a computer. Variables in a program are used to access these memory locations and retrieve the data stored there. In other words, the *variable* is like a sign for a store in a mall: all these stores have an address, which is equivalent to a memory location, but it's much easier to find the store by name than by address. When variables are declared, they're also given a type specification. That type is used to describe the data stored at the address referenced by the variable. In some cases, the type represents data that's stored at the address and, in some cases, it's an address to another location in memory or a pointer.

When discussing a value that only takes up 4 bytes, we could be discussing an integer or a pointer to another memory location. Many different datatypes take up 4 bytes of memory. But this isn't important. What is important is the difference between a memory location that holds data and one that holds an address. The memory location that holds data allows for direct access to the data and is referred to as a *value type*. The memory location that holds an address to another memory location, or a pointer, is referred to as a *reference type*. In addition, value-type data is pushed onto the stack while reference-type data is stored in heap memory. This means that the primary difference between a value type and a reference type is one holds data and the other holds an address.

Type Members

Before we get into discussions on the different types, understanding the elements found in most of these types can help. The .NET documentation refers to these elements as *type members*. Each of these type members can also be assigned different characteristics through the use of keywords when they're declared. Declaring a type member means you're assigning a name, type, and characteristic for that member. Typically the declaration, or definition, of a type member starts with the member's characteristic, followed by the type and name. With Visual Basic, however, the name comes before the type.

The following listing shows the declaration of a `Boolean` named `isValid` in C#, C++, and Visual Basic:

```
[C# and C++]
public bool isValid;


[Visual Basic]
Public isValid As Boolean
```

In the previous example, `public` is a characteristic, `bool` (Boolean) is a type, and the name is `isValid`. As you can guess, many types can be used—in fact, everything in the .NET Framework is considered a type. However, there are less than 20 characteristics defined. As a developer, it's important to learn what those characteristics are and how to use them. But, first, let's look at the different type members.

Table 10-1 shows the different type members that can be assigned to .NET types. The names used for these different members are meant to be generic and aren't related to any specific language. For instance, the method type member, described in Table 10-1, is the same thing as a sub or a function in Visual Basic.NET. When looking through this list, many of these elements should be familiar. Anyone who

Type Member	Description
Event	This is an action to which other objects in an application can capture and respond. Events are typically used to notify other objects when something has changed.
Field	This is a member that describes and contains values within the type. A *field* typically represents a constant or a private variable.
Nested type	This is a datatype nested within the scope of another datatype.
Method	This describes the different operations available on the type. *Constructors* are a method type member called when an object is created.
Property	Properties are members that name a publicly available value. A *property* defines different methods used to get and/or set the value.

Table 10-1   *Type Members*

has worked with classes will recognize these members and come to the conclusion that a class is a datatype, which is a valid conclusion. However, not all of the types in the .NET CTS use these members and they aren't restricted to use in classes only.

As you can see in Table 10-1, not many different type members can be found in a .NET type. In addition, all these members can be declared using different .NET types. For instance, `Public Function GenerateName() as String`, declares a method type member that has a string type. In addition, this declaration has a characteristic assigned to it named `Public`. This characteristic is used to describe the accessibility of the type member. In other words, it describes who can access this member.

Table 10-2 shows all the different characteristics available and the type members that can use them. Note, some of these characteristics apply to types that don't exist as a member of another type. But few types can exist outside another type. In fact, this is one of the major differences between .NET languages, and previous versions of Visual Basic and C++. The .NET Common Language Specification (CLS) doesn't support the use of global variables or methods. As a result, everything exists within the context of another type, which is usually the class type. Even the Visual Basic Module is a specialized version of a class where all the members are shared (static).

NOTE

A method signature consists of the method's name, parameter list, and return type.

Characteristic	Description	Applies To
Public	Indicates that a type is accessible from any other type.	All
Private	Indicates that a type is accessible only from within the same type as the member or within a nested type.	All
Family	Indicates that a type is accessible from within the same type as the member and from subtypes that inherit from it.	All
Assembly	Indicates that a type is accessible only in the same compilation unit, subject to rules set by the specific source language.	All
Family or assembly	Indicates that a type is accessible only from types that qualify for either family or assembly access.	All
Family and assembly	Indicates that a type is accessible only from types that qualify for both family and assembly access.	All
Abstract	Indicates the member doesn't provide any implementation. If a type contains any abstract members, then that type can't be instantiated. Any subtypes that inherit from a type with abstract members must either provide an implementation for that member or declare it as abstract.	Methods, properties, and events
Final	Identifies a member that can't be overridden in a derived type.	Methods, properties, and events
Initialize-only	A value can only be assigned to the field within an initialization block.	Fields
Instance	Members that are neither static nor virtual are called *instance members*.	Fields, methods, properties, and events
Literal	A field assigned a built-in value type at compile time. Literal fields are also referred to as *constants*.	Fields
Newslot or override	Defines how members of a subtype interact with members from the parent that have the same method signature: **Newslot** (default) Hides inherited members with the same signature. **Override** Replaces the definition of an inherited virtual method.	All

Table 10-2   *Member Characteristics*

Characteristic	Description	Applies To
Static	Members that are declared as static (shared in Visual Basic) are similar to global variables. They exist within the scope of an application and can be accessed without instantiating the type they belong to. In addition, all instances of a type that contain static members share a single instance of that member.	Fields, methods, properties, and events
Virtual	A keyword used to indicate a member can be overridden by a member with the same signature in a subtype. During execution, the Runtime Engine determines which instance of a member to use, based on this characteristic. If a member is marked as virtual, the Runtime Engine will look for subtype instances. Otherwise, it will use the instance associated with the type.	Methods, properties, and events

Table 10-2   *Member Characteristics* (continued)

When looking through the different characteristics described in Table 10-2, they probably won't look familiar to anyone who has started developing Visual Basic.NET solutions. For developers using other languages—such as C#—many of these will be familiar, but not all of them. The reason for this is these characteristics aren't meant to describe keywords in each of the languages. Instead, each language defines its own keywords to support the different characteristics described in Table 10-2. The following table shows some of the mappings between characteristics and Visual Basic keywords:

Characteristic	Visual Basic Keyword(s)
Abstract	`MustInherit` and `MustOverride`
Final	`NotInheritable` and `NotOverridable`
Virtual	`Overridable`

Overriding Versus Overloading

These two terms probably cause the most confusion for developers who aren't familiar with object-oriented languages. They both have to do with method signatures, but only one of them deals with inheritance. By this point, you should be able to guess which one refers to inheritance. The characteristics described in Table 10-2 and the Visual Basic keywords help determine that overriding is associated with inheritance. You've learned that when you mark something as virtual, or overridable, the Runtime Engine determines what instance of a member to use by looking at subtypes. But what exactly does that mean?

Overriding

The best way to describe overriding is with an example. Listing 10-1 shows a Base class named `CreditCard` with two procedures: one named `Format` and the other named `Process`. The `Process` class is declared as overridable while the `Format` class isn't. The next class in Listing 10-1 is named `Visa` and it inherits functionality from the `CreditCard` class. The `Visa` class also defines two members—`Format` and `Process`—using the same declaration characteristics. The last class, named `TestClass`, instantiates an instance of `Visa` in the constructor and passes it to a method named `ProcessCard`.

NOTE

A class is considered a reference type in .NET. When discussing examples that use classes, we're also discussing the behavior of other reference types that support the same characteristics.

Listing 10-1   *Overriding Example*

```
Public Class CreditCard
    Public Sub Format()
       'Base class code...
    End Sub
    Public Overridable Sub Process()
       'Base class code...
    End Sub
End Class
Public Class  Visa : Inherits CreditCard
    Public Sub Format()
       'Visa class code...
    End Sub
    Public Overrides Sub Process()
       'Visa class code...
    End Sub
End Class
Public Class TestClass
    Public Sub New()
```

```
      Dim visaCard as CreditCard = new Visa()
      ProcessCard( visaCard )
   End Sub
   Public Sub ProcessCard( ByVal card as CreditCard )
      card.Format()
      card.Process()
      ... do more work
   End Sub
End Class
```

When looking at the definition of the `MyClass.ProcessCard` method in Listing 10-1, you can see it takes a `CreditCard` parameter. In addition, you can see the constructor is passing an instance of `Visa` to `ProcessCard`, which is valid because `Visa` inherits from `CreditCard`. The interesting part comes with the actual member instances that get called inside the `ProcessCard` method. When calling `card.Format()`, the `Format` function in `CreditCard` is called. However, when calling `card.Process()`, the `Process` function in the `Visa` class is called.

The reason for this behavior is because the `Process` method is overridden and the `Format` method isn't. Remember, the `ProcessCard` method is dealing with a type identified as `CreditCard`, which defines both of these methods. As a result, even though the `Visa` instance is passed into it, the `ProcessCard` method only knows it's working with a `CreditCard` type and not a `Visa` type. When the Runtime Engine executes the `Format` function, it uses the instance found in the `CreditCard` class because it wasn't told to look elsewhere. In contrast, when the Runtime Engine executes the `Process` method, it knows to look for the subtype's version because it's marked as overridable. If the Runtime Engine finds an instance in the subtype, it will execute that. If not, it executes the instance found in the Base class.

Overloading

Now that you have a good handle on what it means to override a type member, we need to look at overloading. Overloading has nothing to do with inheritance. Instead, *overloading* is associated with the signature of a method. In the past, if you wanted to write a class that provided different methods used to add two parameters in Visual Basic, you needed to provide a different method name for each type you wanted to handle. With the support of overriding in .NET languages, you no longer have to do that. Instead, you can use the same method name with different parameters and return values. Each variation of parameters and return values creates a new method signature. When calling these functions, the Runtime Engine examines the request and calls the appropriate method whose signature supports the request.

NOTE

For developers familiar with overloading in C++, the .NET implementation is slightly different. With C++, you must have different parameter lists to override methods. Changing the return value alone isn't valid. With .NET languages, you can modify only the return type, parameter list, or both to overload another method.

The following listing shows a class named `MathHelper` with overloaded methods used to add different values. If you call the `Add` function with two integers, the first instance is called. If you call the `Add` function with two strings, however, the second instance is called. That's all overloading involves.

```
Public Class MathHelper
    Public Function Add( ByVal x as Integer, ByVal y as Integer ) As Integer
        Return x + y
    End Function
    Public Function Add( ByVal x as String, ByVal y as String) As Integer
        Return CInt(x) + CInt(y)
    End Function
End Class
```

Now that you understand all the type members and characteristics, let's look at the different value and reference types in .NET.

Value Types

The diagram in Figure 10-2 shows the value types supported by the .NET Framework. The built-in types are all the standard datatypes we're used to as developers, such as *integer* and *string*. In addition, built-in types are identical to the primitive types used by programming languages. Enumerations should be familiar to most developers because they represent a named set of value types. The .NET Framework stores enumeration values in the locations referenced by the names of each field in the set. User-defined types are equivalent to the structure datatype. When you use the `struct` keyword to define a block of data in C#, you're creating a user-defined value type. The common relationship for all these different types is they all store their values in the memory location referenced by the variable.

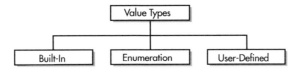

Figure 10-2 *Value types*

Built-In Types

As mentioned previously, built-in types are standard datatypes that are common on most platforms. These datatypes are also considered primitive types because they represent low-level data supported by most languages. In other words, the variable associated with a built-in type represents the actual primitive data. Table 10-3 shows all the .NET built-in value types and the equivalent programming language datatype for VB, C#, and C++. The datatype names are used as type specifiers for variables when they're declared. Table 10-3 also shows the size of each datatype, which is the amount of memory it occupies.

.NET Value Type	Visual Basic	C#	C++	Size
Byte	Byte	byte	char	8 bits (1 byte)
SByte	N/A	sbyte	signed char	8 bits (1 byte)
Int16	Short	short	short	16 bits (2 bytes)
Int32	Integer	int	int or long	32 bits (4 bytes)
Int64	Long	long	__int64	64 bits (8 bytes)
UInt16	N/A	ushort	unsigned short	16 bits (2 bytes)
UInt32	N/A	uint	unsigned int or unsigned long	32 bits (4 bytes)
UInt64	N/A	ulong	unsigned __int64	64 bits (8 bytes)
Single	Single	float	float	32 bits (4 bytes)
Double	Double	double	double	64 bits (8 bytes)
Boolean	Boolean	bool	bool	1 bit (true or false)
Char	Char	char	wchar_t	16 bit (Unicode)
Decimal	Decimal	decimal	Decimal	96 bits (12 bytes)

Table 10-3 *Built-In Types*

One thing that stands out in Table 10-3 is that Visual Basic doesn't provide built-in types for unsigned integers or a signed character. This is because the language doesn't provide an equivalent for these types and doesn't treat them as primitive data. This doesn't mean a Visual Basic program can't use these types of data. It simply means these datatypes will require more overhead because they must be handled by .NET objects.

Boxing

While all these built-in types represent primitive data, they also represent objects with functions and attributes. But this doesn't make sense! How can a datatype represent primitive data and an object at the same time? The functionality that allows this is called boxing. Every one of the value types, which includes built-in types, also have an equivalent reference type that provides additional functionality. When you access that additional functionality, a new object is created that wraps the value type. The process of wrapping the value type is called *boxing*. When a reference type that was boxed is converted back into a value type, that operation is called *unboxing*.

With some languages—such as C# and Visual Basic.NET—you needn't worry about boxing and unboxing values. In other languages, such as C++ .NET, you have to box and unbox value types specifically. The following listing shows an example of how boxing works in C# and C++.

```
[C#]
   int Amount = 100;
   Console.WriteLine( "{0:c}", Amount );

[C++]
   int Amount = 100;
   Console:WriteLine( "{0:c}", __box(Amount) );
```

In the previous example, we're defining an integer type that's equal to 100. Because an *int* is a built-in type, the value is stored at the address location defined by the variable. The next step is to print out the value formatted as a money: $100.00. This is accomplished by using the `WriteLine` function with a formatting specifier. The `WriteLine` function is defined as taking an array of objects after the formatting specifier. However, the datatype we are passing into this function is a value type and not an object. With boxing that is not a problem, and with C# or Visual Basic, you simply pass the value as previously shown. The value type is automatically boxed into a reference type. With C++ you need to do a little more work. Because C++ doesn't support automatic boxing of value types, you need to specifically perform the box operation, using the `__box` language extension.

As mentioned previously, boxing is supported by all the value types, not only the built-in types. In addition, we haven't yet discussed much about reference types or objects, so some of this might still be unclear. The main thing to remember now is all the value types in .NET also have equivalent reference types. When we discus the reference types and .NET Framework classes in the upcoming section "Self-Describing: Class," you'll have another look at boxing.

Enumeration

Enumerations are typically used to define a restricted set of values that can be assigned to a variable. The members of an enumeration can only be defined as one of the signed or unsigned integer types shown in Table 10-3. Another way to think of an enumeration is to use the store name analogy discussed earlier. Instead of using a name to represent data, however, the name represents a specific constant value. Enumerations can be declared without using a type specifier or a specifier can be declared using attributes. If a type specifier isn't used, the types will default to an integer type.

NOTE

Attributes, which are new to Visual Studio languages, provide the capability to declaratively define the behavior of different components in .NET. Attributes can be found in the declaration of classes, methods, structures, enumerations, and other .NET components.

The following listing shows bit-field enumerations in Visual Basic and C#.

```
[Visual Basic]
Public Enum <Flags()> Roles
   None = 0
   Administrator = 1
   Operator = 2
   Customer = 4
   All = Administrator Or Operator Or Customer
End Enum

[C#]
[Flags]
public enum Roles
{
   None = 0,
   Administrator = 1,
   Operator = 2,
```

```
     Customer = 4
     All = Administrator | Operator | Customer
}
```

In the previous code samples, we're using a new datatype to the .NET system called a flag type. The places where you see the keyword `flags` are examples of attributes in .NET. In Visual Basic, attributes are enclosed in angle brackets and, in C# and C++, square brackets are used. A *flag* datatype represents bit values and is typically used when the values need to be combined. The last element in both previous enumerations shows how these bit values can be combined to produce another value.

Enumerations have the following limitations:

► They can't define properties, events, or methods.

► They don't have a constructor.

► They can't extend classes.

► They can't implement interfaces.

User-Defined Types

User-defined types are the same thing as structures in C++ and are similar to user defined types (UDT) in Visual Basic 6.0. Structures are also similar to classes in .NET, but are much more efficient because *structures* are stored as value types instead of reference types. Unlike enumerations, a structure can define methods and properties, as well as implement interfaces. In fact, many of the value types not represented by built-in types, such as Boolean, are defined as structures in the .NET Framework.

The following listing shows some of the value types defined as structures in the .NET Framework:

```
[Visual Basic]
Public Structure Boolean
    Implements IComparable, IConvertible
Public Structure UInt16
    Implements IComparable, IFormattable, IConvertible
 [C#]
public struct Boolean : IComparable, IConvertible
public struct UInt16 : IComparable, IFormattable, IConvertible
```

The `Boolean` and `UInt16` (unsigned 16-bit integer) datatypes are both considered value types because they represent actual values, instead of addresses. As you can see, the .NET Framework accomplishes this by using the structure, which represents a user-defined datatype.

Passing Value Types

By default, when a value type is passed as a parameter to a function in C# or VB.NET, the actual data is copied into the method. Any changes to that data will only be done within the function. This is a change in the VB language, which used to pass the address of parameters by default, instead of the data. This behavior is fine, but can cause some performance problems when passing something like a string or user-defined type, which can be rather large. For instance, your application loads 500 kilobytes of information from a text file into a string and passes that information to another function. When using the defaults, all the data must be copied into a different memory location inside the method. This uses considerable resources and causes extra work. Instead, you might want to pass something like this using the `ByRef` or `ref` keywords, which will only pass the address of the data, and not the data itself.

As mentioned previously, value types can also be converted to reference types when they're passed to functions that expect a reference type through the process known as boxing. During the boxing process, all the value types, including structures and enumerations, are converted into an object. An *object* is nothing more than an instance of a class reference type. When reference types are passed by value, only the reference is passed, not the entire object. This is similar to passing something `ByRef`, but the difference is the original address can't be modified. When passing an object `ByRef`, the original address could be modified by the method called. In the next section, we discuss objects in more detail, along with other reference types that can't be instantiated.

Reference Types

As discussed previously, a reference type is a datatype that stores the address of the value, instead of the actual value. Three different reference types are in the .NET Framework: interface, pointer, and class. The class type can also be divided further into boxed, delegate, and user-defined types. Figure 10-3 shows how all these

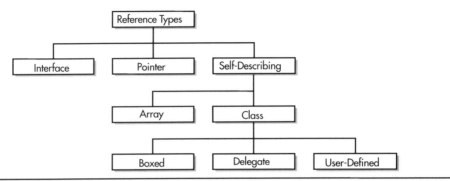

Figure 10-3   *Reference types*

reference types are related to each other. One important thing to note is this: while interface and pointer types are considered reference types, neither of them can hold a reference to an instantiated object. In other words, only the class types and value types represent actual data.

Interface

The *interface* type is used to provide declarations of type members, without providing any implementation. But why would anyone want to do that? What good is providing a declaration without any implementation? These questions have two different answers. The first answer has to do with application design and inheritance. Cases exist where several classes need to provide the same operations, but they must implement each one differently. The second answer has to do with limitations in the .NET language specifications, which isn't a bad thing.

If you look back at the Visa Example in Listing 10-1, we never used the `Process` implementation in `CreditCard`. If we could provide a declaration without any implementation, this would have been more efficient. We could do that by making it abstract with the `MustOverride` keyword, but this would force us to mark the `CreditCard` class as abstract using the `MustInherit` keyword. This means any class that wants the functionality in `CreditCard` must inherit from it. Now, what if we also want to make the `Format` function abstract? We would have a class that provides declarations only and must be inherited, which is basically what an *Interface* is. The reason for defining an *Interface* is to ensure multiple classes will provide the same operations.

With the previous description, you can see why an *Interface* would be useful, but why not simply use abstract classes? According to the specifications, a subtype can only inherit the functionality of one class. On the other hand, a class, or *Interface,* can implement multiple *Interfaces.* Some languages, like C++, enable you to inherit the functionality of several classes, which is called *multiple inheritance.* If you think back to the discussions about overriding and inheritance, however, you can imagine how complicated this gets when multiple classes are involved.

Listing 10-2 shows our `CreditCard` example, rewritten to use an *Interface* instead of inheriting from a class. Notice the members in the *Interface* declaration didn't have any member characteristics associated with it. In addition, each of the members in the `Visa` class that provide the implementation must indicate they're doing so. The syntax used to implement *Interfaces* differ from one language to another. With Visual Basic, you must use more keywords and the implementation is more explicit. With C#, which doesn't have an `Implements` keyword, there's considerable less code, but the implementation isn't as clearly defined.

Listing 10-2   *Interface Example*

```
Public Interface ICreditCard
   Sub Format()
   Sub Process()
End Interface
Public Class Visa : Implements ICreditCard
   Public Sub Format() Implements ICreditCard.Format
      'Visa class code...
   End Sub
   Public Sub Process() Implements ICreditCard.Process
      'Visa class code...
   End Sub
End Class
Public Class TestClass
   Public Sub New()
      Dim visaCard As Visa = New Visa()
      ProcessCard(visaCard)
   End Sub
   Public Sub ProcessCard(ByVal card As ICreditCard)
      card.Format()
      card.Process()
      '... do more work
   End Sub
End Class
```

Probably the most important piece of information in Listing 10-2 is the `ProcessCard` implementation in `TestClass`. This one line of code shows an *Interface* type is valid to use in a declaration. Instead of passing either a value type or a class type, we're passing an *Interface* type. However, we're really passing an instance of a class named `Visa`. The reason this works is the `Visa` class implements the `ICreditCard` *Interface*. The Runtime Engine recognizes this and allows the address of `Visa` to be passed as a reference to an `ICreditCard` Interface. Because the *Interface* type is defined as a reference type that holds address information, this is a valid association.

Pointer

The pointer type shouldn't be confused with C++ pointers, despite some resemblance exists. Because the *pointer type* is a reference type, you know it holds addresses. In addition, when discussing addresses, they're usually referred to as pointers to something. With this information, we can determine that a pointer type is an address to something in memory, but to what? This is something we don't know and something the pointer type doesn't provide. Instead, the pointer type is used to manipulate addresses, instead of the data found at that address.

The pointer type provides the following operations:

▶   You can read a value from, or write a value to, the address referred to by the pointer. In other words, you can change the object it points to.

▶   You can add or subtract integers from a pointer type. This is used to manipulate the address and generate a new address.

▶   You can subtract one pointer from another.

Most of these operations aren't support by the CLS, which means they would only work on unmanaged pointers. The Runtime Engine supports three types of pointers: managed, unmanaged, and unmanaged function. *Managed pointers* are the only ones supported by the CLS, which means unless the language you're using supports unmanaged pointers, you won't be able to work with pointer types. Of the three languages provided by Microsoft with Visual Studio.NET, only the C++ language supports the use of unmanaged pointers.

Self-Describing: Array

The actual definition of an array is somewhat complicated, but an array is nothing more than a multidimensional collection of objects. We haven't discussed objects much yet, but an *object* is an instantiated class. Because the array type holds objects, it makes sense that the array type and class type are at the same hierarchal level. A more detailed description of an *array* is a type that defines an element type, number of dimensions, and the upper and lower bounds of each dimension. Even though the array type supports multiple dimensions, defining more than one is unnecessary and, in most cases, one is all you need. The array type doesn't support zero-dimensional arrays.

The Runtime Engine treats arrays differently from classes and will automatically manage the exact type and definition of the array itself. The type of an array is based on the element types defined for it. If the array is one-dimensional, then its type will be the same as the element. All arrays are derived from the `System.Array` class by the Runtime Engine, regardless of how they are defined. The `System.Array` class provides operations that can be used to manage array dimensions, read and write values, calculate managed pointers to addresses, and query the array for information.

The following listing shows the declaration of a one-dimensional array that holds five integers in C# and Visual Basic:

```
[C#]
int[] myArray = new int[5];

[Visual Basic]
Dim myArray(5) as new Integer
```

Self-Describing: Class

When you step back and consider that the .NET Framework provides an object-oriented programming interface, much of the material we've covered up to this point starts to make more sense. But we still haven't explored exactly what an object is and how it fits into the .NET Framework. Most developers should be familiar with objects. We use them all the time when building applications in Visual Basic and other languages. With Visual Basic 6.0, different types can be instantiated and used as an object, such as forms and classes. With the .NET Framework, only class reference types can be instantiated and used as an object. Value types can be instantiated, but as soon as you use them as an object, they are boxed and converted into a reference type.

When you get down to it, an instance of a .NET class is an object. To take this one step further, all classes in .NET are implicitly derived from a Base class named `System.Object`. Even classes you add as a developer inherit functionality from the `System.Object` Base class, whether or not you want it to do so. This makes a lot of sense when you consider that a Runtime Engine is responsible for managing all the objects. The Runtime Engine needs to have some basic way of identifying and manipulating the different objects it manages. As a result, the `System.Object` class provides operations that can be used to determine the type of an object and see if one object is equal to another.

Because a class type also represents a top-level type, characteristics exist that can be assigned to a class you wouldn't find on type members. Anything within the class is considered a type member and follows the rules associated with member characteristics. This also includes nested classes that exist within the scope of another class. Table 10-4 shows the list of characteristics defined by the .NET language specifications. Some of these are similar to the member characteristics described previously and some are new. In addition to the list shown in Table 10-4, attributes can be used to define additional characteristics for classes and type members.

We've already seen an example of attributes when discussing the enumeration value type. Attributes enable developers to add annotations to types and type members through the use of keywords. An *annotation* is defined as a comment that's attached to a document, but they can also be used to extend the meaning of something. In the case of attributes, they're used to extend the characteristics that can be applied. In a previous example, we defined an enumeration that had a `flags` attribute using the following syntax: `Public Enum <Flags()> Roles`. The `Public` and `Enum` keywords are used to apply characteristics discussed previously. In VB.NET, attributes are enclosed in angle brackets, which is the `<Flags()>` section in our code snippet. This attribute adds an additional characteristic to the `Roles` enumeration indicating it only supports bit fields.

Characteristic	Description
Sealed	Specifies that another class can't be derived from this class.
Implements	Used to identify *Interfaces* the class must implement. A class can implement multiple *Interfaces*.
Abstract	Indicates the class can't be instantiated. Instead, you must derive another class from it.
Inherits	Used to identify a class whose functionality is inherited. A class can only inherit the functionality of one other class. When one class is derived from another using the inherited characteristic, that class exposes all the functionality of the parent class. The derived class can also override any virtual functions from the parent class.
Exported or not exported	Indicates whether a class is visible outside the assembly in which it's defined. This characteristic only applies to top-level classes.

Table 10-4   *Class Characteristics*

Following this section, we'll take a high-level fly-by of the classes provided by the .NET Framework. But, first, you need to learn about the different classifications of class types shown in Figure 10-3. Most of what we deal with as developers are user-defined types: even the .NET Framework classes are considered user-defined. The other two types, Boxed and Delegate, are specialized versions of classes that have additional meanings.

Boxed

We've already spent some time talking about boxing in the discussion on value types. Every value type can be converted into an object for use in operations that require an object. Some languages, such as VB.NET and C#, do the conversion automatically, while other languages require explicit conversion. This conversion is called boxing because it places a box, which is an object, around a value. Value types can also be unboxed when they're converted back into their native type. But, exactly how does this happen and why are Boxed classes different from other classes? The answer is similar to the behavior of arrays discussed previously.

All boxed value types in the system are derived from a Base class named `System.ValueType`. And, like the array type, this is done automatically by the Runtime Engine whenever a value type is boxed. In addition, even though the `System.ValueType` class is marked with a characteristic that requires inheritance, most compilers won't enable you to derive a class from it. The only time you can have a class derived directly from `System.ValueType`, therefore, is when the Runtime Engine creates that class. As discussed previously, the main reason for implementing this type of behavior is to provide the capability to treat all datatypes as objects.

Even though the Runtime Engine treats the `ValueType` object differently than other objects, nothing is special about the operations in this class. The `ValueType` is derived from `System.Object` and provides appropriate implementations of the virtual methods in `System.Object`. In addition, the `ValueType` class doesn't define any other operations than what you'll find on `System.Object`. By now, you should have a good understanding of what overriding is and what it means to have a class that provides different implementations of virtual methods. The main difference is a `ValueType` is created by the Runtime Engine, not by user code, to act as a wrapper around any of the value types that need to be treated as an object.

Delegate

Another class that has specialized behavior is the Delegate class. A Delegate class can only be implemented by the Runtime Engine and it represents a secure, managed object that can't corrupt memory. These objects work something like function pointers in C++, but they can reference static, virtual, and instance datatypes, which you can't do in C++. Here's the reason: a delegate holds more than just a pointer to a function. A delegate also holds a reference to the object instance to which the function belongs. Because they represent a secure location in memory, delegate objects are typically used to implement events and function callbacks in .NET. And, like the `ValueType` object, users can't create delegate objects directly.

The actual class for delegates is `System.Delegate`, which is also marked with a characteristic that requires inheritance. As mentioned previously, you can't derive a class directly from `System.Delegate`, and when you understand what a delegate is, this makes sense. If you think about the term "delegate," one definition that comes to mind is the process of delegating some of your tasks to someone else. That person becomes a proxy for you and performs those tasks as if they were you. A delegate object works the same way. It acts as a proxy for a task that belongs to another object. If you're familiar with Distributed COM (DCOM), you can also relate a delegate to the client side of a DCOM interface, which is also called a *proxy*. The difference is a delegate doesn't need to have the same name as the function it represents. It only needs to have the same signature.

With the understanding that a delegate is nothing more than a typesafe and secure function pointer, we can explore the different types of operations available. When reading through the .NET documentation, they describe a Delegate class as having an invocation list that's used to hold object references. With the `System.Delegate` class, only a single reference can be stored in that list. However, a class named "`MulticastDelegate`", which derives from `System.Delegate`, can hold a list of references. The Delegate class provides operations to add and remove references from this list, as well as combine references from two different delegate objects. Functions are also added by the Runtime Engine to support asynchronous calls to the references contained in the delegate class.

We mentioned that delegates are typically used for callback and event operations, and when you consider what we've discussed, this makes sense. A *callback* is used to allow one method direct access back to another method that called it. With languages like C++, this is handled by passing a function reference to another function, so that function can call back to the reference passed in. With the .NET Runtime Engine and managed memory, this isn't possible. Remember, as discussed in Chapter 9, the Runtime Engine manages all the memory and can move objects around. If we attempt to pass an object reference directly, which the Runtime Engine won't allow, no guarantee exists that the address will be valid when calling back into the original function. By passing a delegate object, we're guaranteed by the Runtime Engine that the object reference will remain valid.

An *event* is an action, such as `OnClick`, that clients want to be notified about. *Event handlers* are functions in a client that handle the notification. Typically, this is implemented by maintaining a collection of references to event handlers that are all called when the action occurs. This is exactly what the `MulticastDelegate` class is designed for: the event is "cast" out to multiple event handlers. As you can guess, this is nothing more than a callback operation but, instead of calling back to one function, multiple functions are called.

Much of this might sound pretty complicated, but the good news is, as developers, you needn't worry about it too much. The Runtime Engine handles all the delegate instantiation for you and chooses the correct type of object to use, based on how delegate methods are declared. In VB.NET, two different keywords can be used to declare delegate methods: `Delegate` and `Event`. The `Delegate` keyword is used to declare the actual Delegate class and method signature it handles. The `Event` keyword is used to declare `MulticastDelegate` instances of a delegate that was previously declared with the `Delegate` keyword.

Listing 10-3 shows a class that defines and uses both a standard Delegate for callbacks and a `MulticastDelegate` for events. As you can see, both the Delegate classes are declared using the `Delegate` keyword and we have an `Event` declaration that is defined as one of the delegate types. When the VB.NET compiler sees the `Event` declaration, it creates a `MulticastDelegate`, instead of a standard Delegate. Inside this class, you also have a method named `ChildName`, which has the same signature as the `MyCallback Delegate` that was declared. In `Sub Main`, we instantiate and use the different delegates that were declared.

Listing 10-3   *Raising Events*

```
Public Delegate Sub MyEventHandler(sender As Object, e As EventArgs)
Public Class MyClass
   Delegate Sub MyCallback( name as String )
   Public Event ClickEvent As MyEventHandler

   Public Sub ChildName( name as String )
      ... Do something with name
   End Sub

   Public Shared Sub Main()
      ' create a delegate and call a function
      Dim myDelegate As New MyCallback(AddressOf ChildName)
      myDelegate("Eleanor")
```

```
      ' raise an event
      Dim e As new EventArgs()
      RaiseEvent ClickEvent(Me, e )
   End Sub
End Class
```

In Listing 10-3, the *singleton,* or *callback,* delegate is instantiated by passing the address of `ChildName` as a parameter to the constructor. What that does is create a typesafe, managed pointer to the `ChildName` method, named `myDelegate`. This delegate instance can be used directly, as shown in the example, or it can be passed to another function that needs to call back into the `ChildName` method. In the example, we call the function through the delegate as if we were calling the actual function.

The next two lines of code in the `main` function found in Listing 10-2 create a new instance of the event arguments, and then use a Visual Basic method to raise the event. If you noticed, we never did anything more than declare `ClickEvent` as an event of type `MyEventHandler`. The compiler creates the code that defines an instance of `ClickEvent` we can use. When this class is added to another class using the `WithEvents` keyword, that class can add a method to the `MulticastDelegate` class by using the `Handles` keyword. Because multiple classes can use this one class, each one can add its own method to the list of references managed by the delegate. When the `RaiseEvent` operation occurs, all the methods added will be called with the parameters passed to the `Event` class.

User-Defined

The final type of class is called a User-Defined class, which represents the majority of classes in the .NET Framework. Just like the Boxed and Delegate types, all User-Defined classes derive from a single class whether or not you want to do so. This class is the `System.Object` class and it represents the superclass of every class in .NET, not only the User-Defined classes. Every one of the class types we discussed previously, such as array, ValueType, and Delegate, all derive from `System.Object`. What this means is all objects can be guaranteed to have specific functionality.

NOTE

All classes in .NET are derived from `System.Object` by the Runtime Engine.

The `System.Object` class defines the following operations:

- ▶ *public static* `Equals`
- ▶ *public static* `ReferenceEquals`

- ▶ *public virtual* Equals
- ▶ *public virtual* GetHashCode
- ▶ *public* GetType
- ▶ *public virtual* ToString
- ▶ *protected virtual* Finalize
- ▶ *protected* MemberwiseClone

The previous list shows the characteristics of each operation in italics. As you can see, most of these are virtual, which means they can be overridden by subclasses, or every class in .NET. You can use these functions in code to get information about every object in .NET. However, some of these functions are targeted at supporting the management of objects by the Runtime Engine. By providing this base functionality and forcing all objects to derive from System.Object, the Runtime Engine is able to implement all the management operations that were discussed in Chapter 9.

Framework Classes

This last section takes a quick pass through the different types of classes provided by the .NET Framework. Hundreds of classes are in the framework, which would take an entire book to describe, so we won't get into much detail. Instead, we'll break things down into the main functionality areas shown in Figure 10-1 and discuss the different namespaces found. In addition, we'll only focus on the System namespace and all namespaces under that. Other namespaces are defined to support different language compilers, such as Visual Basic.NET and Visual C#, but these are outside the context of this discussion.

Namespaces

Before we go much farther, it's important for you to understand the concept of namespaces. Chapter 3 discussed namespaces in the context of XML schemas—the same meaning applies to classes. *Namespaces* provide a way to group names into sections that are isolated from other sections. Imagine how difficult coming up with unique names for hundreds of objects in an application would be. When you consider all the classes in the .NET Framework, and then all the classes you would add to an application, this would be difficult. By using namespaces that provide boundaries around the names, you needn't worry about creating hundreds of unique names.

All the .NET Framework classes can be found in the `System` namespace. But, didn't we just say hundreds of framework classes exist? Yes, we did, but namespaces can also be embedded inside other namespaces, which is how the .NET Framework groups all the classes. You can access all the classes by using the fully qualified namespace. For example: `System.Data.DataSet` is a reference to a class named `DataSet` in the `Data` namespace found in the `System` namespace. You can also tell the compiler you want to include a namespace in your code, which gives direct access to all the classes and other namespaces in the namespace you include.

The following listing shows how namespaces are included in Visual Basic and C#:

```
[Visual Basic]
Imports System.Data

[C#]
using System.Data;
```

When the `System.Data` namespace is included in your classes namespace, you needn't fully qualify the name of a class. For example, `Dim data as new DataSet()`, is valid when the `System.Data` namespace is included. If this namespace hadn't been included, then the system wouldn't recognize the `DataSet` name and the code in our example would fail. Instead, you would need to use `Dim data as new System.Data.DataSet()`, which is sometimes preferable. The reason this might be preferable is every namespace you include has the potential to cause naming conflicts where duplicate names from different namespaces are found.

Base Classes

The Base classes represent all the common support classes needed for basic application development. This includes the special class types we discussed previously, as well as classes that support things like serialization and threading, which are used during execution. The Base classes also include utility classes that can be used to manage collections or manipulate strings.

The following list shows all the namespaces that contain the classes that are considered Base classes:

▶   `System`
▶   `System.Collections`

- ► `System.Configuration`
- ► `System.Diagnostics`
- ► `System.Globalization`
- ► `System.IO`
- ► `System.Net`
- ► `System.Reflection`
- ► `System.Resources`
- ► `System.Runtime.CompilerServices`
- ► `System.Runtime.InteropServices`
- ► `System.Runtime.Remoting`
- ► `System.Runtime.Serialization`
- ► `System.Security`
- ► `System.ServiceProcess`
- ► `System.Text`
- ► `System.Threading`

All the previously discussed class types—ValueType, Enumeration, Delegate, and Array—are found directly under the `System` namespace. This is also where the Object type is defined. The rest of the namespaces shown in the previous list are straightforward. `System.Text` has classes, such as `StringBuilder`, which is used to manipulate strings. `System.Collections` has a Dictionary class that can be used to manage collections of objects. When looking for specific Base classes, the best method is to start with the namespaces, which can help narrow the search.

Data Classes (ADO.NET and XML)

All the classes typically grouped into Data classes are used to provide operations that manage data. Chapters 11 and 12 provide detailed information about the classes in the `System.Data` namespace. These classes are used to interact with databases through a SQL server provider or an OLE DB provider. The classes found under the `System.Xml` namespace are all used to manage XML documents. They provide functionality to load, parse, and transform XML data, along with support for SOAP and other Web service protocols.

The following list shows all the namespaces that contain classes considered Data classes:

- ▶ `System.Data`
- ▶ `System.Data.Common`
- ▶ `System.Data.OleDb`
- ▶ `System.Data.SqlClient`
- ▶ `System.Data.SqlTypes`
- ▶ `System.Xml`
- ▶ `System.Xml.Schema`
- ▶ `System.Xml.Serialization`
- ▶ `System.Xml.XPath`
- ▶ `System.Xml.Xsl`

One of the interesting things to note with these classes is a class in the `System.XML` namespace encapsulates a class in the `System.Data` namespace. This class is the `XmlDataDocument` and it can be used as a wrapper around a `DataSet` object to provide an XML interface into the data. Both objects have access to the same data. The data isn't copied from one to the other. In addition, both these objects are in different namespaces, but they're designed to work together to provide two different access methods into the same data. The same holds true for many other classes in the .NET Framework and specifically for the Data classes discussed here.

ASP.NET Classes

The ASP.NET classes provide functionality for Web Applications and Web services. Most of these classes are discussed in detail in Chapters 14 and 15. The `System.Web` namespace is the base namespace for all these classes. Web service classes can be found in the `System.Web.Services` namespaces and Web Form classes can be found in the `System.Web.UI` namespaces.

The following list shows all the namespaces that contain classes considered ASP.NET classes:

- ▶ `System.Web`
- ▶ `System.Web.Caching`

▶ System.Web.Configuration

▶ System.Web.Hosting

▶ System.Web.Mail

▶ System.Web.Security

▶ System.Web.Services

▶ System.Web.Services.Description

▶ System.Web.Services.Discovery

▶ System.Web.Services.Protocols

▶ System.Web.SessionState

▶ System.Web.UI

▶ System.Web.UI.Design

▶ System.Web.UI.Design.WebControls

▶ System.Web.UI.aspControls

▶ System.Web.UI.WebControls

Windows Forms Classes

The Windows Forms classes provide functionality for developing Windows applications and interacting with graphical devices on a computer. In the past, developers would need to learn about different APIs, such as GDI and User32, in the Windows OS to get the functionality provided by these classes. With the .NET Framework, developers only need to learn about the different operations provided by these classes, without dealing with the complexities involved with interfacing to an OS API. Chapter 16 provides an in-depth look into many of these classes when discussing Windows Forms development.

The following list shows all the namespaces that contain classes considered Windows Forms classes:

▶ System.ComponentModel

▶ System.ComponentModel.Design

▶ System.ComponentModel.Design.Serialization

▶ System.Drawing

- ▶ `System.Drawing.Design`
- ▶ `System.Drawing.Drawing2D`
- ▶ `System.Drawing.Imaging`
- ▶ `System.Drawing.Printing`
- ▶ `System.Drawing.Text`
- ▶ `System.Windows`
- ▶ `System.Windows.Forms`
- ▶ `System.Windows.Forms.Design`

Summary

The main concept that stands out through this chapter is everything in .NET is based on a CTS. You learned about value types and reference types, and how all value types can be converted into reference types through boxing. You learned about different characteristics that can be applied to type members and classes, as well as what effect they have when applied. You also learned how specialized class types, such as Arrays and Delegates, are implemented, and examples were provided. Finally, you learned how the .NET Framework classes are divided into namespaces and saw the different namespaces to get a better understanding of how they are grouped.

The following list covers the main topics discussed:

- ▶ The Common Type System (CTS)
- ▶ Type members and characteristics that can be applied
- ▶ Object-oriented concepts related to member and class characteristics
- ▶ Value types, which include built-in, enumeration, and user-defined types
- ▶ Boxing of value types into objects
- ▶ Reference types, including interface, pointer, and self-describing types
- ▶ Class types, which include Arrays, Delegates, and User-Defined classes
- ▶ Namespaces in .NET and the organization of .NET classes

Integrating SQL Server 2000 with .NET

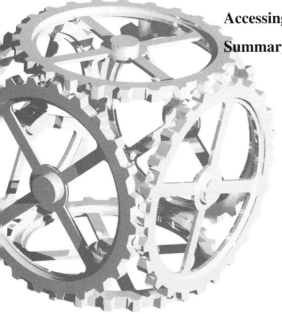

We spent much of the first part of this book discussing XML. This isn't surprising given its considerable impact on the software industry in recent times. But the main reason for paying so much attention to XML is it plays a major role in Microsoft's .NET technology. In fact, XML is the plumbing that runs throughout .NET and its framework. This makes sense, given the emergence recently of XML as the lingua franca for moving information across the Web.

But XML has also taken root with relational databases. XML has been shown as an efficient and effective way to move data in to and out of databases. XML has grown from a simple metalanguage for describing word processing documents to transferring information across distributed applications from the database to the Web and back.

Keeping in line with this trend, Microsoft built SQL Server 2000 with XML as its foundation. This makes integration between .NET and SQL Server 2000 quite seamless, more so than ever before between a development framework and a RDBS.

The Microsoft .NET Framework has made accessing databases quite effortless. We discuss this in detail in Chapters 12 and 13. For now, we explore SQL Server's support of XML, ignoring .NET for the moment. We examine how to build queries that read and write data to the database using XML, and how to create a Web site that offers a direct portal into a SQL Server database.

SQL Server 2000 and XML

SQL Server 2000 was built to natively support XML. This means it offers new features that make developing applications much easier. Perhaps the most obvious new addition is the capability to generate XML using standard `SELECT` queries. But no less important is the way applications can write data to a database using XML, or how applications can access a SQL Server 2000 database over HTTP via a URL.

Microsoft's Own XML Schema Language

While waiting for the XML Schema specification, Microsoft developed its own schema language, XML-DR, or XML Data-Reduced. While XML-DR isn't compatible with the W3C XML Schema discussed in Chapter 3, it is the schema language used by SQL Server 2000. And XML-DR is close enough to the W3C Schema specification that several tools have been written that convert schemas from one to the other.

Microsoft's .NET Framework does comply with the XML Schema specification, however, which is why XML-DR is only sparsely covered in this book. While this chapter focuses on SQL Server 2000, we skip any in-depth explanation of XML-DR, and focus only on the way Microsoft's new SQL Server interoperates with XML.

Returning Data as XML

SQL Server 2000 introduces a new clause for returning XML from queries. Using the FOR XML clause in a SELECT statement, SQL Server returns the results as an XML string. The XML returned is a fragment, rather than a stand-alone XML document. This means the fragments can be assembled with other fragments into a well-formed XML document.

The complete syntax for using this clause is

```
FOR XML mode [, XMLDATA] [, ELEMENTS][, BINARY BASE64]
```

The mode parameter specifies the shape of the resulting XML. It can be one of three values: RAW, AUTO, or EXPLICIT. We will delve into the various modes and how they affect the queries in more detail in the following sections. For now, it is enough to know that the RAW and AUTO modes provide less control over the way the results look than the EXPLICIT mode.

The XMLDATA parameter is optional and specifies an XML-DR schema be returned. We won't discuss this option or use it in any of our examples, as the schema returned doesn't comply with the W3C XML Schema specification.

If the ELEMENTS option is included, the columns from the SELECT statement are returned as subelements of the root element. If this option is omitted, then the columns are returned as attributes. This option can only be used if the mode is specified as AUTO. We will discuss this more in a moment.

The BINARY BASE64 option encodes any binary data returned by the query in base64 format. This must be specified to return binary data when the mode is either RAW or EXPLICIT. When in AUTO mode, binary data is returned as a reference.

AUTO Mode Option

Let's examine how the three mode options affect the XML results SQL Server returns using one particular query. We begin with the AUTO mode. For example, if we run the following query against the Northwind database,

```
SELECT firstName FROM Employees FOR XML AUTO
```

it returns the XML fragment shown in Listing 11-1:

Listing 11-1   *XML Fragment in AUTO Mode*

```
<Employees firstName="Nancy"/>
<Employees firstName="Andrew"/>
<Employees firstName="Janet"/>
<Employees firstName="Margaret"/>
<Employees firstName="Steven"/>
<Employees firstName="Michael"/>
<Employees firstName="Robert"/>
<Employees firstName="Laura"/>
<Employees firstName="Anne"/>
```

Notice four consequences of using the AUTO mode as we examine the results. First, the results of the query were returned as attributes, not as elements. Thus, each row of the results is translated into one XML element, using attributes for the row's columns. Next the case of the column name specified in the query matches the case of the attribute name in the XML fragment. Also, the name of the table, Employees, is specified as the element tag name for each row returned from the query. Finally, the results are returned as an XML fragment and, therefore, are not a well-formed XML document. This fragment would fail if processed standalone by an XML parser. Instead, it could be inserted into an XML document that has an existing root document element.

NOTE

When running this query in SQL Analyzer, not all of the results may be viewable at first. The default size for results in each column can be enlarged to a maximum 8192 bytes. To change this value, go to the Tools menu, and select Options. This brings up an Options dialog box. Click the Results tab and locate the Maximum characters per column text box. Enter a large value, like 8192, to see the entire results of these queries.

The ELEMENTS option can only be used in conjunction with the AUTO mode, so let's see how adding that option to the query changes the XML returned by SQL Server. The original query modified with the ELEMENTS option looks like this

```
SELECT firstName FROM Employees FOR XML AUTO, ELEMENTS
```

and returns the same information, only the XML looks different, as shown in Listing 11-2:

Listing 11-2   *XML Fragment Using the* ELEMENTS *Option*

```
<Employees>
    <firstName>Nancy</firstName>
</Employees>
<Employees>
    <firstName>Andrew</firstName>
</Employees>
<Employees>
    <firstName>Janet</firstName>
</Employees>
<Employees>
    <firstName>Margaret</firstName>
</Employees>
<Employees>
    <firstName>Steven</firstName>
</Employees>
<Employees>
    <firstName>Michael</firstName>
</Employees>
<Employees>
    <firstName>Robert</firstName>
</Employees>
<Employees>
    <firstName>Laura</firstName>
</Employees>
<Employees>
    <firstName>Anne</firstName>
</Employees>
```

The ELEMENTS option has altered the XML so, instead of attributes, each column is contained within its own element. The choice to use this option should be driven by performance and other requirements. Performance may be better without the ELEMENTS option, but other considerations, such as usability and readability, may factor in.

RAW Mode Option

If we change the query to use the RAW mode, like so

```
SELECT firstName FROM Employees FOR XML RAW
```

SQL Server returns (see Listing 11-3):

Listing 11-3   *RAW Mode XML Fragment*

```
<row firstName="Nancy"/>
<row firstName="Andrew"/>
<row firstName="Janet"/>
<row firstName="Margaret"/>
<row firstName="Steven"/>
<row firstName="Michael"/>
<row firstName="Robert"/>
<row firstName="Laura"/>
<row firstName="Anne"/>
```

This looks similar to the first query, but the element name for each row of data is simply `row`. But what if we wanted to perform a join on some tables? Let's examine the query in Listing 11-4.

Listing 11-4   *AUTO Mode Query with Inner Join*

```
SELECT
    firstName = LTRIM(RTRIM(FirstName)),
    lastName = LTRIM(RTRIM(LastName)),
    territoryDescription = LTRIM(RTRIM(TerritoryDescription)),
    regionDescription = LTRIM(RTRIM(RegionDescription))
FROM Employees
INNER JOIN EmployeeTerritories ON
    EmployeeTerritories.EmployeeID = Employees.EmployeeID
INNER JOIN Territories ON
    Territories.TerritoryID = EmployeeTerritories.TerritoryID
INNER JOIN Region ON
    Region.RegionID = Territories.RegionID
WHERE (firstName = 'Andrew') OR (firstName = 'Laura')
ORDER BY lastName
FOR XML AUTO
```

It returns the XML shown in Listing 11-5:

Listing 11-5   *AUTO Mode with Inner Join XML Fragment*

```
<Employees firstName="Laura" lastName="Callahan"
        territoryDescription="Philadelphia" regionDescription="Northern"/>
<Employees firstName="Laura" lastName="Callahan"
        territoryDescription="Beachwood" regionDescription="Northern"/>
<Employees firstName="Laura" lastName="Callahan"
        territoryDescription="Findlay" regionDescription="Northern"/>
<Employees firstName="Laura" lastName="Callahan"
        territoryDescription="Racine" regionDescription="Northern"/>
<Employees firstName="Andrew" lastName="Fuller"
        territoryDescription="Braintree" regionDescription="Eastern"/>
<Employees firstName="Andrew" lastName="Fuller"
        territoryDescription="Louisville" regionDescription="Eastern"/>
<Employees firstName="Andrew" lastName="Fuller"
        territoryDescription="Bedford" regionDescription="Eastern"/>
<Employees firstName="Andrew" lastName="Fuller"
        territoryDescription="Georgetown" regionDescription="Eastern"/>
<Employees firstName="Andrew" lastName="Fuller"
        territoryDescription="Boston" regionDescription="Eastern"/>
<Employees firstName="Andrew" lastName="Fuller"
        territoryDescription="Cambridge" regionDescription="Eastern"/>
```

Even though we joined three other tables, all the information was placed
in the XML attributes of one row. Reverting back to AUTO mode and using the
ELEMENTS clause at the end of this query forces the results to be shaped differently.
Listing 11-6 displays the results of placing the query results within elements instead
of attributes. And, yet, even with the ELEMENTS clause, the original database
structure is lost.

NOTE

*While SORT BY can be used with the FOR XML AUTO clause, GROUP BY and
aggregate functions aren't currently supported. They can be used with the FOR XML RAW
clause. However, because of the output generated by the RAW mode, GROUP BY acts more
like an ORDER BY clause.*

Listing 11-6 *Inner Join Using the ELEMENTS Clause*

```xml
<Employees>
    <firstName>Laura</firstName>
    <lastName>Callahan</lastName>
    <territoryDescription>Philadelphia</territoryDescription>
    <regionDescription>Northern</regionDescription>
</Employees>
<Employees>
    <firstName>Laura</firstName>
    <lastName>Callahan</lastName>
    <territoryDescription>Beachwood</territoryDescription>
    <regionDescription>Northern</regionDescription>
</Employees>
<Employees>
    <firstName>Laura</firstName>
    <lastName>Callahan</lastName>
    <territoryDescription>Findlay</territoryDescription>
    <regionDescription>Northern</regionDescription>
</Employees>
<Employees>
    <firstName>Laura</firstName>
    <lastName>Callahan</lastName>
    <territoryDescription>Racine</territoryDescription>
    <regionDescription>Northern</regionDescription>
</Employees>
<Employees>
    <firstName>Andrew</firstName>
    <lastName>Fuller</lastName>
    <territoryDescription>Braintree</territoryDescription>
    <regionDescription>Eastern</regionDescription>
</Employees>
<Employees>
    <firstName>Andrew</firstName>
    <lastName>Fuller</lastName>
    <territoryDescription>Louisville</territoryDescription>
    <regionDescription>Eastern</regionDescription>
</Employees>
<Employees>
    <firstName>Andrew</firstName>
    <lastName>Fuller</lastName>
    <territoryDescription>Bedford</territoryDescription>
    <regionDescription>Eastern</regionDescription>
</Employees>
```

```
<Employees>
    <firstName>Andrew</firstName>
    <lastName>Fuller</lastName>
    <territoryDescription>Georgetown</territoryDescription>
    <regionDescription>Eastern</regionDescription>
</Employees>
<Employees>
    <firstName>Andrew</firstName>
    <lastName>Fuller</lastName>
    <territoryDescription>Boston</territoryDescription>
    <regionDescription>Eastern</regionDescription>
</Employees>
<Employees>
    <firstName>Andrew</firstName>
    <lastName>Fuller</lastName>
    <territoryDescription>Cambridge</territoryDescription>
    <regionDescription>Eastern</regionDescription>
</Employees>
```

EXPLICIT Mode Option

What if we could preserve this structure in the formation of the XML? The EXPLICIT option offers this capability. It's more powerful than the other options, but also more complex. Unlike the other two options, how the XML looks is up to the developer of the query.

When the EXPLICIT mode is specified in a query, a *universal table* is generated that contains all the information about the XML. Each row in the table represents an XML element and requires two initial columns: Tag and Parent. The first column, Tag, is an integer that identifies the element type. The second column, Parent, is also an integer, and contains the Tag value that is the element's parent. This column may be NULL, which represents the root element of the document. These columns combine to form the parent-child hierarchy for the XML document. Both columns must be named in the query. The remaining columns define the resulting XML per the SQL query.

For example, the following query shown in Listing 11-7:

Listing 11-7   *EXPLICIT Mode Query*

```
SELECT
    1 AS Tag,
    NULL AS Parent,
    Employees.EmployeeID AS [employee!1!employeeID]
```

```
FROM Employees
FOR XML EXPLICIT
```

returns the XML shown in Listing 11-8:

Listing 11-8   *Simple EXPLICIT Mode XML Fragment*

```
<employee employeeID="3" />
<employee employeeID="4" />
<employee employeeID="8" />
<employee employeeID="1" />
<employee employeeID="2" />
<employee employeeID="6" />
<employee employeeID="7" />
<employee employeeID="5" />
<employee employeeID="9" />
```

and the universal table looks like the one shown in Table 11-1.

This is a simple example that doesn't show the power of EXPLICIT queries, but it does offer a basic demonstration of how to query using this mode. Essentially, this example demonstrates that the employee element has a Tag value of 1 and has no Parent. The third column is the attribute of the element, employeeID.

Columns in the universal table, other than the first two columns Tag and Parent, are named using the following format:

```
ElementName!TagNumber!AttributeName!Directive
```

Tag	Parent	employee!1!employeeID
1	NULL	3
1	NULL	4
1	NULL	8
1	NULL	1
1	NULL	2
1	NULL	6
1	NULL	7
1	NULL	5
1	NULL	9

Table 11-1   *EXPLICIT Mode Universal Table*

The first part, `ElementName`, is the name of the element tag. The second part, `TagNumber`, is the tag number of the element, which describes the nesting of the column in the resulting XML. Next is the attribute name if `Directive` isn't specified. Otherwise, if the directive is `xml`, `cdata`, or `element`, it's the name of the child element. The `Directive` is optional. If it isn't specified, then `AttributeName` must be given. If neither `AttributeName` nor `Directive` is provided, then the `element` directive is implied. The `Directive` option can take on one or more of the values, as listed in Table 11-2.

The query in Listing 11-9 demonstrates the use of the `element` directive. From this query, we expect a `firstName` element, a `lastName` element, and a `freightTotal` element will exist.

Directive	Meaning
ID	Specifies an attribute of type `ID`. Attributes of type `IDREF` and `IDREFS` can then refer to this attribute, provided the `XMLDATA` option is included in the query.
IDREF	Attributes specified as this type provide intradocument links, provided the `XMLDATA` option is included in the query.
IDREFS	Attributes specified as this type provide intradocument links, provided the `XMLDATA` option is included in the query.
hide	This hides the specified attribute.
element	This generates a child element, rather than an attribute in the resulting XML. Note, the data is encoded as an entity, meaning characters like < are translated to `&lt;`. Also, this can be combined with `ID`, `IDREF`, or `IDREFS`.
xml	This is similar to the `element` directive, except no encoding is performed. So, < remains <. Also, this can only be combined with the `hide` directive.
xmltext	The data for this attribute is wrapped in a single tag, which is integrated with the remaining document. This column must be of a text type, such as `char`, `varchar`, `text`, and so forth.
cdata	This specifies the content be wrapped in a `CDATA` section without any entity encoding. This directive must be used without `AttributeName` specified. Also, it must be used for data of text type, such as `char`, `varchar`, and `text`. Finally, this can only be combined with the `hide` directive.

Table 11-2   *EXPLICIT Mode Directives*

Listing 11-9   *EXPLICIT Mode Query with Directives*

```
SELECT
    1 AS Tag,
    NULL AS Parent,
    Employees.EmployeeID AS [employee!1!employeeID],
    Employees.FirstName AS [employee!1!firstName!element],
    Employees.LastName AS [employee!1!lastName!element],
    SUM(Orders.Freight) AS [employee!1!freightTotal!element]
FROM Employees
INNER JOIN Orders ON Orders.EmployeeID = Employees.EmployeeID
GROUP BY Employees.EmployeeID, Employees.FirstName, Employees.LastName
FOR XML EXPLICIT
```

And, as we see in Listing 11-10, that is exactly how the XML fragment looks.

Listing 11-10   *EXPLICIT Mode XML Fragment*

```
<employee employeeID="7">
    <firstName>Robert</firstName>
    <lastName>King</lastName>
    <freightTotal>6665.4400</freightTotal>
</employee>
<employee employeeID="6">
    <firstName>Michael</firstName>
    <lastName>Suyama</lastName>
    <freightTotal>3780.4700</freightTotal>
</employee>
<employee employeeID="5">
    <firstName>Steven</firstName>
    <lastName>Buchanan</lastName>
    <freightTotal>3918.7100</freightTotal>
</employee>
<employee employeeID="4">
    <firstName>Margaret</firstName>
    <lastName>Peacock</lastName>
    <freightTotal>11346.1400</freightTotal>
</employee>
<employee employeeID="3">
    <firstName>Janet</firstName>
    <lastName>Leverling</lastName>
    <freightTotal>10884.7400</freightTotal>
</employee>
```

```
<employee employeeID="2">
    <firstName>Andrew</firstName>
    <lastName>Fuller</lastName>
    <freightTotal>8696.4100</freightTotal>
</employee>
<employee employeeID="9">
    <firstName>Anne</firstName>
    <lastName>Dodsworth</lastName>
    <freightTotal>3326.2600</freightTotal>
</employee>
<employee employeeID="1">
    <firstName>Nancy</firstName>
    <lastName>Davolio</lastName>
    <freightTotal>8836.6400</freightTotal>
</employee>
<employee employeeID="8">
    <firstName>Laura</firstName>
    <lastName>Callahan</lastName>
    <freightTotal>7487.8800</freightTotal>
</employee>
```

But, let's say we wanted to join some information together from two tables and have the table join determine the XML hierarchy. How do we define the way the data is organized in the XML fragment? Looking at the query in Listing 11-11, we see it's now more complex. Instead of one SELECT statement, there are two.

Listing 11-11   *EXPLICIT Mode Query with Multiple Elements*

```
SELECT
    1                   as Tag,
    NULL                as Parent,
    Customers.CustomerID as [Customer!1!CustomerID],
    NULL                as [Order!2!OrderID]
FROM Customers
UNION ALL
SELECT
    2,
    1,
    Customers.CustomerID,
    Orders.OrderID
FROM Customers, Orders
WHERE Customers.CustomerID = Orders.CustomerID
ORDER BY [Customer!1!CustomerID], [Order!2!OrderID]
FOR XML EXPLICIT
```

In the first SELECT, all the columns are defined for the universal table. The second SELECT defines how the tables are joined together and displayed for the child element with a Tag number of 2. Note, because the SELECT statements are unioned together, they must have the same number of columns. In the second SELECT, the Tag is specified as 2, with its Parent tag as 1. A partial result of this query is shown in Listing 11-12.

Listing 11-12   *EXPLICIT Mode XML Fragment*

```
<Customer CustomerID="ALFKI">
    <Order OrderID="10643"/>
    <Order OrderID="10692"/>
    <Order OrderID="10702"/>
    <Order OrderID="10835"/>
    <Order OrderID="10952"/>
    <Order OrderID="11011"/>
</Customer>
<Customer CustomerID="ANATR">
    <Order OrderID="10308"/>
    <Order OrderID="10625"/>
    <Order OrderID="10759"/>
    <Order OrderID="10926"/>
</Customer>
```

Using the two SELECT statements together, we can shape the results into whatever form we want. In this example, we made the output from the query look like what you might expect: Customer elements with CustomerID attributes, containing Order child elements each with their own OrderID attributes. Because we can make it look however we want by varying elements and attributes, the EXPLICIT mode is the most powerful mode for pulling data from a database.

Writing Data to the Database Using XML

Now that we have a good handle on querying information from a database in the form of XML, how do we write information back using XML? SQL Server 2000 provides the OPENXML function to insert data into a database. The OPENXML function offers a rowset view using an XML document, which means it can be used within Transact-SQL statements, just like table, view, and OPENROWSET.

The syntax for OPENXML is

```
OPENXML(idoc int [in],rowpattern nvarchar[in],[flags byte[in]])
[WITH (SchemaDeclaration | TableName)]
```

The first parameter, idoc, is an integer containing the handle mapping to the internal XML document. As we will see later on, SQL Server generates the handle for us. The rowpattern is an XML XPath expression that specifies the portion of the XML document to be used in the operation. The optional flags parameter can have the values detailed in Table 11-3.

The optional SchemaDeclaration is the XML-DR schema for the XML document. We won't go into any detail here, other than to say this is where the schema for the XML can be provided to specify how the data is organized. Or, a TableName can be given instead that describes the data schema. The WITH clause is optional. If omitted, an edge table is returned that represents the XML document structure.

To generate the idoc parameter, the sp_xml_preparedocument stored procedure is used. This is shown in Listing 11-13.

In the following examples, we interact once again with the Northwind database, focusing on the Employees and EmployeeTerritories tables. What we want to do is to use XML to insert a new employee with a given employee territory. The Employees table contains an identity column EmployeeID, which generates a new unique value every time a row is inserted. Therefore, we need to reference the newly created employee's primary key when we insert the row into the EmployeeTerritories table.

Value	Meaning
0	This is the default. Using this value specifies attribute-centric mapping.
1	This value specifies the attribute-centric mapping, but can be combined with XML_ELEMENTS. The latter combination means attribute-centric mapping is used first, and then element-centric mapping is used for all the remaining columns.
2	This value specifies the element-centric mapping, but can be combined with XML_ATTRIBUTES. The latter combination means element-centric mapping is used first, and then attribute-centric mapping is used for all the remaining columns.
8	This specifies the consumed data shouldn't be copied to the overflow property. It can be combined (logical OR) with XML_ATTRIBUTES or XML_ELEMENTS.

Table 11-3   *Flag Values for* OPENXML *Function*

Let's start by first using OPENXML to select data. Listing 11-13 is a query that prepares an XML document, and then uses it to perform the query.

Listing 11-13   *Simple* OPENXML *Query*

```
DECLARE @idoc int
DECLARE @xml char(2000)

SELECT @xml =
'<root>
    <employee FirstName="Bugs" LastName="Bunny">
        <territory TerritoryID="01581"/>
    </employee>
</root>'

--Prepare the internal XML document
EXEC sp_xml_preparedocument @idoc OUTPUT, @xml

--Perform the query
SELECT * FROM OPENXML(@idoc, 'root/Employees')

--Remove the internal XML document
EXEC sp_xml_removedocument @idoc
```

The optional WITH clause was omitted in this query. The result shown in Table 11-4 is an edge table that describes the XML hierarchy and content.

id	parent id	node type	local name	prefix	name spaceuri	data type	prev	text
2	0	1	employee	NULL	NULL	NULL	NULL	NULL
3	2	2	FirstName	NULL	NULL	NULL	NULL	NULL
7	3	3	#text	NULL	NULL	NULL	NULL	Bugs
4	2	2	LastName	NULL	NULL	NULL	NULL	NULL
8	4	3	#text	NULL	NULL	NULL	NULL	Bunny
5	2	1	territory	NULL	NULL	NULL	NULL	NULL
6	5	2	TerritoryID	NULL	NULL	NULL	NULL	NULL
9	6	3	#text	NULL	NULL	NULL	NULL	01581

Table 11-4   *Edge Table from Simple* OPENXML *Query*

If we remove the SELECT statement from the SQL in Listing 11-13 and replace it with INSERT statements, we can create a stored procedure to insert data into the Employees and EmployeeTerritories table, as shown in Listing 11-14.

Listing 11-14   *OPENXML Insert*

```
CREATE  PROCEDURE sp_putNewEmployee(@xmlIn char(2000)) AS
BEGIN
    DECLARE @idoc int

    --Prepare the internal XML document
    EXEC sp_xml_preparedocument @idoc OUTPUT, @xmlIn

    INSERT INTO Employees SELECT * FROM OPENXML(@idoc, 'root/employee')
    WITH Employees

    INSERT INTO EmployeeTerritories (EmployeeID, TerritoryID)
    SELECT
        EmployeeID = @@IDENTITY,
        territoryID FROM OPENXML(@idoc, 'root/employee/territory')
    WITH EmployeeTerritories

    --Remove the internal XML document
    EXEC sp_xml_removedocument @idoc
END
```

This procedure takes a string parameter and uses it to create an internal XML document. The information in the XML is then pulled out and used in two INSERT statements: the first insert creates a new row Employee table; the second insert creates a new EmployeeTerritory row. It uses the new identity value of the Employee table and the TerritoryID from the internal XML to populate this new row. Listing 11-15 shows how to call this procedure with some XML.

Listing 11-15   *Calling the OPENXML Stored Procedure*

```
sp_putNewEmployee
'<root>
    <employee FirstName="Bugs" LastName="Bunny">
        <territory TerritoryID="01581"/>
    </employee>
</root>'
```

Notice the attributes of the XML match the case of the column names in the tables. This is important because the `WITH` clauses in Listing 11-14 specify the table schemas. These schemas pull their descriptions straight from SQL Server 2000, and XML is, of course, case-sensitive. When the procedure is run with the given XML, a new row is created in the `Employees` table with a first name of "`Bugs`" and a last name of "`Bunny`." Then, a new row in the `EmployeeTerritories` table is created, populated with the `EmployeeID` of the new `Employees` row and the `TerritoryID` from the XML.

Accessing SQL Server 2000 over HTTP

Providing information from a database over the Web is one of the most common requirements of business today and is becoming a necessity for survival. SQL Server 2000 provides a new feature that enables a developer to build Web sites that have direct access to a specified database. This means application users can view information directly through the Web, as if their browsers were a window into the database.

These Web portals into SQL Server databases have a variety of applications. First and foremost is providing reports to clients. Because these portals return data from queries, reporting is a natural implementation of this feature. In fact, any type of static content, or data, updated over time or calculated, would be a good candidate for this type of application. For example, this feature could even provide help systems for online applications if the help content is stored in a database.

Setting Up a SQL Server Web Site

SQL Server 2000 provides direct access to its databases through the use of a tool, *IIS Virtual Directory Management for SQL Server,* which creates Web sites that incorporate a special ISAPI filter. This ISAPI filter—the magic behind accessing databases over HTTP—allows SQL queries to be executed directly against a specified database with the results displayed as XML on the Web page. The tool, an MMC snap-in, makes it easy to set up a Web site aimed at a particular database.

Let's walk through setting up a SQL Server Web site for the `Northwind` database. From the Start menu, select the Microsoft SQL Server folder. Clicking Configure SQL XML Support in IIS opens the MMC snap-in. From there, expand the server icon. Right-clicking the Default Web site pops up a menu. Clicking New brings up the Properties dialog box, as shown in Figure 11-1. Enter the name of the new Web site, along with the local pathname.

Moving to the next tab, Security, enter the credentials to log in to the SQL Server database based on the authentication methods used when SQL Server was installed. Figure 11-2 shows the Web site set up for Windows Integrated Authentication.

On the Data Source tab, select the database server and database this Web site will expose through HTTP. Figure 11-3 shows the virtual Web site referencing the `Northwind` database and pointing to the local database.

The remaining tabs help to configure the Web site. The Settings tab has several options for the type of queries the Web site supports. SQL Server supports URL queries, which use the `HTTP GET` command to process dynamic SQL. Also on this tab are options for Template Queries and XPath Queries, both of which are discussed later in this chapter. The `HTTP POST` command is the final option. As

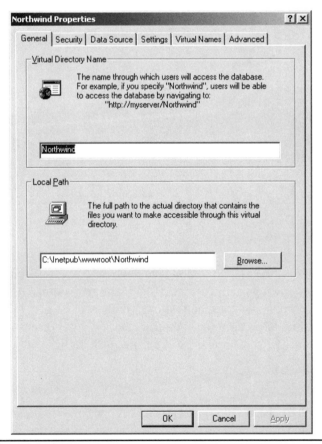

Figure 11-1   *New Virtual Directory properties*

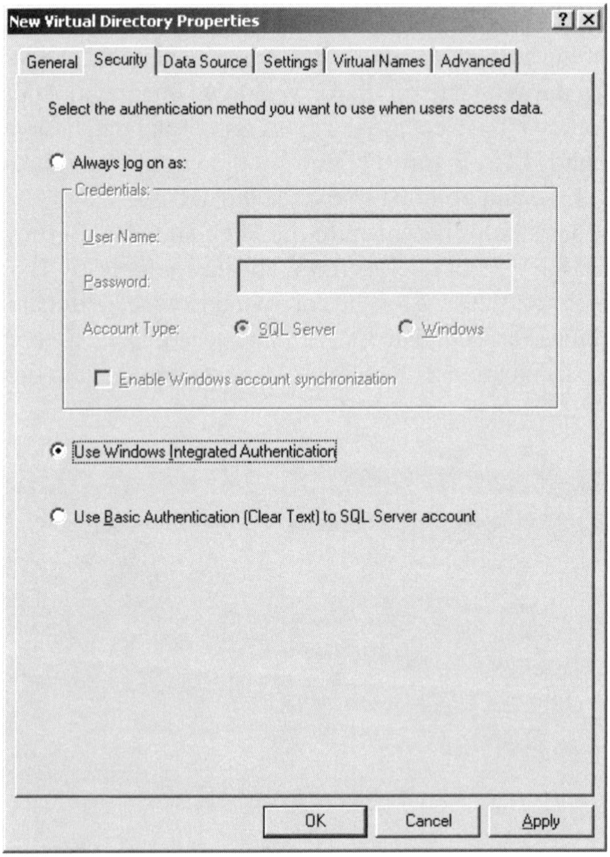

Figure 11-2   *Virtual Directory Security settings*

shown in Figure 11-4, the default option is to have only Allow Template Queries selected. For the following examples, select the first three options: Allow URL Queries, Allow Template Queries, and Allow XPath.

The Virtual Names tab is used for Template Queries and is discussed later. The last tab, Advanced, is used to customize the Web site further.

URL Queries

Once this Web site has been set up, queries can be made against it using simple query strings. For example, this URL queries against the new Web site

```
http://localhost/Northwind?SQL=SELECT+FirstName+,+LastName+FROM+Employees+
FOR+XML+AUTO&root=root
```

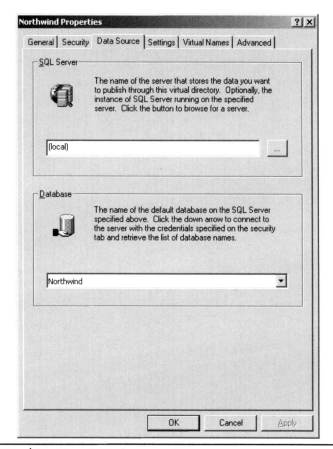

Figure 11-3   *Virtual Directory Data Source settings*

which returns the results, shown in Figure 11-5.

NOTE

The `&root=root` at the end of the query places a single document root element called `root` around the XML returned by SQL Server. Remember, SQL Server returns XML fragments and not XML documents. The clause at the end easily solves this problem.

Template Queries

The results shown in Figure 11-5 are of dynamic SQL tacked on to the end of a URL. This, of course, isn't the most effective way for an application to have its users access a database. Template queries provide something close to stored procedures, but they

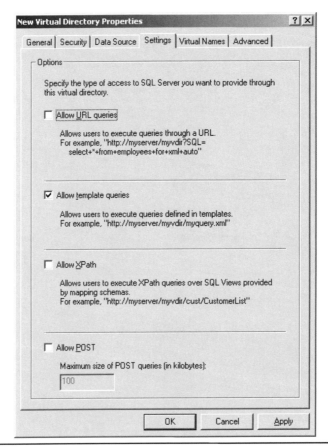

Figure 11-4   *Virtual Directory Options settings*

are written in XML. Using the tool, a virtual alias can be applied to an XML file that contains a SQL query. The XML uses a special namespace developed for SQL Server: xml-sql. Using this namespace, an XML document can be written that provides the appropriate information to the ISAPI filter to perform the desired query.

For example, let's add a template to the Northwind virtual Web site. Using the Properties dialog box, click the Virtual Names tab, and then click the New button. This brings up another dialog box, as shown in Figure 11-6. Enter the name **ByEmployeeID** as the template name, specify this is a template, and then specify the location of the file: ByEmployeeID.xml. Click Save, and then the template is created for the Web site, as shown in Figure 11-7. The source for this file is shown in Listing 11-16.

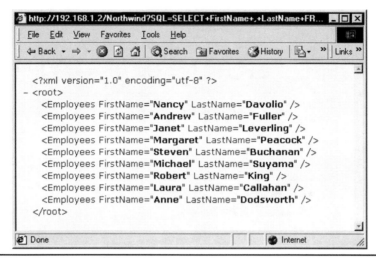

Figure 11-5   *Browser view of HTTP query*

Listing 11-16   *Northwind Employee Template Query as* `ByEmployeeID.xml`

```xml
<?xml version="1.0"?>
<root xmlns:sql="urn:schemas-microsoft-com:xml-sql">
    <sql:header>
        <sql:param name="EmployeeID"/>
    </sql:header>
    <sql:query>
        SELECT FirstName, LastName FROM Employees WHERE EmployeeID =
        @EmployeeID FOR XML AUTO, ELEMENTS
    </sql:query>
</root>
```

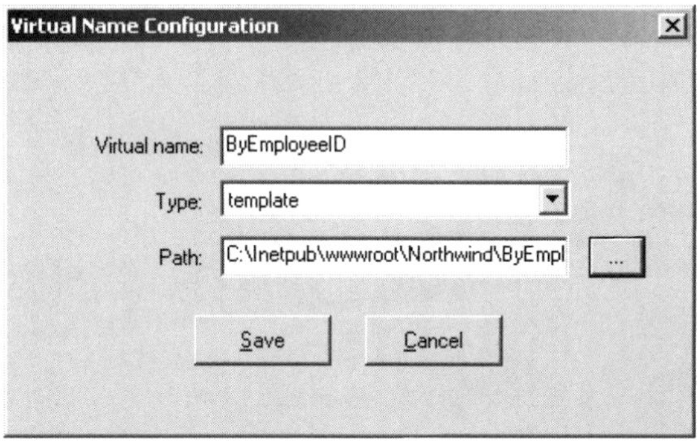

Virtual Name Configuration

Virtual name: `ByEmployeeID`

Type: `template`

Path: `C:\Inetpub\wwwroot\Northwind\ByEmpl`

Save   Cancel

Figure 11-6   *Adding a template*

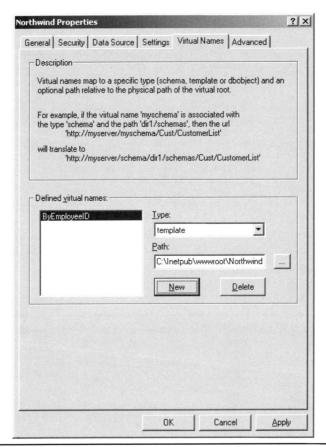

Figure 11-7   *New ByEmployeeID template*

This XML document uses the `xml-sql` namespace to specify that a parameter `EmployeeID` will be specified in the URL. This parameter is used in the query to return the employee with the given ID. The following URL demonstrates how to call this template query:

```
http://localhost/Northwind/ByEmployeeID?EmployeeID=1
```

Entering this URL in a browser generates the results shown in Figure 11-8.

Now, if we wanted to display this information using an XSL stylesheet, we could modify our original template query to reference a particular XSL file, much like any

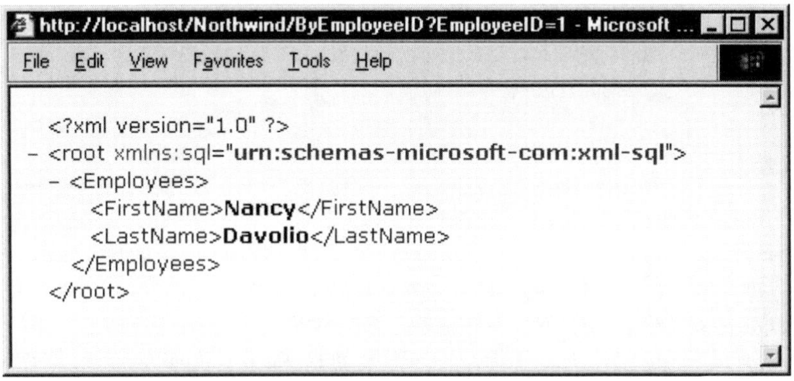

Figure 11-8 *Browser view of template query*

other XML document. However, we need to create two more template aliases: one for the new XML query, and one for the XSL stylesheet it references. Both of these are added in the same manner as before. Listing 11-17 provides the listing for the file `ByEmployeeIDWithXSL.xml`.

Listing 11-17 *Template Query with XSL Specified as* `ByEmployeeIDWithXSL.xml`

```
<?xml version="1.0"?>
<?xml-stylesheet
    type="text/xsl"
    href="http://localhost/Northwind/EmployeeIDXSL"?>
<root xmlns:sql="urn:schemas-microsoft-com:xml-sql">
    <sql:header>
        <sql:param name="EmployeeID"/>
    </sql:header>
    <sql:query>
        SELECT EmployeeID, FirstName, LastName FROM Employees WHERE
        EmployeeID = @EmployeeID FOR XML AUTO, ELEMENTS
    </sql:query>
</root>
```

The stylesheet in this example is quite simple. Listing 11-18 lists the stylesheet previously referenced. Again, both this stylesheet and the XML document `ByEmployeeIDWithXSL.xml` need to be added as templates using the Virtual Names tab of the properties page. Specify `XSLByEmployeeID` and `EmployeeIDXSL` respectively.

NOTE

EmployeeIDXSL is referenced explicitly in the XML template ByEmployeeIDWithXSL.xml, and the template name doesn't match the filename. This last change has to do with a bug in the ISAPI filter. The problem is it doesn't distinguish between ByEmployeeID and ByEmployeeIDWithXSL. Apparently, the filter stops at the first template that partially matches the given template name. Distinguishing it by placing the XSL part of the template name first avoids this problem.

Listing 11-18   *XSL Stylesheet for Template Query*

```
<?xml version="1.0" encoding="UTF-8"?>
<xsl:stylesheet version="1.0"
    xmlns:xsl="http://www.w3.org/1999/XSL/Transform"
    xmlns:fo="http://www.w3.org/1999/XSL/Format">
    <xsl:template match="/">
        <xsl:apply-templates/>
    </xsl:template>
    <xsl:template match="Employees">
        <h1>Employee ID #<xsl:value-of select="./EmployeeID"/></h1>
        <hr><h1><xsl:value-of select="./LastName"/>, <xsl:value-of
        select="./FirstName"/></h1></hr>
    </xsl:template>
</xsl:stylesheet>
```

Using the following URL

```
http://localhost/Northwind/XSLByEmployeeID?EmployeeID=2
```

returns the information shown in Figure 11-9.

XPath Queries

XPath queries use the same template functionality of template queries, but look a little different. For example, Listing 11-19 lists the `ByEmployeeIDXPath.xml`

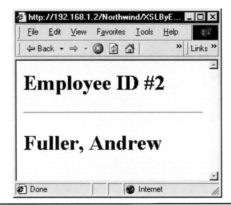

Figure 11-9   *Browser view of template query with XSL specified*

file. This can be installed as another template to query the `Employees` table for a particular row with a specific `EmployeeID` using XPath.

Listing 11-19   *XPath Query as* `ByEmployeeIDXPath.xml`

```
<?xml version="1.0"?>
<root xmlns:sql="urn:schemas-microsoft-com:xml-sql">
    <sql:header>
        <sql:param name="EmployeeID"/>
    </sql:header>
    <sql:xpath-query mapping-schema="EmployeeSchema.xml">
        Employees[@EmployeeID=$EmployeeID]
    </sql:xpath-query>
</root>
```

NOTE

Pay attention to how the `EmployeeID` *column is specified using the attribute notation,* `@`, *and the* `$` *prefixes the XPath variable* `EmployeeID`. *Do not be confused by the use of these symbols in XPath queries and the way they are used in SQL queries.*

To make this work, however, the attribute `mapping-schema` must be assigned a Microsoft XML-DR schema file for the `Employees` table. A schema for this table can be obtained in XML-DR format, using SQL Server 2000. The XML-DR for the `Employees` table is shown in Listing 11-20.

Listing 11-20 *Microsoft XML-DR Schema for* `Employees` *Table as EmployeeSchema.xml*

```
<Schema name="Schema1" xmlns="urn:schemas-microsoft-com:xml-data"
                       xmlns:dt="urn:schemas-microsoft-com:datatypes">
    <ElementType name="Employees" content="empty" model="closed">
        <AttributeType name="EmployeeID" dt:type="i4" />
        <AttributeType name="LastName" dt:type="string" />
        <AttributeType name="FirstName" dt:type="string" />
        <AttributeType name="Title" dt:type="string" />
        <AttributeType name="TitleOfCourtesy" dt:type="string" />
        <AttributeType name="BirthDate" dt:type="dateTime" />
        <AttributeType name="HireDate" dt:type="dateTime" />
        <AttributeType name="Address" dt:type="string" />
        <AttributeType name="City" dt:type="string" />
        <AttributeType name="Region" dt:type="string" />
        <AttributeType name="PostalCode" dt:type="string" />
        <AttributeType name="Country" dt:type="string" />
        <AttributeType name="HomePhone" dt:type="string" />
        <AttributeType name="Extension" dt:type="string" />
        <AttributeType name="Photo" dt:type="uri" />
        <AttributeType name="Notes" dt:type="string" />
        <AttributeType name="ReportsTo" dt:type="i4" />
        <AttributeType name="PhotoPath" dt:type="string" />
        <attribute type="EmployeeID" />
        <attribute type="LastName" />
        <attribute type="FirstName" />
        <attribute type="Title" />
        <attribute type="TitleOfCourtesy" />
        <attribute type="BirthDate" />
        <attribute type="HireDate" />
        <attribute type="Address" />
        <attribute type="City" />
        <attribute type="Region" />
        <attribute type="PostalCode" />
        <attribute type="Country" />
        <attribute type="HomePhone" />
        <attribute type="Extension" />
        <attribute type="Photo" />
        <attribute type="Notes" />
        <attribute type="ReportsTo" />
        <attribute type="PhotoPath" />
    </ElementType>
</Schema>
```

```xml
<?xml version="1.0" ?>
- <root xmlns:sql="urn:schemas-microsoft-com:xml-sql">
    <Employees EmployeeID="3" LastName="Leverling" FirstName="Janet"
      Title="Sales Representative" TitleOfCourtesy="Ms." BirthDate="1963-
      08-30T00:00:00" HireDate="1992-04-01T00:00:00" Address="722
      Moss Bay Blvd." City="Kirkland" Region="WA" PostalCode="98033"
      Country="USA" HomePhone="(206) 555-3412" Extension="3355"
      Photo="FRWvAAIAAAANAA4AFAAhAP////9CaXRtYXAgSW1hZ2UUGFpbnQ
      Notes="Janet has a BS degree in chemistry from Boston College
      (1984). She has also completed a certificate program in food
      retailing management. Janet was hired as a sales associate in 1991
      and promoted to sales representative in February 1992."
      ReportsTo="2"
      PhotoPath="http://accweb/emmployees/leverling.bmp" />
  </root>
```

Figure 11-10   *Browser view of XPath query*

Again, this is the XML Data-Reduced schema format, so it looks different from the schemas we're used to seeing, as discussed in Chapter 3.

Both of these template files can be installed using the `Template` tab of the `Properties` dialog box in the same way as the other templates. Again, be careful how you name the XPath template. It needs to be different in the way it begins from all the other template names. For example, naming it `XPathByEmployeeID` works fine. Enter the following URL into the browser:

```
http://localhost/Northwind/XPathByEmployeeID?EmployeeID=3
```

Figure 11-10 shows the results.

Summary

SQL Server 2000 offers several new features that involve XML. First, a new clause was introduced for `SQL SELECT` statements, `FOR XML`. This clause returns the results of the query in the form of an XML fragment. This clause has three different modes: `AUTO`, `RAW`, and `EXPLICIT`. The `AUTO` mode provides the easiest way to return results as XML with the data as either attributes or child elements. The `RAW` mode is more basic and compresses each row in the result set into one XML element. And, finally, the `EXPLICIT` mode, while more complex, is the most powerful. It enables developers to shape the XML any way they desire.

Second, the `OPENXML` function translates a given XML document into a rowset that can be used just like `table`, `view`, and `OPENROWSET`. This rowset is powerful because it can be used not only by `SELECT` statements, but also `UPDATE` and `INSERT` statements.

And, finally, SQL Server 2000 offers HTTP access to its databases. Developers can use an intuitive tool to provide a Web portal directly into any SQL Server database. These Web portals can accept dynamic SQL queries, template queries, and XPath queries. The dynamic SQL queries are entered directly in the browser's URL address by the end user. If the developer wants to provide an easier application, however, templates can be used to generate the SQL queries. XPath queries use the same template concept, but employ XPath to generate the queries.

These new features make SQL Server an even more powerful database. With the capability to generate results in XML, and to accept updates and inserts as XML, SQL Server 2000 has taken the next step, extending itself to the latest transport of data over the Internet: XML.

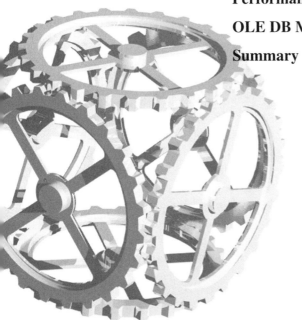

ADO.NET Overview

This chapter focuses on Microsoft's new ADO.NET class library, which is a departure from previous versions of ADO in several ways. *ADO.NET* is built from the ground up to meet the demands of the Web's distributed environment and it's no longer an add-on component library. All the classes and functionality are integrated right into the development environment.

In this chapter, you learn how ADO.NET fits in with the rest of the .NET Framework, paying special attention to the Managed Providers. *Managed Providers* can be thought of as OLE DB Providers for a given data source. You learn how to use the four main classes in the SQL Server Managed Provider. Then, you explore how to connect to a data source, how to execute SQL queries against a database, and how to use the Managed Providers interact with the disconnected portion of ADO.NET. The next chapter delves deeper into ADO.NET's distributed and disconnected classes.

Evolution of ADO

One of the biggest changes Microsoft has made to its development platform with the introduction of the .NET Framework is the incorporation of its ActiveX Data Object (ADO) library. While ADO has been evolving consistently over time into an optimized and simple interface for moving data between a client application and a database, it still has been unable to clear the last hurdle and run in the multiplatform world of the Internet. ADO is platform-specific; it relies on the client having not only the same operating system (OS), but the same platform libraries as well. On disparate systems, clients can't consume ADO recordsets. The Web's greatest asset is its capability to bring people and their computers together, regardless of location, computer platform, or OS. To avoid being left out of the tidal wave that is Web development, Microsoft encouraged developers to build Web servers that consumed the recordsets themselves, transforming them into static HTML. This HTML could be sent down to any and all client browsers, thus, keeping in line with the primary goal of the Web. But this wasn't so much a solution as a workaround. Something else was needed.

ADO.NET is dramatically different from previous versions of ADO, having been written from the ground up to be ready for the Web and its distributed environment. This coincides with the mission goals of Microsoft's .NET initiative to make the Web its development platform. And, yet, major similarities also exist to prior versions, which you see when you look closely at each of the classes. Furthermore, applications built with the .NET Framework needn't include any special components or add any additional libraries: the ADO.NET class library is built right into the Class Framework. Figure 12-1 shows how ADO.NET fits in with the rest of the .NET Framework.

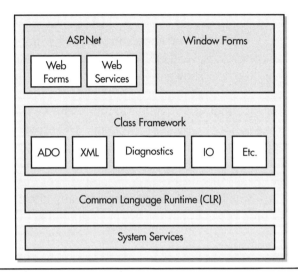

Figure 12-1   *Microsoft .NET Framework*

ADO.NET Object Models

ADO.NET is composed of two object models. First is the *connected layer,* also known as the *Managed Provider,* which is responsible for connecting and interacting with a specific data source. The second object model is *the disconnected layer,* centering on the DataSet class found in the `System.Data` namespace. This chapter provides an overview of ADO.NET and the Managed Providers. Chapter 13 focuses on `DataSets` in more detail.

SqlClient Managed Provider

The `System.Data.OleDb` and the `System.Data.SqlClient` namespaces are the two Managed Provider class libraries. The former is the generic version and the latter is optimized for SQL Server. For the majority of the chapter, we focus on the `SqlClient` namespace, though the two namespaces are quite similar. The classes and methods of one are mirrored in the classes and methods of the other. Only the class prefixes change. For example, both `OleDbDataAdapter` and `SqlDataAdapter` derive from the base `DbDataAdapter`, which resides in the `System.Data.Common` namespace and is abstract. Both of these derived classes perform the same functionality and behave in exactly the same way. The difference between them is that the OleDbDataAdapter class can be used with a variety of data sources, while the SqlDataAdapter class must be used with SQL Server.

Both class libraries consist of several classes used to provide interaction with a data source. Of these classes, the ones shown in Figure 12-2 are most commonly used.

Focusing on the SqlClient namespace, the SqlCommand and SqlConnection classes should be familiar to those who've used ADO before. These classes function similarly to their ancestors in ADO providing connections to, and executing SQL against, the specified data source. The Managed Provider classes should also be familiar because, together, they act like an OLE DB Provider. These two classes, and more specifically their OleDb namespace cousins OleDbCommand and OleDbConnection, abstract the peculiarities of any given data source. To the developer, the data source becomes a black box with a familiar API.

SqlConnection

To open a connection, you must first provide the connection string, just as you did with prior versions of ADO. So, for example, the following lines in Listing 12-1 create and initialize a new SqlConnection object, and establish the connection:

Listing 12-1   *Creating a SqlConnection Object*

```
using System.Data.SqlClient;
…
// initialization code omitted for brevity
…
SqlConnection m_connection = new SqlConnection();
m_connection.ConnectionString = "data source=localhost;initial catalog=" +
                                 "Northwind;user id=someuser;" +
                                 "password=password;";
m_connection.Open();
```

Note, this example uses the System.Data.SqlClient namespace. The first line of code creates a new instance of the SqlConnection class. The second line sets the connection string; it contains the information needed to initialize the connection. In this case, it uses standard name value pairs to specify the OLE DB provider, server, and the database. Because we're using the SqlClient namespace, we needn't specify the Provider. The data source represents the name of the database server and the initial catalog specifies the Northwind database. The user id and password values are the security credentials for a valid login to the database. If

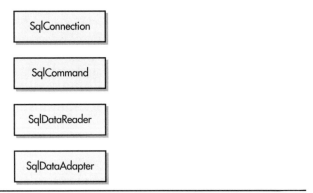

Figure 12-2 *Primary Managed Provider classes*

these are omitted, you can use Window's integrated security specified through the attribute `integrated security=SSPI`. Again, this would be in place of the `user id` and `password` attributes.

Finally, the code calls the `Open()` method to establish the connection. If an error occurs, it will be either an exception of type `IllegalOperationException` or, because we're using the `SqlClient` namespace, an exception of type `SqlException`.

`SqlConnection` offers developers the means to create transactional connections to a data source. The `BeginTransaction()` method begins the transaction by creating an instance of the `SqlTransaction` class. The `SqlTransaction` class has a `Commit()` method and a `Rollback()` method. The first is used to commit the changes, while the second is used to undo, or roll back, the changes incurred during the life of the transaction. These methods don't take any parameters. The `BeginTransaction()` method must be called after the call to `SqlConnection.Open()`. The `Commit()` method must be called after the `BeginTransaction()` method, but before a call to `Rollback()`. And, of course, the `Rollback()` method must be called after the `BeginTransaction()` method, but before any call to the `Commit()` method. The instance of `SqlTransaction`, created by the call to `BeginTransaction()`, must be passed to all other Managed Provider objects that want to participate in the transaction.

SqlCommand

Once a connection has been established, SQL commands can be executed against the data source. Once again, this class, like its cousin class `OleDbCommand`, has three principal methods: `ExecuteReader()`, `ExecuteNonQuery()`, and

ExecuteScalar(). The first, ExecuteReader(), returns the results of the SQL command as a SqlDataReader. Be aware that the SQL might not return the desired result if the query uses SQL SET commands. ExecuteNonQuery() is used for INSERT, UPDATE, DELETE, and SET statements, as these commands don't return any results. Finally, the ExecuteScalar() method returns a single value, usually an aggregate, as an Object.

NOTE

*The **ExecuteReader()** method invokes commands using the system stored procedure, **sp_executesql**. This method might yield undesired results if used to carry out commands, such as Transact-SQL SET statements.*

The SqlCommand class has an additional method, ExecuteXmlReader(), which executes the SQL and returns the results in an instance of the XmlReader class. Normally, the query will contain a FOR XML clause, which causes SQL Server to return the results in XML format. All the features and options available with the FOR XML clause, as discussed in Chapter 11, are possible here. Or, if the XML is stored in an ntext field in the table, the SqlCommand query can build the XmlReader by simply pulling the XML from this column.

To participate in a transaction, the Transaction property must be set to an existing instance of the SqlTransaction class. As you saw earlier, these instances are generated by the BeginTransaction() method found on the SqlConnection class.

Visual Studio .NET makes generating SqlCommands easy for forms in an application. When in Design mode, a developer can establish a connection to a data source, and then drag-and-drop tables, stored procedures, or views on to a form. The act of dragging-and-dropping a stored procedure, for example, on to the design surface of a form automatically generates an instance of a SqlConnection configured against the given data source and an instance of a SqlCommand configured to execute the stored procedure.

Let's walk through dropping a stored procedure on a form. If you create a new C# Windows application, it will contain a Windows Form with the name Form1.cs. Now, if you click on the Server Explorer window at the top-left corner of the designer page, a window with a tree view slides in from the left, containing a list of the servers it could find in the network. It also contains a list of data sources. Initially, this list is empty. Let's add one by right-clicking the Data Connections leaf and selecting Add Connection… from the pop-up menu.

The Data Link Properties dialog box is displayed as shown in Figure 12-3. Enter the information for the connection, such as the name of the database server and the

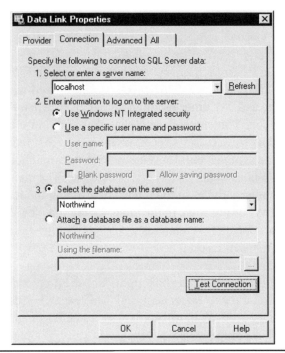

Figure 12-3   *Data Link Properties*

default database. The other important setting is security. You have the option of using Windows Integrated authentication, or a specific user name and password. Once these values are entered, you can test the connection, or click the OK button and create the data connection.

Once the connection to the data source is established, you can peruse the various tables, views, stored procedures, diagrams, and functions. Any of these can be expanded to select the desired database object. Once you choose an object, such as a table or a stored procedure, it can be dragged-and-dropped on to any design surface, such as a form, a Web page, or a Web service. When the object is dropped on the design surface, Visual Studio generates an instance of the `SqlConnection`, called `sqlConnection1`, on the bottom of the form designer page. If one already exists, then no instance is generated. If the chosen database object is a stored procedure, Visual Studio also generates an instance of the `SqlCommand` named "`sqlCommand1`" tied to the selected procedure. This, too, appears in a little window at the bottom of the form designer page. These objects can be renamed easily by left-clicking them, and then entering a new name in the `Name` property of the Properties window. If the database object dropped on to the design surface was a table or view, then Visual Studio creates an instance of a `SqlDataAdapter`. We will discuss data adapters later in this chapter.

Inside the `InitializeComponents()` method of the form or Web page, the `SqlConnection` and `SqlCommand` objects are initialized with their connection strings, query strings, and any other required values from when they were dropped on to the design surface. You can now reference them in your code to execute queries against the data source. Let's see how this works in a real example.

The following code samples build a Windows Forms application that obtains data from the `Employees` table in the `Northwind` database. The main form displays a grid listing the current employees in the table. By pressing the Refresh button, the list is updated with the current rows in the table. When the New Employee button is clicked, a dialog box appears that contains fields to enter the first and last name. Pressing the OK button will insert a new row into the `Employees` table with the given first and last names.

To create the New Employee dialog box, right-click the project name in the Solution Explorer window, select the Add menu item, and then select the Add Windows Form… menu item. Or, select the Add Windows Form… menu item from the Project menu from the main menu bar. Then, drop two labels, two text boxes, and a button on to this new form. In our example, the first label and the first text box have been renamed to `m_lblFirstName` and `m_txtFirstName` respectively. The second label and text box have also been renamed `m_lblLastName` and `m_txtLastName`. The button is named `m_btnOK`.

Now use the Server Explorer to add a connection to the `Northwind` database. Next, expand the connection until the Stored Procedures directory is displayed. Right-click this entry and add the following stored procedure:

```
CREATE PROCEDURE sp_putNewEmployee(@FirstName varchar, @LastName varchar)
AS
BEGIN
    INSERT INTO Employees (FirstName, LastName)
    VALUES (@FirstName, @LastName)
END
```

Save this stored procedure to add it to the database. Now, from within the Stored Procedures directory on the Server Explorer window, drag-and-drop it on to our New Employee dialog box. This generates instances of the `SqlConnection` and `SqlCommand` classes: rename them to `m_sqlConnection` and m_sqlCmdNewEmployee. The dialog box should appear as shown in Figure 12-4. Note the m_sqlConnection and m_sqlCmdNewEmployee objects in the small window below the form.

Finally, view the properties for the OK button by selecting the control in design mode and pressing the F4 key. Then, select the Events view by clicking the lightning bolt at the top of the Properties window. If the Properties window is organized by category, find the Action section, and then type in a name of a routine for the Click event. For our example, we'll call it "clickInsertNewEmployee". Press ENTER

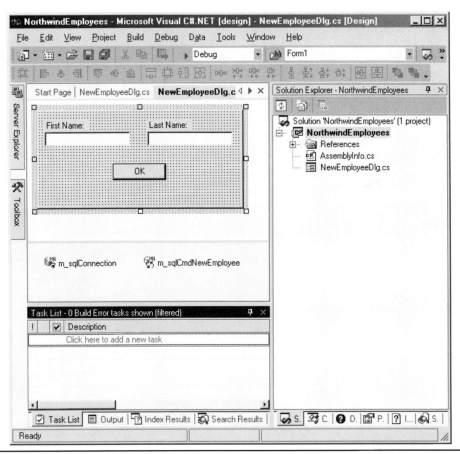

Figure 12-4   *New Employee dialog box*

and you'll be taken directly to the code. There, you'll find a new event added to your code to handle the `Click` event for the OK button. The code is shown in Listing 12-2.

NOTE

*When using **SqlCommand** objects, you must explicitly open and close the connection to the data source. When using data adapters, you needn't be concerned with managing the connection. The code in Listing 12-2 uses the **finally** block to ensure the connection is always closed before you leave this method.*

Listing 12-2   *Insert New Employee Method*

```
private void clickInsertNewEmployee(object sender, System.EventArgs e)
{
    try
    {
        m_sqlConnection.Open();
        m_sqlCmdNewEmployee.Parameters["@FirstName"].Value =
            m_txtFirstName.Text;
        m_sqlCmdNewEmployee.Parameters["@LastName"].Value =
            m_txtLastName.Text;
        m_sqlCmdNewEmployee.ExecuteNonQuery();
    }
    catch (Exception ex)
    {
        System.Console.WriteLine(ex.Message);
    }
    finally
    {
        if (m_sqlConnection != null)
        {
            if (m_sqlConnection.State ==
System.Data.ConnectionState.Open)
            {
                m_sqlConnection.Close();
            }
        }
    }
}
```

This code should look familiar to the old style of ADO. All the code to set up the `SqlConnection` and `SqlCommand` objects is done in the `InitializeComponent()` method. This method is found within the Windows Form Designer generated code region. Among the settings for the various controls we dropped on to this dialog box, this method initializes our `SqlConnection` and `SqlCommand` objects, as shown in Listing 12-3.

Listing 12-3 *Hidden Initialization Code*

```
//
// m_sqlConnection
//
this.m_sqlConnection.ConnectionString = "data source=MyServer;" +
    "initial catalog=Northwind;integrated security=SSPI;persist " +
    "security info=False;packet size=4096";
//
// m_sqlCmdNewEmployee
//
this.m_sqlCmdNewEmployee.CommandText = "dbo.sp_putNewEmployee";
this.m_sqlCmdNewEmployee.CommandType =
    System.Data.CommandType.StoredProcedure;
this.m_sqlCmdNewEmployee.Connection = this.m_sqlConnection;
this.m_sqlCmdNewEmployee.Parameters.Add(
    new System.Data.SqlClient.SqlParameter(
        "@RETURN_VALUE", System.Data.SqlDbType.Int, 4,
        System.Data.ParameterDirection.ReturnValue, true,
        ((System.Byte)(10)), ((System.Byte)(0)), "",
        System.Data.DataRowVersion.Current, null));
this.m_sqlCmdNewEmployee.Parameters.Add(
    new System.Data.SqlClient.SqlParameter(
        "@FirstName", System.Data.SqlDbType.Char, 1,
        System.Data.ParameterDirection.Input, true, ((System.Byte)(0)),
        ((System.Byte)(0)), "", System.Data.DataRowVersion.Current, null));
this.m_sqlCmdNewEmployee.Parameters.Add(
    new System.Data.SqlClient.SqlParameter(
        "@LastName", System.Data.SqlDbType.Char, 1,
        System.Data.ParameterDirection.Input, true, ((System.Byte)(0)),
        ((System.Byte)(0)), "", System.Data.DataRowVersion.Current, null));
```

NOTE

For all the example source code in this chapter, if your data source is on your local machine, then the value of `data source` in the connection string should be changed from `MyServer` to `localhost`. Otherwise, it should be changed to the name of the computer running SQL Server.

The method in Listing 12-2 first opens a connection to the data source using the `SqlConnection.Open()` method. The connection string, specified in Listing 12-3, identifies the data source, the database, and the type of authentication to be used—Windows Integrated Authentication—in this case.

Next, the parameters for the stored procedure in the `SqlCommand` object are assigned the values in the text boxes. Normally, you would provide checks here to make sure these fields aren't blank. After the parameters have been set, the `ExecuteNonQuery()` method is invoked to insert the new row into the database. This method is used because your stored procedure doesn't return any results.

The remaining code consists of a `catch` block to handle any exceptions and a `finally` clause to ensure you close the connection before you leave. This allows proper clean up of the connection to the data source.

SqlDataReader

The `ExecuteNonQuery()` method from the previous example executes SQL that doesn't return any results. But what if you want to obtain results from the database? `SqlCommand` uses the `ExecuteReader()` method to return values in a `SqlDataReader`.

A `SqlDataReader` is used to provide a forward-only stream of data from a data source. It has no public constructor; instead, instances of this class are created by using the `ExecuteReader()` method of the `SqlCommand` class. Classes can't inherit from this class. Once created, a `SqlDataReader` can move through the results one row at a time, until all the results are processed. In addition, the methods of this class that access the data for each row (see Table 12-1) don't generate new copies of the data but, instead, reuse the same values each time they're called. For these reasons, the `SqlDataReader` is the most efficient and fastest way to retrieve data from SQL Server. We explore performance in more detail in the section "Performance: DataAdapter Versus DataReader."

Because this class is part of the ADO Managed Provider, it must remain connected to the data source to function. In fact, no other operations can be executed on the connection until the `SqlDataReader` has been closed. Once closed, little can be done with this class, other than call the `IsClosed` and `RecordsAffected` properties.

Let's examine a `SqlDataReader` in action. If you want to obtain the first and last name of every employee in the `Employees` table, you can use the code from Listing 12-4 to populate a `SqlDataReader`.

Listing 12-4 *Populating a SqlDataReader*

```
SqlCommand sqlCmd = new SqlCommand();
sqlCmd.CommandText = "SELECT FirstName, LastName FROM Employees";
sqlCmd.CommandType = CommandType.Text;
sqlCmd.ActiveConnection = sqlConnection;
SqlDataReader sqlDataReader = sqlCmd.ExecuteReader();
```

This example assumes an active connection is already established. Using the `SqlCommand.ExecuteReader()` method, a `SqlDataReader` is created and returned.

Listing 12-5 illustrates how to retrieve the results. Each call to the `Read()` method obtains one row from the database, until no more results exist. Each time through the loop, the values of the first two columns are retrieved and written to the out console. The *{0} {1} string* is a format string used to specify how the output should be displayed. The *{0}* represents the first argument of the format expression, and *{1}* represents the second. The `SqlDataReader` class has many methods to convert values into different datatypes as we see in Table 12-1. Each of these methods takes an integer as the ordinal value specifying the column of the row to retrieve. In the example in Listing 12-5, you're seeking the string representations of the first and last names. Because these are already represented as strings, no conversion occurs and the strings are simply returned.

Listing 12-5 *Processing the SqlDataReader*

```
while (sqlDataReader.Read())
{
    System.Console.Out.WriteLine
    (
        "{0} {1}",
        sqlDataReader.GetString(0),
        sqlDataReader.GetString(1)
    );
}
// always close the SqlDataReader when you are done
sqlDataReader.Close();
```

Method	Description
GetBoolean	Returns the value of the specified column as a Boolean
GetByte	Returns the value of the specified column as a byte
GetBytes	Returns the value of the specified column as a byte array
GetChar	Returns the value of the specified column as a character
GetChars	Returns the value of the specified column as a character array
GetDataTypeName	Returns the name of the back-end datatype
GetDateTime	Returns the value of the specified column as a DateTime object
GetDecimal	Returns the value of the specified column as a Decimal object
GetDouble	Returns the value of the specified column as a double-precision floating point number
GetFieldType	Returns the Type Class that is the datatype of the object
GetFloat	Returns the value of the specified column as a single-precision floating point number
GetGuid	Returns the value of the specified column as a globally unique identifier
GetInt16	Returns the value of the specified column as a 16-bit signed integer
GetInt32	Returns the value of the specified column as a 32-bit signed integer
GetInt64	Returns the value of the specified column as a 64-bit signed integer
GetName	Returns the name of the specified column
GetOrdinal	Returns the ordinal value given the name of the column
GetSByte	Returns the value of the specified column as an SByte
GetString	Returns the value of the specified column as a string
GetTimeSpan	Returns the value of the specified column as a TimeSpan
GetUInt16	Returns the value of the specified column as a 16-bit unsigned integer
GetUInt32	Returns the value of the specified column as a 32-bit unsigned integer
GetUInt64	Returns the value of the specified column as a 64-bit unsigned integer
GetValue	Returns the value of the specified column in its native format
GetValues	Returns all the columns in the collection for the current record

Table 12-1   *SqlDataReader Accessor Methods*

SqlDataAdapter

As said previously, the SqlDataReader is an effective way of obtaining results from queries quickly and easily but, again, a connection to the data source must be maintained. This might not be the most effective way to retrieve results in a distributed environment. Microsoft .NET, by its very title, is a platform for building applications over a distributed environment.

To achieve a disconnected representation of query results, .NET provides the DataSet class found in the System.Data namespace. This class is discussed in great detail in the next chapter but, for now, we'll focus on the SqlDataAdapter class, which is used to populate DataSet objects.

DataSet objects are important, though, because unlike SqlDataReaders, DataSets can also update, delete, and insert information. They do all this through the use of the SqlDataAdapter class. Because a DataSet is connectionless, changes made to the data in a DataSet aren't propagated back to the database automatically. Through the use of a SqlDataAdapter object, however, these changes can be migrated back to the original data source.

If you assign the SqlDataAdapter object to a specific table or view in the data source, it generates dynamic SQL to perform the necessary inserts, updates, and deletes. If you don't want to use dynamic SQL, you can create your own stored procedures and assign them to the data adapter. In any case, each time you assign or specify SQL or stored procedures to a data adapter, it generates a SqlCommand object to carry out the respective operation. These SqlCommand objects are assigned to a SqlDataAdapter using the SelectCommand, InsertCommand, UpdateCommand, and DeleteCommand properties. So, if you have a stored procedure to insert a row into a table and you configure a data adapter to use that procedure, what you're doing is setting the InsertCommand property equal to an instance of the SqlCommand class and initializing the instance to use the given stored procedure.

The SqlDataAdapter is essential for a given DataTable within a DataSet. A one-to-one correlation exists between DataTables and data adapters. So, a given DataSet can use several data adapters to communicate with the data source. *Data adapters* are the hub for disconnected operations using DataSets. The four operations performed on a data source are often referred to as CRUD: Create, Retrieve, Update, and Delete. So, if you had a SqlDataAdapter mapped to the Employee table in the Northwind database, you could assign the necessary SqlCommands that perform all the CRUD operations to the four SqlCommands of the SqlDataAdapter. You would populate the DataTable in the DataSet using this data adapter. Then, you could modify its data as needed—adding rows, updating existing rows, and deleting others. Once satisfied with your desired changes to the data, you would pass it back to the `SqlDataAdapter` to update the data source. It would require no additional code or SQL on your part because you would have already configured the data adapter with all the know-how to perform these operations.

Let's create an application that puts these ideas into action. This application will use a grid to display the current list of employees in the `Northwind` database. The grid, a Microsoft `DataGrid`, has several useful properties. These properties, which it has in common with many other Microsoft controls, can be used to bind a `DataTable`, a `DataView`, a `DataSet`, or a `DataSetView`. Once bound, the control—a grid in this case—displays the contents of the object.

To begin, create a new C# Windows application. Rename the main form to "Employees.cs". This can be done by right-clicking the form name in the Solution Explorer window and selecting Rename. Or, you could modify the File Name property of the form. You also need to search and replace the `Form1` class name globally with `Employees` throughout the source code.

Next, go to the Toolbox window located on the slim window on the left of Visual Studio. Select the Windows Forms tab, and then drag-and-drop a `DataGrid` on to your form.

To set up your database objects, you should already have a connection to the data source from your previous examples using `SqlCommand`. You reuse the connection in this application. This time, instead of dragging-and-dropping a stored procedure, you drop the `Employees` table on to your form. When you do this, you see Visual Studio has created `sqlConnetion1`, as before, but it's also created `sqlDataAdapter1`. Visual Studio creates an instance of the `SqlDataAdapter` class in this case because, behind the scenes, it generated dynamic SQL for all desired CRUD operations, coalescing them into four `SqlCommand` objects, managed by the single data adapter. Unfortunately, the SQL it generated for these commands is a bit like SQL on steroids because each column of the `Employees` table is referenced individually, but this isn't a problem.

Well, this isn't a problem except in the case of updates. For this example, you must modify the SQL used to perform updates, which was generated by Visual Studio, so the `WHERE` clause references only the `EmployeeID` column. Otherwise, you'll have some concurrency issues. You can do this one of several ways. The most direct way is to modify the source code by first expanding the `Windows Form Designer generated code` region. Under the portion of the initialization code that assigns the SQL for the update command, you remove the additional columns in the `WHERE` clause. The SQL now looks like this:

```
"UPDATE Employees SET LastName = @LastName, FirstName = @FirstName, " +
   Title = @Title, TitleOfCourtesy = @TitleOfCourtesy, BirthDate = " +
   "@BirthDate, HireDate = @HireDate, Address = @Address, City = @City" +
   ", Region = @Region, PostalCode = @PostalCode, Country = @Country" +
   ", HomePhone = @HomePhone, Extension = @Extension, Photo = @Photo" +
   ", Notes = @Notes, ReportsTo = @ReportsTo, PhotoPath = @PhotoPath " +
   "WHERE (EmployeeID = @Original_EmployeeID); SELECT EmployeeID, " +
   "LastName, FirstName, Title, TitleOfCourtesy, BirthDate, HireDate, " +
   " Address, City, Region, PostalCode, Country, HomePhone, Extension, " +
   "Photo, Notes, ReportsTo, PhotoPath FROM Employees WHERE " +
   "(EmployeeID = @Select_EmployeeID)"
```

For a more elegant approach, you can select the data adapter from the form's design surface and press the F4 key to view the Properties window. From here, we expand the `UpdateCommand` property. This reveals several subordinate properties. Select the `CommandText` property and click the … next to the value. This displays the Query Builder dialog box. You can now edit the dynamic SQL directly in the text box provided.

NOTE

Normally, you would create a stored procedure that performed the update and you wouldn't use the code generated by Visual Studio. Stored procedures execute faster than dynamic SQL and are easier to maintain. But, for this simple example, using the dynamic SQL meets our needs.

As you can see, Visual Studio generates a lot of code. All the code for this sample application can be found at the McGraw-Hill/Osborne Web site at **www.osborne.com** in the Downloads section of the site.

The important thing to learn here is this: using a `SqlDataAdapter`, along with a `DataSet`, enables you to display the list of employees in the `Employees` table, modify them in any way, and then propagate the changes back to the data source.

The next step is to create a `DataSet`. Visual Studio has a special wizard that makes this process extremely easy. All you must do is select your `sqlDataAdapter1` object on the form's design surface, and then display the Properties window. To do this, press the F4 key while the data adapter is still highlighted or select the Properties window menu item from the View menu. Once you have the Properties window with the data adapter in focus, you can click the Generate Dataset… link at the bottom. A Generate DataSet dialog box is displayed. You can choose to use an existing derived `DataSet` or create a new one. Because you haven't created a derived `DataSet` yet, select the New option. Now type in the class name for your derived `DataSet`. As Figure 12-5 shows, you named the `DataSet` "EmployeesDS". When you click the OK button, the dialog box disappears and you see that Visual Studio has created

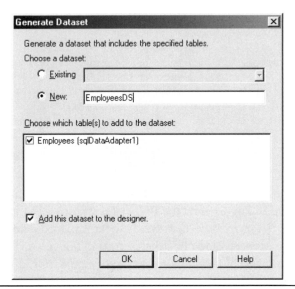

Figure 12-5   *Generate Derived DataSet*

an Employees.xsd schema file in your Solution Explorer window, and an
`employeesDS1` object next to the `sqlDataAdapter1` object.

The `employeesDS1` object is an instance of the `EmployeesDS` class you
created. This isn't shown in the Solution Explorer window, but it can be seen in the
Class View window.

Now you can bind this `DataSet` to the `DataGrid` on your form. Click the
`DataGrid` and press F4 to view the Properties window. Choose the
`employeesDS1` selection from the drop-down menu for the `DataSource`
property of the `DataGrid`. The last thing you need to do is add some code to fill
the `DataSet`. Listing 12-6 shows this code.

Listing 12-6   *Bind a DataSet to a DataGrid*

```
/// <summary>
/// Constructor for this class
/// </summary>
public Employees()
{
    //
    // Required for Windows Form Designer support
```

```
    //
    InitializeComponent();

    // display the employees
    displayEmployees();
}

/// <summary>
/// Displays the employees in the gird by populating the DataSet
/// </summary>
protected void displayEmployees()
{
    try
    {
        // fill the employees data table
        sqlDataAdapter1.Fill(dsEmployees1.Employees);
    }
    catch (Exception ex)
    {
        System.Diagnostics.Debug.WriteLine(ex.ToString());
    }
}
```

This isn't a lot of code; most of it is exception handling.

Now, if you run this application as is, you can display the employees in the Employees table and make modifications, but you have no way of sending the changes back to the database. To do this, you need to add an Update button and some more code to your form.

From your Windows Form tab on the toolbox, drag-and-drop a button—button1—on to your form and label it Update. Now, you need to add an event for this button. Select the button and view its properties. You switch the view so it lists the events by clicking the lightning bolt at the top of the Properties window. In the Click event, type **updateEmployees** and press the ENTER key. Visual Studio adds the new event to the form, creates a new event handler for the button, and automatically positions you in the handler to implement the event. Listing 12-7 contains the complete code listing.

Listing 12-7 *updateEmployees( ) Event Routine*

```
/// <summary>
/// Updates the data source with the changes made in the DataGrid
```

```
/// </summary>
/// <param name="sender"></param>
/// <param name="e"></param>
private void updateEmployees(object sender, System.EventArgs e)
{
    try
    {
        // update the data source with the changes to the given data table
        sqlDataAdapter1.Update(dsEmployees1.Employees);
    }
    catch (Exception ex)
    {
        System.Diagnostics.Debug.WriteLine(ex.ToString());
    }
    finally
    {
        // refresh the display
        displayEmployees();
    }
}
```

NOTE

When you add the `updateEmployees()` *event, Visual Studio modifies the code in the* `InitializeComponent()` *method to create a new* `System.EventHandler` *and assigns it to the Click property of the button.*

Again, this isn't a lot of code. If you run this application now, you can add, delete, or modify the rows in the grid as desired. When you click the Update button, the changes are sent to the database and the display is refreshed. Figure 12-6 shows the initial view of this application, Figure 12-7 shows the app with some new rows and values, and, finally, Figure 12-8 shows the application with the new rows deleted.

Note, the `updateEmployees()` method, under the covers, updates the changes to the database, closes the connection, and reopens the connection to refresh the display. This might not be the most optimized way to do this, but it ensures you always close your connections. When using a data source like SQL Server, which has a connection pool, opening and closing connections does not incur any real performance penalties. Furthermore, if you want to place the update within a transaction, you could do so without having a separate connection object to retrieve the data.

One reason for the small amount of code you had to write is, in part, because of the amount of code Visual Studio generates for you. You saw some of that code when you modified the update SQL statement earlier.

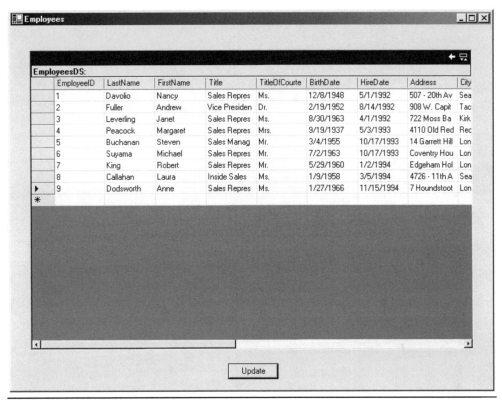

Figure 12-6   *Initial view of the DataGrid*

Performance: DataAdapter Versus DataReader

Performance can be a tricky subject because it isn't always about speed. A number of different factors must be considered when deciding whether to employ `DataSets` or `DataReaders`.

NOTE

For clarity in this section, we use the term `DataReaders` *(or data readers) to represent both* `SqlDataReaders` *and* `OleDbDataReaders`. *And, when we refer to* `DataSets`, *we're referring to both* `SqlDataAdapters` *and* `OleDbDataAdapters`, *in combination with* `DataSets`.

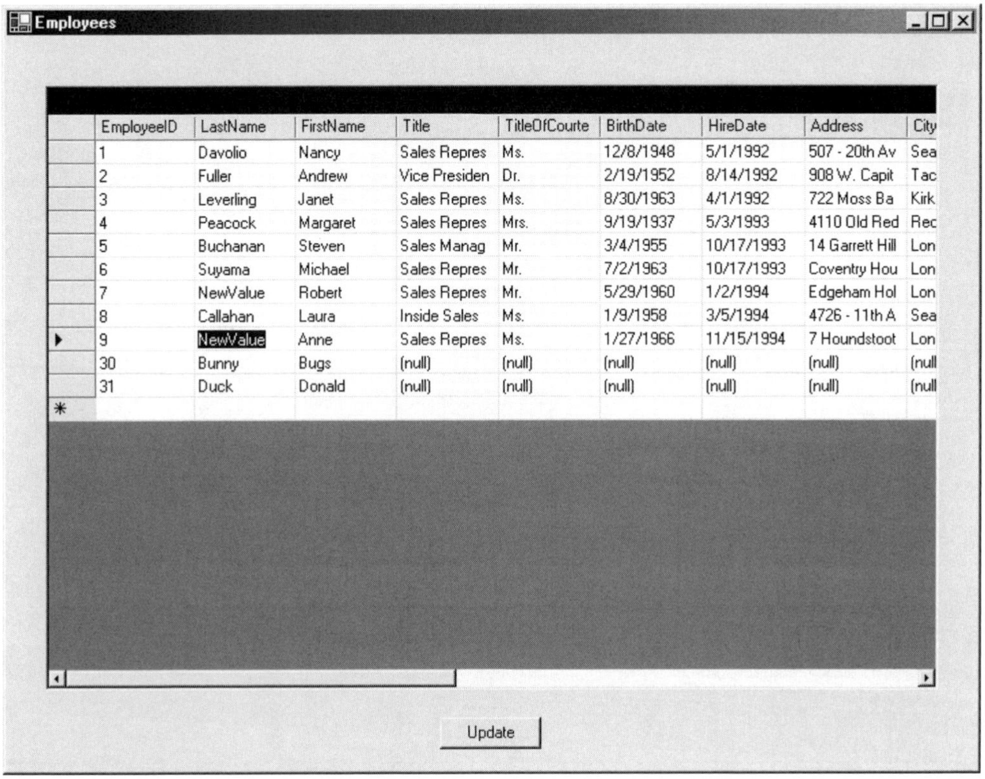

Figure 12-7 *DataGrid with modifications*

But ways exist to tackle this issue. By determining what each functional or vertical slice of an application requires, this can help to clarify which decision to make. The following questions are a few you might want to ask when you determine which class to use:

▶ Is this portion of the application only retrieving data or will it also be modifying the data?

▶ How important is speed for this portion of the application?

▶ Do I want to spend less time in the development of the application so I can get something up and running?

If a particular vertical slice of an application is intended only to retrieve data from the database, `DataReaders` are a better choice because `DataReaders` extract

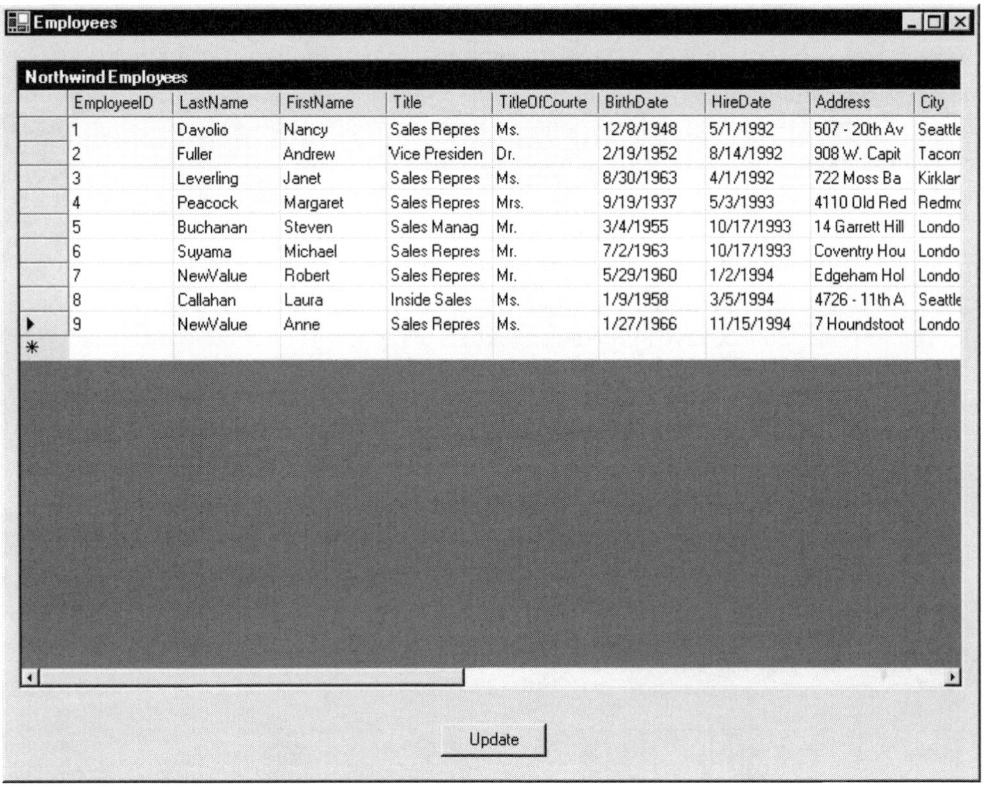

Employees

Northwind Employees

EmployeeID	LastName	FirstName	Title	TitleOfCourte	BirthDate	HireDate	Address	City
1	Davolio	Nancy	Sales Repres	Ms.	12/8/1948	5/1/1992	507 - 20th Av	Seattle
2	Fuller	Andrew	Vice Presiden	Dr.	2/19/1952	8/14/1992	908 W. Capit	Tacom
3	Leverling	Janet	Sales Repres	Ms.	8/30/1963	4/1/1992	722 Moss Ba	Kirklar
4	Peacock	Margaret	Sales Repres	Mrs.	9/19/1937	5/3/1993	4110 Old Red	Redm
5	Buchanan	Steven	Sales Manag	Mr.	3/4/1955	10/17/1993	14 Garrett Hill	Londo
6	Suyama	Michael	Sales Repres	Mr.	7/2/1963	10/17/1993	Coventry Hou	Londo
7	NewValue	Robert	Sales Repres	Mr.	5/29/1960	1/2/1994	Edgeham Hol	Londo
8	Callahan	Laura	Inside Sales	Ms.	1/9/1958	3/5/1994	4726 - 11th A	Seattle
9	NewValue	Anne	Sales Repres	Ms.	1/27/1966	11/15/1994	7 Houndstoot	Londo

Update

Figure 12-8 *DataGrid with rows deleted*

data from a data source faster than a `DataAdapter`. `DataReaders` are optimized to scroll forward through a result set and pull the data from the stream. On the other hand, if this portion of the application will also need to handle modifications to the data, then `DataAdapters` are a better choice. As you've seen, `DataAdapters`—together with `DataSets`—have a number of features that make this much easier than `DataReaders`.

If speed in obtaining the data is critical to a portion of the application, then `DataReaders` should be used. Ultimately, modifications can be sent back to a database using `SqlCommands` and either dynamic SQL or stored procedures. This is more work and, most likely, will take longer to develop, but it must be weighed against the importance of speed.

This brings us to our last criterion. If development time is an issue or the technical expertise of the developers is in question, then consider `DataAdapters`. They are much easier to code against, and Visual Studio has many features to enable Rapid Application Development (RAD). For example, Visual Studio provides a number of wizards to automatically generate `DataAdapters` and `DataSets`. In addition, Visual Studio comes with several controls both for Windows Forms and Web Pages that can be bound to `DataSets` and `DataViews`.

To see the difference in development time, consider the small code snippet in Listing 12-8. It retrieves some information for a Web Application that's used to display the rankings of football players based on a variety of statistics. This application is reviewed more in Chapter 14. But, for now, the listing shows the portion of code that retrieves this data as XML using a `DataSet`.

Listing 12-8   *Generating XML from a Data Source Using a DataSet*

```
m_sqlDAGetPlayersByPosition.Fill(m_playersByPositionDS);
// some code omitted for clarity
xmlDoc.LoadXml(m_playersByPositionDS.GetXml());
```

This is quite simple. But look at the code in Listing 12-9 that's needed to do the same thing using a `SqlDataReader`.

Listing 12-9   *Generating XML from a Data Source Using a DataReader*

```
SqlDataReader sqlDataReader =
    m_sqlDAGetPlayersByPosition.SelectCommand.ExecuteReader();
m_xmlDoc = new XmlDocument();
XmlElement xmlRoot = m_xmlDoc.CreateElement("PlayersByPositionDS");
XmlElement xmlElement = null;
while (sqlDataReader.Read())
{
    XmlElement xmlRow = m_xmlDoc.CreateElement("sp_getPlayersByPosition");
    for (int index = 0; index < sqlDataReader.FieldCount; index++)
    {
        xmlElement = m_xmlDoc.CreateElement(sqlDataReader.GetName(index));
        xmlElement.InnerText = sqlDataReader.GetValue(index).ToString();
        xmlRow.AppendChild(xmlElement);
    }
```

```
    xmlRoot.AppendChild(xmlRow);
}
m_xmlDoc.AppendChild(xmlRoot);
sqlDataReader.Close();
```

As you can see in Listing 12-9, quite a bit more code is needed than in Listing 12-8, and some additional knowledge is also required. Ultimately, if the process of encoding the XML from the `DataReader` is more complex than this simple example, employing a `DataReader` might take longer than using the combination of a `DataAdapter` with a `DataSet`.

You might not always need to pull data from a data source and encode it as XML, however. Sometimes, you only need data to execute business logic or to perform a calculation. Or, maybe, you're simply populating a drop-down menu on a Web page. In these situations, using `DataReaders` probably makes more sense.

As you can see, no clear-cut winner exists. Choosing which class to use isn't always based on speed alone. And, usually, it won't be a straightforward decision. Careful consideration of the application requirements, the expertise of the development team, and what each portion of the application is trying to do leads to the best decision. Often, applications contain a hybrid of techniques, mixing the different ways for manipulating data in a data source.

OLE DB Managed Provider

Up until now, we've been discussing the `System.Data.SqlClient` namespace, which serves as the .NET SQL Server Managed Provider. `System.Data.OleDb` serves as the namespace for the .NET OLE DB Managed Provider. The collection of classes in this namespace is a mirror image of those in the SQL Server Managed Provider but, because the OLE DB provider is designed to be generic, it doesn't benefit from any optimizations the way its sibling namespace does. Otherwise, these two namespaces are quite similar. As with the SQL Server Managed Provider, the OLE DB Managed Provider consists of four main classes: the `OleDbConnection`, the `OleDbCommand`, the `OleDbDataReader`, and the `OleDbDataAdapter`.

To demonstrate how similar these providers are from the perspective of a developer, let's examine Listing 12-10.

Listing 12-10 *Comparing OleDb and SqlClient Namespaces*

```
this.oleDbDataAdapter1 = new System.Data.OleDb.OleDbDataAdapter();
this.oleDbSelectCommand1 = new System.Data.OleDb.OleDbCommand();
this.oleDbConnection1 = new System.Data.OleDb.OleDbConnection();
this.sqlDataAdapter1 = new System.Data.SqlClient.SqlDataAdapter();
this.sqlSelectCommand1 = new System.Data.SqlClient.SqlCommand();
this.sqlConnection1 = new System.Data.SqlClient.SqlConnection();
//
// oleDbDataAdapter1
//
this.oleDbDataAdapter1.SelectCommand = this.oleDbSelectCommand1;
this.oleDbDataAdapter1.TableMappings.AddRange(
    new System.Data.Common.DataTableMapping[]
    {
        new System.Data.Common.DataTableMapping(
            "Table", "CustOrdersDetail",
        new System.Data.Common.DataColumnMapping[]
        {
            new System.Data.Common.DataColumnMapping(
                "ProductName", "ProductName"),
            new System.Data.Common.DataColumnMapping(
                "UnitPrice", "UnitPrice"),
            new System.Data.Common.DataColumnMapping(
                "Quantity", "Quantity"),
            new System.Data.Common.DataColumnMapping(
                "Discount", "Discount"),
            new System.Data.Common.DataColumnMapping(
                "ExtendedPrice", "ExtendedPrice")
        })
    });
//
// oleDbSelectCommand1
//
this.oleDbSelectCommand1.CommandText = "CustOrdersDetail";
this.oleDbSelectCommand1.CommandType =
    System.Data.CommandType.StoredProcedure;
this.oleDbSelectCommand1.Connection = this.oleDbConnection1;
this.oleDbSelectCommand1.Parameters.Add(
    new System.Data.OleDb.OleDbParameter(
        "RETURN_VALUE", System.Data.OleDb.OleDbType.Integer, 4,
        System.Data.ParameterDirection.ReturnValue, true,
        ((System.Byte)(10)), ((System.Byte)(0)), "",
        System.Data.DataRowVersion.Current, null));
this.oleDbSelectCommand1.Parameters.Add(
    new System.Data.OleDb.OleDbParameter(
        "OrderID", System.Data.OleDb.OleDbType.Integer, 4,
```

```
            System.Data.ParameterDirection.Input, true, ((System.Byte)(10)),
            ((System.Byte)(0)), "", System.Data.DataRowVersion.Current, null));
//
// oleDbConnection1
//
this.oleDbConnection1.ConnectionString = @"Provider=SQLOLEDB.1;" +
    "Integrated Security=SSPI;Persist Security Info=False;Initial " +
    "Catalog=Northwind;Data Source=localhost;Use Procedure for " +
    "Prepare=1;Auto Translate=True;Packet Size=4096;Workstation ID=" +
    "localhost;Use Encryption for Data=False;Tag with column collation " +
    "when possible=False";
//
// sqlDataAdapter1
//
this.sqlDataAdapter1.SelectCommand = this.sqlSelectCommand1;
this.sqlDataAdapter1.TableMappings.AddRange(
    new System.Data.Common.DataTableMapping[]
    {
        new System.Data.Common.DataTableMapping(
            "Table", "CustOrdersDetail",
        new System.Data.Common.DataColumnMapping[]
        {
            new System.Data.Common.DataColumnMapping(
                "ProductName", "ProductName"),
            new System.Data.Common.DataColumnMapping(
                "UnitPrice", "UnitPrice"),
            new System.Data.Common.DataColumnMapping(
                "Quantity", "Quantity"),
            new System.Data.Common.DataColumnMapping(
                "Discount", "Discount"),
            new System.Data.Common.DataColumnMapping(
                "ExtendedPrice", "ExtendedPrice")
        })
    });
//
// sqlSelectCommand1
//
this.sqlSelectCommand1.CommandText = "CustOrdersDetail";
this.sqlSelectCommand1.CommandType =
    System.Data.CommandType.StoredProcedure;
this.sqlSelectCommand1.Connection = this.sqlConnection1;
this.sqlSelectCommand1.Parameters.Add(
    new System.Data.SqlClient.SqlParameter(
        "@RETURN_VALUE", System.Data.SqlDbType.Int, 4,
        System.Data.ParameterDirection.ReturnValue, true,
        ((System.Byte)(10)), ((System.Byte)(0)), "",
        System.Data.DataRowVersion.Current, null));
this.sqlSelectCommand1.Parameters.Add(
```

```
      new System.Data.SqlClient.SqlParameter(
          "@OrderID", System.Data.SqlDbType.Int, 4,
          System.Data.ParameterDirection.Input, true, ((System.Byte)(10)),
          ((System.Byte)(0)), "", System.Data.DataRowVersion.Current, null));
//
// sqlConnection1
//
this.sqlConnection1.ConnectionString = "data source=localhost;initial " +
    "catalog=Northwind;integrated security=SSPI;persist " +
    "security info=False;workstation id=RDA-LADER;packet size=4096";
```

The code in Listing 12-10 was generated by dragging-and-dropping an
`OleDbDataAdapter` and a `SqlDataAdapter` on to a Windows Form from
the Data tab on the Toolbox window. The two data adapters were set up to use the
`CustOrdersDetail` stored procedure in the `Northwind` database. Notice how
similar the code is to initialize the representative classes of the two providers. The only
real difference shows up in the connection strings. Otherwise, the code is identical.

Some differences can be found when exploring the two Managed Providers.
For example, the `ExecuteReader()` method on the `OleDbCommand` object
operates differently from the `SqlCommand`; the latter invokes commands using the
`sp_executesql` system stored procedure. And the `OleDbCommand` class doesn't
have the `ExecuteXmlReader()` method found on the `SqlCommand` class.

With respect to the connection classes, the `SqlConnection` class provides an
optimized connection to a SQL Server data source. Because the provider is defaulted
to SQL Server, specifying the provider in the connection string is unnecessary. The
`OleDbConnection` doesn't benefit from any optimizations and it must specify
the provider in its connection string. When connecting to SQL Server databases prior
to version 7.0, or to non-SQL Server data sources, you must use the
`OleDbConnection` class.

Summary

This chapter explored ADO.NET's Managed Providers. You learned how to connect
to a data source using the `Open()` method of the `SqlConnection` class. You
also examined how to execute SQL queries. These behave much as they had with
prior versions of ADO. Today, with ADO.NET, you use the `SqlCommand` class.
The `ExecuteNonQuery()` method allows the `SqlCommand` object to execute
SQL without any results returned. The `ExecuteReader()` method executes SQL
queries in conjunction with the `SqlDataReader` class, which allows a forward-only

cursor to iterate through the results. In addition, you began to explore the disconnected portion of ADO.NET with the `SqlDataAdapter` class, using the `Fill()` method to populate `DataSets`.

You also examined the issues of performance with respect to accessing data. In some cases, when the vertical slice is only retrieving data, retrieving data using `DataReaders` makes sense. On the other hand, if the application also needs to update data, data adapters and `DataSets` make more sense.

You also looked at the OLE DB Managed Provider. This is a generic Managed Provider, which operates, for the most part, like the SQL Server Managed Provider class library, but was designed to be used for any data source. Unlike the SQL Server provider, its generic nature prevents it from taking advantage of any optimizations for improved performance.

All the classes discussed in this chapter work together to provide connected access to a given data source. They provide quick access to data and have the capability to insert, update, and delete data. But this is only half of the story. The next chapter delves into the rest of ADO.NET: `DataSets`.

ADO.NET DataSets

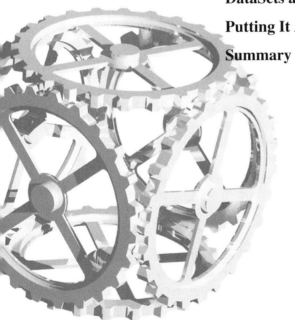

Τhis chapter picks up where the last chapter ended, delving into the powerful features of Microsoft's new disconnected class for managing relational data, the ADO.NET `DataSet`. We'll study how to use this class to provide information over a distributed environment and interact with a data source. Some of the areas we examine are

▶ Creating `DataSets` from scratch

▶ Deriving a class from a `DataSet`, based on a table, view, or stored procedure in a data source

▶ Modifying data within a `DataSet`

▶ Updating a data source using data modified in a `DataSet`

▶ Validating changes in a `DataSet`

▶ Obtaining an XML representation of a `DataSet`

DataSet Class

The most powerful class in the ADO.NET class library is the `DataSet` class. It can be described as a replacement for the old ADO `Recordset` class, but it's much more than a simple replacement. With XML built into the design, developers can interact with the data in a `DataSet` by modifying the XML or by accessing the information directly using `accessor` methods. Its rich class hierarchy makes modeling databases, both real and virtual, quite simple. And its disconnected nature eliminates the need to maintain costly connections and is ideal for transporting content across the Internet.

The `DataSet` class is found in the `System.Data` namespace. The `DataSet` class, along with its constituent classes, comprises the most versatile and powerful classes in the ADO.NET library. It can be thought of as an in-memory database, caching data and relationships.

Figure 13-1 lists the primary classes in the `DataSet` class hierarchy. Using classes for tables, rows, and columns, the `DataSet` class is able to model a database. Relationships can be established between the columns of one table and the columns of another. A `DataSet` can simulate a database without ever interacting with one.

This is an important feature. With the growing use of XML, a `DataSet` can easily represent the hierarchical content of an XML document. `DataSets` were designed with XML in mind and can readily translate data received from a data source into XML.

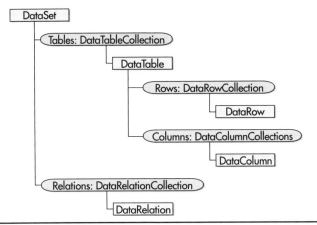

Figure 13-1   *Primary DataSet classes*

Using DataSets

The following sections describe how `DataSets` are typically used in applications.
`DataSets` needn't be based on a data source; they can serve as a data warehouse
for in-memory storage as well. And that's where we'll begin, by examining how to
create a `DataSet` from scratch.

Creating DataSets

Listing 13-1 illustrates how to create a `DataSet` that contains two tables:
`Authors` and `Books`.

Listing 13-1   *Creating a DataSet from Scratch*

```
// create a new DataSet object
m_dataSet = new DataSet("AcmeBooks");

// add a table
m_dataSet.Tables.Add("Authors");

// now add some columns
DataTable dt = m_dataSet.Tables["Authors"];
```

```
dt.Columns.Add("AuthorID", Type.GetType("System.Int32"));
dt.Columns.Add("AuthorName", Type.GetType("System.String"));

// ...and set its primary key
DataColumn [] primaryKeys = new DataColumn[1];
primaryKeys[0] = dt.Columns["AuthorID"];
dt.PrimaryKey = primaryKeys;

// ...and add another table
m_dataSet.Tables.Add("Books");

// ...and some columns to that table
dt = m_dataSet.Tables["Books"];
dt.Columns.Add("BookID", Type.GetType("System.Int32"));
dt.Columns.Add("FK_AuthorID", Type.GetType("System.Int32"));
dt.Columns.Add("Title", Type.GetType("System.String"));
dt.Columns.Add("PublishDate", Type.GetType("System.DateTime"));
dt.Columns.Add("ISBN", Type.GetType("System.String"));

// ...and set its primary key
primaryKeys[0] = dt.Columns["BookID"];
dt.PrimaryKey = primaryKeys;

// now lets relate these two tables
DataColumn parentCol =
m_dataSet.Tables["Authors"].Columns["AuthorID"];
DataColumn childCol =
m_dataSet.Tables["Books"].Columns["FK_AuthorID"];
m_dataSet.Relations.Add("Authors_Books", parentCol, childCol);
```

Let's examine this code. After constructing an instance of the `DataSet` class, the next line creates a new instance of a `DataTable` named `"Authors"`. After the table has been created, we obtain a reference to the `DataTable` and begin adding columns. Using the `DataColumnCollection.Add()` method, we add a column named `"AuthorID"` that is of type `System.Int32`. Next, using the same method, we add a column called `"AuthorName"` that is of type `System.String`.

Now we need to set the primary key for this table. The `DataTable.PrimaryKey` property takes an array of `DataColumns` as its value. Because our primary key consists of only one column, we create an array of columns with a length of one. Then we assign this new column array to the column named `"AuthorID"`. Now, we can assign this array of columns to the `DataTable.PrimaryKey` property and we have established a primary key for this table.

At this point, we begin the process again and add another table to the `DataSet` called `"Books"`. We add a few more columns in the same way we added columns to the other table. Once again, we use an array of columns with a length of one to assign the column `"BookID"` as our primary key for this table. Pay attention to the column named `"FK_AuthorID"`. This column will serve as our foreign key to the `"Authors"` table.

So, now our `DataSet` has two tables, each with its own primary key. As just noted, we want to relate these two tables together. We can do this by creating a `DataRelation` and adding it to the `DataRelationCollection` of the `DataSet`. First, though, we need to identify the columns that will serve to relate these two tables. The parent column is identified as the `"AuthorID"` of the `"Authors"` table and the child column as the `"FK_AuthorID"` of the `"Books"` table. Once these two have been assigned to the `parentCol` and `childCol` variables, we can add the `DataRelation` to the `DataSet`. The `DataRelationCollection.Add()` method takes as parameters both the parent and child column, and, optionally, a name for the relationship. In this case, we have named the relationship `"Authors_Books"`, and have passed in the `parentCol` and `childCol` objects.

Strongly Typed DataSets

As we've seen, we can easily construct a mini-database using the `DataSet` class and creating tables, columns, primary keys, and even foreign keys. This can be a lot of work, however, if we're trying to mimic a large database, or worse, an enterprise-level database.

Fortunately, Visual Studio comes to the rescue. It provides a wizard to walk the developer through the process of generating a class derived from the `DataSet` class, configuring it for a particular result set like a table in the database. These derived `DataSets` are referred to as *strongly typed DataSets.*

Before this wizard can be invoked, we must first have a `SqlConnection` and a `SqlDataAdapter` available on a form. This can be accomplished with just one step—by dragging-and-dropping a table or a view from a data source on to a design surface—as we did in Chapter 12. Alternatively, we could drag-and-drop a `SqlDataAdapter` from the Data tab of the Toolbox window on to the design surface. This action invokes the DataAdapter Configuration Wizard. The wizard walks you step-by-step through the process of defining the data adapter in relation to an element of the database (that is, tables, views, stored procedures, and so forth). As you saw in Chapter 12, dropping these objects on to a Windows form generates the initialization code in the `InitializeComponents()` method hidden in the Windows Form Designer generated code region. If dropped on to a Web form, the initialization code is generated in the same method inside the Web Form Designer generated code region.

NOTE

If the data source isn't Microsoft SQL Server or is a version of SQL Server that's earlier than 7.0, then instances of `OleDbDataAdapter` *and* `OleDbConnection` *must be used instead.*

Once these have been added to a form, you can click the `SqlDataAdapter1` object in the small window below the design surface. Once selected, we display the Properties view for this object by pressing F4. At the bottom of this window is a hyperlink to the Generate DataSet... Wizard. Or, you could right-click the data adapter and select the Generate Dataset... menu item.

In either case, the Generate DataSet dialog box is displayed. Now, we follow the procedures outlined in Chapter 12 to create a new strongly typed `DataSet`. The first step is to select the New option. We type in the class name for our derived `DataSet`. Typically, you want this name to bear some relation to the name of the tables, views, or stored procedures associated with the `SqlDataAdapter`. For this example, let's assume we dragged the `Employee` table from the `Employee` database on to our form.

NOTE

The `Employee` *database was first introduced in Chapter 6.*

As Figure 13-2 shows, we named the `DataSet` "DSEmployee". This becomes the name of the class derived from the base `DataSet` class and the name of the W3C XML Schema file that represents the structure of this table.

On the bottom of the dialog box, we see the name of the database elements (and, in parentheses, the name of the data adapter associated with that database element) we're associating with our strongly typed `DataSet`. If more database elements had been dropped on to our form, we could choose from more options. And, we could select more than one. Finally, a check box is on the bottom of the dialog box. If checked, an instance of this new strongly typed `DataSet` is created and added to the form.

When we click the OK button, the dialog box disappears. We see Visual Studio has created an DSEmployee.xsd schema file in our Solution Explorer window and a `dsEmployee1` object next to the `sqlDataAdapter1` object below the form. And, if we look in the Class View (the tab next to the Solution Explorer tab), we see there's `DSEmployee.cs` class. This class is hidden from the Solution Explorer window.

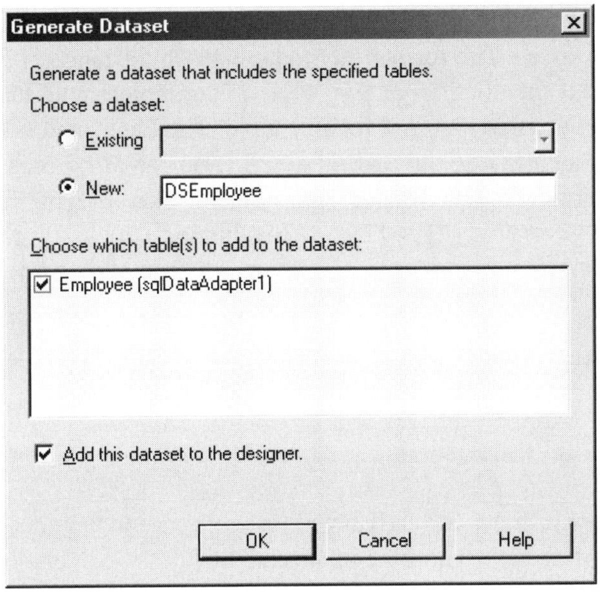

Figure 13-2   *Generating a strongly typed DataSet*

We can now use this `DataSet` with the data adapter to send and retrieve data from our data source. If our `DataSet` had been associated with more than one database element, then we could use it with each data adapter, specifying which `DataTable` in our `DataSet` to use with each `DataAdapter`. We explore `DataTables` more later in this chapter. For now, it's enough to know we can use the `Fill()` and `Update()` methods of the data adapter to get and put information to and from our data source.

And, finally, we can bind this strongly typed `DataSet` to various Windows or Web controls dropped on our form. Binding the `DataSet` to a control automatically populates the control with the information in the `DataSet`. As you see in later chapters, there are only a few properties to set and only a couple lines of code to add to bind a `DataSet` to a control.

There are many added benefits to using strongly typed `DataSets`. For example, we can bind controls to specific `DataTables` or even specific `DataColumns` in the case of text boxes. Each `DataTable` in a strongly typed `DataSet` is actually a class derived from `DataTable`, which provides two special methods: `New<TableName>Row()` and `Add<TableName>Row()`. So if the table's name is `Employees`, then these methods would be `NewEmployeesRow()` and

AddEmployeesRow(). These methods make it easier to manipulate DataRows specific to these classes. The former method creates an instance of a class derived from DataRow but specific to that DataTable, complete with the columns and other schematic properties required for that table. The latter method accepts rows of this class type, adding it to the DataTable. You can also access column values directly using these derived DataRow classes. For example, the following code shows how, given a strongly typed DataSet named DSEmployees, you can create an instance of a derived DataRow using the methods we just described, access the FirstName column, and then add it to the DataTable:

```
DSEmployees.EmployeesRow employeeRow =
dataSet.Employees.NewEmployeesRow();
employeeRow.FirstName = "Michael";
dataSet.Employees.AddEmployeesRow(employeeRow);
```

As this example illustrates, strongly typed DataSets and their derived DataTable and DataRow classes have a number of special methods worth exploring. One group of methods, not shown here, enables developers to quickly and easily check for null values. For each column in a row, there is a complimentary method that returns true if the column's value is null and false otherwise.

Populating DataSets from a Data Source

As you saw in Chapter 12, the Fill() method from the OleDbDataAdapter and SqlDataAdatper classes is used to populate a DataSet from a given data source. To review, the code snippet in Listing 13-2 illustrates how to populate a DataSet with the Employee table in the Employee database. This is the database first introduced in Chapter 6.

Listing 13-2   *Populating a DataSet*

```
private System.Data.SqlClient.SqlConnection sqlConnection1;
private System.Data.SqlClient.SqlDataAdapter sqlDataAdapter1;
private DataSetExercise.DsEmployee dsEmployee1;
...
// initialization code omitted for brevity
...
sqlConnection1.Open();
sqlDataAdapter1.Fill(dsEmployee1,
                     dsEmployee1.Tables[0].ToString());
```

In the example, the dsEmployee1 variable is an instance of a class created using the Generate Dataset… Wizard described earlier. This is derived from the DataSet and defined specifically for the Employee table of the Employee database.

If we want to display the DataSet values in a console window, we could iterate through each of the rows and columns of the DataTable. For example, the snippet in Listing 13-3 illustrates how to access the first and last name of each row in the results.

Listing 13-3   *Selecting Columns from a DataSet*

```
DataTable table = dsEmployee1.Tables[0];
for (int iIndex = 0; iIndex < table.Rows.Count; iIndex++)
{
    DataRow row = table.Rows[iIndex];
    System.Diagnostics.Debug.WriteLine("First Name: " +
                        row["FirstName"] +
                        ", Last Name: " +
                        row["LastName"]);
}
```

Notice rows and columns can be accessed using integer indexes or named values.

If the control is data-ready, then we can assign the DataSource property to the DataSet. This automatically populates the control. For example, if we want to fill a Windows Forms DataGrid control, first we assign the DataSource property of the control to our DataSet. We can do this from the Properties window or using the following code:

```
DataGrid1.DataSource = dsEmployee1;
```

As we discussed, a DataSet can have more than one DataTable, so we need to set the DataMember property to the DataTable we want to display. And we set the DataKey field to the column that serves as the primary key for our table. This last field is optional. Finally, we populate our DataSet using the Fill() method of our data adapter, and then invoke the following call:

```
DataGrid1.DataBind();
```

This binds the associated DataTable of the DataSet to the control, populating it with the values automatically. This is a much easier and more efficient alternative to iterating through the DataSet by hand.

Modifying Data in a DataSet

As you've just seen, `DataSets` are an excellent way for obtaining information from a data source across a distributed environment. But they're also useful for making changes to the data from a remote location. The disconnected nature of the `DataSet`, and its powerful capability to reflect the structure and relationships of its data source, makes it easy for us to change existing data, and to add and delete rows.

A number of different ways exist to modify data. As stated, columns in existing rows can be updated, new rows can be added to the `DataSet`, and rows can be deleted from the `DataSet`. You might be familiar with the way previous versions of ADO kept track of changes made to its Recordsets, updating a batch of changes to a data source all at once. Well, ADO.NET `DataSets` can do this and more. One of the limitations of previous ADO versions was that updating a data source with such modifications had to be done to one table at a time. `DataSets` improve on this giving us the capability to change many tables at once, even tables related through foreign keys. How do they do this? Read on.

Updating a DataSet

Let's begin by updating some columns. To update values in existing rows, the values in the rows are modified. Listing 13-4 demonstrates how this works.

Listing 13-4   *Updating a Column's Value*

```
DataRow row = dsEmployee1.Tables["Employee"].Rows[0];
row["FirstName"] = "Bugs Bunny";
```

The code in Listing 13-4 sets the variable `row` to the first row in the `DataTable` specified by the index `"Employee"`. The first row in the `DataRowCollection` is obtained using the collection's indexer, providing it with a value of `0`. The snippet of code then assigns `"Bugs Bunny"` to the `DataColumn` specified by the index `"FirstName"`. Both the `DataTableCollection` indexer and the `DataRow.Item` property can access `DataTables` and column values, respectively, using a name or a numerical index.

Adding a New Row

To add a new row, the first thing we need to do is to create and populate a new DataRow. While creating a new DataRow is simple enough, we want it to match the schema of the DataTable. We could do this by hand or we could have the DataTable do it for us. Because the latter choice is much simpler, we'll use the NewRow() method of the DataTable to create and initialize our new DataRow.

Once we initialize the new row, we need to fill in any required values. The snippet of code in Listing 13-5 demonstrates how to create a new row, populate it, and add it to the DataSet.

Listing 13-5   *Inserting a New Row*

```
DataRow newRow = dsEmployee1.Tables[0].NewRow();
newRow["FirstName"] = "Daffy";
newRow["LastName"] = "Duck";
newRow["OfficePhone"] = "1234567890";
newRow["OfficeManagerID"] = "1";
newRow["EmployeeID"] = 1000;
dsEmployee1.Tables[0].Rows.Add(newRow);
```

The last line in Listing 13-5 is what actually adds the row to the first DataTable in the DataSet.

Deleting a Row

Deleting a row from a DataSet is quite easy. From the DataRowCollection class, we can either call the Remove() or the RemoveAt() method. The methods are shown in the following:

```
public void Remove(DataRow row);
public void RemoveAt(int index);
```

The first method, Remove(), takes a DataRow as its argument. This is the row deleted from the collection. The other method, RemoveAt(), takes an integer. This is a standard 0-based index into the array of DataRows in the DataRowCollection.

Reviewing the Changes

One feature of the `DataSet` is its capability to identify those rows that have changed in some way. So, after modifying a `DataSet` in one of the ways previously described, a `DataSet` can generate another `DataSet` that contains only the `DataRows` that were modified in some way.

The method, `GetChanges()`, is responsible for creating a `DataSet` that contains the equivalent `DataTables` as the original, except the `DataTables` contain only the `DataRows` that were modified. If no rows were modified for a given `DataTable`, then the `DataRowCollection` is empty for that `DataTable`.

The following code

```
DataSet ds = dsEmployee1.GetChanges();
```

generates a `DataSet` named `ds` that contains any and all changes made to the `DataTables` within the `dsEmployee1` object.

Checking for Errors

`DataSets` provide a convenient way to check for errors. If errors exist, `DataSets` and the subsequent classes provide properties and methods to isolate the errors.

The HasErrors Property

Once the changes have been isolated in a `DataSet` using the `GetChanges()` method, we can check it for errors using the `HasErrors` property. This property returns a Boolean value of `true` if any `DataTable` in the `DataSet` contains an error. The `HasErrors` property is also available on the `DataTable` class. The `DataSet.HasErrors` value is determined by checking each `HasErrors` property on each `DataTable` in the `DataSet`.

Setting and Getting Errors

A number of properties and methods exist that the `DataSet` and its requisite classes can use to get and set error strings. For example, the `DataTable.GetErrors()` method returns an array of `DataRows` that have been assigned an error. The `DataRow.RowError` property returns the error string for a particular `DataRow`. Also, the `DataRow.GetColumnError()` method can return the error string for a particular column.

Setting error strings can be done using the `DataRow.SetColumnError()` method on a column-by-column basis. To set an error string for a given row, use the `DataRow.RowError` property.

The code in Listing 13-6 illustrates how to use some of these properties and methods to display errors in a text box.

Listing 13-6   *Checking for Errors*

```
if (dataSet.HasErrors)
{
    textBox.Text = "";
    foreach(DataTable dt in dataSet.Tables)
    {
        if (dt.HasErrors)
        {
            DataRow [] errorRows = dt.GetErrors();
            for(int iIndex = 0; iIndex < errorRows.Length; iIndex++)
            {
                foreach(DataColumn col in dt.Columns)
                {
                    textBox.Text += col.ColumnName + " " +
                    errorRows[iIndex].GetColumnError(col) + "\n";
                }
            }
        }
    }
}
```

Merging Changes with the Original DataSet

Once the errors are addressed, the corrected `DataSet` can be merged back in with the original. To do this, we use the `DataSet.Merge()` method. A number of overloads exist for this method but, essentially, the rows from the second `DataSet` replace the existing rows of the first `DataSet`.

```
dsEmployee1.Merge(ds);
```

Updating the Data Source with the Changes

Once the `DataSet` has had the changes merged back into its `DataTables`, it's time to update the data source. This can be done using the appropriate data adapter.

In this case, we're using SQL Server 2000, so we'll use the class optimized for this data source, `SqlDataAdapter`. As described in Chapter 12, we use the `Update()` method to send the changes back to the data source. For example,

```
sqlConnection1.Open();
sqlDataAdapter1.Update(dsEmployee1);
```

this code opens a connection to the data source and updates it with the given `DataSet`. This code assumes the `DataSet` was populated using the `SqlDataAdapter.Fill()` method while connected to the same data source.

Accepting or Rejecting the Changes

The `DataSet` class, along with its constituent `DataTable` and `DataRow` classes, provide us with a way of modifying data without validation. For instance, if we have certain restrictions on data like unique constraints or foreign keys, modifying a `DataSet` can be difficult without generating validation events when only part of the data has been entered.

One way around this is to use a combination of the `BeginEdit()` and `AcceptChanges()` methods. The `BeginEdit()` method allows data to be entered without checking any constraints. Once all the information has been updated in the `DataSet`, we can then either accept or reject the changes. Let's start by first determining how to accept changes made to a `DataSet`.

Accept Changes

The `DataSet` hierarchy has several ways to do this. The `DataSet`, `DataTable`, and `DataRow` classes all have an `AcceptChanges()` method. Changes can be accepted by `DataRow`, which apply the changes to just that row. Changes can also be accepted at the `DataTable` level by using the `AcceptChanges()` method to apply the changes to an entire table. When `AcceptChanges()` is invoked on a `DataTable`, `AcceptChanges()` is called for each `DataRow` in the `DataTable`. Or, changes can be applied to an entire `DataSet`. This calls `AcceptChanges()` on each `DataTable` in the `DataSet`, which, in turn, calls `AcceptChanges()` on each of its `DataRows`. Therefore, invoking `DataSet.AcceptChanges()` enables you to affect changes to all the `DataSet`'s subordinate objects with just one call.

Before accepting the changes, we can examine both the original and modified values by passing in `DataRowVersion.Original` or `DataRowVersion.Proposed` for the version argument of the `DataRow.Item` property. Edits to a row can be cancelled by invoking the `DataRow.CancelEdit()` method.

NOTE

The `AcceptChanges()` method should never be invoked on a `DataTable` until after updating the data source with the changes to the `DataSet` using the data adapter `Update()` method.

When `AcceptChanges()` is invoked, whether it be by a `DataSet`, `DataTable`, or `DataRow`, the `DataRow.EndEdit()` method is implicitly invoked, applying all the `DataRow`'s constraints against the changes. Once the changes are accepted, the editing session ends.

Reject Changes

Just as `AcceptChanges()` methods exist for each of the `DataSet`, `DataTable`, and `DataRow` classes, a `RejectChanges()` is also on each of these classes. And, just as the `DataSet.AcceptChanges()` cascaded the `AcceptChanges()` invocation down the class hierarchy, `DataSet.RejectChanges()` causes `RejectChanges()` to cascade down to all the `DataTables` and all the `DataRows`.

When `RejectChanges()` is invoked on a `DataRow`, the `DataRow.CancelEdit()` method is implicitly called. This ends the editing session and rolls back any changes. If the `RowState` was `Deleted` or `Modified`, the row returns to its original state and the `RowState` becomes `Unchanged`. If the `RowState` was `Added`, then the row is removed.

DataSets and XML

`DataSets` were built to interact with XML. `DataSets` come ready with several methods that enable you to read XML from and write XML to `DataSets`. Reading XML into a `DataSet` populates the `DataTables` and `DataRows` with the contents of the XML document. The `DataSet` can infer the schema for the XML and establish the appropriate tables or it can use the inline schema, if available.

`DataSets` can also write XML out, creating XML documents that represent the contents of the `DataSet`. We'll begin there, learning how to retrieve XML from a `DataSet`.

Writing XML out of a DataSet

The easiest way to get XML from a `DataSet` is to use the `GetXml()` method. This returns a string containing an XML representation of the information stored in a `DataSet`. Returning the XML as a string, though, requires a bit of overhead.

Another way to get XML from a `DataSet` that uses less resources is the `WriteXml()` method. This method has several overloads that can be used to output the XML to a file, a `TextWriter`, an `XmlWriter`, or a `Stream`, as the following shows:

```
public void WriteXml(string);
public void WriteXml(Stream);
public void WriteXml(TextWriter);
public void WriteXml(XmlWriter);
public void WriteXml(string, XmlWriteMode);
public void WriteXml(Stream, XmlWriteMode);
public void WriteXml(TextWriter, XmlWriteMode);
public void WriteXml(XmlWriter, XmlWriteMode);
```

Additional overloads send the XML to the same outputs, but also use a second argument: an `XmlWriteMode` value. The values of the `XmlWriteMode` enumeration are detailed in Table 13-1.

Value	Description
DiffGram	Using this value generates the entire `DataSet` as a `DiffGram`, including the original and current values. To create a `DiffGram` containing only changed values, use the `DataSet.GetChanges()` method, and then call `WriteXml()` as a `DiffGram` on the returned `DataSet`. The `DiffGram` can be used with SQL Server because it's a subset of an `UpdateGram`.
IgnoreSchema	This value outputs the contents of a `DataSet` as XML, without an XSD schema. If no data is loaded into the `DataSet`, nothing is written.
WriteSchema	This is the default value. Using this value generates the contents of a `DataSet` as XML with the XSD schema inline. If no data exists, then only the schema is written. If there's no schema, then nothing is written.

Table 13-1   *XMLWriteMode Enumerations*

`DataSets` also provide a way to get the XML Schema for the underlying content of the `DataSet`. The `GetXmlSchema()` method returns a string that contains the XSD Schema representation of the `DataSet`.

Matching the symmetry of the `WriteXml()` and `GetXml()` methods, the `WriteXmlSchema()` method complements the `GetXmlSchema()` method. This method writes out the `DataSet`'s XML Schema to a file, a `Stream`, a `TextWriter`, or an `XmlWriter`. The various overloads are listed here:

```
public void WriteXmlSchema(Stream);
public void WriteXmlSchema(string);
public void WriteXmlSchema(TextWriter);
public void WriteXmlSchema(XmlWriter);
```

Reading XML into a Dataset

The symmetry of the `DataSet` methods continues with the `ReadXml()` method, which provides equal, but opposite, functionality to the `WriteXml()` method. `ReadXml()` is used to read an XML document into a `DataSet`. The XML can be read in from a file, a `Stream`, a `TextReader`, or an `XmlReader`. The method overloads are listed here:

```
public XmlReadMode ReadXml(string);
public XmlReadMode ReadXml(Stream);
public XmlReadMode ReadXml(TextReader);
public XmlReadMode ReadXml(XmlReader);
public XmlReadMode ReadXml(string, XmlReadMode);
public XmlReadMode ReadXml(Stream, XmlReadMode);
public XmlReadMode ReadXml(TextReader, XmlReadMode);
public XmlReadMode ReadXml(XmlReader, XmlReadMode);
```

And, like the `XmlWriteMode` enumeration for the `WriteXml()` method, there's an `XmlReadMode` enumeration for the `ReadXml()` method as we see in Table 13-2.

The `ReadXmlSchema()` method is used to read an XML schema into the `DataSet`. The schema can be read in from a file, a `Stream`, a `TextReader`, or an `XmlReader`. The following shows the overloads:

```
public void ReadXmlSchema(string);
public void ReadXmlSchema(Stream);
public void ReadXmlSchema(TextReader);
public void ReadXmlSchema(XmlReader);
```

Value	Description
Auto	This is the default value. Using this value, the method executes the ReadXml() operation using the most appropriate of these actions: —If the data is a DiffGram, then the method sets the XmlReadMode to DiffGram. —If an existing schema is in the DataSet or if the XML contains an inline schema, then the XmlReadMode ReadSchema value is used. —If the XML doesn't include an inline schema and the DataSet doesn't have an existing schema, then the XmlReadMode value InferSchema is used.
DiffGram	This value is used to read in a DiffGram. The changes are applied to the DataSet, much like the way the Merge() method works, preserving RowState values. The only DiffGrams passed to the ReadXml() method should be those created by the WriteXml() method using WriteXmlMode set to DiffGram. The DiffGram schema must match the schema of the DataSet. If not, the ReadXml() method will fail, throwing an exception.
Fragment	This value reads XML documents containing inline XDR schema fragments. These fragments may be those generated from executing FOR XML statements in SQL Server, as long as the results include inline XDR schema.
IgnoreSchema	This value is used to ignore any inline schema, reading data into the DataSet's existing schema. If some of the data doesn't match this schema, it's ignored (this includes data from different namespaces defined for the DataSet). If the XML document is a DiffGram, then this parameter value has the same functionality as DiffGram.
InferSchema	Passing in this value causes the DataSet to ignore any inline schema, inferring schema from the data instead. The DataSet loads the data. If the DataSet is already using a schema, the current schema is extended by adding columns to the existing tables. Also, new tables are added if they don't already exist. The DataSet will throw an exception if a column already exists and has an incompatible mapping type property.
ReadSchema	This value is used to read any inline schema and loads the data. If the DataSet is already using a schema, new tables may be added, but an exception is thrown if any tables in the inline schema already exist in the DataSet.

Table 13-2   *XmlReadMode Enumeration*

The schema can contain table, relation, and constraint definitions. Usually, this method is invoked just prior to the `ReadXml()` method to establish the schema for the XML document. Once the schema is in place, the data can be read in directly.

Putting It All Together

Now that we've covered the majority of the uses of `DataSets`, let's see them in action. This section describes a simple Web Application that displays certain information about employees assigned to a particular project. The application, `EmployeeNet`, consists of a single page that uses an ASP.NET drop-down control to select from several different projects. Initially the page is blank, but when a project is selected from the drop-down control, the application pulls the appropriate information from the database and renders the page with the new data.

The Web page shown in Figure 13-3 shows the Web page the first time it's displayed. Note the combo box at the bottom of the page is filled with various project names, but the rest of the contents of the page are empty.

Figure 13-3   *Initial EmployeesByProject page*

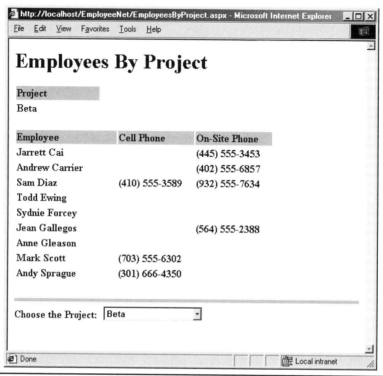

Figure 13-4   *Beta project*

Now, as you can see in Figure 13-4, a project has been selected from the drop-down control and the information for the employees working on the `Beta` project is shown.

One of the beautiful things about ASP.NET is how it manages to make Web pages simpler. We get into this more in later chapters, but let's look at Figure 13-5 to see how a user can select another project, say, project `Alpha`, from the drop-down list.

Once the user selects this project, the submission is automatically posted back to the server and new results are generated, as shown in Figure 13-6.

You learn more about how ASP.NET works its magic later in the book but, for now, let's examine how this Web page works. Listing 13-7 shows the code Microsoft's Visual Studio generates when you drop controls on to the Web page—`EmployeesByProject.aspx`—in this case. Normally, this code is hidden inside a collapsed region, but we're showing it here to give you an idea of the code automatically created when controls are added in Design mode. Most of the essential code exists within the private method `InitializeComponent()` that falls inside this collapsed region and is invoked when the `OnInit()` event handler is called.

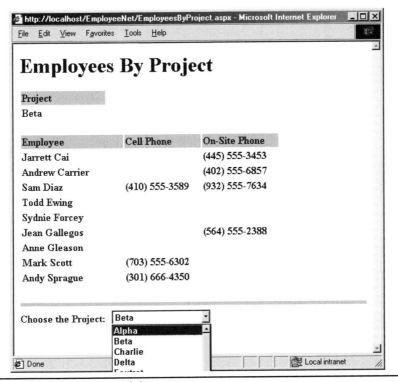

Figure 13-5   *Selecting project Alpha*

The `InitializeComponent()` method initializes the various data and GUI controls dropped on to the Web form designer page. To make the `EmployeesByProject.aspx` page do what we want, we have dropped several data components including a `SqlConnection`, a `SqlCommand`, a `SqlDataAdapter`, and a derived `DataSet`. When we dropped these controls on the page, we were able to set various properties that show up in Listing 13-7. For example, the connection string for the variable `m_sqlConnection` is defined here. The SqlCommand `m_sqlCmdGetProjectList` is assigned the stored procedure it will use to query the list of projects. And even the ASP.NET drop-down control `m_drpChooseProject` is initialized in this section to be data-bound to the `m_projectListDataSet` DataSet.

This latter data member—`m_projectListDataSet`—is an instance of a strongly typed `DataSet` named `ProjectListDataSet`. `ProjectListDataSet` is a `DataSet` class derived from the results of the stored procedure used to return a list of projects. It was generated using the Generate DataSet… command. This command becomes available on the Properties page when focus is placed on the

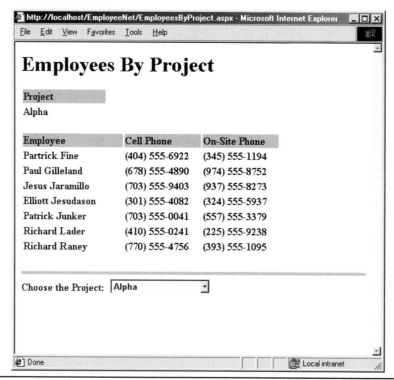

Figure 13-6 *Displaying project Alpha*

SqlDataAdapter m_sqlDAGetProjectList. The stored procedure returns a list of projects and the associated ProjectID for each project name.

Listing 13-7 *Code Generated by Visual Studio*

```
this.m_sqlConnection = new System.Data.SqlClient.SqlConnection();
this.m_sqlDAGetProjectList = new System.Data.SqlClient.SqlDataAdapter();
this.m_sqlCmdGetProjectList = new System.Data.SqlClient.SqlCommand();
this.m_projectListDataSet = new EmployeeNet.ProjectListDataSet();
this.m_sqlDAGetEmployeesByProject =
    new System.Data.SqlClient.SqlDataAdapter();
this.m_sqlCmdGetEmployeesByProject = new System.Data.SqlClient.SqlCommand();
this.m_employeesDataSet = new EmployeeNet.EmployeesDataSet();
((System.ComponentModel.ISupportInitialize)
```

```
    (this.m_projectListDataSet)).BeginInit();
((System.ComponentModel.ISupportInitialize)
    (this.m_employeesDataSet)).BeginInit();
this.m_drpChooseProject.SelectedIndexChanged +=
    new System.EventHandler(this.displayNewProject);
//
// m_sqlConnection
//
this.m_sqlConnection.ConnectionString = "data source=localhost;" +
    "initial catalog=Employee;persist security info=False;" +
    "user id=sa;packet size=4096";
//
// m_sqlDAGetProjectList
//
this.m_sqlDAGetProjectList.SelectCommand = this.m_sqlCmdGetProjectList;
this.m_sqlDAGetProjectList.TableMappings.AddRange(
    new System.Data.Common.DataTableMapping[] {
        new System.Data.Common.DataTableMapping("Table", "ProjectList",
            new System.Data.Common.DataColumnMapping[] {
                new System.Data.Common.DataColumnMapping("ProjectID",
                    "ProjectID"),
                new System.Data.Common.DataColumnMapping("Name", "Name")})});
//
// m_sqlCmdGetProjectList
//
this.m_sqlCmdGetProjectList.CommandText = "[sp_getProjectList]";
this.m_sqlCmdGetProjectList.CommandType =
    System.Data.CommandType.StoredProcedure;
this.m_sqlCmdGetProjectList.Connection = this.m_sqlConnection;
this.m_sqlCmdGetProjectList.Parameters.Add(new
    System.Data.SqlClient.SqlParameter("@RETURN_VALUE",
    System.Data.SqlDbType.Int, 4,
    System.Data.ParameterDirection.ReturnValue, false, ((System.Byte)(10)),
    ((System.Byte)(0)), "", System.Data.DataRowVersion.Current, null));
//
// m_projectListDataSet
//
this.m_projectListDataSet.DataSetName = "ProjectListDataSet";
this.m_projectListDataSet.Locale =
    new System.Globalization.CultureInfo("en-US");
this.m_projectListDataSet.Namespace =
    "http://www.tempuri.org/ProjectListDataSet.xsd";
//
```

```
// m_sqlDAGetEmployeesByProject
//
this.m_sqlDAGetEmployeesByProject.SelectCommand =
    this.m_sqlCmdGetEmployeesByProject;
this.m_sqlDAGetEmployeesByProject.TableMappings.AddRange(new
    System.Data.Common.DataTableMapping[] {
        new System.Data.Common.DataTableMapping("Table", "Employees",
            new System.Data.Common.DataColumnMapping[] {
                new System.Data.Common.DataColumnMapping("FirstName",
                    "FirstName"),
                new System.Data.Common.DataColumnMapping("MiddleInitial",
                    "MiddleInitial"),
                new System.Data.Common.DataColumnMapping("LastName",
                    "LastName"),
                new System.Data.Common.DataColumnMapping("CellPhone",
                    "CellPhone"),
                new System.Data.Common.DataColumnMapping("SitePhone",
                    "SitePhone"),
                new System.Data.Common.DataColumnMapping("ProjectName",
                    "ProjectName")})});
//
// m_sqlCmdGetEmployeesByProject
//
this.m_sqlCmdGetEmployeesByProject.CommandText =
    "[sp_getEmployeesByProject]";
this.m_sqlCmdGetEmployeesByProject.CommandType =
    System.Data.CommandType.StoredProcedure;
this.m_sqlCmdGetEmployeesByProject.Connection = this.m_sqlConnection;
this.m_sqlCmdGetEmployeesByProject.Parameters.Add(new
    System.Data.SqlClient.SqlParameter("@RETURN_VALUE",
    System.Data.SqlDbType.Int, 4,
    System.Data.ParameterDirection.ReturnValue, false, ((System.Byte)(10)),
    ((System.Byte)(0)), "", System.Data.DataRowVersion.Current, null));
this.m_sqlCmdGetEmployeesByProject.Parameters.Add(new
    System.Data.SqlClient.SqlParameter("@ProjectID",
    System.Data.SqlDbType.Int, 4, System.Data.ParameterDirection.Input,
    false, ((System.Byte)(10)), ((System.Byte)(0)), "",
    System.Data.DataRowVersion.Current, null));
//
// m_employeesDataSet
//
```

```
this.m_employeesDataSet.DataSetName = "EmployeesDataSet";
this.m_employeesDataSet.Locale =
    new System.Globalization.CultureInfo("en-US");
this.m_employeesDataSet.Namespace =
"http://www.tempuri.org/EmployeesDataSet.xsd";
this.Load += new System.EventHandler(this.Page_Load);
((System.ComponentModel.ISupportInitialize)
    (this.m_projectListDataSet)).EndInit();
((System.ComponentModel.ISupportInitialize)
    (this.m_employeesDataSet)).EndInit();
```

This is also where event handlers are associated with the controls that raise the events. The `m_drpChooseProjectList` is assigned the handler `displayNewProject()` for the `SelectedIndexChanged` event and the form itself is assigned the `Page_Load()` handler when the `Load` event is raised.

As we said, the first thing the Web page does in the `OnInit()` event handler method is call `InitializeComponent()`, which runs all the code in Listing 13-7. After this returns, an instance of our internal `DataSet`—`m_dataSet`—is created. Then, as you can see in Listing 13-8, the page load event handler, `Page_Load()`, checks to see if the Web page has been loaded previously. If the page hasn't yet been displayed, then it populates the drop-down control.

Listing 13-8   *Populate the Drop-Down Control*

```
if (! this.IsPostBack)
{
    try
    {
        m_sqlDAGetProjectList.Fill(m_projectListDataSet.ProjectList);
        m_drpChooseProject.DataBind();
        renderPage();
    }
    catch (Exception ex)
    {
        System.Diagnostics.Debug.WriteLine(ex.ToString());
    }
}
```

NOTE

The first line of Listing 13-8 is extremely important. It returns true the first time the page is loaded and false each time a Web control posts back to the server. In this example, the drop-down control posts back when the user selects a different project. This generates an event that's handled by the `displayNewProject()` *method, discussed later in Listing 13-11.*

We're using the `m_sqlConnection` and `m_sqlDAGetProjectList` objects that were initialized already in the `InitializeComponents()` method. The `SqlConnection` object—`m_sqlConnection`—was initialized to connect to the `Employee` database and the `SqlDataAdapter` object— `m_sqlDAGetProjectList`—was tied to the SQL stored procedure, `sp_getProjectList`. Notice that because we are using data adapters, we do not need to open or close the connection. The `m_drpChooseProject` is a `DropDownList` control also dropped on to this page. Using a `DataSet` derived from the results of the stored procedure, this control was data-bound to `m_projectListDataSet`, an instance of the `ProjectListDataSet` class. You can see this data-binding in the ASP.NET source code for the `DropDownList` control shown in Listing 13-9.

Listing 13-9 *Data-Binding the Drop-Down Control*

```
<asp:DropDownList
    id="m_drpChooseProject"
    AutoPostBack="true"
    style="Z-INDEX: 101; POSITION: relative"
    runat="server"
    DataSource="<%# m_projectListDataSet %>"
    DataTextField="Name"
    DataValueField="ProjectID"
    DataMember="sp_getProjectList"
    Width="154px"
    Height="22px"
    Font-Bold="True">
</asp:DropDownList>
```

After populating the control, a call is made to our `renderPage()` method. After this routine executes, the page looks as it does in Figure 13-3.

Listing 13-10 details how the page is rendered with the `renderPage()` method. In a nutshell, we use the `System.Xml` and `System.Xml.Xsl` namespaces to read in XML and transform it into HTML using a stylesheet.

Listing 13-10   *Render the Web Page*

```
private void renderPage()
{
    try
    {
        // create an XML Document object
        XmlDocument xmlDoc = new XmlDocument();
        // load it with the XML from the DataSet
        xmlDoc.LoadXml(m_dataSet.GetXml());
        // create an XSL Transform object
        XslTransform xslDoc = new XslTransform();
        // and an XPath Document object to navigate the XML Document
        XPathDocument xPath =
                new XPathDocument(new XmlNodeReader(xmlDoc.DocumentElement));
        // load the XSLT Stylesheet
        xslDoc.Load(this.Server.MapPath("EmployeesByProject.xsl"));
        // transform the XML using the Stylesheet and
        // place the output in an XML Reader object
        XmlReader reader = xslDoc.Transform(xPath, null);
        // re-use the XML Document, and load it with the XML Reader
        xmlDoc.Load(reader);
        // and now place the transformed XML (now HTML)
        // into the output of the Web Page
        m_placeHolder.Controls.Add(new LiteralControl(xmlDoc.OuterXml));
    }
    catch (Exception ex)
    {
        System.Diagnostics.Debug.WriteLine(ex.ToString());
    }
}
```

The xmlDoc object is an XmlDocument that's initialized with the XML string returned from the DataSet. The first time the page is loaded, this string is empty; otherwise, it would contain the XML representation of the data returned from the data source. An XPathNavigator is created and initialized using the xmlDoc object. Specifically, it's created from the beginning of the root element using the DocumentElement property. This allows the XslTransform object— xslDoc—to traverse the XML and transform it using the stylesheet "EmployeesByProject.xsl". The output from this transformation is returned as XML as an instance of the XmlReader class, in this case, the reader object.

The xmlDoc object is then reused by reinitializing it with the new reader object. We then access the XML in the xmlDoc object using the OuterXml property, which is actually the HTML output resulting from the transformation. We use it to create and initialize an instance of a LiteralControl, which is added to our PlaceHolder Web control. Essentially, this places our HTML output on the page exactly where we want it.

When the user selects a different project, the displayNewProject() event handler is called.

Listing 13-11   *Drop-Down Changed Event Handler*

```
private void displayNewProject(object sender, System.EventArgs e)
{
    try
    {
        // obtain the new project ID from the ASP.NET drop down control
        string strProjectID =
        m_drpChooseProject.Items[m_drpChooseProject.SelectedIndex].Value;
        // now get the new project list based off of this new project ID
        m_sqlDAGetEmployeesByProject.SelectCommand.Parameters
            ["@ProjectID"].Value = strProjectID;
        m_sqlDAGetEmployeesByProject.Fill(m_employeesDataSet.Employees);
        renderPage();
    }
    catch (Exception ex)
    {
        System.Diagnostics.Debug.WriteLine(ex.ToString());
    }
}
```

Let's step through the code in Listing 13-11. First, we need to get the ProjectID value from the drop-down control. The control was bound in Design mode to the ProjectID and Name fields from the strongly typed DataSet. Therefore, the control is able to associate the ProjectID value with the textual name of the project the user selected from the drop-down control. Obtaining the unique identifier using the SelectedIndex and Value properties is quite easy. The value is returned as a string. This value is then assigned to the parameter for the stored procedure used by this data adapter. The DataSet is then filled with the results of the query, and then renderPage() is invoked to display the Web page.

Summary

As you've seen, `DataSets` make viewing data in controls on a form easy. They also make it easy to modify data in a distributed environment and to update the data source with the new information. Some of the key principles we discussed are

▶ `DataSets` can be created programmatically to represent data with the benefit of an actual database. This is useful when you want to represent XML data, or some small section of information, without requiring an entire database or connecting to a data source.

▶ Strongly typed `DataSets` can be generated using data adapters to associate the `DataSet` with objects in a data source. These classes are easy to generate using wizards associated with data adapters that have been dropped on to a design surface.

▶ Of course, `DataSets` can be populated from a data source using the `Fill()` method from a data adapter.

▶ Using the `GetChanges()` method, you can easily review only the `DataRows` that have changed within a `DataSet`.

▶ `DataSets` have a robust set of methods for checking for errors, including the `HasErrors()` properties.

▶ Once changes are checked for validity, they can be merged back with the original `DataSet` using the `Merge()` method.

▶ The data source can be updated with all the modifications made to a `DataSet` using the `Update()` method on a data adapter. Typically, the `DataSet` or `DataTable` was first populated using the same data adapter via the `Fill()` method.

▶ Changes can be accepted or rejected, based on whether they validate against the constraints defined under the `DataSet`.

▶ `DataSets` were designed from the outset with XML in mind. Therefore, exchanging information between XML and `DataSets` is easy. The `GetXml()` and `WriteXml()` methods generate XML from the contents of a `DataSet`. And the `ReadXml()` method populates a `DataSet` from an XML document. `DataSets` can also return an XML schema using either the `GetXmlSchema()` and `WriteXmlSchema()` methods. And, XML schemas can be used to establish `DataTables`, `DataRelations`, and other constraints using the `ReadXmlSchema()` method.

.NET Services and Applications

OBJECTIVES

▶ Explore how to build robust, scalable, and secure Web services using ASP.NET, and learn how to consume a Web service in ASP.NET applications.

▶ Provide an overview of building Web Applications with ASP.NET, and write a sample Web Application that uses events and delegates.

▶ Discuss the programming model for ASP.NET server controls, and learn how to build and use Custom controls and User controls.

▶ Learn how to design and build Windows Forms applications that use DataSets, Custom controls, and User controls.

▶ Learn how Windows Forms applications interface with Web services, including Java Web services.

ASP.NET Web Services

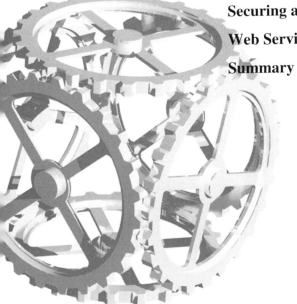

Thus chapter focuses on ASP.NET Web services. It examines how to build ASP.NET Web services and how to make them secure. You learned in Chapter 8 that Web services are powerful mechanisms that provide application services across distributed environments. In that chapter, you also learned Web services are programmable interfaces that use standard Web protocols. Built on top of the universally accepted and established HTTP and XML protocols, Web services can be implemented on a wide array of platforms, providing a never-before-seen interoperable environment. COM+ applications can call J2EE Web services and Java applications can invoke Web services built with Microsoft's .NET platform. Any combination is possible.

The caller, or Web service client, is completely unconcerned with the implementation of the service, becoming language- and platform-agnostic. Instead, the consumer of the Web service only needs to know how to invoke the call, what parameters to send, and what to expect in return. As you learned in Chapter 8, Web services provide this information to a client using an XML file, the Web Services Description Language (WSDL). This file describes the interfaces for Web services, giving the client application the vital information it needs to invoke the Web service methods or Web methods. Figure 14-1 shows a client application metaphorically peeking over a wall into a Web service. The periscope represents the WSDL, while the wall represents the boundary that prevents the client from looking inside. Clearly, from the outside, Web services are black boxes—their Web methods are the only way to interact with them—and the WSDL is the instruction manual. This is crucial because it changes the way we think about how to design and encode our business layers as Web services. This is discussed in the section "Web Service Design."

Another representation of client interaction with Web services is depicted in Figure 14-2. The wall is again the boundary that prevents consumers of the Web

Figure 14-1   *Client peeking at a Web service*

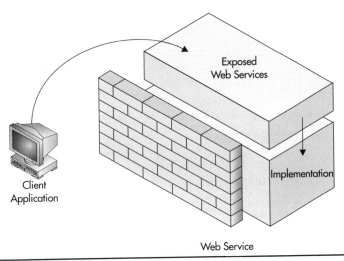

Web Service

Figure 14-2   *Abstraction from a Web service*

service from discerning any information about how it was designed and implemented. The consumer is ignorant of the operating system (OS), the language, and even of what objects were used to build the Web service. This is important because by ignoring compatibility, developers can concentrate on designing and building the actual service.

The diagram provides a simple overview of how client applications interact with Web services. Web services provide loosely coupled, self-describing interfaces. The loose coupling abstracts the implementation. As long as the service adheres to the interface contract, both the client and the server can communicate. And the self-describing information contained in the WSDL enables clients to determine how to use the services at design time or even at run time.

Microsoft, IBM, and other companies have pioneered the Simple Object Access Protocol (SOAP) 1.1 specification. *SOAP* is an implementation of XML that allows messages to be sent across protocols, such as HTTP. Web services use SOAP to send RPC-like messages to invoke application services across a network.

Web services are certainly revolutionary. They make possible communication and information exchange between applications of all types, across all types of boundaries. But when built entirely by hand, Web services require a lot of work. WSDL must be generated for a service and either provided directly to the clients or advertised in Universal Description, Discovery, and Integration (UDDI). SOAP handlers must be crafted for both the client and the server applications. SOAP calls must be processed properly, so the appropriate objects are instantiated, the right methods are called, and the return values—if any—are returned to the caller in a new SOAP message.

If only they were easy to build. With Microsoft ASP.NET, they aren't only easy to build, they're also fun.

ASP.NET Web Services

ASP.NET, along with Visual Studio, simplifies the task of creating Web services because much of the difficult infrastructure and plumbing for the Web service exists already as part of the .NET Framework. This is the real advantage to building a Web service with .NET.

What's left for developers to build is the actual Web service. Because you don't have to implement the SOAP handlers or write the time-consuming WSDL for your service, you can focus on what's important: the actual application.

It's important to note that .NET is highly flexible and extensible. For example, the framework comes with existing SOAP handlers, but like everything else in the framework, these are classes that can be extended to provide additional functionality. So, while .NET makes building Web services simple and quick, it doesn't preclude building sophisticated services that add different or new functionality into the basic Web service plumbing.

Building a Web Service with .NET

So how do you build a .NET Web service? Let's begin by creating a new project with Visual Studio. Your Web service will center around football stats. In this example, your database will be fed player statistics from an imaginary source. The purpose of the service is to present these statistics to service clients, based on query parameters. For example, a client could request the stats for all the quarterbacks.

From the New Project wizard, choose the ASP.NET Web Service template. As shown in Figure 14-3, the Web service is named "FootballStats". When you click OK in this dialog box, a Web Application is created under Microsoft's Internet Information Server (IIS) and a new project is created for Visual Studio.

NOTE

Typically, Web Applications are created under the directory path C:\Inetpub\wwwroot, which equates to http://localhost. This is where Visual Studio places its project files and source for the Web service. However, Visual Studio has many options, which include setting it to create projects in different locations.

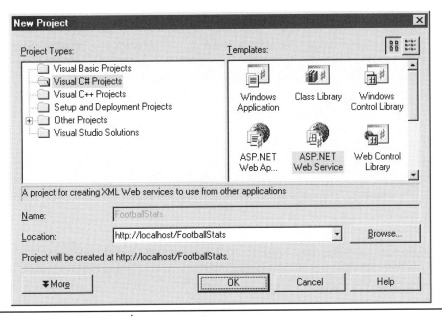

Figure 14-3 *Creating a Web service project*

How .NET Organizes Web Services into Classes

Let's examine the files Visual Studio has created for this project. First, it created
an empty Web service page named "Service1.asmx".This is our Web service for this
project. You can add more Web services but, for now, use this one. Microsoft .NET
maps each Web service that a project exposes to an individual Web service class. Each
Web service class exposes zero or more Web methods. *Web methods* are exactly like
regular class methods or properties except they're designated as Web service methods
and are, thus, Web-callable. Both Web service classes and Web service methods use
compiler attributes, `WebService` and `WebMethod`, respectively, to indicate their
special status (these attributes are discussed in a moment). ASP.NET Web service
projects can contain more than one Web service classes, and thus, can expose more
than one Web service. These Web services are grouped together under one URL where
they're physically located on the Web server. The Web services in a given ASP.NET
Web service project are uniquely identified by providing them with their own
namespace. The namespace, assigned using a property of the `WebService` attribute,
typically consists of the URL, plus a unique name for the individual Web service.

NOTE

ASP.NET Web service pages have the extension .asmx. This extension has no special meaning. ASP.NET Web Forms have the extension .aspx, which differentiates them from the older ASP pages. In both cases, the pages can use Code Behind for the actual source code. These files are given the extensions .asmx.cs and .aspx.cs, respectively. Of course, if you use a language other than C#, say, VB.NET, then the extensions would be .asmx.vb and .aspx.vb.

Now, back to your first Web service class. To make it more meaningful, let's rename it to `PlayerStats`. Do this by right-clicking the file in Solution Explorer and selecting the Rename menu item. You rename the file to PlayerStats.asmx, but this doesn't affect the class name. Then, you right-click the file again but, this time, select View Code to see the C# Code Behind for this page. Next, simply search and replace `Service1` with `PlayerStats` to rename the class.

Right now, if you were to build this Web service, it would do nothing. You exposed a Web service, but it has no methods. So, now it's time to add your first function to your Web service. If you look at the source code, you see some code that was generated when Visual Studio created the project. This code is commented out, but it describes how to expose a Web service method.

WebService and WebMethod Attributes

The main thing to notice is the method attribute `[WebMethod]` on the line above the method declaration. This attribute tells the compiler this method is to be treated as an exposed Web service method. Methods and properties with this attribute can receive and process SOAP messages. If they return any values, they're wrapped up as SOAP messages as well. Again, all this serialization and deserialization of SOAP messages is handled by ASP.NET.

NOTE

Attributes are specified using the [and] characters in C# and are positioned on the line above the class, property, or method. VB.NET uses the < and > characters to signify attributes and places the attributes on the same line.

One other attribute we'll use is the following, placed just above the class declaration:

```
[WebService(Namespace="http://someurl.net/FootballStats/PlayerStats")]
public class PlayerStats : System.Web.Services.WebService
```

This serves to specify a namespace for the Web service. Each Web service should have its own unique namespace, so clients can differentiate between them on the Web. If we were to add another Web service to this application, say, TeamStats.asmx, then we would use the following namespace attribute:

```
[WebService(Namespace="http://someurl.net/FootballStats/TeamStats")]
```

C# WebService Attribute Syntax

If we were using VB.NET, instead of C#, we would specify the attribute this way:

```
<WebService(Namespace:="http://someurl.net/FootballStats/TeamStats")>
Public Class TeamStats
```

VB.NET WebService Attribute Syntax

NOTE

Several other attributes can be applied to ASP.NET classes, properties, and methods that can affect compilation, but they aren't discussed here because they don't refer to Web services.

Finally, we could add a description to this Web service class using another property of the attribute, like so:

```
[WebService(Namespace="http://someurl.net/FootballStats/PlayerStats",
Description="Returns football players' statistics for the 2000 season")]
public class PlayerStats : System.Web.Services.WebService
```

If we remove the commented code from our service and add the following method from Listing 14-1, we have our first Web service method.

Listing 14-1   *Our First Web Service Method*

```
/// <summary>
/// Returns an XML string containing the stats of football players
/// for a particular position from last season
/// </summary>
/// <param name="position">
/// This parameter is the integer value that specifies the desired position
/// </param>
/// <returns>
/// Returns an XML string containing the player's statistics
/// </returns>
[WebMethod]
public string getPlayerStats(int position)
{
    return "<root/>";
}
```

WebService Attribute

You've seen that .NET Web services make use of two attributes. While not required, the `WebService` attribute has some useful properties. But, first, let's discuss attribute-property syntax. When specifying a property, the proper syntax for C# is

```
[AttributeName (PropertyName="value")]
```

while the syntax for VB.NET is

```
<AttributeName (PropertyName:="value")>
```

Remember, VB.NET attributes are inline, while C# attributes are placed on the previous line.

The `WebService` attribute applies to the Web service class, but doesn't make the methods callable. Instead, it helps to document the Web service, providing information for the Web service page that ASP.NET generates and the WSDL. The `WebService` attribute has three possible properties. Table 14-1 describes these properties.

WebMethod Attribute

Returning to the `WebMethod` attribute, you can specify several values. Table 14-2 lists the different properties for the `WebMethod` attribute and their meanings.

Property	Description
Description	The string used here describes the entire Web service. It shows up in the Web page ASP.NET generates when a user browses against the Web service directly. It's also added to the WSDL.
Name	This property can be used to assign a name for the Web service in the WSDL. The string used here is assigned to the `name` attribute of the `service` element in the WSDL.
Namespace	This property assigns a unique namespace to the Web service. As you've seen, this ensures the Web methods exposed by the Web service are unique. By default, the namespace is `http://tempuri.org`.

Table 14-1   *WebService Attribute Properties*

Running the Web Service

For now, the code in Listing 14-1 returns a hard-coded XML string of `<root/>`. This will change once you hook this service up to the database. But, if you build and run this application, you see the page ASP.NET automatically generates for you in Figure 14-4.

If you click the Service Description hyperlink, you're given the WSDL for this Web service. Listing 14-2 has the complete WSDL description.

Property	Description
BufferResponse	This allows the developer to control how large responses are sent back to the caller. If a method is returning a large amount of data, sometimes it's more optimal to return the data as the Web service receives it, rather than waiting for the entire response. Possible values are `true` and `false`. By default, this is set to `true` to buffer the entire response.
CacheDuration	This property allows a method to cache the return value for a specific duration. Rather than obtaining the return value(s) each time a request is made, this property instructs the method to cache the results, optimizing the performance. This is of great value when the Web method is obtaining the same data from a database each time.
Description	This property can be used to provide a description of the Web method. The string used to describe the method shows up in the page that ASP.NET generates automatically when a user visits the Web service directly. The string is also used when generating the WSDL for the Web service.
EnableSession	This turns Session State on or off. Possible values are `true` and `false`. Using Session State requires additional overhead. Session State violates the concept of Web services to some degree because Web services are intended to be stateless. Use this with care. Because Session State is persisted using cookies, it's available only when the SOAP protocol uses HTTP. This is disabled by default.
MessageName	Used to provide an alias to a given Web method. This is useful if two Web methods in a class share the same name, as in the case of overloading a method. This property can provide different public Web method names to these routines, differentiating them for the consumer of the Web service.

Table 14-2   *WebMethod Properties*

Property	Description
TransactionOption	Transactions can only begin in a Web service. Transactions can't flow into Web services that were begun by another application. Several options exist for this property: —**Disabled** Automatic transactions can't be controlled on this Web method. —**NotSupported** This method won't run within the scope of a transaction. —**Supported** The method will run in the scope of an existing transaction. If one doesn't exist, it will execute without one. —**Required** This method requires a transaction. If a transaction doesn't exist, it will create one. This is the default. —**RequiresNew** This method will always create a new transaction each time it's executed. When this property is used, `SetAbort()` and `SetComplete()` aren't required. If no exceptions are thrown, `SetComplete()` is called automatically. Otherwise, `SetAbort()` is called. These two methods are part of the `ContextUtil` class, in the `System.EnterpriseServices` namespace.

Table 14-2   *WebMethod Properties* (continued)

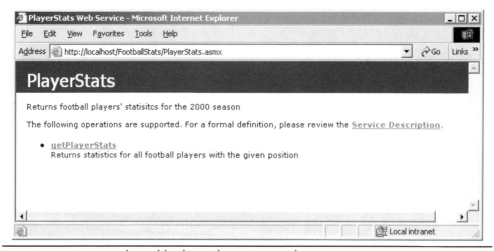

Figure 14-4   *Running the stubbed-out PlayerStats Web service*

Listing 14-2   *PlayerStats WSDL*

```
<?xml version="1.0" encoding="UTF-8"?>
<definitions xmlns:http="http://schemas.xmlsoap.org/wsdl/http/"
xmlns:soap="http://schemas.xmlsoap.org/wsdl/soap/"
xmlns:s="http://www.w3.org/2001/XMLSchema"
xmlns:s0="http://someurl.net/FootballStats/PlayerStats"
xmlns:soapenc="http://schemas.xmlsoap.org/soap/encoding/"
xmlns:tm="http://microsoft.com/wsdl/mime/textMatching/"
xmlns:mime="http://schemas.xmlsoap.org/wsdl/mime/"
targetNamespace="http://someurl.net/FootballStats/PlayerStats"
xmlns="http://schemas.xmlsoap.org/wsdl/">
  <types>
    <s:schema elementFormDefault="qualified"
      targetNamespace="http://someurl.net/FootballStats/PlayerStats">
      <s:element name="getPlayerStats">
        <s:complexType>
          <s:sequence>
            <s:element minOccurs="1" maxOccurs="1" name="position"
              type="s:int"/>
          </s:sequence>
        </s:complexType>
      </s:element>
      <s:element name="getPlayerStatsResponse">
        <s:complexType>
          <s:sequence>
            <s:element minOccurs="0" maxOccurs="1"
              name="getPlayerStatsResult" type="s:string"/>
          </s:sequence>
        </s:complexType>
      </s:element>
      <s:element name="string" nillable="true" type="s:string"/>
    </s:schema>
  </types>
  <message name="getPlayerStatsSoapIn">
    <part name="parameters" element="s0:getPlayerStats"/>
  </message>
  <message name="getPlayerStatsSoapOut">
    <part name="parameters" element="s0:getPlayerStatsResponse"/>
  </message>
  <message name="getPlayerStatsHttpGetIn">
    <part name="position" type="s:string"/>
```

```
    </message>
    <message name="getPlayerStatsHttpGetOut">
      <part name="Body" element="s0:string"/>
    </message>
    <message name="getPlayerStatsHttpPostIn">
      <part name="position" type="s:string"/>
    </message>
    <message name="getPlayerStatsHttpPostOut">
      <part name="Body" element="s0:string"/>
    </message>
    <portType name="PlayerStatsSoap">
      <operation name="getPlayerStats">
        <input message="s0:getPlayerStatsSoapIn"/>
        <output message="s0:getPlayerStatsSoapOut"/>
      </operation>
    </portType>
    <portType name="PlayerStatsHttpGet">
      <operation name="getPlayerStats">
        <input message="s0:getPlayerStatsHttpGetIn"/>
        <output message="s0:getPlayerStatsHttpGetOut"/>
      </operation>
    </portType>
    <portType name="PlayerStatsHttpPost">
      <operation name="getPlayerStats">
        <input message="s0:getPlayerStatsHttpPostIn"/>
        <output message="s0:getPlayerStatsHttpPostOut"/>
      </operation>
    </portType>
    <binding name="PlayerStatsSoap" type="s0:PlayerStatsSoap">
      <soap:binding transport="http://schemas.xmlsoap.org/soap/http"
        style="document"/>
      <operation name="getPlayerStats">
        <soap:operation
          soapAction=
            "http://someurl.net/FootballStats/PlayerStats/getPlayerStats"
          style="document"/>
        <input>
          <soap:body use="literal"/>
        </input>
        <output>
          <soap:body use="literal"/>
        </output>
      </operation>
```

```xml
    </binding>
    <binding name="PlayerStatsHttpGet" type="s0:PlayerStatsHttpGet">
      <http:binding verb="GET"/>
      <operation name="getPlayerStats">
        <http:operation location="/getPlayerStats"/>
        <input>
          <http:urlEncoded/>
        </input>
        <output>
          <mime:mimeXml part="Body"/>
        </output>
      </operation>
    </binding>
    <binding name="PlayerStatsHttpPost" type="s0:PlayerStatsHttpPost">
      <http:binding verb="POST"/>
      <operation name="getPlayerStats">
        <http:operation location="/getPlayerStats"/>
        <input>
          <mime:content type="application/x-www-form-urlencoded"/>
        </input>
        <output>
          <mime:mimeXml part="Body"/>
        </output>
      </operation>
    </binding>
    <service name="PlayerStats">
      <documentation>Returns football players' statistics for the 2000
          season</documentation>
      <port name="PlayerStatsSoap" binding="s0:PlayerStatsSoap">
        <soap:address
          location="http://localhost/FootballStats/PlayerStats.asmx"/>
      </port>
      <port name="PlayerStatsHttpGet" binding="s0:PlayerStatsHttpGet">
        <http:address
          location="http://localhost/FootballStats/PlayerStats.asmx"/>
      </port>
      <port name="PlayerStatsHttpPost" binding="s0:PlayerStatsHttpPost">
        <http:address
          location="http://localhost/FootballStats/PlayerStats.asmx"/>
      </port>
    </service>
</definitions>
```

This is what the client's SOAP handler uses to determine how to bundle up requests to this Web service and what to expect in return. It also tells the client where to find the Web service. In this case, the Web service is simple: it requires an integer and returns a string. Despite the simplicity of the call, the WSDL contains considerable information.

Yet, even with all this information, the WSDL doesn't define the contents of the string in any way. Nothing in the WSDL defines the contents of the returned string as XML or provides the XML Schema for the string. If the client and the Web service are developed together, and they share an XML Schema, this isn't a problem. If this is a public Web service, however, it might be beneficial to specify you're returning an XML string, and provide the XML Schema. We'll return to this shortly.

First, let's see what happens when you invoke our Web service, `getPlayerStats`. When you click this hyperlink from your original page, you see the results shown in Figure 14-5.

This page contains a lot of information. First, it provides a field to enter the parameter for this Web service and a button to invoke it. Second, it lists samples

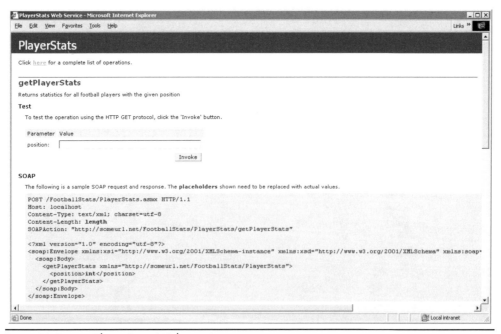

Figure 14-5   *getPlayerStats Web service*

of SOAP messages that could be used to invoke this Web service, if the client must build its SOAP messages by hand. Third, it shows examples of `HTTP GET` and `HTTP POST` requests and responses, which demonstrate how a browser can be used to access the service, letting it do the work of bundling and unbundling the SOAP messages. This is informative for clients using a public Web service, who don't have the advantage of a development environment like Visual Studio for .NET.

Let's see what happens when we provide the service with an integer and click the Invoke button. As you see in Figure 14-6, you get back some XML that contains your string value of `<DSPlayerStats/>`.

Providing Data Access to a Web Service

As Figure 14-6 clearly shows, the `getPlayerStats` Web service, in its current state, isn't useful. To make it provide some real information, hook it up to your database. The SQL to generate the tables, along with some sample data, is provided on the Web at **www.osborne.com**.

Once the database is created and the sample data imported, we're ready to add our stored procedure. This procedure, shown in Listing 14-3, will retrieve player stats based on the given position. Using Visual Studio .NET, you can use the IDE to create and edit your stored procedures. You can even debug them, stepping through them, line-by-line.

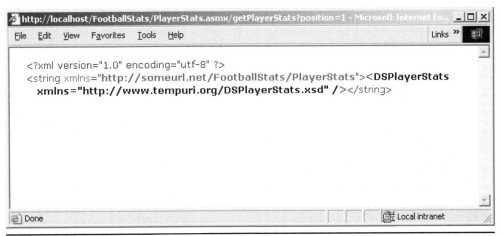

Figure 14-6 *getPlayerStats results*

Listing 14-3   *sp_getPlayersByPosition Stored Procedure*

```
CREATE PROCEDURE sp_getPlayersByPosition(@PositionID int) AS
BEGIN
    SELECT
        Players.PlayerID,
        FirstName,
        LastName,
        Teams.TeamName,
        GamesPlayed,
        PassingCompletions,
        PassingAttempts,
        PassingYards,
        PassingTouchdowns,
        Interceptions,
        Carries,
        RushingYards,
        RushingTouchdowns,
        Receptions,
        ReceptionYards,
        ReceptionTouchdowns,
        TDReturn,
        2PointConversion,
        Fumbles
    FROM Players WITH (NOLOCK)
    INNER JOIN Teams ON Teams.TeamID = Players.TeamID
    WHERE Players.PositionID = @PositionID
ORDER BY PassingYards DESC
END
```

Now, the easy part. All you need to do is create a `SqlDataAdapter` that's configured to use this particular stored procedure. You do this as described in Chapter 13. You add a connection to the database using the Server Explorer, locate the `Players` table, and then drag-and-drop it on to the PlayerStats.asmx page (sometimes referred to as a *surface*) in design mode. This creates the now-familiar `sqlConnection1` and `sqlDataAdapter1` objects on the page. If you had dragged-and-dropped the stored procedure, you would have created a `SqlCommand` object, which doesn't let you generate a strongly typed `DataSet`. Rename the two objects on your page to `m_sqlConnection` and `m_sqlDAPlayerStats`.

The next step is to configure the `m_sqlDAPlayerStats` object to use the stored procedure. You can right-click this object and select the Configure Data

Adapter… menu item or you can look in the Properties window and click the Configure Data Adapter… hyperlink. Either way, the Data Adapter Configuration Wizard dialog box is displayed. You step through this wizard, accepting the given connection, and then choose to use existing stored procedures. The next step enables you to pick stored procedures for each of the four types of `SqlCommands` available within a `SqlDataAdapter`. In this case, you're only interested in selecting values from the database, not in inserting, updating, or deleting anything. Therefore, you select the `sp_getPlayersByPosition` stored procedure, and leave the other drop-downs blank. You click Finish and you have configured your data adapter.

Before you generate your `DataSet`, make sure you appropriately name some properties in your instances of the `SqlDataDapter`. Begin by examining the Properties window for `m_sqlDAPlayerStats`, and then expand the `SelectCommand` property and modify the `Name` property to `m_sqlCmdPlayersByPosition`. This names the `SqlCommand` member variable used by the `SqlDataAdapter`. Next, click the … in the `TableMappings` property. This brings up the TableMappings dialog box. All you need to do here is change the name of the `DataSet` table from `sp_getPlayersByPosition` to `PlayerStats`. Now, when you generate your strongly typed `DataSet`, you'll have a more appropriately named `DataTable` within your `DataSet`. This is important because the action that generates your `DataSet` also creates inner classes for `DataTables` and `DataRows` that are named based on this value.

Now, you can generate your strongly typed `DataSet`. Again, as you did in Chapter 13, bring up the Generate DataSet dialog box. Make sure the `PlayerStats` table is checked and enter the name `DSPlayerStats` in the text box next to the New radio button. This names the XML Schema file and the C# class based on this value. Finally, make sure the check box to add an instance of this `DataSet` to the designer is *not* checked. Now click OK.

This generates a strongly typed `DataSet` for your Web service. All that's left to do is modify your Web service method to retrieve the data using the data adapter and return the XML string from the `DataSet`. Listing 14-4 shows the new method.

Listing 14-4   *Completed PlayerStats Web Method*

```
[WebMethod]
public string getPlayerStats(int position)
{
    // create a new empty DataSet
    DSPlayerStats dataSet = new DSPlayerStats();
```

```
try
{
    // set the required parameter for the select command's
    // stored procedure using the given value
    m_sqlDAPlayerStats.SelectCommand.Parameters["@PositionID"].Value =
        position;
    // and fill the DataSet
    m_sqlDAPlayerStats.Fill(dataSet.PlayerStats);
}
catch (Exception ex)
{
    System.Diagnostics.Debug.WriteLine(ex.ToString());
}

// return the XML string from the DataSet
return dataSet.GetXml();
}
```

The code to fill the `Dataset` is simple enough. Set the appropriate parameter of the `SqlCommand`, the one associated with the select command of the data adapter, to the given value, and then call the data adapter's `Fill()` method. Then, return the `DataSet` as an XML string using the `GetXml()` method.

NOTE

You needn't explicitly open and close your `SqlConnection` when you use data adapters. These classes manage the connection for you automatically. If you were using `SqlCommand` objects only, you would need to open and close the connections manually.

Now, when you run the Web service and invoke the `getPlayerStats` Web service method, you see the results in Figure 14-7. There certainly is a lot of information and the browser window doesn't show it all. But, as you can see, you're getting an XML string that contains a significant amount of information. The client application can then choose how to use this data and, perhaps, present it to the user in a more digestible format.

Application-Specific Settings in the web.config File

When you dragged-and-dropped your table on to the Web service, it generated a `SqlConnection` object for you. You used this object intrinsically to connect to your data source. However, sometimes you want to use a different connection string

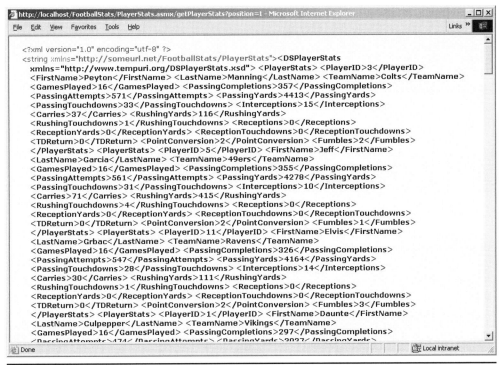

Figure 14-7   *getPlayerStats Web method results as a string*

that relies on a specific user and password combination to protect your data resources. Or, perhaps you simply want the connection string to be configurable. When deploying Web Applications to servers that use distributed database servers, having an easily configurable connection string becomes important.

However, you'll probably want to leave the connection string as it's specified in the `InitializeComponent()` method. This enables you to generate your `DataSets`, and to continue dragging-and-dropping other data elements on to your Web service. If you delete it or edit it in any way, Visual Studio will drop another connection object on to the Web service page with the settings you specified when you created the connection to the data source in the Data Connections element of the Server Explorer window. So, while you might not want to configure this setting during design time, you definitely want to be able to adjust the connection string at run time.

How do you do this? The solution is quite simple. First, you add the following XML lines to your web.config file, placing them before the `system.web` element, but inside the document root element, `configuration`. In the interest of clarity, we have ignored all the other settings in the web.config file. It should now look like this:

```
<configuration>
    <appSettings>
        <add key="ConnectionString"
            value="data source=localhost;initial catalog=FootballStats;
                    user id=sa;password=;packet size=4096"/>
    </appSettings>

    <system.web>
        <!--The settings here have been removed for brevity -->
    </system.web>
</configuration>
```

NOTE

In this example, we used `localhost` *for our data source. In fact, the database server is usually another machine on the local network and can be specified here in place of* `localhost`, *typically using the value specified by the IDE.*

The `appSettings` element enables you to add application-specific name-value pairs in your web.config file. The values can then be retrieved by name during run time. You can add other name-value pairs, using as many `add` elements as you need. This is a powerful feature because now we can configure our Web Applications as needed, without using Microsoft's Registry. Furthermore, because this is a text file, you only need to modify the values. You needn't recompile. You can change the connection string value and save the file. The next time the Web service is instantiated, it will use the new value. And the web.config file is protected from the outside world by ASP.NET, so you needn't worry about Web users poking around the file. You have no registry keys to worry about and no unwanted access. Plus, you have easy configuration. This is powerful and easy.

But now, how do you access these values during run time? First, you need to decide when and where you want to obtain your value. In the case of assigning a value to your connection string, the best place to do this would be in the class constructor. So, you modify the constructor to look like this:

```
public PlayerStats()
{
    //CODEGEN: This call is required by the ASP.NET Web services Designer
    InitializeComponent();
```

```
    // obtain the connection string from the web.config file
    m_sqlConnection.ConnectionString =
        System.Configuration.ConfigurationSettings.AppSettings
        ["ConnectionString"];
}
```

Now, when you run your service, your `SqlConnection` object uses the value in the web.config file for its connection string. You placed this line of code *after* the call to `InitializeComponent()`. Remember, that method still initializes your connection string to the design-time value. You want to leave it that way, but you want to adjust the value during run time to use the web.config value.

Using the web.config file to configure your Web Applications is easy. You can add as many name-value pairs to the file as you need. Once you add the code to obtain these values, they can be changed without having to recompile any of the code—and the file is protected by ASP.NET. And we haven't even discussed the other settings in the file! You learn how to use it to secure your Web Applications in the section "Securing a .NET Web Service."

Error Handling

Notice in Listing 14-4 that we wrapped the code of a Web service method within a generic `try/catch` block. We don't want to allow exceptions to escape unhandled. Normally, you would process the exception, in addition to writing its output to the Visual Studio output window and you can do this in a number of ways. One way is to process the exception, generating a `DataTable` representation of the error. This could be added to the `DataSet` that's returned to the client. This is useful when performing updates that can generate business logic errors. By throwing an exception when the new data violates a business rule, the *error handler* can package the error up in a `DataTable`, tack it on to the `DataSet` it was given, and return the whole thing to the client. This way, the client application is able to show the users what's wrong with the information they entered, and given them a chance to correct the problem.

The code in Listing 14-5 is an XML Schema for a list of errors. You might recognize this from Chapter 3 where XML Schemas were discussed.

Listing 14-5 *ErrorList XML Schema*

```xml
<?xml version="1.0" encoding="UTF-8"?>
<xsd:schema xmlns:xsd="http://www.w3.org/2001/XMLSchema"
    elementFormDefault="qualified" targetNamespace="ErrorList"
    xmlns:err="ErrorList">
    <xsd:element name="DSErrorList">
```

```
        <xsd:complexType>
            <xsd:sequence>
                <xsd:element name="Error" type="err:ErrorType"
                             maxOccurs="unbounded"/>
            </xsd:sequence>
        </xsd:complexType>
    </xsd:element>
    <xsd:complexType name="ErrorType">
        <xsd:sequence>
            <xsd:element name="Number" type="xsd:integer"/>
            <xsd:element name="Message" type="xsd:string"/>
            <xsd:element name="Source" type="xsd:string"/>
            <xsd:sequence minOccurs="0">
                <xsd:element name="Module" type="xsd:string"/>
                <xsd:element name="LineNumber" type="xsd:integer"/>
            </xsd:sequence>
        </xsd:sequence>
        <xsd:attribute name="Severity" use="required">
            <xsd:simpleType>
                <xsd:restriction base="xsd:NMTOKEN">
                    <xsd:enumeration value="info"/>
                    <xsd:enumeration value="warning"/>
                    <xsd:enumeration value="critical"/>
                    <xsd:enumeration value="fatal"/>
                </xsd:restriction>
            </xsd:simpleType>
        </xsd:attribute>
    </xsd:complexType>
</xsd:schema>
```

The schema has been modified a little, but it's essentially the same. Note, this schema was generated by hand, not autogenerated by the IDE. You can use this to generate a strongly typed `DataSet`, named "`DSErrorList`". By right-clicking the view of the schema and selecting the Generate DataSet menu item, you can specify that Visual Studio generate a `DataSet` whenever you save the schema. You can then create an error-handler class with static methods to generate `DataTables` given an exception. Listing 14-6 shows how this is done.

Listing 14-6 *ErrorHandler Class*

```
class BusinessException : Exception {}

public class ErrorHandler
{
    static private string EventLogSource = "ApplicationName";

    enum ErrorSeverities
    {
        Information = 1,
        Warning,
        Critical,
        Fatal
    };

    public static string DataTableName
    {
        get { return "Error"; }
    }

    internal static void writeErrorToLog(Exception ex, int errorNumber)
    {
        // if not a business error, write error to the Application Event Log
        EventLog eventLog = new EventLog();
        eventLog.Source = EventLogSource;
        eventLog.WriteEntry(ex.GetType().Name + ": " + ex.Message +
            "\n\n***\n\nThis error occurred" + ex.StackTrace,
            EventLogEntryType.Error, errorNumber, 0);
    }


    /// <summary>
    ///
    /// </summary>
    /// <param name="ex"></param>
    /// <returns></returns>
    static public DSErrorList.ErrorDataTable handleError(Exception ex,
        DataSet dataSet)
    {
        const int dummyErrorNumber = 1000;

        DSErrorList.ErrorDataTable dataTable = (DSErrorList.ErrorDataTable)
            dataSet.Tables[ErrorHandler.DataTableName];
        if (dataTable == null)
        {
            // create a new table if the one we're given is null
            dataTable = new DSErrorList.ErrorDataTable();
```

```
        // and add it to the DataSet
        dataSet.Tables.Add(dataTable);
    }

    DSErrorList.ErrorRow dataRow = dataTable.NewErrorRow();
    dataRow.Message = ex.Message;
    dataRow.Number = dummyErrorNumber;
    dataRow.LineNumber = 0;
    dataRow.Module = ex.StackTrace;
    dataRow.Source = ex.Source;

    if (typeof(BusinessException) == ex.GetType())
    {
        dataRow.Severity = ErrorSeverities.Business.ToString();
    }
    else
    {

        dataRow.Severity = ErrorSeverities.Critical.ToString();
        writeErrorToLog(ex, dummyErrorNumber);
    }

    dataTable.AddErrorRow(dataRow);
    // log error to output window
    System.Diagnostics.Debug.WriteLine(ex.ToString());

    return dataTable;
    }
}
```

This code first defines a `BusinessException` as a specific type of `Exception`. Your application can then throw these when a business rule is violated. The error handler behaves differently with exceptions of this type, forgoing the part about adding the error to the Event Log. But, in each case, a `DataRow` is generated from the exception and added to a `DataTable`. The `DataTable` is returned to the caller, typically in a `catch` block, like so:

```
catch (Exception ex)
{
    ErrorHandler.handleError(ex, dataSet);
}
```

This allows Web methods to process any exceptions easily and return the errors to the client. If the error was a business rule violation, the client application can then show the user the business error and give them a chance to correct the mistake.

If, on the other hand, the error is a system error—perhaps a connection to the database server is lost—the client application can report a system error has occurred and provide a phone number the user can use to call a help desk. The help desk would then be able to view the error in the Event Viewer log of the OS.

The point to take away here is never allow exceptions to go unhandled in a Web method. Otherwise, you get an ugly SOAP message about unhandled exceptions. A `try`/`catch` block should always surround the code in the Web method. And, furthermore, some sort of error handler should be invoked to process the exceptions.

Exposing XML Schema in the WSDL — Returning DataSets

Earlier, you learned how your Web service method returns a string. This means the WSDL doesn't specify the string is XML and it doesn't provide an XML Schema so clients would know what to expect. A way does exist to have the WSDL provide clients with this information. ASP.NET provides an easy technique to do this through the use of `DataSets`. When a Web service returns a `DataSet`, it serializes the class into its XML form, including the XML Schema for the `DataSet`. So, let's modify our Web service method to look like Listing 14-7.

Listing 14-7   *Modifying the Web Method to Return a DataSet*

```
[WebMethod]
public DSPlayerStats getPlayerStats(int position)
{
    // create a new empty DataSet
    DSPlayerStats dataSet = new DSPlayerStats();

    try
    {
        // set the required parameter for the select command's
        // stored procedure using the given value
        m_sqlDAPlayerStats.SelectCommand.Parameters["@PositionID"].Value =
            position;
        // and fill the DataSet
        m_sqlDAPlayerStats.Fill(dataSet.PlayerStats);
    }
    catch (Exception ex)
    {
        System.Diagnostics.Debug.WriteLine(ex.ToString());
```

```
    }

    // return the DataSet
    return dataSet;
}
```

As you can see, the method remains essentially as it was before. Only two changes occurred. The method declaration has been modified to return your strongly typed `DataSet` instead of a string. And the last line was changed to return the `DataSet` and not the XML representation of the `DataSet`.

When you run the service now and invoke the Web method, you see that you get a much different result. As Figure 14-8 shows, the return value is XML, containing an inline XML Schema, along with the data.

Returning XML instead of a string provides much more value to the client application. It takes advantage of XML Schemas, so the client can explicitly know what to expect and how to extract the information. And, as you see in the next chapter, if the client application was built using .NET, the application can rehydrate the original strongly typed `DataSet`. This adds tremendous value to the developers building the client application.

NOTE

When returning a `DataSet` from a Web service method, you should consider the implications. If it's a public service, revealing so much of the inner workings of your Web service might be a security risk.

Consuming Web Services

Consuming a Web service from a client application that wasn't built with .NET can be a manual process. As you saw in Chapter 8, developers first need to decide whether they're going to use a specific, well-known Web service or if they'll use discovery services to locate the desired service. This is often referred to as looking inside or looking outside the firewall. Web services built within a firewall are typically services built for specific client applications. These client applications are probably on the same network or intranet as the Web service. And, probably both the Web service and client applications were written for the same company or a friendly organization. Such close relationships support a lot of open communication back and forth about the design of the Web service.

Figure 14-8 *getPlayerStats Web method results as XML*

Sometimes, though, the decision is to find a Web service outside the firewall, written by some unknown group of people. The latter can be a bit more complex because it means building a client that responds to an existing Web service contract. To make this work, you need to obtain the WSDL, and then build your SOAP messages based on that specification.

When building a Web client using .NET, both situations become much easier. When a .NET client application consumes a Web service, the .NET Framework creates a proxy for the service, allowing the service to be treated as if it were a local DLL. This makes the code much easier to write because Visual Studio has interpreted the WSDL for you and even uses its IntelliSense to help you with the parameters for the Web service methods. Also, you benefit from compile-time type checking, so your calls to the Web service execute properly the first time. In fact, if both the Web service and the client are built using .NET, you can debug both the client and the Web service in one debug session.

To consume a Web service from a .NET project, select the Add Web Reference… menu item from the Project menu.

NOTE

We can also add Web references by right-clicking the project name in the Solution Explorer window, and then selecting the Add Web Reference… menu item.

This displays the Add Web Reference dialog box. You have the option at this point to click the UDDI Directory link or the Test Microsoft UDDI Directory link. The first link enables you to identify a business that has registered its Web services in a public UDDI directory. The second link lets you test your client application against test Web services on Microsoft's test UDDI directory. If none of these links suit your purpose—perhaps the Web service exists on another server in your local network—you can type the URL to this service in the Address window at the top of the dialog box. If the service will always be located on the same machine as the client, you can replace the server name with `localhost`.

A catch exists, however. In beta releases of Visual Studio .NET, searching for .vsdisco files revealed the Web services for the entire Web server. These files were basically empty XML files used by Visual Studio to generate the proper files needed to consume the Web service. Microsoft changed the default nature of this policy to disallow developers from advertising their services so easily. The reasoning behind this change is the original setting allowed undesirable access to information on the Web servers. The final evolution of these decisions is the dialog box shown in Figure 14-9. It can be restored by altering the file, but the intention is that you create your own .disco files for consumption, or navigate to the Web service directly. The advantage of the .disco files is that they advertise only those services you want exposed.

To create a .disco file, you can write one by hand. Or, you can use the disco.exe tool that comes with Visual Studio .NET to generate one for you. This tool is used from the command line for each Web service to be consumed. If more than one Web service is in a particular Web service project or, in other words, more than one

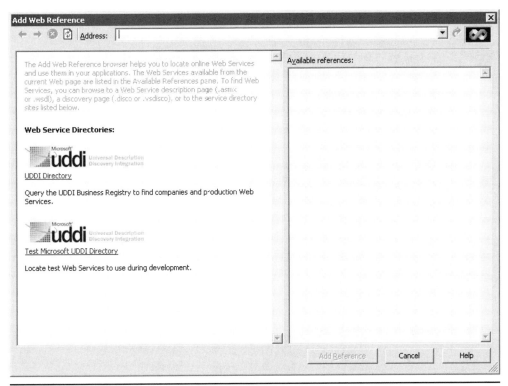

Figure 14-9 *Add Web reference*

Web service in a given namespace, then the disco.exe utility should be run on each service. In general, you invoke the utility with the URL of the Web service with any of the optional arguments placed before the URL. In the case of the `FootballStats` namespace, the disco.exe application would be called from the command line, like so:

```
disco /o:"disco" http://localhost/FootballStats/PlayerStats.asmx
```

The `/o` specifies the output directory, which, in this case, is the subdirectory `"disco"`. The tool generates several files for each Web service. They are the .disco file itself, a .wsdl file, a .discomap file, and any XML Schema files. The schema files are the result of returning strongly typed `DataSets`. If several Web services from a particular namespace are to be referenced, the .disco files can be merged together into one file to reduce complexity. Once you have the final .disco file, you can consume it by using the dialog box in Figure 14-9.

NOTE

To override the default behavior and allow Visual Studio to use .vsdisco files, first open the machine.config file located in the C:\WINNT\Microsoft.NET\Framework\v1.0.3705\CONFIG directory with a simple editor like notepad.exe. Locate the line containing the verb for .vsdisco files that's commented out within the `httpHandlers` *element. Uncomment this line and Visual Studio will allow dynamic discovery. Be aware, however, doing this on a public Web server allows anyone to poke around the site and possibly obtain sensitive information.*

You can use the Add Web Reference dialog box to browse for a particular .disco file. The dialog box displays the contents of the .disco file in the left panel and describes the list of services in the right panel. The Add Reference button is now enabled and you can add the service to your application. When you search your local server for the `FootballStats` Web service you just built, you see the screen as shown in Figure 14-10.

If you know the Web service will *always* remain on the same machine as the client machine, then you have the option of avoiding SOAP altogether and invoking the service directly as a project reference. By right-clicking on the References folder

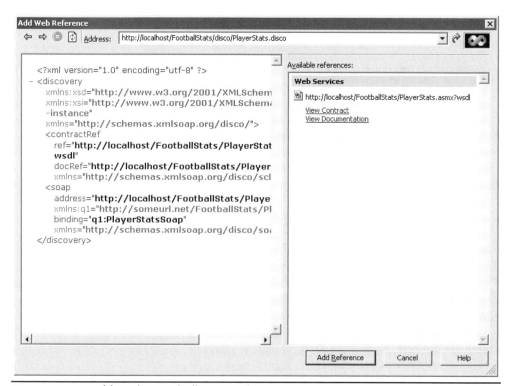

Figure 14-10 *Adding the FootballStats Web service*

in the Solution Explorer, and selecting the Add Reference… menu, you can add a reference to a .NET class library, a COM/COM+ component, or one of your own .NET projects. By selecting this last tab, Projects, you can add a reference to another project in the same solution, or browse for one on the same machine or local network. This is a huge advantage because now the two projects interact as if the Web service really was a local DLL. No SOAP is used at all; instead, it uses straight invocations to the Web service DLL. If you browse for a project reference outside of the solution, you may want to add the project to the solution for simplified debugging.

You can add an existing project to the solution by selecting the Add Project menu item from the File menu, which, in turn, has three child menu items of its own: New Project…, Existing Project…, and Existing Project From Web…. When you choose to create a new project, you use the same dialog box as you would if you were creating a brand new .NET project. Only after you're finished is the new project added to the existing solution. If you select an existing project on the same machine or a project on another machine via a URL, that project is then added to the project solution. You can then edit, compile, and debug that project, along with the original project, without having multiple instances of Visual Studio. This saves a lot of time, especially for projects on remote machines.

Web services, in particular, offer the added advantage of eliminating SOAP when they're added as project references, rather than Web references. The reason they can be added in this way is ASP.NET compiles all the code-behind files for Web Applications and Web services into a single DLL. The .aspx and .asmx files are compiled at run time. In the case of Web services, however, the .asmx files are essentially empty, so there's nothing to compile. Therefore, placing the DLL from a Web service into the bin directory of a Web Application is just like placing the DLL from a class library into the bin directory. You could say that setting a project reference to the Web service equates to using the Web service like a class library. Calls are made directly into the exposed Web methods as if they were public methods on a class.

NOTE

When invoking other Web Applications or services from an existing Web Application, the values and settings in the web.config file of the startup application will override those of the other projects. Therefore, it might be prudent to copy any application settings from other projects in the solution to the startup application's web.config file.

The code is more efficient and less complex, and you avoid the need for SOAP handlers altogether. The Web service can still be used like a Web service, using the SOAP and HTTP protocols. However, the client application that uses it as a project reference doesn't need to use SOAP.

Securing a .NET Web Service

Security is always an in issue for Web Applications. We're all aware of the numerous issues associated with applications built for the Web. When you deploy an application for the Web, suddenly, millions of people have access to your Web site. Most have good intentions. To keep out the few who don't, like the thief scaling the wall in the following illustration, you need to implement some form of security. Although this chapter focuses on Web services, the same issues apply for Web Applications. So, this section applies to both applications and services built for the Web using the .NET Framework.

Web security means many different things to different people and it can often be misinterpreted. The term is normally used as an umbrella that encompasses three issues: encryption of data transmitted between Web client and server, authentication, and authorization. In this section, we focus on authentication and authorization.

First, let's agree on the definitions. *Authentication* refers to the portion of the application that serves as gatekeeper, like the giant hand shown in the next illustration. It determines who the user is that's accessing the Web Application or service, and then either allows or denies that individual access to the site. When a user visits your Web site, there's *always* some form of authentication. This is done through the exchange of credentials, typically, a user ID and password. In open, public Web sites, the authentication is minimal, allowing all users to visit the site through the use of some sort of anonymous user. This is usually the default. But, for secure Web sites, authentication limits who can visit the site, allowing only specific users through and rejecting everyone else.

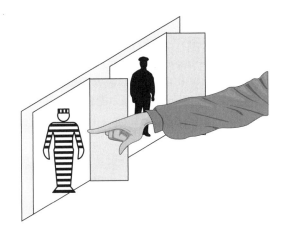

Once through, authorization takes over. Getting access to the site is one thing, but actually viewing and interacting with the site falls under the domain of *authorization*. Here, issues of permissions and roles define what an authenticated user is allowed to do with a particular Web site. Can the users see this menu item? Can they click that button? Are they allowed to navigate from this page to that page? Controlling what they can and can't do is what authorization is all about.

Windows Authentication

ASP.NET has three offerings for handling authentication and authorization: Windows Authentication, Passport Authentication, and ASP.NET's Forms Authentication. The first, *Windows Authentication,* is the familiar security framework that uses existing Windows users and groups to provide access to resources. To use Windows Authentication, NTLM or Clear-Text/Basic Authentication must be enabled through IIS for the given Web site.

Windows Authentication is strictly enforced through the use of standard browser behavior. When a user visits a Web site with either NTLM or ClearText/Basic Authentication enabled, the browser automatically pops up a dialog box, requesting the user's ID and password. While not all clients can or will support NTLM, almost all support ClearText/Basic Authentication. While it's not as sophisticated as the hash algorithm used by NTLM, Basic Authentication encodes the credentials using Base64. Although hidden, they aren't hard to decode. By itself, this form of encryption usually isn't sufficient. Used in conjunction with HTTPS, however, this technique of authentication is more than adequate and is globally accepted.

You can access the credentials of an authenticated user with the `User` property from the `WebService` class. This property returns an instance of the `IPrincipal` interface. This interface has one public method, `IsInRole()`, and one public property, `Identity`. The method takes a string containing the name of a role and returns `true` or `false`, depending on whether the authenticated user belongs to the specified role. The `Identity` property returns an instance of the `IIdentity` interface. This interface has three important public properties:

▶ **AuthenticationType**   This returns the authentication type as a string.

▶ **IsAuthenticated**   This returns true if the user was authenticated.

▶ **Name**   Returns the name of the user as a string.

Other properties and methods obviously hang off the base interfaces. These contain additional information about the user and how they were authenticated. The ones discussed here, though, provide Web service developers with the essential information to determine programmatically how to manage a user's rights and permissions.

Passport Authentication

The *.NET Passport Authentication Service* is Microsoft's distributed authentication service. It's a Web service that uses a previously established set of credentials stored elsewhere to validate visitors. Using a separate and distributed authentication service has its advantages and its disadvantages. It saves time and resources that would normally be spent designing and implementing a similar service, and no need exists to store user information in a database. But it does mean all your application's users must subscribe to this distinct service, registering their user identification password to visit and use your Web site. For smaller, more private applications, this might not be the best route. For public Web sites that attract large numbers of visitors, however, this might be adequate.

Although perhaps only adequate for security purposes, other reasons beyond security actually make the .NET Passport Authentication Service desirable. Essentially, a Web service like this allows a Web Application to join a community of other applications that share a single sign-on. By joining this community, your Web Application is now available to an even larger community of users that have registered with this service. If you're building a public application, such as commerce application, this is a major advantage.

In addition, other user information can be registered with the .NET Passport service. This information, such as gender, address, birth date, and so forth can be shared among all the applications that rely on this service. This allows a community of applications to share key information about a user that would normally take up space on their own databases.

If application security is more important than public access or if reducing the database size isn't critical, then a service like this might not be your first choice. Typically, commerce applications with a large user base would select this form of authentication.

Forms Authentication

Finally, *Forms Authentication* is ASP.NET's internally integrated authorization and authentication framework. Using user-defined users and roles, or even existing users and groups from Windows, developers indicate who can access the site and how. Forms Authentication uses the web.config XML file found in each .NET Web site. This configuration file, though an XML text file, is extremely powerful, and allows a developer to control access to the site by typing a few lines and saving the file. Saving the file causes the Web site to act differently the next time a new user requests a page from the Web site. You saw this earlier when we added application-specific name-value pairs to the file. Attempts to visit pages in the Web site directly are thwarted automatically by redirecting the visitor to a user-defined login page. Once validated, the visitor is redirected back to their desired page.

Of the three forms of security offered by ASP.NET, Forms Authentication is the simplest to implement. It enables you to use an HTML form of your design to request a user's credentials. These credentials can then be validated against any data source, whether it's our own database or a Windows Active Directory. Once properly validated, a cookie is sent to the client and used for subsequent requests.

The web.config File

Each .NET Web site has its own web.config file, which is an XML file used to configure various settings, as well as include user-defined keys. web.config files are hierarchical, that is, the web.config file in the local Web directory overrides the root web.config file.

To use Forms Authentication in a .NET Web Application, replace the existing `authentication` element in the web.config file with the lines of code shown in Listing 14-8.

Listing 14-8   *Implementing Forms Authentication in the web.config File*

```
<configuration>
    <system.web>
```

```
<!--  AUTHENTICATION
      This section sets the authentication policies of the application.
      Possible modes are "Windows", "Forms", "Passport" and "None"
-->
    <authentication mode="Forms">
       <forms name="NameOfApplication" path="/" loginUrl="Login.aspx"
           protection="All" timeout="15"/>
    </authentication>
    <authorization>
       <deny users="?"/>
    </authorization>
    <!-- other settings omitted for brevity -->
  </system.web>
</configuration>
```

Other settings exist inside the system.web element, but this example is meant to highlight the authorization and authentication settings. The first section contains the element authentication. This specifies the type of authentication the site will use. In our example, we specified Forms Authentication. This forces visitors to log in before giving them access to the site. The loginUrl attribute specifies the login page, Login.aspx, in this case. The name attribute provides a name for the cookie created when the user is verified. The path attribute specifies the portion of the Web Application that's protected by the authentication scheme. In this case, the / value specifies the entire Web Application. The protection attribute controls how the cookie is sent: possible values include All, None, Encryption, and Validation. Finally, the timeout attribute is used to measure the amount of time, measured in minutes, between requests before the cookie times out.

Another element, credentials, a child to the authentication element, could also be added here. This element would contain a list of user IDs and passwords. This would serve as a minidatabase of users. Users could be authenticated programmatically with the Authenticate() method from the System.Web.Security.FormsAuthentication class. This class contains static methods called by .NET Web Applications to implement Forms Authentication. The Authenticate() method takes a user ID and a password as parameters, and then compares them against the values listed in the credentials section of the web.config file. It returns true or false, depending on whether it could validate the credentials. The chief problem with this method is we're placing user IDs and passwords in a text file. While remote users and clients can never see this file (.NET protects the web.config file), it does enable developers to see these passwords. You could use .NET's hash algorithms to encrypt the passwords first, and then place the encrypted text in the web.config file.

A more sophisticated approach, however, would be to place these user IDs and passwords in a secure database or use Windows Active Directory. Then, instead of using the `Authenticate()` method to check the web.config file, you would perform your own validation against the database (or Active Directory).

Regardless of how you determine if the credentials are valid, once you're sure they're correct, then you would use the `SetAuthCookie()` method to create the authentication cookie and redirect them to a desired page, like so:

```
System.Web.Security.FormsAuthentication.SetAuthCookie(UserID.Text, false);
Server.Transfer("HomePage.aspx");
```

The second parameter of the `SetAuthCookie()` method indicates you don't want a persistent cookie that lives beyond browser sessions. Alternatively, you could invoke the `RedirectFromLoginPage()` method, which also creates the cookie but, in addition, redirects them back to the original page they tried to visit:

```
System.Web.Security.FormsAuthentication.RedirectFromLoginPage(
    UserID.Text, false);
```

Again, the second parameter here is used to determine whether you want a persistent cookie. This latter technique is useful when a visitor to the site tries to go directly to a specific Web page. After being redirected to the login page and entering valid credentials, the user is directed back to their original page.

NOTE

Using `Server.Transfer(string url)` is much more efficient to direct a user to a specific page. The `Response.Redirect(string url)` method creates more round trips to the client because, first, the server sends an HTTP header back to the client instructing the client browser to request the new URL. Then the client browser responds by requesting the actual URL. `Server.Transfer()` simply stops the execution of the current page and begins a new thread with the new page. A catch exists, however. Be aware that when stopping the execution of a page, .NET forces the thread to abort using the `Thread.Abort()` method. Whenever a thread is terminated in this fashion, a `ThreadAbortException` is thrown. It's very important not to catch these exceptions when you use the `Server.Transfer()` method. The thread needs to see this exception occur to clean itself up. If you catch it and prevent the page's thread from seeing it, then the page never has a chance to clean itself up.

The `authorization` element is used to control who does and who doesn't have access to the Web pages and files. In this case, we're denying specific users access to the Web site. The use of the `?` signifies anonymous access, a fairly typical implementation, which provides access only to valid users and prohibits anonymous users.

Basically, this section contains a list of `allow` and `deny` elements. Each element can contain the attributes described in Table 14-3. The `verbs` attribute is optional, but a `users` attribute or a `roles` attribute must be present. The `users` and `roles` attributes can be used together, however.

The use of `*` for the value of the `users` or `roles` attributes indicates all users or all roles, while using a `?` indicates the anonymous identity. The following snippet shows one way these elements can work together:

```
<authorization>
    <allow verb="POST" users="*"/>
    <allow verb="GET" users="mike"/>
    <deny verb="GET" users="*"/>
</authorization>
```

Here, you specified all users can use the `POST` verb, but only Mike can use `GET`. The rules are sorted out by having the one closest to the top overriding those below it. Thus, if you reverse the last two lines, you would deny everyone, including Mike, the capability to do a `GET`.

Web Service Design

As you saw earlier in the chapter, Web services provide client applications with a contract, the WSDL, which the clients use to invoke Web methods. Other than the WSDL, the consumers of a Web service have no insight into how the service was designed, what language was used to build it, or even on what platform it runs. The use of globally accepted protocols like HTTP make these questions disappear.

Attribute	Description
users	This is a comma-separated list of users that are either granted or denied access to a particular resource. When specifying a user from a specific domain, use this format: `"<domainname>\<username>"`. For example, `"mydomain\john"`.
roles	A comma-separated list of desired roles for this element.
verbs	Defines the HTTP verbs the user can or can't access. For example, `GET`, `POST`, and `HEAD`. This attribute is optional.

Table 14-3 *Allow and Deny Element Attributes*

The only information the client has about the Web service are the exposed Web methods. These Web methods are all a client application has to interact with a Web service. So, in reality, the Web methods represent the entire functionality of a Web service, boiled down to only a few exposed functions. This is interesting because it's a subtle, but important, shift in how we think about designing our business layers or middle tiers as Web services.

Before the prevalence of Web services, middle tiers were built as COM/COM+ components, or even as just DLLs, tightly coupled to the client applications that consumed them. The tight coupling meant joint development, or even collaboration, between the consumers of the middle tier and the developers of the middle tier. This might not be a bad thing, but it forced limitations on the middle tier. When XML appeared on the scene, everyone building business layers began using it in their interfaces to loosen the coupling between client and server. Once the XML interfaces were designed and agreed on, developers of the client applications could begin building their applications and, at the same time, developers of the middle tier could go off and build their components. This was a huge step forward.

NOTE

Using ASP.NET, you can pass strongly typed `DataSets` back and forth between the presentation layer and the Web service business layer. `DataSets` are serialized as XML across Web boundaries, containing both their data and their XML Schema. This enables clients not built with .NET to still interact with the Web service in the same loosely coupled fashion. When built with ASP.NET, however, Web clients have the added advantage of deserializing the XML into the original, strongly typed `DataSet`. The fully functional `DataSet` can then be bound to Web controls and the internal data can be modified more easily.

But consumers of these components were still bound by platform, language, and even the design of the business layers. So when Web services came along and abstracted all of this, it made it possible for the middle tier developers to go off and build their services any way they wanted, just as long as they exposed a formal contract using a standard format: WSDL.

Why is this so important? Because, at times, large-scale object-oriented design (OOD) can be cumbersome and it can even get in the way of designing small, efficient business services. If we want to build a Web service that processes credit card orders over the Web, do we need to have a `CreditCard` class, a `Money` class, and a `Customer` class? Maybe. Maybe not. The implementation isn't important any longer, but the functionality of the Web service is. Instead of making sure your Web service classes follow the OOD of a larger design, we can ask questions of our classes more suited to our smaller purpose:

▶   What information is needed to process a single credit card order?

▶   Does the Web service accept all forms of credit cards?

▶   Does the service report unauthorized credit-card transactions?

The design focus has shifted to what the Web service does, rather than how and who will be using them. Everything else is distilled out and what's left is the real important stuff. In reality, Web services are only functions, exposed to the public via the Web, and organized into meaningful containers, called Web services. This is good because now developers aren't distracted by platform, language, or, most important, how they have to build their Web services. This new focus has two important by-products. First, Web services are organized and designed with specific functionality in mind. And, second, the classes that support them are designed for that specific functionality only, with no intention of supporting any larger purpose.

The first by-product means our services are well organized and efficient. They exist only to expose their Web methods and for no other reason. This single-minded approach provides clarity to the developers. They know exactly what they're building and what they need to fulfill the functionality. For example, if we were to build a simple version of the credit-card Web service, what would it do? Perhaps it would simply accept a credit card order and return an order number. Behind the scenes, it might store the order information in a database, generate a unique order number, and place the order on a message queue to be processed later. But, as far as the exposed functionality, it's only one method, say, `PlaceOrder()`. This Web method takes a customer's order information and returns a unique order number. That's it. That's all there is to our simple Web service. So, with this single function in mind, we go off and design the supporting cast for the Web service—that is, the underlying implementation.

Such clarity when designing the implementation leads to the second by-product. Here, we look inside the Web service itself and see all the classes used to support the exposed functionality. What classes do we design? Do we still use OOD? Of course, OOD will probably always be necessary. We're still designing classes and instantiating objects. But *strict* OOD, the concept of one class for each object modeled in the analysis phase, doesn't have to be used when designing the classes that support Web services.

So, what's so important about not using strict OOD? Let's delve into the credit-card Web service just mentioned. Here, we're discussing the classes that support the Web service, not the Web service class itself. If you want to create a `CustomerOrder` class rather than distinct `Customer` and `Order` classes, we could. This might not conform to strict OOD, but the `CustomerOrder` class would provide you with exactly the information you would need when executing the particular credit card request for a particular customer. Why make it any more complicated than necessary? You have merged two classes into a more meaningful one.

This is perhaps an oversimplified example, but it serves to demonstrate the clarity you can achieve when you wipe away the distractions of building components as part of a larger application. In the past, when we built these components, we might have shared classes with the very client applications that call our business layers. Class reuse is an important and useful principle in software design. But, in the case of Web services, more often than not, it muddies the waters. Our components would be incorporating `Customer` classes, for example, that serve not only the business layer, but the presentation layer as well. In these scenarios, the business layer would be shoehorning its needs in with the needs of the presentation layer, building a class with overloaded purposes. Collaboration and reuse in these situations isn't always a positive.

Web services let you design and code to the beat of your own drum, in your own sand box. You are building black boxes that are beholden only to the interfaces you expose through the WSDL, nothing more. This shift in design focus is powerful, providing you with clarity and freedom. This doesn't mean you can abandon all you know and have learned from years of software design. Instead, it means be smart. Be minimalist. Build small, efficient classes that serve their simple purpose. You needn't worry about some grand design, you don't need to know who will be using your Web service, or how. This freedom isn't an excuse for poor design or obfuscated code. You must remain disciplined and apply the same design principles you've always used. You now have the autonomy to think smaller, and to design your Web services for its own simpler needs. This is a liberating change. Use it well.

Summary

ASP.NET Web services aren't revolutionary. They operate and behave like every other Web service built today. What is amazing about ASP.NET is how easy it makes the process of creating and building Web services. Combined with the ease of accessing data from a data source using ADO.NET, ASP.NET Web services become a breed apart.

In this chapter, you learned how Web services fit into the new world of Web computing. You saw how to build a Web service using ASP.NET. You examined how to add error handling to your Web methods and you delved into Web security.

You also learned about shifts in designing business layers and middle tiers as Web services. The following list summarizes these topics:

▶ ASP.NET enables developers to create Web services more easily because the .NET Framework provides default SOAP handlers for processing the SOAP messages back and forth. ASP.NET also generates the WSDL for the Web service.

▶ ASP.NET organizes Web services into .asmx and .asmx.cs files (or .asmx.vb depending on the programming language).

▶ The `WebMethod` attribute must be applied to a method for it to be exposed on a Web service.

▶ The `WebMethod` attribute has several properties that can be used to control how data is returned, whether session state has been enabled, and the description of the method.

▶ The `WebService` attribute can be applied to a Web service class to name the service uniquely within a namespace.

▶ `DataSets` returned by Web services are serialized into XML that contains enough information to deserialize it back into strongly typed `DataSets` on the client side.

▶ ASP.NET Web services can be referenced as a project from within another .NET project, bypassing SOAP, and calling the Web methods directly.

▶ ASP.NET can use Windows Authentication, a distributed service like Microsoft Passport, or ASP.NET Forms Authentication to secure a Web Application or service.

▶ Designing business layers as Web services enables developers to focus on smaller problem domains, building to specific functionality. This makes the design more focused and alleviates the problem of having to build strict OOD components that serve a larger design.

15

ASP.NET

IN THIS CHAPTER:

ASP.NET Web Pages

Web Page Events

Postbacks

ASP.NET Controls

Summary

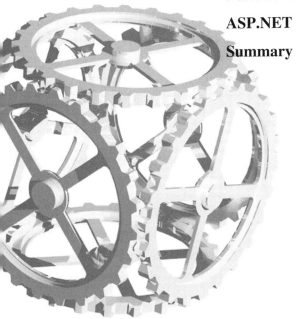

A SP.NET encompasses Web services, as you learned in the last chapter, but it also encompasses Web Applications. ASP.NET has evolved from Microsoft's Application Server Pages (ASP). Under ASP.NET, you can build powerful Web Applications using server-side controls. While you can still use script for the server-side code, developers are more likely to choose more powerful programming languages like C# and VB.NET to develop their pages.

In this chapter, you gain an overview of ASP.NET. You build a Web Application and learn how to use some of the more common server-side controls. We'll consume a Web service and we'll even build our own custom control. There's a lot to cover, so let's begin.

ASP.NET Web Pages

The Web is a strange medium for business applications. Because browsers expect HTML and different browser vendors implement different standards, an unfortunate lowest-common denominator prevails for HTML content. What's more, HTML is best suited for static content, something contradictory to most business needs. But, whatever the reasons, HTML has become the lingua franca of Web browsers.

To support the needs of dynamic content generation and user interaction, businesses have required software platforms to develop client-side and server-side script languages that can be executed for a single Web page. The server-side script generates the HTML for the page and the client-side script aids in user interaction. Eventually, the server-side script evolved into platforms that could also respond to the information a user submitted for a given page. Now, as developers, we can control what is sent to the browser, how the user interacts with the content in the browser, and then what the user sends back to the server.

Similar to ASP.NET Web Service pages, ASP.NET Web pages follow the pattern of code behind the page. An ASP.NET Web page file has the extension .aspx, and the code behind the Web page has the extension .aspx.cs for C#, and .aspx.vb for VB.NET. The .aspx page contains the server-side HTML that provides the design view of the page, while the code behind page—.aspx.cs, for example—contains the code developers write to respond to Web page events.

Web Page Events

When a page is requested by the user, four critical events occur. While we, as developers, might not need to write handlers for each of these events, we'll discuss them here, so you know how to use them if and when you need them. The diagram in Figure 15-1 shows you the order of the events for an ASP.NET Web page: first, the `Init` event; second, the `Load` event; third, an event raised by a Web control; and, fourth, the `Unload` event.

When a page is created by Visual Studio, a handler for the `Init` event is generated automatically in the Web Form Designer generated code region. We examine this region of code later on but, for now, understand an `OnInit()` method responds to the `Init` page event.

In addition, when a Web page is first created by Visual Studio, it creates the `Page_Load()` method to handle the `Load` event. The biggest difference between these two events is the Web controls are guaranteed to be fully loaded for the `Load` event. If the page is called from a postback, the controls might not be properly initialized to the values contained in the ViewState in the `Init`. We discuss postbacks and ViewState in the upcoming section "Postbacks" but, for now, the concept to remember is the `Load` event marks the point at which the page's controls are fully initialized and loaded.

The first two events always occur when a page is run. They are generated by the internals of .NET. If the page is being executed in response to user interaction with a Web control, however, then the next event the page responds to after the `Load` event is the Web control's event. This is basically the definition of a postback. If the page is loading for the first time, no postback event occurs and, thus, there's no additional event to handle. If, on the other hand, the page has already been loaded and the user clicks a Submit button, for example, then the page will be responding to the button's postback event.

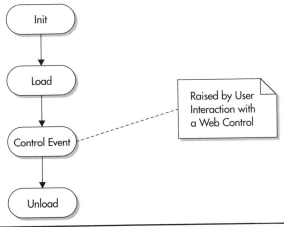

Figure 15-1   *The four basic ASP.NET Web page events*

Finally, once the page handles all these events and the page is to be unloaded from memory, the `Unload` event is fired. This is typically used to clean up any resources allocated for the page.

Events and Delegates

As you can see, a Web page is either responding to the request to load the page for the first time or to an event raised by some user interaction with a Web control on the Web page: in other words, a postback. Before we get too far along, we should first discuss what events are and how they're used within the .NET Framework. If you've done any development in the past few years, you're probably familiar with the term "event." Essentially, *event* describes an asynchronous call, generated in some way by the interaction between the user and the application. For example, when the user clicks a button, an event is generated. If the user chooses to exit the application, an event is generated. Within ASP.NET, we've seen that when the user requests a particular Web page, two events are always generated: `Init` and `Load`.

Events are typically processed using a handler. A *handler* is simply another subroutine, a function designed for the specific purpose of being called when a certain event is generated. You can write a `handleButtonClick()` function that's invoked each time the user clicks a particular button. You can code a routine, `handleAppExit()`, which cleans up any resources allocated by the application when the user chooses to exit the program. And, you can provide code for the `OnInit()` and `Page_Load()` methods that respond to the page initialization and page load events.

Delegates

So, how do you map a particular event with a particular handler? With ASP.NET, we use delegates. In the world of software development, delegates have different meanings. In the world of ASP.NET, a *delegate* is a structure that refers either to a static method or to an instance method written for a class. If you have a C or C++ background, then an *ASP.NET delegate* is nothing more than a class wrapper for a function pointer. The *function pointer* references a method having a particular signature. The delegate allows some code elsewhere in an application to invoke either a static method or an instance method of a particular object anonymously. A method's signature is defined by the number and types of parameters it takes, and the type of value it returns.

We said a delegate is a class wrapper for a function pointer. Let's see what this means. When we write the following line of code in C#

```
public delegate void AnimalDelegate(Animal animal);
```

.NET internally creates a class. When you look at this class using the Microsoft .NET Framework IL Disassembler (ILDasm.exe), you can see it extends the `System.MulticastDelegate` and it has several methods. The other classes shown in Figure 15-2 are part of an application called `EventsAndDelegates`, which we'll discuss shortly. The methods created on our behalf enable us to invoke the target of this delegate, either synchronously or asynchronously. For this discussion, we'll focus on the synchronous invocations.

Once we create our delegate, we can use it to call any method from any class, as long as those methods have the signature specified by the delegate. Certainly, this has intriguing implications that become clearer when we tie them together with events. But, for now, imagine we have a fictional class `SomeClass`. Let's add a method to it that mirrors the signature of the `AnimalDelegate`:

```
public void doAnimalAction(Animal animal)
{
    // do something
}
```

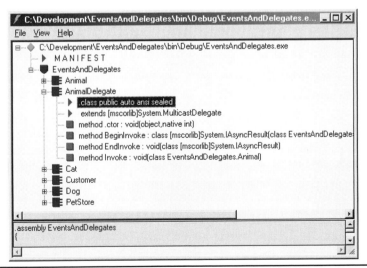

Figure 15-2   *ILDasm.exe of AnimalDelegate*

This method matches the signature because it takes an instance of the class `Animal` as its only parameter, and then returns `void`. Now, we add another method to our class `SomeClass` that will accept an instance of `AnimalDelegate` as a parameter:

```
public void delegateFunction(AnimalDelegate animalDelegate)
{
    Animal animal = new Animal();
    animalDelegate(animal);
}
```

To make this class a running application, we need to add an application entry point. We do this by providing `SomeClass` with a static method called `Main()`. Here, we create an instance of `SomeClass` and create an instance of our delegate. It looks like this:

```
public static void Main(string [] args)
{
    SomeClass someClass = new SomeClass();
    someClass.delegateFunction(new
        AnimalDelegate(someClass.doAnimalAction));
}
```

When we run this class, the `doAnimalAction()` method is called when we invoke the `delegateFunction()` method, passing in an instance of the `AnimalDelegate`. We construct the `AnimalDelegate` instance using the name of the method we want called, `doAnimalAction`.

So what's the big deal? Well, the importance of delegates becomes more obvious when we discuss them in conjunction with events. For now, though, the key is that the method, `delegateFunction()`, has no idea what method it's invoking. And it doesn't know the class or even the instance of the class. This is all completely anonymous. This has value because it means this function can call a variety of methods on a variety of classes using very little code, if all the methods share the same signature as the delegate. For example, we could change the `delegateFunction()` method to the following:

```
public void delegateFunction(ArrayList delegates)
{
    Animal animal = new Animal();
    foreach (AnimalDelegate animalDelegate in delegates)
    {
        animalDelegate(animal);
    }
}
```

Now it takes an `ArrayList` of `AnimalDelegates`. The `ArrayList`, a class found in the `System.Collections` namespace, could consist of delegates containing methods from all types of classes, as long as they match the `AnimalDelegate` signature. Such anonymity makes delegates powerful indeed.

Events

Delegates are important to .NET, but become more so when you begin talking about events. Events are exactly what you would expect: events are calls to a particular method generated by some action. Typically, events are generated by user interaction with a program.

In .NET, we declare an event using the keyword `event`, like so:

```
public event AnimalDelegate NoiseEvent;
public event AnimalDelegate PlayEvent;
```

These two lines of C# code declare the events `NoiseEvent` and `PlayEvent`, and associate them with the delegate, `AnimalDelegate`. Again, .NET does some things behind the scenes for you, creating two methods and a private static class for each `event` statement. If you look in ILDasm.exe, you see it added an `add_NoiseEvent()` method, an `add_PlayEvent()` method, a `remove_NoiseEvent()` method, and a `remove_PlayEvent()` method to the `Animal` class. We examine the `Animal` class, along with several other classes, that demonstrate events and delegates shortly. In the meantime, as you see in Figure 15-3, it also added a private, static class `NoiseEvent` and `PlayEvent`. So, for each event statement, .NET adds an `add_XXX()` method, a `remove_XXX()` method, and a private, static class.

When you think of events as invocations of function calls generated by user interaction, you get a real feel for how events and delegates work together. Let's work through a small application to see how they fit together. The program, `EventsAndDelegates`, is a console application that has several classes. There is an `Animal` class, which is an abstract class and serves as a base class for two other classes: `Cat` and `Dog`. The *base classes* impose that both derived classes must implement the `makeNoise()` and `play()` methods. The `makeNoise()` implementation for the `Cat` writes out "Meow!" while the `Dog` implementation writes out "Bark!" For the `play()` method, the `Cat` class bats a ball of string, while the `Dog` class retrieves a stick. There's also a `PetStore` class and a `Customer` class.

To re-create this application yourself, create a new console application, named `EventsAndDelegates`, using Visual Studio. After removing the generic class—`Class1`—from the project, add in the `Animal`, `Cat`, `Dog`, `PetStore`, and

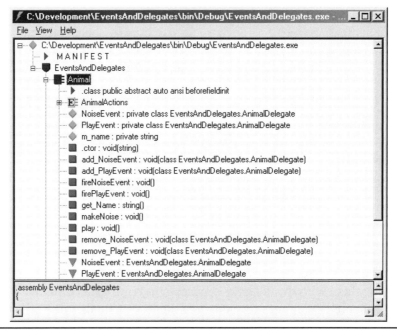

Figure 15-3   *ILDasm.exe of events*

Customer classes. Then, in one of the classes, say, the Animal class, add the delegate to the EventsAndDelegates namespace. The delegate should look like this:

```
public delegate void AnimalDelegate(Animal animal);
```

Let's begin with the Animal class first. Listing 15-1 shows you the entire class.

Listing 15-1   *Animal Class*

```
public abstract class Animal
{
    private string m_name = null;
    public event AnimalDelegate NoiseEvent;
    public event AnimalDelegate PlayEvent;
    public enum AnimalActions
    {
        AnimalActionListen = 0,
        AnimalActionPlay,
        AnimalActionCount
```

```
    };

    public Animal(string name) { m_name = name; }

    public string Name
    {
        get { return m_name; }
    }

    public void fireNoiseEvent() { NoiseEvent(this); }
    public void firePlayEvent() { PlayEvent(this); }

    public abstract void makeNoise();
    public abstract void play();
}
```

This class declares the two events you saw earlier: `NoiseEvent` and `PlayEvent`.
This class also has two abstract methods: `makeNoise()` and `play()`. These
methods force polymorphism on all derived classes to be instantiated, ensuring that
each implements a particular sound for the animal and a specific mode of play. Two
other methods exist: `fireNoiseEvent()` and `firePlayEvent()`. These methods
are extremely simple and invoke the `NoiseEvent()` and `PlayEvent()` events,
respectively. These methods are required because events can be invoked *only* from
within the class that declares them. In other words, events can only be raised by
other methods defined for the class. Therefore, methods of type `fireXXX()` will
most likely exist for any class that declares any type of event.

   Moving on to the `Cat` class, Listing 15-2 shows you how this class implements
the two abstract base class methods.

Listing 15-2   *Cat Class*

```
public class Cat : Animal
{
    public Cat(string name) : base(name) { }

    public override void makeNoise()
    {
        System.Console.WriteLine(Name + " says \"Meow!\"");
    }

    public override void play()
```

```
    {
        System.Console.WriteLine(Name + " bats the ball of string....");
    }
}
```

Listing 15-3 does the same for the Dog class.

Listing 15-3   *Dog Class*

```
public class Dog : Animal
{
    public Dog(string name) : base(name) { }

    public override void makeNoise()
    {
        System.Console.WriteLine(Name + " says \"Bark!\"");
    }

    public override void play()
    {
        System.Console.WriteLine(Name + " retrieves the stick....");
    }
}
```

Now, we move on to the PetStore class. As you can see in Listing 15-4, this is a bit more complex than the last two classes. Comments have been removed for brevity. The PetStore class has an ArrayList of cages. In the constructor, these cages are populated with instances of the Cat and Dog classes. After the cages have been filled, a foreach loop assigns a delegate to the two events exposed by the Animal base class.

Listing 15-4   *PetStore Class*

```
public class PetStore
{
    private ArrayList m_cages = null;
    private string m_name = null;

    public PetStore(string name)
    {
```

```csharp
        m_name = name;
        m_cages = new ArrayList();
        m_cages.Add(new Cat("Fluffy"));
        m_cages.Add(new Cat("Sneaky"));
        m_cages.Add(new Dog("Wolfie"));
        m_cages.Add(new Cat("Lioness"));
        m_cages.Add(new Dog("Rex"));
        m_cages.Add(new Dog("Terror"));

        foreach(Animal animal in m_cages)
        {
            animal.NoiseEvent += new
                AnimalDelegate(this.handleListenToAnAnimalEvent);
            animal.PlayEvent += new
                AnimalDelegate(this.handlePlayWithAnAnimalEvent);
        }
    }

    public string Name
    {
        get { return m_name; }
    }

    public int AnimalCount
    {
        get { return m_cages.Count; }
    }

    public Animal getAnimal(int index)
    {
        return (Animal) m_cages[index];
    }

    public void handleListenToAnAnimalEvent(Animal animal)
    {
        animal.makeNoise();
    }

    public void handlePlayWithAnAnimalEvent(Animal animal)
    {
        animal.play();
    }
}
```

As you can see, these delegates are constructed by passing in the names of two methods contained in this class: `handleListenToAnAnimalEvent()` and `handlePlayWithAnAnimalEvent()`. As you would expect, these methods follow the signature of the `AnimalDelegate`. Notice we assign these delegates using the `+=` operator. The `+=` operator and the `-=` operator are the only two ways you can interact with these properties. The former operator hooks up the specified delegate to the event and the latter operator unhooks a delegate from the event.

When you examine the two delegate functions, you can see they invoke the `makeNoise()` and `play()` methods on the `Animal` class. When an event for a given animal is raised, these handlers are called and the correct polymorphic method is executed. These are the most important elements to this class. The rest of the class is relegated to defining a property or two that help the `Customer` class do its job.

Speaking of the `Customer` class, Listing 15-5 shows you what this class is all about.

Listing 15-5   *Customer Class*

```
public class Customer
{
    private string m_name = null;

    public Customer(string name) { m_name = name; }

    public void visitPetStore(PetStore petStore)
    {
        System.Random random = new System.Random((int)
            System.DateTime.Now.Ticks);

        System.Console.WriteLine(m_name + " visits the " + petStore.Name +
            " pet store.");
        System.Console.WriteLine("");

        for (int index = 0; index < 10; index++)
        {
            Animal animal =
                petStore.getAnimal(random.Next(petStore.AnimalCount));
            Animal.AnimalActions animalAction = (Animal.AnimalActions)
                random.Next((int) Animal.AnimalActions.AnimalActionCount);
            interactWithAnimal(animal, animalAction);
        }
    }
```

```
    public void interactWithAnimal(Animal animal,
                                   Animal.AnimalActions animalAction)
    {
        if (animalAction == Animal.AnimalActions.AnimalActionListen)
        {
            System.Console.WriteLine(m_name + " goes to " + animal.Name +
                "'s cage, and listens to it.");
            animal.fireNoiseEvent();
        }
        else
        {
            System.Console.WriteLine(m_name + " goes to " + animal.Name +
                "'s cage, and plays with it.");
            animal.firePlayEvent();
        }
    }

    public static void Main(string [] args)
    {
        Customer customer = new Customer("John");
        PetStore petStore = new PetStore("Pets-R-Us!!");

        customer.visitPetStore(petStore);
    }
}
```

This class simulates a customer visiting a pet store. The customer goes around to a random set of cages and either listens to an animal or plays with it. The `visitPetStore()` method sets things up by creating a random number generator, using the number of computer ticks counted by the computer as a seed. Then it loops ten times and selects a random animal from the cages in the pet store. It also generates a random action: listen or play. Once this is determined, it calls the `interactWithAnimal()` method.

This method then writes out the action of the customer, based on the given parameter. The customer either listens or plays with the given animal. The method then raises the appropriate event by calling the appropriate `fireXXX()` method on the `Animal` class.

The `Main()` method is the entry point for this console application. It starts everything off by creating a `Customer` object and a `PetStore` object. Then it calls the `visitPetStore()` method and the magic begins.

So what happens when we run this application? Let's begin by stepping through the `interactWithAnimal()` method of the `Customer` class, as shown in Listing 15-5. As you can see in Figure 15-4, the first time through the loop, John, the Customer, visits Fluffy's cage. John listens to Fluffy, who meows at him. So, when we walk through this method, we must have executed the following line:

```
animal.fireNoiseEvent();
```

As you saw in Listing 15-1, this method invokes the `NoiseEvent` on the `Animal` class. And, as you saw in the `PetStore` class, in Listing 15-4, each animal in the `m_cages` `ArrayList` was assigned a delegate. In the case of the `NoiseEvent`, that delegate was `handleListenToAnAnimalEvent()`. So, in fact, when this event is fired, this handler is called. Inside this handler, the code calls the `makeNoise()` method for the given instance of the animal. In the case of Fluffy, that method is the `Cat.makeNoise()` method. This writes out the string "Fluffy says Meow!"

What's important about this application, though, is it's a metaphor for how events and delegates are used within a real application, with real user interaction. A direct correlation exists between the classes in this application and the classes used in ASP.NET. If you think of the `PetStore` class as a Web page, its corresponding

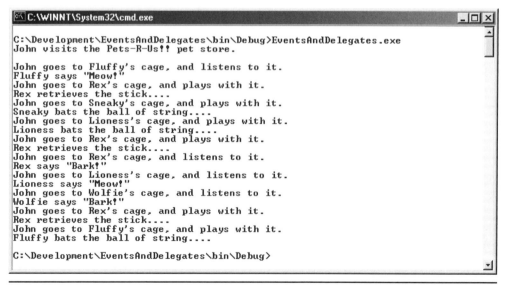

Figure 15-4   *Running the EventsAndDelegates application*

class is `System.Web.UI.Page`. The `m_cages ArrayList` can be thought of as the Controls property that returns the `System.Web.UI.ControlCollection`. And, of course, the `Animal` class, which populated the cages, corresponds with the `System.Web.UI.WebControls.WebControl` base class. The `ControlCollection` is usually populated with instances of `WebControls`. And, finally, the `Customer` class corresponds with no class at all, but is, in fact, the user, clicking merrily on buttons and drop-down menus, and filling in text. For each action the user takes, an event is fired, and an appropriate delegate is called.

How ASP.NET Uses Events and Delegates

How does all this work with actual ASP.NET controls? To find out, let's make a simple Web page that contains a text box and a Submit button. Create a new application and select the ASP.NET Web Application template from the New Project dialog box. Let's call this application WebEvents. When Visual Studio creates the project, it creates a Web page for us, named "WebForm1.aspx". Let's rename that to "MainPage.aspx." Web page names are class names and they should be more informative than WebForm1.aspx, WebForm2.aspx, and so forth. Remember also to rename the class to `MainPage`.

NOTE

When renaming a class, remember to rename the filename by right-clicking the file in the Solution Explorer and also to rename the class. When renaming the class, make sure you do a global search and replace within the file to rename all the occurrences of the class name or you'll get compiler errors.

From the Toolbox tab, drag-and-drop a text box and a button on to this page. Anywhere will do. Notice the TextBox control is named `TextBox1` and the button is named "`Button1`". By themselves, they'll function normally enough, but no code is behind them to respond to any user interaction.

To add an event, you need to go to the Visual Studio Property window. In Design mode, you click the button, and either press F4 or right-click and select the Properties menu item. Toward the top of the Property window, you can see a toolbar. In this toolbar is a lightning bolt. When you click the lightning bolt, you see the list of available events for the Button control, as shown in Figure 15-5.

Of these, use the `Click` event. Now, if we want to, you could simply double-click the event. Visual Studio will generate a name for the event handler by concatenating the name of the control, `Button1`, and the name of the event, `Click`, to form the event handler `Button1_Click`. Most developers have some sort of coding standards that usually include naming conventions. So, instead

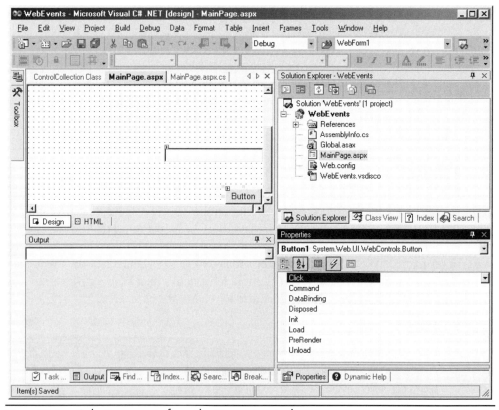

Figure 15-5   *Selecting events from the Property window*

of double-clicking the event, type in **handleButtonClickEvent** in the space provided, and then press the ENTER key.

Whether you double-click or type in your own name for the event, Visual Studio generates a method in the `MainPage` class and positions your cursor inside the method. In this case, the method is named `handleButtonClickEvent()`. What you don't see is what it added inside the collapsed Web Form Designer generated code region. If you expand this region, you see the code in Listing 15-6.

Listing 15-6   *Visual Studio Generated Code*

```
#region Web Form Designer generated code
override protected void OnInit(EventArgs e)
{
    //
```

```
    // CODEGEN: This call is required by the ASP.NET Web Form Designer.
    //
    InitializeComponent();
    base.OnInit(e);
}

/// <summary>
/// Required method for Designer support - do not modify
/// the contents of this method with the code editor.
/// </summary>
private void InitializeComponent()
{
    this.Button1.Click += new
        System.EventHandler(this.handleButtonClickEvent);
    this.Load += new System.EventHandler(this.Page_Load);

}
#endregion
```

Essentially, this code is unchanged from when the form was first created, except for the addition of one line. The first line of the `InitializeComponent()` method should look familiar:

```
this.Button1.Click += new System.EventHandler(this.handleButtonClickEvent);
```

This is assigning a delegate to the `Click` event of the `Button1` control. In most cases, ASP.NET Web Controls use the `EventHandler` delegate found in the `System` namespace. Some exceptions exist but, for now, let's examine this delegate. When you pressed the ENTER key in the Events window, Visual Studio assigned the delegate to the `Click` event, using the name of the handler you provided.

Visual Studio also created the handler for you, positioning you inside the new method. The code in Listing 15-7 is the handler Visual Studio generated for you.

Listing 15-7   *Button Click Event Handler*

```
private void handleButtonClickEvent(object sender, System.EventArgs e)
{

}
```

As you can see, this empty method has a particular signature that matches the `System.EventHandler` delegate's signature. As shown in Listing 15-8, the declaration for this delegate is

Listing 15-8   *EventHandler Delegate*

```
public delegate void EventHandler(object sender, EventArgs e);
```

and the declaration for an event using this delegate is

```
public event EventHandler SomeEvent;
```

You can assume the `Button` control class declares an event named `Click` using the previous format. This delegate requires two parameters: the variable `sender`, which is an instance of object and also the source of the event, and the variable `e`, which contains the event data, if any.

Within the method in Listing 15-7, you can add any code you like. For example, if you add the following line of code

```
System.Diagnostics.Debug.WriteLine("The user entered \"" +
                             TextBox1.Text + "\" in the text box.");
```

you can record what the user entered in the text box to Visual Studio's debugger Output window. While this line of code doesn't do anything dramatic, it does demonstrate you're catching the event when the user clicks the button and you can manipulate the controls server-side, obtaining the values the user entered client-side. When you debug this application in Visual Studio, the Web page appears displaying your text box and button. If you type **hello world!** in the text box and click the button, the Output window of Visual Studio will contain the following line:

```
The user entered "hello world!" in the text box.
```

This is a minor demonstration meant to ignite your imagination with possibilities. For example, imagine how easy it would be if, for some reason, you wanted to store these values in a database somewhere. Using what you now know of Web services and ADO.NET, this would be quite simple. In the last few chapters, you have moved from the database to the business layer via ADO.NET and Web services, and then to a user's Web browser via ASP.NET. With .NET events and delegates, you initiated the round-trip back to the server-side application, which eventually led you back to where you began: the database.

Postbacks

When the user clicks the Button control in the last example, the page sends all the information back to the server in the form of an HTTP POST. Microsoft .NET refers to this as a *postback*. This term was discussed earlier in the chapter when we talked about loading a Web page. This is similar to the way things worked with ASP. But, unlike before, you needn't rely only on a collection of name-value pairs in the `Forms` property to obtain the values the user entered. Don't fear, this mechanism still exists. You can access it using the `Request.Form` property that hangs off the `Page` class. This property returns a `NameValueCollection` from within the `System.Collections.Specialized` namespace.

As you saw in the last section, however, you can also reference the values directly in your controls. How is this possible? This is accomplished through a hidden control on every ASP.NET Web page named "`__VIEWSTATE`". This field is used to send the state of the controls between the client and the server. Because ASP.NET events perform postbacks to the same ASP.NET Web page, you could be potentially sending the state of the controls back and forth many times. The ViewState information is stored as an instance of `StateBag`, a class in the `System.Web.UI` namespace, which is transmitted in the form of a string. For the small ASP.NET application you just built for the last section, it looks like this:

```
<input type="hidden" name="__VIEWSTATE" value="dDwxNDg5OTk5MzM3Oz4=" />
```

Obviously, the more controls on a given page, the larger the size of the ViewState information passed back and forth. On the other hand, each ASP.NET control on a page needn't persist its state. While it defaults to a value of true, a developer can turn off a control's use of ViewState by setting the `EnableViewState` property to false. This can also be set at the page level, so no ViewState is used at all. You can use the setting on individual controls to tune the amount of information sent back to the server, balancing the need to obtain the user's modifications against obtaining the best performance.

A postback occurs when the user performs an action on the Web page that fires an event previously hooked up with an event handler. If no event handler is specified, no event is fired. The event posts back to the original .aspx page, executing the page server-side. As you saw in Figure 15-1, when an .aspx page is executed, first the `Init` and `Load` events are fired. Then, because this is a postback, the specified event handler is invoked. The event handler typically follows the delegate of the type shown previously in Listing 15-8, though other events like those of the DataGrid have different delegate signatures.

Event	Description
DataBinding	Fired when the server control is bound to a data source.
Disposed	Fired when the server control is released from memory. This is the last stage in a control's lifecycle.
Init	Fired when the server control is initialized. This is the first stage in a control's lifecycle.
Load	Fired when the server control is loaded into the page.
PreRender	Fired when the server control is about to render itself to the containing page.
Unload	Fired when the server control is unloaded from memory.

Table 15-1   *Basic Web Control Events*

All ASP.NET Web controls have six basic events, which are shown in Table 15-1. All controls that derive from the WebControl class inherit these events. But controls that provide additional user interaction supply their own supplementary events. For example, buttons and text boxes provide events like the `Click` event and the `TextChanged` event. DropDownList controls provide the `SelectedIndexChanged` event. For each type of control you use, you need to examine the events they expose and decide which ones need event handlers.

Deciding which event handlers to implement can sometimes also involve weighing performance. Remember, for every event handler you write, the Web page will respond to the user's action by posting back to the server. For small Web pages without much information, this isn't a performance problem. For larger Web pages that make use of a large amount of ViewState, however, developers should consider the consequences of responding to particular events. Responding to the click of the Submit button is certainly a necessity. But, in case of other events that can occur quite often before the final submit of the page, sometimes an alternative solution might improve the user-friendliness of the Web page.

ASP.NET Controls

Now that you understand how events and delegates work within ASP.NET, we should discuss how ASP.NET Web controls use them. Visual Studio .NET is probably the richest developer environment for designing forms in an application. This is even more true when you consider the environment for building Web Applications. Creating good-looking Web pages has never been easier.

A big part of this is the rich set of controls that can be dragged-and-dropped on to a Web page. Among the TextBox and Button controls, are DropDownList controls, DataGrid controls, and AdRotator controls. And, another whole group of controls exists, called Validators. We examine them shortly. The best part about all these controls is all you have to do is drag-and-drop them on to a page to start using them.

HTML and Design Mode

When you drag a control on to a Web page's surface, be aware that Visual Studio not only generates code in the `InitializeComponent()` method in the code behind the page, as you saw in Listing 15-6, but it also generates server-side HTML. You can see the HTML it creates by clicking the HTML tab at the lower-left corner of the Web page. Two tabs, Design and HTML, enable you to switch between the Design view and the HTML view of the Web page. You can think of the Design view as the logical representation or preview of the page, as it will appear in a browser, and the HTML view as the actual, textual contents of the .aspx page.

As you manipulate the control in the Design view, you affect the values assigned to the attributes of the controls in the server-side HTML. For example, when you wrote the small application to demonstrate events and delegates, you dropped a TextBox and a Button on to the Web page. As you played and manipulated these controls, the HTML was automatically modified for you. When you dropped the TextBox on the page, Visual Studio generated the following code:

```
<asp:TextBox id="TextBox1" style="Z-INDEX: 101; LEFT: 344px;
    POSITION: absolute; TOP: 184px" runat="server"></asp:TextBox>
```

Note the following about this snippet: all ASP.NET Web controls use the `asp` XML namespace and they all contain the attribute `runat` with a value of `"server"`. This tells ASP.NET to execute these controls at the server. When you view this page in a browser, you see the following:

```
<input name="TextBox1" type="text" id="TextBox1"
    style="Z-INDEX: 101; LEFT: 344px; POSITION: absolute; TOP: 184px" />
```

As you can see, ASP.NET compiled the control at the server and emitted the appropriate HTML to represent the text box in a Web browser.

Code Behind

We've touched on the code behind a Web page. This is the actual server-side code written in another file. Having code behind a particular Web page isn't necessary.

You can write your C# or VB.NET code right inside the .aspx file if you want using the familiar `script` element.

But using code behind when writing ASP.NET Web pages has two advantages. The first is you can separate the look and feel of a page from the server-side code. As long as the type and number of controls remain the same for a given page, one developer can work on how the page looks, while another works on the server-side code in the code behind file. This improves the development process, especially if developers have particular skills in one area over another.

The other advantage is organization. Code organization is critical on medium-sized to large applications. Mixing server-side code in with the layout of TextBox and Button controls can be confusing and make it very difficult to debug, test, and maintain the code in the future. Separating the code out into two files makes it much easier to read, debug, test, and modify the code throughout the entire lifecycle of the Web Application.

When you use code behind, the .aspx file includes two attributes in its `@Page` directive. These are the `Inherits`, which specifies the class name of the class in the code behind, and `Codebehind`, which specifies the pathname to the code behind file. In a moment, we'll build an application called FootballViewer, which consumes the PlayerStats Web service built in Chapter 14. We'll take a quick peek into this application and examine only the first line of HTML for the main .aspx Web page. The `@Page` directive looks like this:

```
<%@ Page language="c#" Codebehind="Viewer.aspx.cs" AutoEventWireup="false"
    Inherits="FootballViewer.Viewer" %>
```

NOTE

The `AutoEventWireup` attribute is used by ASP.NET to call events automatically with predefined handler names. A good idea is to leave this attribute set to false. This way, you can specify your own method names for the handlers you implement.

DataGrid

One of the most powerful and versatile controls ASP.NET offers is the DataGrid control. An entire book could be written on this control alone and an author is probably working diligently on the topic right now. We'll cover only the highlights here.

The most obvious and straightforward thing you can do with DataGrids is to display information in a grid-like fashion on a Web page. No big deal, right? Add in the capability to sort this data interactively on a particular column, paging functionality, and the capability to bind to a variety of data sources, such as an `ArrayList`, a `DataSet` or a `DataView`, and you have a powerful Web control.

But, like a game show host discussing the prize you've won, that's not all. Have you ever wanted to edit the information in a grid inline, like you would in a Windows Forms application? Well, the DataGrid also lets users do this. You can even write some simple code to insert rows to the grid as well.

We had a preview of this control in other chapters before now. Let's start off simply and display some data. Let's say you're delivered a DataSet from a Web service, and you want to display the contents of the DataSet on a Web page. You can use the FootballStats Web service you created in Chapter 14 and consume the `DataSet` from the PlayerStats Web service.

Consuming a Web Service

We touched on this topic in Chapter 14. You saw how to add a Web reference to a Web service. Now we'll complete the process. Let's create a Web Application called FootballViewer and rename the WebForm1.aspx page to "Viewer.aspx." Then, following the steps from the last chapter, add a Web reference to the FootballStats Web service. Your project should now look like Figure 15-6.

The first step is to drag-and-drop a DataGrid from the Toolbox tab. Visual Studio takes care of generating all the code behind and server-side HTML, and names it "`DataGrid1`".

Once you position the DataGrid where you want it, the next step is to place the strongly typed `DataSet` on your page. Return to the Toolbox tab and select the Data tab. Then drag-and-drop a `DataSet` on to the page, and the Add DataSet dialog box appears. As you see in Figure 15-7, it defaults to the one and only typed `DataSet` in the solution: `DSPlayerStats`. Click the OK button and Visual Studio adds an instance of this `DataSet`—`dsPlayerStats1`—to the page.

Next, examine the properties of the DataGrid. With the DataGrid selected, choose the `DataSource` property in the Properties window. From the drop-down box, choose `dsPlayerStats1` as your data source. Magically, the DataGrid has morphed on the Web page to represent all the columns of the `DataSet`. If you examine some of the other properties for the DataGrid, you can see that you can modify the look and feel of the header, and even add alternating colors for every other row. When you expand the `HeaderStyle` property, you can set the `BackColor` property to DeepSkyBlue from within the Web tab. Then, you can go to the `AlternatingItemStyle` and expand that property. Here, you set the `BackColor` to CornSilk, again from the colors in the Web tab. If you want to set the font for the entire control, expand the `Font` property and set the `Name` property to Arial.

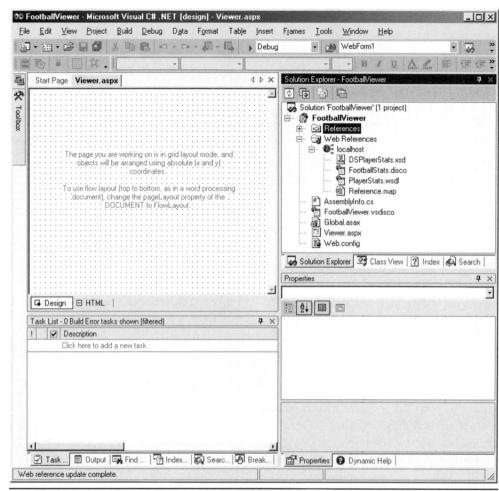

Figure 15-6 *Added Web reference to the FootballStats Web service*

You're almost done. Move on to the code behind page and add the following lines to the `Page_Load()` method:

```
localhost.PlayerStats playerStats = new localhost.PlayerStats();
dsPlayerStats1 = playerStats.getPlayerStats(1);
DataGrid1.DataBind();
```

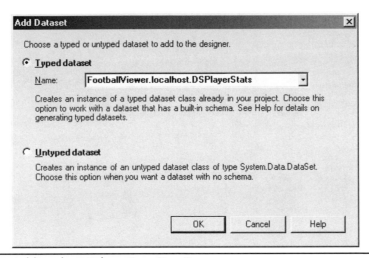

Figure 15-7   *Adding the DSPlayerStats DataSet*

Use the `localhost` namespace because this is where your Web service is added
when you generated the Web reference to the FootballStats Web service project.
From there, you instantiate the PlayerStats Web service. Call the `getPlayerStats()`
method, passing in the number 1 for the position, and assign the results to
`dsPlayerStats1`. The last thing you do is call the `DataBind()` method on
the grid. Or, you could have called `DataBind()`, which would have bound all the
controls on the page, but this is your only control.

NOTE

*When you add a Web reference, Visual Studio creates the subdirectory, Web References. This
directory contains other directories that contain our reference information, such as .vsdisco files
and WSDL files.*

Now let's run the application. You can see the statistics for Quarterbacks in
Figure 15-8 when you pass in a value of 1 to the Web service. The only problem
with this display is there's a lot of data to show—both many columns and many
rows. How can you make the display easier to see?

DataGrid Columns

Let's deal with the number of rows in a minute. First, you can control the number
of columns by clicking the ... on the `Columns` property of the DataGrid. As you

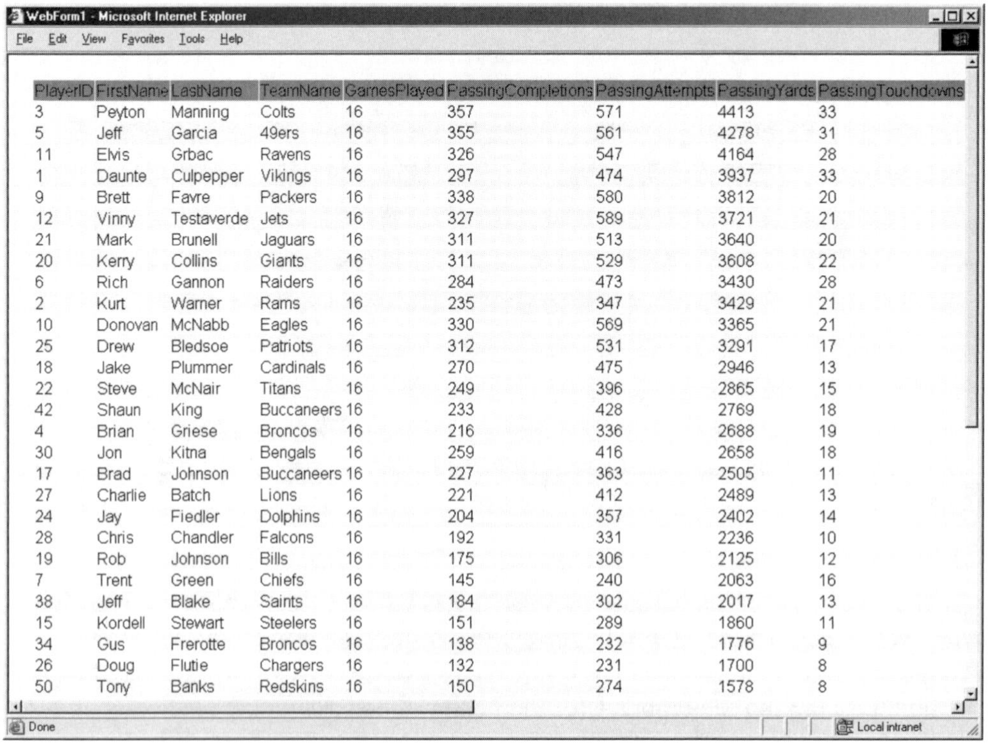

PlayerID	FirstName	LastName	TeamName	GamesPlayed	PassingCompletions	PassingAttempts	PassingYards	PassingTouchdowns
3	Peyton	Manning	Colts	16	357	571	4413	33
5	Jeff	Garcia	49ers	16	355	561	4278	31
11	Elvis	Grbac	Ravens	16	326	547	4164	28
1	Daunte	Culpepper	Vikings	16	297	474	3937	33
9	Brett	Favre	Packers	16	338	580	3812	20
12	Vinny	Testaverde	Jets	16	327	589	3721	21
21	Mark	Brunell	Jaguars	16	311	513	3640	20
20	Kerry	Collins	Giants	16	311	529	3608	22
6	Rich	Gannon	Raiders	16	284	473	3430	28
2	Kurt	Warner	Rams	16	235	347	3429	21
10	Donovan	McNabb	Eagles	16	330	569	3365	21
25	Drew	Bledsoe	Patriots	16	312	531	3291	17
18	Jake	Plummer	Cardinals	16	270	475	2946	13
22	Steve	McNair	Titans	16	249	396	2865	15
42	Shaun	King	Buccaneers	16	233	428	2769	18
4	Brian	Griese	Broncos	16	216	336	2688	19
30	Jon	Kitna	Bengals	16	259	416	2658	18
17	Brad	Johnson	Buccaneers	16	227	363	2505	11
27	Charlie	Batch	Lions	16	221	412	2489	13
24	Jay	Fiedler	Dolphins	16	204	357	2402	14
28	Chris	Chandler	Falcons	16	192	331	2236	10
19	Rob	Johnson	Bills	16	175	306	2125	12
7	Trent	Green	Chiefs	16	145	240	2063	16
38	Jeff	Blake	Saints	16	184	302	2017	13
15	Kordell	Stewart	Steelers	16	151	289	1860	11
34	Gus	Frerotte	Broncos	16	138	232	1776	9
26	Doug	Flutie	Chargers	16	132	231	1700	8
50	Tony	Banks	Redskins	16	150	274	1578	8

Figure 15-8 *Showing off the DataGrid*

see in Figure 15-9, this brings up the Properties dialog box for the DataGrid, with the Columns Property selected on the left. Notice that the Create columns Automatically At Run Time check box at the top has been selected. Checking this box causes the DataGrid to pull the columns it displays from the object assigned to the `DataSource` property, in this case, the `DSPlayerStats DataSet`.

If you clear this check box, you can select which columns you want to see. For example, if you choose to show only the FirstName, LastName, TeamName, GamesPlayed, and PassingCompletions columns, you greatly reduce the width of the grid. You also have the option to specify the name displayed for each of the columns by changing the string in the Header Text field. This means you can change FirstName to "First Name" and GamesPlayed to "Number of Games Played,"

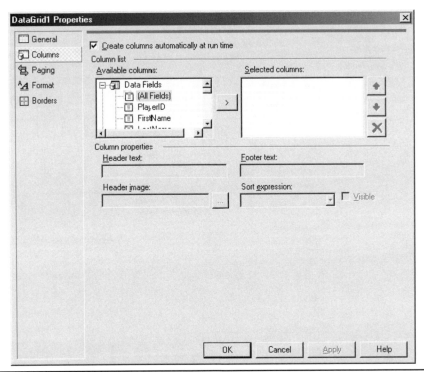

Figure 15-9 *DataGrid Properties dialog box*

and so on. It's entirely up to you how these columns are displayed. Figure 15-10 demonstrates how we made these modifications.

DataGrid Pagination

So, you adjust the number of columns. But what do you do to control the number of rows you see? To make things look a little neater, you could paginate the grid. The first step is to set the `AllowPaging` property to true. When this is turned on, the grid will display only the number of rows specified by `PageSize` property. This property defaults to ten.

The second step is to change the way the page loads. Remember, the DataGrid is bound in the `Page_Load()` event handler. However, you only want it to load in this fashion when no postback exists, for example, when the page is loading for the

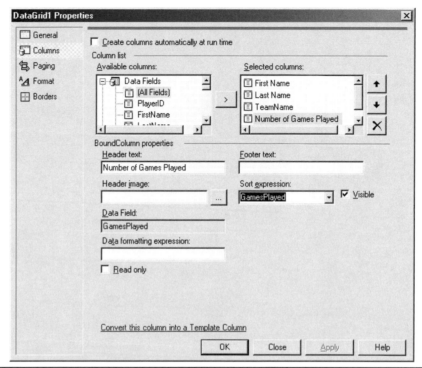

Figure 15-10   *Modifying DataGrid columns*

first time. If a postback event occurs, you want to let the event handler bind the DataGrid. So, as Listing 15-9 shows, you first check to see if you're being called from a postback.

Listing 15-9   *Binding to the DataGrid on the Load Event*

```
private void Page_Load(object sender, System.EventArgs e)
{
    if (! this.IsPostBack)
    {
        bindDataGrid();
    }
}

private void bindDataGrid()
```

```
{
    localhost.PlayerStats playerStats = new localhost.PlayerStats();
    dsPlayerStats1 = playerStats.getPlayerStats(1);
    DataGrid1.DataBind();
}
```

If not, then you bind the DataGrid. Notice you moved the lines of code to bind the grid into a separate method: `bindDataGrid()`. That is because you'll be invoking this method from other event handlers.

The third, and final, step is to handle the `PageIndexChanged` event. This is generated when the user requests the next page of rows. Let's go to the list of events for the DataGrid, select the `PageIndexChanged` event, and enter `handlePageIndexChanged` in the space provided. Visual Studio hooks up this handler with the event and positions you within the method. You add code to make it look like Listing 15-10.

Listing 15-10   *PageIndexChanged Event Handler*

```
private void handlePageIndexChanged(object source,
    System.Web.UI.WebControls.DataGridPageChangedEventArgs e)
{
    DataGrid1.CurrentPageIndex = e.NewPageIndex;
    bindDataGrid();
}
```

NOTE

The delegate for the `DataGrid`'s events is different from other controls. Notice that the second parameter isn't an instance of `EventArgs` like other controls, but is, instead, an instance of the `DataGridPageChangedEventArgs` class.

Now, according the diagram in Figure 15-1, when the user requests the next page of data, the `Page_Load()` method is invoked first, but it does nothing. Then the handler for the `PageIndexChanged` event is called. As you can see in Listing 15-10, you modify the `CurrentPageIndex` property of the DataGrid to the new page index passed to you from the event, and then bind the grid. Figure 15-11 shows you what the application looks like now. This is much cleaner than what you saw originally in Figure 15-8.

First Name	Last Name	TeamName	Number of Games Played	PassingCompletions
Donovan	McNabb	Eagles	16	330
Drew	Bledsoe	Patriots	16	312
Jake	Plummer	Cardinals	16	270
Steve	McNair	Titans	16	249
Shaun	King	Buccaneers	16	233
Brian	Griese	Broncos	16	216
Jon	Kitna	Bengals	16	259
Brad	Johnson	Buccaneers	16	227
Charlie	Batch	Lions	16	221
Jay	Fiedler	Dolphins	16	204

< >

Figure 15-11   *New DataGrid*

NOTE

You might realize you're retrieving the `DataSet` *on each postback. For large amounts of data, this could cause performance problems. This is the perfect example of when to implement caching on the Web service method. Caching the data returned by the* `PlayerStats.getPlayerStats()` *method will improve the performance dramatically on repeated postbacks because the Web service won't have to return to the database each time it's called. Remember, from Chapter 14, you turn caching on using the* `CacheDuration` *property of the* `WebMethod` *attribute, which is applied to the* `getPlayerStats()` *method in the Web service.*

You can improve the grid's look and feel further by examining the `PagerStyle` property. When you expand this property, it has the usual font properties, but it also enables you to control the placement of your page index within the grid, the mode of the page index, and the text display based on the Pager mode. For example, if you change the `Mode` property from `NextPrev` to a value of `NumericPages`, the grid instead displays page numbers. Now, rather than flipping page-by-page through the data, you can go directly to Page 3, 6, or whatever page you want, simply by clicking the number. If you leave the mode as `NextPrev`, then you can modify the

< and > symbols in the `PrevPageText` and `NextPageText` properties to other strings like previous and next. The DataGrid is flexible and you can easily make it look however you want.

Inline Editing

What if you want to edit the grid, updating your data source with the changes? Well, that's simply another exercise of hooking up the right events. The first thing you need to do is add some buttons to the grid that enable you to edit the rows. Go to the Properties window with the grid selected, and click the ... next to the `Columns` property. This brings up the Properties dialog box for the DataGrid. Then scroll down through the list of Available columns, until you reach the Button Column entry. You expand that out, and add the Edit, Update, Cancel column to the grid, as you can see in Figure 15-12.

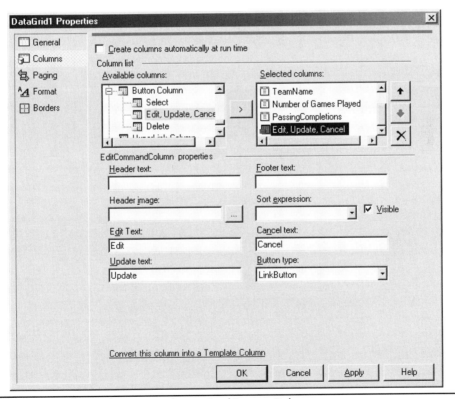

Figure 15-12   *Edit, Update, Cancel DataGrid Button Column*

Now, return to the Properties window for the grid and select the view of the grid's events. Next to the `CancelCommand`, type **handleCancelRow**. For the `EditCommand`, enter **handleEditRow**. And, for the `UpdateCommand` event, type **handleUpdateRow**. Your code for these event handlers can be seen in Listing 15-11.

Listing 15-11   *Cancel, Edit, and Update Event Handlers*

```
private void handleCancelRow(object source,
    System.Web.UI.WebControls.DataGridCommandEventArgs e)
{
    // end the editing session
    DataGrid1.EditItemIndex = -1;
    bindDataGrid();
}

private void handleEditRow(object source,
    System.Web.UI.WebControls.DataGridCommandEventArgs e)
{
    // begin the editing session with the given row
    DataGrid1.EditItemIndex = e.Item.ItemIndex;
    bindDataGrid();
}

private void handleUpdateRow(object source,
    System.Web.UI.WebControls.DataGridCommandEventArgs e)
{
    foreach (TableCell cell in e.Item.Cells)
    {
        if (cell.Controls[0].ToString().EndsWith("TextBox"))
        {
            // update the database with the changes
            // add code here to update the changes to the database
            System.Diagnostics.Debug.WriteLine(((TextBox)
                cell.Controls[0]).Text);
        }
    }

    // end the editing session
    DataGrid1.EditItemIndex = -1;
    bindDataGrid();
}
```

The `handleEditRow()` handler is quite simple. All you need to do is specify the row you're editing in the grid using the given value, passed in as part of the `DataGridCommandEventArgs` parameter. As you saw earlier, the DataGrid's delegates for its event handlers are different from the standard delegates. You assign the value to the `EditItemIndex` property and the grid changes its display to enable the user to edit the row. Figure 15-13 demonstrates how this looks.

The `handleCancelRow()` method reverses this process. The user no longer wants to edit the row, so assign -1 to the `EditItemIndex` property.

The `handleUpdateRow()` handler is where the action is. If you make some changes and clicks the Update button, then you need to update the data source with the changes. Of course, updating a data source with new information is simple enough using ADO.NET `DataSets` or even an ADO.NET `SqlCommand`. In Listing 15-11, we demonstrate how to access the values of the updated DataGrid row by writing out the values to the Visual Studio Debugger Output window. If you had updated your database with the changes, then you would call the `DataSet.AcceptChanges()` method. Finally, you end the editing session by assigning -1 to the `EditItemIndex` property of the grid, and then binding the grid to the updated `DataSet`.

That's all there is to editing the grid inline. The DataGrid is perhaps the most versatile and extensible control in ASP.NET's offering. You've now seen how easy it is to bind `DataSets` and `DataViews` to the control. And, you learned how to customize the display, from the colors of the headings and rows to the fonts used by the DataGrid to which columns it shows, as well as the number of rows it displays. But there are still other controls of interest to developers.

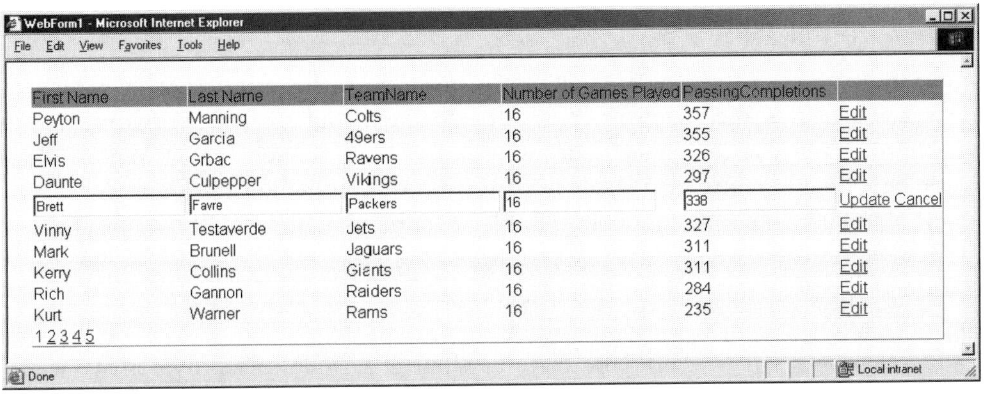

Figure 15-13   *Editing the DataGrid inline*

Validator Controls

ASP.NET provides a whole other group of Web controls used only to perform
client-side validation. When you drop one of these controls on a page, it's assigned
a specific control on the page to validate. Then, based on the type of validator control,
when the user enters invalid information or tries to submit a page of information
without certain fields filled in, these controls display error messages that describe
the problem. Once the user corrects the problem by inputting proper values, the
error messages disappear and the user can submit the form.

One of the simpler validator controls is the RequiredFieldValidator. When you
drop this control on a page, you see the default error text RequiredFieldValidator.
Each validator control enables you to customize the error message by typing in text
for the `ErrorMessage` property. Once you type in some reasonable string, such as
You must enter your e-mail address, you can assign the validator to watch a
particular control. All validator controls have the `ControlToValidate` property.
This drop-down menu enables the developer to choose which Web control to validate
with this validator control. Select the desired control and you're done. That's all
there is to it. If the assigned Web control is empty when a Submit button or similar
control is clicked, this validator swallows the event and reports the error.

Any Web control with the `CausesValidation` property, such as a button, will
cause the Web page to examine the validator controls in its `Validators` collection.
The `Validators` property returns a `ValidatorCollection`. This collection
contains any and all validator controls dropped on to the Web page. When a validator
reports an error, the page prevents the postback to server from firing. The validator
control(s) in error report their messages on the page.

User-Defined Controls

Everything in .NET is a class, which means most of .NET's classes can be extended.
This is also true of Web controls. You can extend existing controls, providing new
functionality, or you can create your own controls from scratch. If you want to add
some new functionality, say, to the TextBox Web control, you can extend the
`TextBox` class and refine it to accept only numeric text entry, for example. If you
want to start from scratch, then you can extend the `WebControl` class in the
`System.Web.UI.WebControls` namespace. Whatever your needs, ASP.NET
proves its richness through its extensibility.

Regardless of what type of control you're building, ASP.NET provides two ways
to make them available to Web pages. You can create a WindowsControlLibrary
project from within Visual Studio or you can add a Web User Control to an existing

Web Application project. To add a user-defined control to a Web Application project, right-click the project in the Solution Explorer window. From the Add menu item, select the Add Web User Control… menu item.

NOTE

ASP.NET uses the extensions .ascx and .ascx.cs (or .ascx.vb for VB.NET) for user-defined controls. Similar to the way the Web pages are organized, the .ascx pages contains the server-side HTML and the .ascx.cs (or .ascx.vb) files contain the code behind the control.

If you build a control outside the project, using a WindowsControlLibrary project, for example, you need to make it available to other projects. You do this by clicking the Toolbox bar in Visual Studio when a Web page is in Design mode. Hover your mouse over the Toolbox slide-out window. When the Web Forms tab is selected, right-click the toolbar, and select the Customize Toolbox… menu item. The Customize Toolbox dialog box appears. Select the .NET Framework Components tab, as shown Figure 15-14.

From here, click the Browse… button. Using the familiar File Open dialog box, search for the .dll file that contains the Web control you created. Once you select this control, and then select Open, the new control is added to the list of controls in the

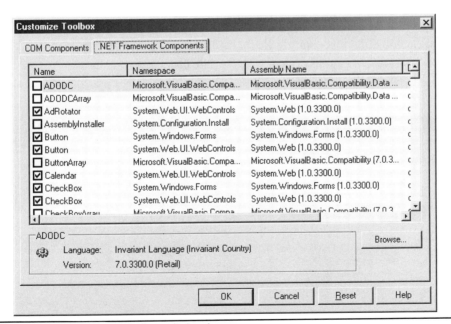

Figure 15-14 *Customize Toolbox dialog box*

Customize Toolbox dialog box, with its check box checked. Now click the OK button and your own user-defined control is available from the Toolbox slide-out window.

Composite Controls

Sometimes the wide array of controls that comes with ASP.NET just isn't enough. Then it's time to build your own. Plenty of examples exist of how to create custom controls derived from existing controls. Sometimes, though, what you need isn't a custom DropDownList or Textbox, but a combination of controls.

A good example would be a Web calendar control. The one provided by ASP.NET is nice, but it requires multiple round trips, or *postbacks,* to arrive at a desired date. This can be frustrating to the user who wants to scroll through a wide range of dates and is forced to wait between each click. If you want to provide a more responsive calendar control for the user, which also looks a little nicer, a composite control might be the ticket.

Let's walk through how to build a calendar composite control. Figure 15-15 gives you an early glimpse of what you're going to build. This looks like three DropDownList controls in a row, but they're one control that contains and manages three DropDownList controls. The single control has only one date value as a property, allowing other developers to get and set the control's date. When a new date value is assigned to the control, it automatically assigns the proper month, day, and year to the respective DropDownList controls.

How do you build this control? Begin by creating a new Web Control Library project. This creates a small project with a single class, `WebCustomControl1.cs`. First, let's rename this class to something meaningful, like `DateControl.cs`.

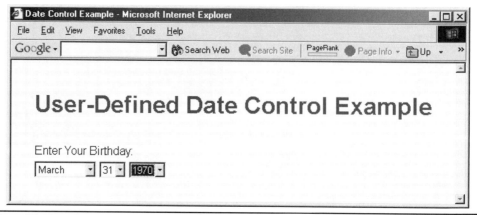

Figure 15-15   *Composite Date Control*

Let's examine the skeleton code generated by Visual Studio for your custom control in Listing 15-12. First, the class derives from WebControl in the System.Web.UI.WebControls namespace. You could derive your control from Control in the System.Web.UI namespace, but that would limit your options to some degree. For example, if you want ASP.NET validators to validate this control, you must derive from the WebControl class.

Listing 15-12   *WebControl Skeleton Class*

```
using System;
using System.Web.UI;
using System.Web.UI.WebControls;
using System.ComponentModel;

namespace WebControlLibrary1
{
    /// <summary>
    /// Summary description for WebCustomControl1.
    /// </summary>
    [DefaultProperty("Text"),
        ToolboxData("<{0}:WebCustomControl1
                    runat=server></{0}:WebCustomControl1>")]
    public class WebCustomControl1 : System.Web.UI.WebControls.WebControl
    {
        private string text;

        [Bindable(true),
            Category("Appearance"),
            DefaultValue("")]
        public string Text
        {
            get
            {
                return text;
            }

            set
            {
                text = value;
            }
```

```
        }

        /// <summary>
        /// Render this control to the output parameter specified.
        /// </summary>
        /// <param name="output"> The HTML writer to write out to </param>
        protected override void Render(HtmlTextWriter output)
        {
            output.Write(Text);
        }
    }
}
```

Another thing to notice about your skeleton is Visual Studio assigned two attributes to the class: `DefaultProperty` and `ToolboxData`. We'll add a third but, for now, these two specify the default property for the control, and the default tag generated when the control is dragged from the toolbox and dropped on to a Web page.

The last thing to notice is the custom control skeleton implements its default property specified by the class attribute as `Text`, and the method `Render()` to render the control's HTML output. The property has been assigned three attributes itself. The first, `Bindable(true)`, says it can be data bound. This is important if you want to bind this control to values in `DataSets`, `DataViews`, or other bindable objects. The next one, `Category("Appearance")`, says where this property should be placed in the property view when the properties are displayed by categories. In this case, it says this property belongs in the "Appearance" category. And, last, the `DefaultValue("")` attribute provides an empty string as the default value.

Now, because you're going to build a composite control, you need to make a few changes. First, you don't need any of the code Visual Studio generated inside the class. Second, you need your class to implement `INamingContainer` interface. We explain why you need the `INamingContainer` interface shortly. So now your control class should look like Listing 15-13.

Listing 15-13   *Initial Class for Composite Control*

```
using System;
using System.Web.UI;
```

```
using System.Web.UI.WebControls;
using System.ComponentModel;

namespace ControlLibrary
{
    /// <summary>
    /// Summary description for DateControl.
    /// </summary>
    [DefaultProperty("Value"),
    ValidationPropertyAttribute("Value"),
    ToolboxData("<{0}:DateControl runat=server></{0}:DateControl>")]
    public class DateControl : WebControl, INamingContainer
    {
    }
}
```

You've changed the `DefaultProperty` attribute to specify `"Value"` as the default property. You also added a new attribute, `ValidationProperty Attribute("Value")`, which specifies ASP.NET validator controls should use the Value property when checking this control for validity. This is discussed more in a following section.

The first thing you need to do now is add some class member variables. You're going to have three DropDownList controls, one each for the month, day, and year. You'll also want to have some constants for the day range and some variables for the year range. So, let's add the code in Listing 15-14 to the beginning of your class.

Listing 15-14 *Data Members for the Class*

```
private const int m_minDay = 1;
private const int m_maxDay = 31;
private int m_minYear = 1950;
private int m_maxYear = 2020;
private DropDownList m_month;
private DropDownList m_day;
private DropDownList m_year;
```

Notice you made the day range as constants, while the year range consists of variables. The reason for this is you'll allow the developer to adjust the year range when designing the form. On the other hand, you'll always be using a range of 1 to 31 for your days.

Now, let's add a constructor for this control:

```
/// <summary>
/// Constructor -- makes sure the controls exist
/// </summary>
public DateControl() { EnsureChildControls(); }
```

The constructor is extremely simple. All it does is call the base class method
`EnsureChildControls()`. This method is a protected virtual method of the
`Control` class and checks to see if the composite controls were created by
examining `ChildControlsCreated`, a protected bool property, which is false
when the child controls haven't yet been created. If this flag is false, it calls the
protected virtual method `CreateChildControls()` method, also a member of
the `Control` class.

You'll override this class to create our child controls, namely the three DropDownList
controls. Listing 15-15 shows your implementation of this method. Every time a
developer drops your custom control on to a Web page in Design mode, your constructor
will ensure that you create the controls. This way, the developer can accurately
determine the size and shape of your control with respect to the rest of the layout
of the page.

Listing 15-15   *CreateChildControls Implementation*

```
/// <summary>
/// Creates the composite controls for this user-defined control.
/// Should only be called once.
/// </summary>
protected override void CreateChildControls()
{
    int index;

    // create the month control
    m_month = new DropDownList();
    m_month.Items.Add(new ListItem("January", "1"));
    m_month.Items.Add(new ListItem("February", "2"));
    m_month.Items.Add(new ListItem("March", "3"));
    m_month.Items.Add(new ListItem("April", "4"));
    m_month.Items.Add(new ListItem("May", "5"));
    m_month.Items.Add(new ListItem("June", "6"));
    m_month.Items.Add(new ListItem("July", "7"));
```

```
m_month.Items.Add(new ListItem("August", "8"));
m_month.Items.Add(new ListItem("September", "9"));
m_month.Items.Add(new ListItem("October", "10"));
m_month.Items.Add(new ListItem("November", "11"));
m_month.Items.Add(new ListItem("December", "12"));
Controls.Add(m_month);

// add a space
Controls.Add(new LiteralControl(" "));

// create the day control
m_day = new DropDownList();
for (index = m_minDay; index < m_maxDay + 1; index++)
{
    m_day.Items.Add(new ListItem(index.ToString(), index.ToString()));
}
Controls.Add(m_day);

// add a space
Controls.Add(new LiteralControl(" "));

// create the year control
m_year = new DropDownList();
populateYears();
Controls.Add(m_year);
}
```

We've overridden the `CreateChildControls()` method to create three
DropDownList controls, separated by single spaces. Each DropDownList control is
populated with the appropriate values. At the end of this method, you call a separate
routine, `populateYears()`, to fill in the possible choices for the year drop-down
control. This is in a separate method because you'll need to repopulate the
ListItems in this control if and when the developer changes the range of years.
The code for this method is shown here:

```
/// <summary>
/// Populate the drop down list with the years based on the
/// min and max values.
/// </summary>
protected void populateYears()
{
    m_year.Items.Clear();
```

```
        for (int index = m_minYear; index < m_maxYear + 1; index++)
        {
            m_year.Items.Add(new ListItem(index.ToString(),
                index.ToString()));
        }
}
```

You specified your default property is the Value property, so let's implement this property. Listing 15-16 contains the code for this property.

Listing 15-16   *The Value Property*

```
/// <summary>
/// Default property that gets/sets the System.DateTime
/// value for this control
/// </summary>
[Bindable(true),
Category("Appearance"),
DefaultValue("")]
public object Value
{
    // this is the get portion of the property
    get
    {
        object date = null;
        // make sure the controls exist before using them
        EnsureChildControls();
        try
        {
            // obtain a date value from each of the 3 drop downs
            // if it fails to create the date, then the control returns null
            date = new DateTime(Convert.ToInt32(m_year.SelectedItem.Value),
                Convert.ToInt32(m_month.SelectedItem.Value),
                Convert.ToInt32(m_day.SelectedItem.Value));
        }
        catch (Exception)
        {
        }
        return date;
    }

    // this is the set portion of the property
    set
    {
        // make sure the controls exist before using them
```

```
        EnsureChildControls();
        try
        {
            // takes the given value and separates it into its
            // composite parts --month, day, year
            DateTime theValue = (DateTime) value;
            m_year.SelectedIndex = theValue.Year - m_minYear;
            m_month.SelectedIndex = theValue.Month - 1;
            m_day.SelectedIndex = theValue.Day - m_minDay;
        }
        catch (Exception)
        {
            // the given value was not a valid date, so
            // set all of the drop downs to selected index -1
            m_year.SelectedIndex = -1;
            m_month.SelectedIndex = -1;
            m_day.SelectedIndex = -1;
        }
    }
}
```

This is fairly simple. The `get` routine tries to construct a `System.DateTime` value from the three values in the DropDownList controls. If they form a valid date, this is what's returned. If not, an exception is thrown and the value `null` is returned. The `set` routine attempts to take the given value and convert it to a `DateTime` value. If successful, it takes its commensurate parts and assigns them to each of the three DropDownList controls. Otherwise, the value isn't a valid date and it sets the controls to the first item in their lists.

Only one major part is left. To have this control validated on the client-side, you need to use an ASP.NET CustomValidator. The CustomValidator enables you to specify either a VBScript or a JavaScript function that it will use to validate a control on the client-side. So, you need to provide some client-side script. Do this by registering a script block in the `OnPreRender()` event handler. Listing 15-17 shows you how to do this.

Listing 15-17   *Pre-Render the Control*

```
protected override void OnPreRender(System.EventArgs e)
{
    base.OnPreRender(e);
    Page.RegisterClientScriptBlock("DateControlValidator" + ClientID,
        @"<SCRIPT LANGUAGE=""javascript"">
```

```
function Validate" + ClientID + @"(source, arguments)
{
    arguments.IsValid = true;
    month = document.all[""" + ClientID + @":_ctl0""].value;
    day = document.all[""" + ClientID + @":_ctl1""].value;
    year = document.all[""" + ClientID + @":_ctl2""].value;
    testDate = new Date(year, month - 1, day);
    // test if it is valid
    if (testDate.getDate() != day)
    {
        arguments.IsValid = false;
    }
}
</SCRIPT>");
}
```

Because you're overriding the base class `OnPreRender()` method, the first thing you do is call the base class's implementation of this method. The second line of code registers the block of script. The script operates on the actual HTML elements emitted to the client browser, so to determine if the date is valid, it tries to create a date using the values from the three drop-down menus. When ASP.NET emits the HTML for your composite control, it breaks the HTML down into its child controls, giving each a unique name by prefixing it with the name of the composite control and adding a `_ctl` suffix. This suffix is made unique by appending a number, one for each child control, beginning with zero. The `_ctl` suffix comes from a private member, `automaticIDPrefix`, on the `Control` class. You use this knowledge to identify the child controls in the JavaScript. If the values obtained from the DropDownList controls are invalid, JavaScript then creates a date with a different value. Using this, compare the values and when they aren't the same, you set the `arguments.IsValid` property to false.

When you're ready, you'll add a CustomValidator to this page. The CustomValidator is one of the supplied .NET validator controls. You simply drag-and-drop it on to your page's design surface. The next thing you need to do is assign the `ClientValidationFunction` property the name of your JavaScript function. The property expects the method signature to be in the following form:

```
functionName(source, arguments)
```

The arguments variable has two properties: `Value` and `IsValid`. When you set the `IsValid` property to false, the CustomValidator perceives that the control isn't

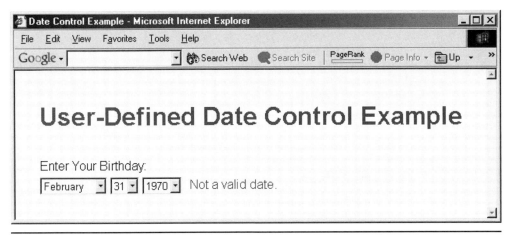

Figure 15-16   *Exercising the custom validator on your Date Control*

valid and displays its error message. After dropping a custom validator beside your control on the Web page, assigning the `ClientValidationFunction` property with the name of your JavaScript method, and mapping it to validate your custom control, you're ready for client validation. As you see in Listing 15-17, the function name is dependent on the `ClientID` value. Therefore, the value you assign the `ClientValidationFunction` property of your validator control is different for each instance of your composite control. Figure 15-16 shows you what happens when the user enters an invalid date.

You can now make your composite control a little fancier by providing additional functionality. For example, to make this consistent with other controls on a Web page, you can expose the `Enable` and `BackColor` properties. Because your base class already exposes such properties, you must specify that you're overriding them. Listing 15-18 shows you how to override these properties.

Listing 15-18   *Exposing the Enable and BackColor Properties*

```
public override System.Drawing.Color BackColor
{
    get
    {
        EnsureChildControls();
        return m_month.BackColor;
    }
```

```
        set
        {
            EnsureChildControls();
            m_month.BackColor = value;
            m_day.BackColor = value;
            m_year.BackColor = value;
        }
    }

    public override bool Enabled
    {
        get
        {
            EnsureChildControls();
            return (m_month.Enabled && m_day.Enabled && m_year.Enabled);
        }

        set
        {
            EnsureChildControls();
            m_month.Enabled = value;
            m_day.Enabled = value;
            m_year.Enabled = value;
        }
    }
```

Notice that in both the `get` and `set` methods of both properties, you always call the `EnsureChildControls()` method first. As mentioned earlier, this method first checks the `ChildControlsCreated` property, a Boolean flag, which is false when the child controls haven't yet been created. If this flag is false, then this method calls the `CreateChildControls()` method. So, by calling the `EnsureChildControls()` method, you can be assured your child controls exist.

Finally, we decided earlier to make the minimum and maximum values for the year range variables, rather than constants. We did this so developers could adjust the range of dates for this control. To give the developer the capability to modify the range at design time, you need to expose two properties, as shown in Listing 15-19.

Listing 15-19   *Min and Max Year Properties*

```
public int MaxYear
{
    get { return m_maxYear; }
    set
    {
        m_maxYear = value;
        EnsureChildControls();
        populateYears();
    }
}

public int MinYear
{
    get { return m_minYear; }
    set
    {
        m_minYear = value;
        EnsureChildControls();
        populateYears();
    }
}
```

These properties repopulate the year control each time they're modified. They do this by calling the `populateYears()` method.

That's pretty much all the code needed for a simple, composite date control, but you can certainly do more with this control. For instance, you could add some labels beneath the drop-down controls that specify month, day, and year. You can also expose other properties of the `WebControl` base class to make your composite control more customizable.

This example gives you a basis for building composite controls. You can take the basic concepts shown here to build other kinds of composite controls. For example, you could design a Social Security Number composite control that contains three text boxes, each allowing only numeric text entry. Other examples include phone number controls and ZIP code controls. The possibilities are limited only by your imagination.

Summary

You have learned a lot in this chapter. ASP.NET encompasses .NET's entire Web Application offering. In the last chapter, you learned how ASP.NET provides developers with Web services. In this chapter, you learned how to build Web Applications, consume Web services, use the provided Web controls, and even build your own custom controls. In summary, we discussed the following:

▶ ASP.NET and Visual Studio make building Web Applications easy. ASP.NET offers a rich set of Web controls that can easily be dragged-and-dropped on to Web page surfaces.

▶ ASP.NET Web files consist of .aspx files and an optional code behind page, .aspx.cs (or .aspx.vb, if you're using VB.NET).

▶ ASP.NET uses events and delegates to handle user interaction with Web pages. Events are posted back to the server-side code, sending information back and forth using ViewState.

▶ ASP.NET makes consuming Web services easy using Web references. Instead of manually generating WSDL files or downloading them from the Web service itself, ASP.NET generates the WSDL and the proxy files automatically.

▶ The DataGrid is an exceptionally versatile Web control. You can modify how the columns, rows, and headings are displayed. You can control the fonts used. You can paginate the DataGrid. And, you can perform inline editing of the control's rows.

▶ You can build custom controls in ASP.NET. Custom controls use .ascx files (and .ascx.cs or .ascx.vb code behind files).

▶ You can easily develop composite controls with ASP.NET.

Windows Forms

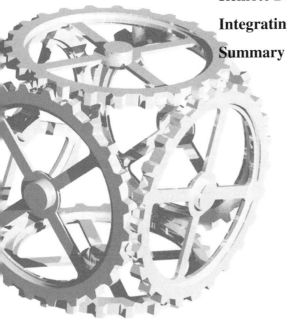

507

I n Chapter 15, you learned how to develop ASP.NET applications using Web Forms. In this chapter, the focus is on developing Windows applications using the Windows Forms model. You'll find that developing a Windows application hasn't changed too much from the Visual Basic model, but you'll also find it's much more powerful. Throughout this chapter, you look at the features that make this model so powerful and build samples that take advantage of this power. Instead of trying to cover the entire `Windows.Forms` namespace, the focus is on developing and expanding an application, while we add new features and modify its design. We also discuss best practices for designing applications that are both extensible and maintainable.

Throughout this chapter, the application we develop and evolve is used to view and manage employee information for a fictitious company. The source code for all our samples can be found at **www.1osborne.com/** in the Downloads section of the McGraw-Hill/Osborne Web site. The database used for our sample application is the same one first introduced in Chapter 6, and then used again in Chapters 7 and 8. In addition, the samples in this chapter use the same XSD schemas defined in Chapter 8. We start with a stand-alone Windows application and evolve it into a distributed Windows application that uses the Web services developed in Chapter 8. Toward the end of this chapter, we examine a sample that demonstrates how to integrate .NET applications with Java applications through the use of Web services. That's a lot of material to cover, so let's begin.

New Windows Application

The first application we'll build is a form-based application that interfaces directly with a database, and provides operations to view and save data. The first step in developing any application should be a good analysis phase. We can assume, however, that the analysis has already been performed and we're ready to start building our first form— named "AcmeEmployees". This is a Windows application that enables users to get a list of employees, to view detail information on each employee, and to update employee specific information. The first place to start is by launching Visual Studio.NET (VS.NET) and choosing New Project from the start page or File | New | Project from the File menu.

The following New Project dialog window shows the settings we need for our first project. For this example, we'll use C# as the language choice. We're developing a Windows application, which is shown in the templates window. The location shown in the dialog box that follows is "d:\Examples\Chapter16", however, you can choose any location on your system you want. The name for our new project is

"AcmeEmployee", which is also shown in the next dialog box. Complete the operation by pressing OK, which creates a new subdirectory under the location you chose, using the same name as the project.

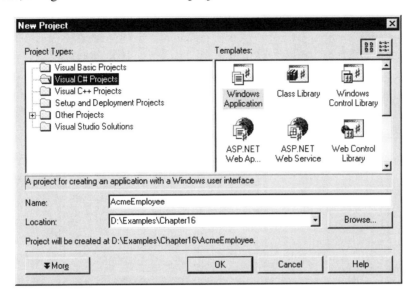

Inside the new project directory, you'll find several files created by VS.NET as a starting point for building the application. Figure 16-1 shows the Visual Studio development environment with our new project loaded and stubbed-out. Before getting into development details, let's look at some of the different windows in the development environment. This discussion assumes that you are using the "Visual Studio Default" layout, which can be set in the MyProfiles tab of the Start Page. Starting at the top right, we have a *Solution Explorer,* which lists the different elements that make up the solution. In our example, we have one project in the solution named AcmeEmployee, which contains References, AssemblyInfo, an application icon, and a default form for our application named Form1. Below the Solution Explorer is a *Properties* window, which displays the properties of any item or component that's currently active. The properties displayed in Figure 16-1 are for the Form1 window, which is the active component.

The main Development window shown on the left in Figure 16-1 can contain different types of windows, which are based on the type of work being performed. If you're placing controls on a form, the window is a designer. If you're working on code, the window will contain a code editor. In addition, each window you open will have a tab at the top that can be used to switch between the open windows during development. To the left of the main Development window is a menu named

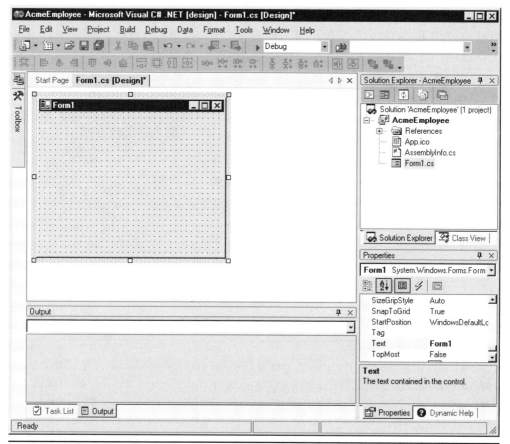

Figure 16-1   *AcmeEmployee stub-out*

Toolbox. The Toolbox menu is typically referred to as *the toolbox* and it contains submenus with different types of controls. Later in this chapter, you'll add Custom controls to the Components menu of the toolbox.

We haven't discussed all the sections in the development environment, however, the documentation with VS.NET is comprehensive. The help system has been completely redeveloped, and it contains more information and samples than ever before. The main reason we discussed the windows in Figure 16-1 was to set a foundation for terms that will be used throughout the rest of this chapter. When we discuss selecting the TextBox control from the Windows Forms menu in the toolbox, you'll know what that means. Another term we need to clarify is *Context menu,* which is a menu associated with a specific item. The way to display a context menu is to select the item and press the right-mouse button, which is called *right-clicking* the item.

Now that you have a high-level overview of the different terms we're going to use, let's start writing code. The first thing you need to do is remove the default form and add a new form named "Directory". The following steps describe how to add the form.

1. Select Form1 in the Solution window and select Delete from the Context menu or the Edit menu. Answer yes to all prompts.

2. Select the AcmeEmployee project in the Solution window and select Add | Add Windows Form from the Context menu. The following dialog box is displayed:

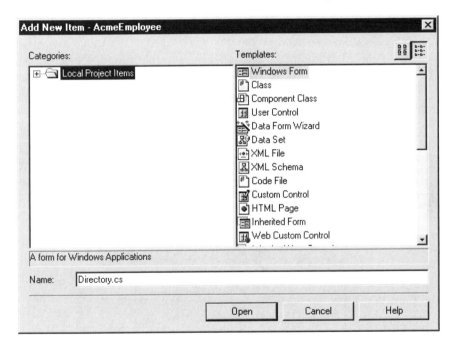

3. Make sure the Windows Form template is selected and change the name to Directory.cs.

4. Click the Open button to create the new form.

Now, you could have simply renamed Form1 to Directory, but that means you'd also have to change names in the code behind. It's much easier to delete the default and add your new form.

Adding Controls

The next step is to add all the controls used to display and manage data from the database on to your form. If you're used to developing Windows applications using older versions of Visual Basic, this will be familiar. The toolbox contains controls for editing text, displaying lists, executing commands, and nearly anything else needed by an application. A control is added to the form by selecting it in the menu and dragging it on to the form. You can also double-click any of the controls and they'll be added to the active form. In your first application, you'll be using Button, ComboBox, Label, ListBox, and TextBox controls.

Figure 16-2 shows the Directory form in a Designer window with all the controls added. The form has also been named "Employee Directory", which is shown in the title bar. To set the title, you need to update the Text property of the Directory form with the text displayed in Figure 16-2. Rather than walk through step-by-step instructions for adding the controls, we'll list each control starting at the top left, moving left-to-right and top-to-bottom. Table 16-1 shows this list with the type of control and the values used for the name and text properties on each control.

When you look through the list of controls in Table 16-1, they should all be familiar to most Windows developers. We're using the ListBox in Figure 16-2 to display a list of employees, and then show detailed information for each employee in the Label and TextBox controls on the form. The difference between this implementation and the previous example in Chapter 8 is we'll also support the capability to update

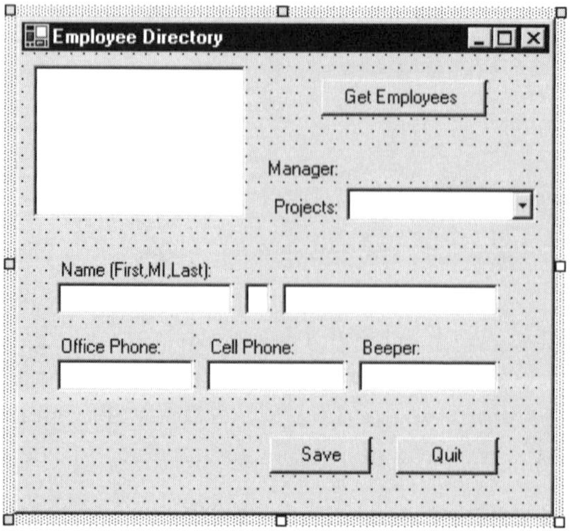

Figure 16-2   *Form designer*

Type	Name	Text
ListBox	lstEmployees	
Button	btnEmployees	Get Employees
Label	Label1	Manager:
Label	lblManager	
Label	Label2	Projects:
ComboBox	cboProjects	
Label	Label3	Name (First,MI,Last):
TextBox	txtFirst	
TextBox	txtMI	
TextBox	txtLast	
Label	Label4	OfficePhone:
Label	Label5	Cell Phone:
Label	Label6	Beeper:
TextBox	txtOffice	
TextBox	txtCell	
TextBox	txtBeeper	
Button	btnSave	Save
Button	btnQuit	Quit

Table 16-1   *Employee Directory Controls*

employee information. With this last step, we now have a bunch of controls on a form and we need to do something with those controls.

Instead of using traditional approaches where text attributes on each control are set, and then read when the user presses save, we'll bind the controls to DataSets. By now, you should have a good understanding of the important role that DataSets play in the .NET Framework. Almost every sample program in this book has used DataSets in one way or another. In addition, we'll use the same DataSets created for Chapter 8 in this chapter. We'll also use DataAdapters to populate the DataSets, but we won't take advantage of the wizards and designers that can be used to generate database commands automatically. Instead, the approach used to query data will be the same as Chapter 8 and we'll use OPENXML to update the database. Once you understand the reason for this approach, it will make sense. Right now, you probably have some questions.

Adding DataSets

You can read data from a database using ADO.NET in two basic ways: `DataSets` or `DataReaders`. It's a little more involved than that, but these two components represent the main interfaces. The *DataReader* has a performance advantage, but it only allows static, read-only access to the data, and it remains connected while the data is processed. The *DataSet* supports the capability to pass data between tiers, allows manipulation of data without being connected to a database, and supports binding to controls. For these examples, we'll use `DataSets` to take advantage of binding in Windows Forms and use their remoting capabilities as we evolve the application. In addition, by taking advantage of the power `DataSets` provide, we can write business components that focus on applying business rules to data, instead of managing the data.

Data Abstraction

As mentioned previously, we won't take advantage of the wizards in the DataAdapter used to generate SQL. Instead, the methods we use to retrieve and update data in the database are designed to provide a data abstraction layer between the application and physical structure of the tables in the database. If we'd decided to take advantage of the DataAdapter wizards, they would create SQL code that binds us to the physical database structure. These statements would be embedded throughout our application, which makes it difficult to adjust the database and maintain the application over time.

To provide a data abstraction layer between the business components and the database tables, we'll use stored procedures. By using stored procedures, we can rename and restructure database tables with almost no impact on the data returned. This is accomplished by using aliases and Transact SQL statements to join tables together, which control the structure returned. In addition, the stored procedures that perform updates and inserts will use a new feature available with SQL Server 2000 named `OPENXML`. With the use of `OPENXML` to update the database, you can pass the XML into a stored procedure, which then uses the data from the XML to update fields in the database tables. We only have one parameter on the stored procedure, which is the XML data, and it's much easier to handle data type conversions between the XML fields and database fields.

Previously, we mentioned you would be using the `DataSets` from Chapter 8, which means the first step to adding `DataSets` is to copy them. The only files that need to be copied are EmployeesDS.xsd and EmployeeDetailDS.xsd. You don't need the .xsd.cs or .xsd.xsx files that have the same name. Once the files are copied over, you need to generate the `DataSets` you left behind with the .xsd.cs files. The reason you have to generate, and not copy, the .xsd files is because the Chapter 8 project contains custom information you wouldn't have in your project and Visual Studio would create a second `DataSet` with a 1 appended to the name. To generate a `DataSet`, you need to open the .xsd file in Design view. When the Designer window opens, you should see tables. Right-click anywhere inside the Designer window and select Generate DataSet from the Context menu. That's it, the Framework will automatically generate the code behind (.xsd.cs) and resource (.xsd.xsx) files for this project.

The last step is to add the `DataSets` to the Form Designer window, so you can bind controls to them. It's not as easy as dragging them from the Solution Explorer and dropping them on to the Designer window, however. Instead, you need to use one of the controls in the toolbox to add the `DataSet`. The following steps describe how to add the `EmployeesDS DataSet` to the Designer window.

1. Open the Data submenu in the toolbox.

2. Select `DataSet` from the menu, and then drag-and-drop it on to the Designer window. The following dialog box is displayed.

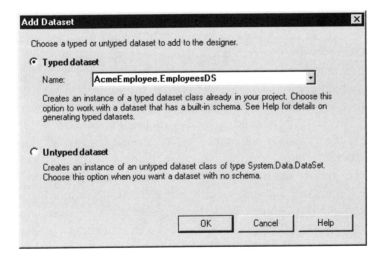

3. Make sure that `Typed DataSet` is selected and the `AcmeEmployee.EmployeesDS DataSet` is displayed in the drop-down box.

4. Choose OK to add the `DataSet` to the Designer window.

Once the `DataSet` has been added, rename it to mEmployeesDS. Follow the same steps to add the `EmployeeDetailDS` and rename the new designer-based `DataSet` to mDetailDS.

Binding DataSets to Controls

Now that you have the `DataSets` defined and your controls are added to the form, it's time to tie, or bind, them together. Binding the controls of Windows Forms is easy to do and somewhat different from ASP.NET. With ASP.NET, you associate `DataSets` with components and the framework uses that relationship to access the data when generating HTML: the relationship is one-way only. This has to do with the disconnected programming model in Web applications. When actions on a Web page are processed, the `DataSets` bound to controls won't contain any data because the original `DataSet` used to generate the HTML has been released. Even calling DataBind on the page won't transfer data into the `DataSet`. Instead, you need to write code that reinitializes the `DataSet` and loads it with data passed in from the client in the ASP Form object.

With a Windows Forms application, the control and `DataSet` are bound together in real-time because they have a much longer life span. The relationship is maintained during the lifetime of these objects and a two-way relationship exists between them. When a control is updated, the `DataSet` bound to it is updated, and when the `DataSet` is updated, the bound control is updated. This makes writing code to access and manage data in the controls easy. You have little need to access individual controls. Instead, you simply need to manipulate `DataSets`.

We're getting ahead of ourselves, though. Instead of talking about updates, we need to focus on getting the `DataSets` bound to the controls. That data is bound in several different ways and we'll examine the two most common types of binding in this example. The first type of binding deals with binding a `DataSet` to some type of List control, like a ListBox, a ComboBox, and even a Grid. With these controls, you need to specify a DataSource, which can include a `DataSet` or DataTable, and then you need to specify the fields that will be managed by the control. The second type of binding deals with binding specific properties to fields in a `DataSet` without specifying a DataSource. These bindings are used for controls that can only hold a single value, like a TextBox or Label. Let's examine these bindings in a little more detail, and then we'll list all the bindings you need to set on the controls.

In our example, the ListBox control is bound to the list of employees in the `mEmployeesDS DataSet` using three properties. The first property is *DataSource,* which is bound to the `Employee` DataTable. The second property is *DisplayMember,* which represents the field displayed in the list and is bound to the `LastName` field in the `Employee` DataTable. The last property is the *ValueMember,* which holds the value represented by a selection and is bound to the `EmployeeID` field in the `Employee` DataTable. When this control is rendered, it will display all the employees in the `DataSet` with the `LastName` displayed and the `EmployeeID` stored as the value for each item in the list.

The TextBox controls in this example are bound to single fields in the `DataSet` and don't require the use of a DataSource. The only property bound to a field is the Text property, which is bound to a field in the `Employee` DataTable in this example. One drawback to binding is you can't specify multiple fields in the `DataSet` for a single property and it doesn't support calling methods as does ASP.NET binding. As a result, you need to modify some of the fields in our example before binding them to controls. We look at the code used to modify the data when discussing the `Get Employees` method in the next section.

The following table shows the data-binding values set for the controls in our example that use a DataSource.

Control Name	DataSource	DisplayMember	ValueMember
lstEmployees	mEmployees.Employee	LastName	EmployeeID
cboProjects	mDetails.Project	Name	(not used)

Because the cboProjects ComboBox is only meant to display the list of projects, we didn't need to set a ValueMember. In addition, these controls have additional properties we aren't using, which supports the binding of selected properties to other `DataSet` fields.

The next table lists all the TextBox controls and the binding information defined for them.

Control Name	Text
txtFirst	mDetailsDS.Employee.FirstName
txtMI	mDetailsDS.Employee.MiddleInitial
txtLast	mDetailsDS.Employee.LastName
txtOffice	mDetailsDS.Employee.OfficePhone
txtCell	mDetailsDS.Employee.CellPhone
txtBeeper	mDetailsDS.Employee.Beeper

As you can see, this is straight-forward. Each Text property is bound to a single field in the `mDetailsDS DataSet`. By binding these text boxes to a single `DataSet`, you can perform set-based operations on this data. For instance, when you need to update employee information, all we need to do is pass the `mDetailDS DataSet` to a procedure that updates the database with information in the `DataSet`. No need exists to access the individual text properties when performing an update: the data is already extracted through the binding process. This might not seem like a big deal when building a stand-alone application with access to all the controls, but it does become significant when you want to interact with remote services.

Writing the Code

Now that you've finished adding the controls and `DataSets`, and you've defined the binding, you need to write some code. The class diagram in Figure 16-3 shows three classes that will be added to the project. This diagram follows the same design principles discussed in Chapter 8: the operations are divided into a business class and a data access class. The *business class* is responsible for implementing business rules and the *data access class* is responsible for interacting with the database. In some cases, the business class methods act as a pass-through, but by implementing a consistent model, any updates that require new business rules will be easy to add. In addition, if the database interaction needed modification, no impact would occur to business objects. In other words, the main reason for separating these operations is to provide maximum maintainability and extensibility.

The business class in Figure 16-3 is prefixed with `bc` and the data access class is prefixed with `dc`. By using these prefixes on the class names, it's easy to identify which classes have business rules and which classes are used to interact with the database. The last class shown in Figure 16-3 is a utility class named DataManager. This class provides helper functions used to manage connections, create, and initialize DataAdapters, execute nonquery SQL commands, and convert `DataSets` into XML. We'll also add code to the Directory.cs class, which contains code for the

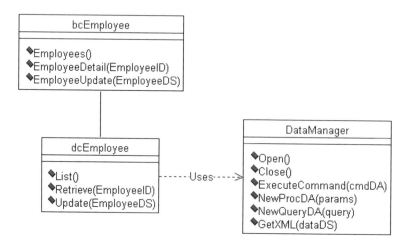

Figure 16-3   *AcmeEmployee class diagram*

Directory form. In addition, we'll modify the application config file to add connection information, instead of hard-coding that into the application.

Four different operations can be performed by the controls shown in Figure 16-2. The Get Employees button initiates an action that retrieves a list of employees and loads them into the lstEmployees ListBox. When an item is selected in the ListBox, another action is initiated that will retrieve detail information for the selected employee and display the information using the Label and TextBox controls, as shown in Figure 16-2. The next operation is initiated when the Save button is clicked. The Save operation uses the `DataSet` bound to TextBox controls to update the database. The last operation, initiated when the Quit button is pressed, is used to unload the form and quit the application. We don't need to examine the details behind the Quit operation, but we do need to examine how the other three operations interact with the database and interact with the bound controls.

Get Employees

Get Employees is the first step users will perform when they interact with this application. When the Get Employees button is pressed, it calls an event function, which is shown in Listing 16-1. This event can be added by double-clicking the button in the Designer window, shown in Figure 16-2. You can also add events by selecting the Event icon in the Properties window for any object that has events. The Properties window, shown in the following, displays the events available to the Get Employees button with the `Click` event filled in. The icon that looks like a lightning bolt in the Properties window is used to display the list of events. If this icon doesn't exist, make sure a Designer window is open. Otherwise the object doesn't have events.

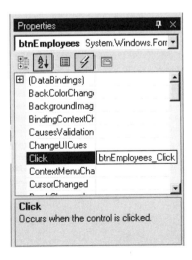

Listing 16-1 *Get Employees*

```
private void btnEmployees_Click(object sender, System.EventArgs e)
{
    // get the list
    bcEmployee emp = new bcEmployee();
    EmployeesDS empDS = emp.Employees();

    // update the Last name field
    foreach( EmployeesDS.EmployeeRow row in empDS.Employee.Rows )
    {
        string mi = "";
        if( row.IsMiddleInitialNull() == false )
        {
            mi = row.MiddleInitial;
        }
        // get the full name
        row.LastName = GetFullName(row.FirstName, mi, row.LastName);
    }
    // Update the list box.
    lstEmployees.BeginUpdate();
    lstEmployees.DataSource = empDS.Employee;
    lstEmployees.EndUpdate();
}
// Helper used to build full name information
protected string GetFullName( string first, string mi, string last )
{
    string fullName = last + ", " + first;
    if( mi != null && mi.Length > 0 )
    {
        fullName += " " + mi + ".";
    }
    return fullName;
}
```

The first function in Listing 16-1 is the event handler for the `btnEmployees Click` event. The first operation in this event handler is to call our business component to retrieve a list of employees from the database. Listing 16-2 shows the business and data access code used to perform this operation. The first function in Listing 16-2 is called from the event handler code in Listing 16-1. In the business class, we're instantiating a new instance of the `EmployeesDS DataSet` and passing that to a data access function that will fill it with data.

Listing 16-2   *Get Employees—Business and Data Access Code*

```
[bcEmployee.cs]
// get a list of employees
public EmployeesDS Employees()
{
   EmployeesDS EmployeeDS = new EmployeesDS();
   dcEmployee EmpData = new dcEmployee();
   EmpData.List( EmployeeDS );

   return EmployeeDS;
}
```
```
[dcEmployee.cs]
// get a list of employees
public void List( DataSet destDS )
{
   if( destDS != null )
   {
      // instantiate the Data Manager component and open a connection
      DataManager dataMgr = new DataManager();
      dataMgr.Open();

      // Initialize a data adapter
      string sQuery = "SELECT EmployeeID, FirstName,
                     LastName, MiddleInitial FROM Employee";
      SqlDataAdapter listDA = dataMgr.NewQueryDA( sQuery );
      listDA.Fill( destDS, "Employee" );

      // close the connection
      dataMgr.Close();
   }
}
```

The data access function, shown in Listing 16-2, is used to interact with the database and fill the `DataSet` passed in with data from the query. You might have noticed we're using a SQL command in this query, which is contradictory to our earlier statement about using stored procedures for everything. Because this is an example application, we want to demonstrate how SQL queries can be used. In practice, however, we would use a stored procedure here, instead of the SQL query. The data access function in Listing 16-2 uses our `DataManager` utility class to create a new DataAdapter initialized with the query, and then uses that adaptor to fill the `DataSet` that was passed in.

Once the `DataSet` is returned to the event handler in Listing 16-1, you can perform operations on that data. Because of the limitations in binding that only allow one field to be bound to a property on the control, you need to format some of the data for your display. The lstEmployees DisplayMember is bound to the LastName, however, you want to display the full name of your users in this list. As a result, you're using the `foreach` operator to iterate through the `DataSet` and update the LastName field with a formatted full name using other fields in the `DataSet`. This is an acceptable operation because the data is read-only and you won't be attempting to update the database with this formatted data. The second function in Listing 16-1 is used to format the name information.

Once the `DataSet` is formatted and ready to use, you need bind that data to the lstEmployees ListBox control. One approach would have been to merge the `DataSet` returned from the business component with the page-specific `DataSet` bound to the control. This causes a problem, however, which results in locking up the application during the merge process. As a result, the best approach with a list is to replace the DataSource on the control with the new one we just filled with data. Because this is the same `DataSet` type used in the binding statements, your bind operations will work with no problems. The `BeginUpdate()` and `EndUpdate()` functions in Listing 16-1 are used to keep the control from painting while you update it, which results in better performance.

Get Details

Now that the lstEmployees ListBox is filled with data, we'll use the `SelectedIndexChanged` event on the ListBox to retrieve detail information. This event will fire when the ListBox is first populated and anytime the user selects a different item in the list. Listing 16-3 shows the event-handler function, along with the business and data access functions called.

Listing 16-3   *Get Detail—Event, Business, and Data Access Code*

```
[Directory.cs]
private void lstEmployees_SelectedIndexChanged(object sender,
                                              System.EventArgs e)
{
   // Get the EmplyeeID from the selected value
   int empID = int.Parse(lstEmployees.SelectedValue.ToString());

   // get the details
   bcEmployee emp = new bcEmployee();
   EmployeeDetailDS detailDS = emp.EmployeeDetail( empID );
```

```
   // Make sure we have employee information
   if( detailDS.Employee != null )
   {
      // update the Manager name... this is read-only
      if( detailDS.Manager.Rows.Count > 0 )
      {
         EmployeeDetailDS.ManagerRow row = detailDS.Manager[0];
         row.LastName = GetFullName( row.FirstName, null, row.LastName);
      }
      // clear any previous data in the Form DataSet and
      // merge the Data from the database into it.
      mDetailDS.Clear();
      mDetailDS.Merge( detailDS );
   }
}
```

[bcEmployee.cs]

```
// get employee details from three different sources
public EmployeeDetailDS EmployeeDetail( int EmployeeID )
{
   // initialize a DataSet
   EmployeeDetailDS DetailDS = new EmployeeDetailDS();

   // get the EmployeeData
   dcEmployee oEmp = new dcEmployee();
   oEmp.Retrieve( DetailDS, EmployeeID );

   // return the result
   return DetailDS;
}
```

[dcEmployee.cs]

```
// Get employee detail information
public void Retrieve( DataSet destDS, int employeeID )
{
   if( destDS != null )
   {
      // instantiate the Data Manager component and open a connection
      DataManager dataMgr = new DataManager();
      dataMgr.Open();

      // Initialize a stored proc data adaptor
      SqlDataAdapter employeeDA = dataMgr.NewProcDA( "uspEmployeeDetail",
                                              "@EmployeeID",
                                              employeeID );
```

```
    // set the table names
    employeeDA.TableMappings.Add( "Table", "Employee" );
    employeeDA.TableMappings.Add( "Table1", "Manager" );
    employeeDA.TableMappings.Add( "Table2", "Project" );

    // invoke the query.
    employeeDA.Fill( destDS, "Table" );

    // close the connection
    dataMgr.Close();
  }
}
```

The first step in the event handler, shown in Listing 16-3, is to get the value of the currently selected item, which is the `EmployeeID`, and convert it into an integer. Next, the `EmployeeID` is passed into a business function used to retrieve the detail information. When you return from the business function, a new `DataSet` is populated with detail information for the selected employee. In this case, use the `Merge()` function to load the bound data set with your new data. In addition, before calling the `Merge()` function, you need to `Clear()` any existing data from the `DataSet`. Because the detail `DataSet` is bound to multiple TextBox controls, we didn't have the same option of replacing a DataSource as we did with the ListBox control, plus we need to use the bound `DataSet` when performing the update operation.

The business and data access functions shown in Listing 16-3 are similar to the functions shown in Listing 16-2. The business function initializes a `DataSet`, passes that `DataSet` to the data access class, and then returns it to the caller. The data access class uses a stored procedure, however, and includes some additional operations, discussed briefly in Chapter 8. The stored procedure we're calling has three `SELECT` statements, which will return three different tables. We need to adjust the names of the tables returned to load our `EmployeeDetailDS DataSet`. To adjust the names, you need to modify the TableMappings on the DataAdapter used to perform the query. The example in Listing 16-3 changes the name identified in the fill command to the appropriate names needed by the `DataSet`.

As soon as the Merge function in Listing 16-3 is called, all the TextBox, Label, and ComboBox controls bound to the `mDetailDS DataSet` are loaded with data. The user can now manipulate this data using the controls on the form. This includes modifying the data in the TextBox controls, and then saving those updates to the database.

Save

Listing 16-4 shows the event, business, and data access code for the Save operation. Similar to the Get Employees operation, we're using the Click event of the Save button to initiate saving employee data. For this operation, all you need to do is pass the detail DataSet bound to the controls on the page into your business function. Inside the business function, you would normally add business rules to validate the operation, but in this example, you're simply passing the DataSet into the data access function. Inside the data access function, we are converting the DataSet into an XML string and then passing that to a stored procedure, which uses the XML data to update the database. Because this command doesn't return data, you can use the ExecuteCommand function on the DataManager to execute the command.

Listing 16-4 *Save—Event, Business, and Data Access Code*

```
[Directory.cs]
private void btnSave_Click(object sender, System.EventArgs e)
{
    // Call the update function.
    bcEmployee emp = new bcEmployee();
    emp.EmployeUpdate( mDetailDS );
}
[bcEmployee.cs]
// Update the employee
public void EmployeUpdate( EmployeeDetailDS detailDS )
{
    // Invoke the update
    dcEmployee oEmp = new dcEmployee();
    oEmp.Update( detailDS );
}
[dcEmployee.cs]
// Update the data in the database
public void Update( EmployeeDetailDS empDS )
{
    // instantiate the DataManager and get the data
    // from the DataSet as XML
    DataManager dataMgr = new DataManager();
    string xml = dataMgr.GetXML( empDS );

    // Open a connection and initialize a stored proc data adapter
    dataMgr.Open();
```

```
    SqlDataAdapter employeeDA = dataMgr.NewProcDA( "uspEmployeeUpdate",
                                                   "@data", xml );
    // execute the query and close the connection
    dataMgr.ExecuteCommand( employeeDA );
    dataMgr.Close();
}
```

One interesting item in Listing 16-4 that might raise questions is the use of a method on the DataManager class to convert the `DataSet` into XML. If you're familiar with the XmlDataDocument class, you might be wondering why that wasn't used to get an XML representation of the data instead. The *XmlDataDocument* is a wrapper around the `DataSet` and can be used to perform XML-based operations against the data, but some issues occur with namespaces. When a strongly typed `DataSet` is created, it's given a namespace value that binds it to the XSD file. This namespace is carried into the XmlDataDocument, which means all XML operations must use the namespace to perform queries against the data. This behavior causes a problem when you try to use this data with operations that don't support namespaces, such as the OPENXML operation in SQL Server 2000.

According to the `System.Xml` documentation in the .NET Framework, you should be able to retrieve XML in a string format using the innerXML properties. This is a read-write property that should return XML data without namespaces added. In reality, what happens is the namespace on the base element is set to an empty string, which should work, but the original namespace attribute is added to all the child elements. This behavior makes the resulting XML difficult to use because you have to know that the parent element doesn't have a namespace, but all child elements do. As a result, we added a custom reader to the DataManager class that will completely remove any namespace attributes from the XML as it reads it from the source passed in. By using this method, we can convert the strongly typed `DataSet` into an XML string that can be used by SQL Server 2000.

Listing 16-5 shows the SQL Server stored procedure developed to perform the update operation. All the stored procedures used by the examples can be found with the source code for this chapter. The data access code in Listing 16-4 shows we're passing one parameter into the `uspEmployeeUpdate` stored procedure named "@data". This parameter is a string that contains the XML from our `mDetailDS` `DataSet`. Inside the stored procedure shown in Listing 16-5, you load that XML into memory using the `sp_xml_preparedocument` stored procedure, which initializes a handle that can be used in the OPENXML statements.

Listing 16-5 *uspEmployeeUpdate*

```
DECLARE @hDoc   int
-- Load our XML document
EXEC sp_xml_preparedocument @hDoc OUTPUT, @data

-- Now update the Employee information
UPDATE dbo.Employee
SET
    LastName        = xmlEmp.LastName
,   FirstName       = xmlEmp.FirstName
,   MiddleInitial   = xmlEmp.MiddleInitial
,   OfficePhone     = xmlEmp.OfficePhone
,   CellPhone       = xmlEmp.CellPhone
,   Beeper          = xmlEmp.Beeper
FROM OPENXML(@hDoc, '//Employee', 2)
WITH (
    EmployeeID      int             'EmployeeID'
,   LastName        nvarchar(50)    'LastName'
,   FirstName       nvarchar(50)    'FirstName'
,   MiddleInitial   nvarchar(1)     'MiddleInitial'
,   OfficePhone     nvarchar(10)    'OfficePhone'
,   CellPhone       nvarchar(10)    'CellPhone'
,   Beeper          nvarchar(10)    'Beeper'
) xmlEmp
WHERE
    dbo.Employee.EmployeeID  = xmlEmp.EmployeeID

-- Unload our XML document
EXEC sp_xml_removedocument @hDoc
```

The OPENXML statement in Listing 16-5 enables you to map fields in the XML document to database attributes that are used in the SET command. Because these fields are mapped to type safe variables, SQL server automatically performs conversion operations on the data found in the DataSet. If one of the XML elements can't be converted into the specified type, SQL server raises an error that can be caught in the data access class. By using OPENXML, performing set-based operations on XML data is also much easier, which means the same code shown in Listing 16-5 could be used to update several Employee elements at the same time. In addition, you can add fields to the DataSet without having to update code through all layers in the application. In other words, you never need to update the data access code if fields in the DataSet are modified.

Executing the Application

Once you finish adding all the code, you can build the application. Before you run this application, however, you have one more task to accomplish. We didn't discuss the DataManager class in detail, but it uses connection string information from a configuration file to connect to the database. You need to add this information to the configuration file for the application. The .NET Framework supports the capability to add configuration files to any .NET application. These configuration files use XML structures and are automatically handled by the framework. The .NET Framework provides a default handler, which can be used to add and read name/value pairs of data. You can also develop custom handlers and add custom elements to the configuration files. For this example, we'll take advantage of the default handlers.

The following XML element can be found in the configuration file for your application. The following `connString` key is the one that was added to hold connection information for the DataManager class. You need to update this configuration setting to change the data source at a minimum. The data source should be set to the name of your database, which usually defaults to the name of your machine. The rest of the following entries shown were added by Visual Studio.

```
<configuration>
  <appSettings>
    <!--   User application and configured property settings go here.-->
    <!--   Example: <add key="settingName" value="settingValue"/> -->
    <add key="lstEmployees.MultiColumn" value="True" />
    <add key="connString" value="data source=IVREL;initial
catalog=Employee;persist security info=False;user id=sa;packet size=4096" />
  </appSettings>
</configuration>
```

The config file in the project is named app.config and it was automatically added when you started adding controls. If this file doesn't exist, you can manually add one and name it app.config. When the application is built, the compiler will look for this file in the root directory of the project and copy it to the output directory, using the assembly name appended with .config. You can review Chapter 9 for more detail on assemblies, however, for this example, you simply need to know that AcmeEmployee.exe is considered an assembly. As a result, the config file generated for the application is named AcmeEmployee.exe.config.

When the .NET Framework sees the config file, it will implement handlers you can use to get values that were added to the `appSettings` block. The following code snippet shows the line used to initialize the connection string in the DataManager class.

```
// initialize the connection object
dataCN = new SqlConnection();
```

```
dataCN.ConnectionString =
    ConfigurationSettings.AppSettings.Get("connString");
```

By using the config file to hold this information, you needn't recompile code if the database connection information is changed.

Figure 16-4 shows our sample application after retrieving a list of employees. All the detail information for the first employee in the list is displayed and a user can modify that data. You now have your first fully functional Windows Forms application that performs read and update operations against a database. You're not finished, though. The phone numbers are difficult to read and there's no way to tell if data has been modified. You could add operations to format all the phone numbers, and then validate them as the user makes changes. You can also track when a user changes anything and set a local variable to determine if the changes should be saved.

The problem with adding a lot of formatting and validation code is you'll have to repeat the same code in any other forms that need to display phone numbers or manipulate employee data. With a large application, this translates to considerable duplication of code. In addition, we've introduced the possibility that formats and behavior will be inconsistent from one form to another. The solution to make formatting consistent is creating Custom controls that handle formatting based on a format property. To wrap all the employee-specific controls into a single unit, you can create a User control that contains all the individual employee controls in your application.

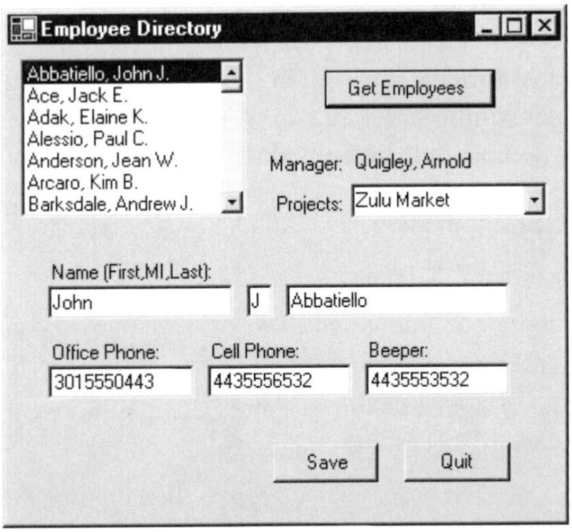

Figure 16-4 *First Windows Forms application*

New Controls

Both ASP.NET and Windows Forms applications support two different types of controls: Custom controls and User controls. At a high level, a *Custom control* is analogous to one of the Windows Forms controls we added to the AcmeEmployee application. Custom controls represent low-level controls that handle all their own painting and property management. It's possible, however, to inherit functionality from one of the Windows Forms controls and simply extend that functionality. On the other hand, User controls are considered much higher-level controls, used to group several low-level controls together. One big difference between User controls in Windows Forms and User controls in Web Forms is the Windows Forms User controls can't be dropped on to a designer from the Solution Explorer like the Web Forms User controls can.

For the AcmeEmployee application, we identified two different controls that would make developing additional forms in the application easier. The first control is a TextBox control that will handle application-specific formatting and validation for you. The second one is a User control that will group all the employee-specific controls into one control. As you can guess, the TextBox control represents a Custom control, which we'll develop by extending the Windows Forms TextBox control. Before you can start adding controls, however, you need to add a new project to your solution.

Adding a Control Library Project

To build controls that can be added to a Windows Forms application, you need to create a new Control Library application. For this example, you'll add the new project to your current solution, so you can work on both projects at the same time. The following steps demonstrate how to add a new project to the existing solution.

1. Right-click the Solution and select Add | New Project from the Context menu.

    or

    Select the Solution, and then select Add Project | New Project from the main File menu.

2. Make sure this is a Visual C# project and Select Windows Control Library from the list of templates on the right.

3. Make sure the Location is set correctly, and then change the name to AcmeControls. The following screenshot shows the correct configurations:

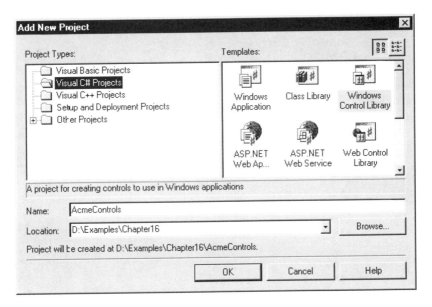

4. Select OK to create the new project and add it to your solution.

Figure 16-5 shows the development environment with the new Windows Control Library project added. Similar to what we found when creating the new Windows Forms application, VS.NET has added several files, with some stubbed-out code to get things started. Instead of starting with a Custom control, however, the default behavior is to create a default User control named "UserControl1". You should also notice the User control starts with a blank Designer window that will be used to hold other controls. Giving us a starting point is all well and good but, once again, we don't want to use the default. Instead, we're going to start by replacing the default User control with a Custom control.

Custom Controls

As mentioned previously, a Custom control represents a low-level control that handles its own painting and property management. The base class used for a Custom control is `System.Windows.Forms.Control`, which provides support for standard control properties and screen management. In addition, Custom controls can inherit functionality from existing controls and extend that functionality, which is preferred to building one from scratch. In our example, we'll only add one Custom control.

The new Custom control we're going to add is a TextBox control that extends the functionality of the `System.Windows.Forms.TextBox` control. Using the

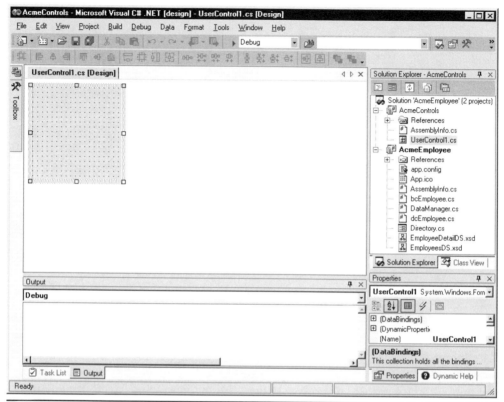

Figure 16-5   *New Windows Control Library project*

same steps described earlier in this chapter to add a new Form, replace UserControl1 in Figure 16-5 with a new Custom control named TextBoxEx.cs. This creates new files with stubbed-out code and opens a Designer window. This Designer window is used for Server or Data controls and isn't the same Designer window used for Windows Forms controls. The first thing you need to do is open the code window and change the class declaration to derive your control from TextBox. Listing 16-6 shows the updated class declaration for TextBoxEx, along with an enumeration that was added to the AcmeControls namespace. Notice the TextBoxEx class shown in Listing 16-6 is derived from the `System.Windows.Forms.TextBox` control, as previously described.

Listing 16-6   *TextBoxEx Class*

```
namespace AcmeControls
{
   public enum EditFormat
   {
      None,
      Phone
   }
   /// <summary>
   /// Summary description for TextBoxEx.
   /// </summary>
   public class TextBoxEx : System.Windows.Forms.TextBox
   {
      private EditFormat    mFormat = EditFormat.None;

      protected override void OnPaint(PaintEventArgs pe)
      {
         // Calling the base class OnPaint
         base.OnPaint(pe);
      }
   }
}
```

The enumeration shown in Listing 16-6 is named EditFormat and it represents the different formats supported by this control. Currently, those formats are None and Phone. The TextBoxEx class in Listing 16-6 has a private `EditFormat` member named `mFormat`, which is initialized with the value `EditFormat.None`. Not shown in Listing 16-6 is a property with `get` and `set` operations used to update this member variable. The only other code shown in Listing 16-6 is the `OnPaint` function. This function is called when the control is rendered and it needs to paint to the form. In our example, we don't have any custom painting and we'll use the default behavior supplied by the base class, which will draw our text box.

Listing 16-7 shows the Text property, along with functions used to `Trim` and `Format` data that will be displayed in the text box. For this control, we overrode the Text property in our base class, so we can format strings before adding them to the base. We also need to strip formatting characters from the text displayed in the text box when accessing the Text property. The reason for stripping off the format characters is we don't want to store format information with the data in the database. The private methods shown in Listing 16-7 are used to handle the actual `Trim` and `Format` operations.

Listing 16-7 *TextBoxEx Format Support*

```csharp
// overriding the text property to trim and
// format the text.
public override string Text
{
   get
   {
      return TrimText(base.Text);
   }
   set
   {
      base.Text = FormatText(value);
   }
}
// private function used to trim format characters
private string TrimText( string text )
{
   switch( mFormat )
   {
      case EditFormat.None:
         return text;
      case EditFormat.Phone:
         return Phone.Trim(text);
   }
   return text;
}
// private function used to format characters.
private string FormatText( string text )
{
   switch( mFormat )
   {
      case EditFormat.None:
         return text;
      case EditFormat.Phone:
         return Phone.Format(text);
   }
   return text;
}
```

Both the `TrimText` and `FormatText` functions shown in Listing 16-7 use the `mFormat` property to determine how it should handle the text. If the format property is set to Phone, they both use static functions from another custom object we added, named Phone.cs. This object is simply a new C# class we added that has support to format, trim, and validate phone numbers. The reason for putting this in another class is we can use the same functions from other controls or classes, and be assured of consistent formatting and validation throughout the application.

Once you have the control complete, you need to build it and add it to the toolbox to use it. You can build the AcmeControls by right-clicking the project and selecting Build from the Context menu. The following steps can be used to add your custom TextBox control:

1. Open the Directory form in a Designer window.

2. Open the Components submenu in the toolbox.

NOTE

If you don't have the Form Designer window open, this submenu won't be available.

3. Right-click the menu and select Customize Toolbox from the Context menu, which opens a dialog box used to add controls.

4. Make sure the .NET Framework Components tab is selected in the dialog box, and then click the Browse button to bring up a File dialog box.

5. Using the File dialog box, navigate to the AcmeControls\Bin\Debug directory and open the AcmeControls.dll. This will close the File dialog box and add your control to the list, which is shown in the following screenshot.

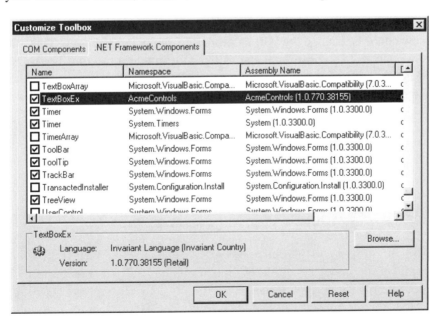

6. Select OK on the Customize Toolbox dialog box, which will add your Custom control to the Components menu, shown in the following screenshot.

The last step is to replace all the TextBox controls for the Phone numbers in Figure 16-2 with the new TextBoxEx controls you just added. When replacing the old TextBox controls, use the same name and binding information on the new TextBoxEx controls. The only additional property that needs to be set is the Format property you added to the control. Because this is defined as an enumeration, the Property window will display a combo box used to select the Format value. For all three of the new controls, change the Format property from None to Phone. That's it! You now have controls that will format and validate information for you. The following shows a new version of the AcmeEmployee application with the controls you added.

User Controls

When building a large application, cases exist where a group of controls is repeated on several different forms. Rather than copy those controls and code to each form, you can create something called a User control. *User controls* enable you to group multiple Windows Forms controls into a single unit. In fact, the designer for a User control, shown in Figure 16-5, is the same designer used to build Windows Forms. In other words, a User control is really just another type of form embedded inside a Windows Form. The difference is that User controls are dropped on to a form from the toolbox, just like any other Windows Forms control.

The AcmeEmployee example we've been working on throughout this chapter has a group of controls for employee information that could be grouped into a User control. Now, we have to admit this is somewhat contrived, but it's possible this same group of controls would be needed on several different forms in the same application. As a result, we're going to create a new User control named EmployeeInfo and add it to the AcmeControls project. This control will contain all the employee specific text boxes and it will expose a type-specific DataSource, so you can continue to bind your `EmployeeDetailDS DataSet` to the fields in this control. The use of a `DataSet` shared across multiple projects does cause some additional consideration, which we'll address shortly, but first you need to start with updating your current projects.

One of the major benefits to developing and deploying .NET applications is that you no longer have to deal with registration details. You can simply copy an application into a directory and run it with no additional setup required. This same ease of deployment is also carried over into VS.NET projects. All you need to do is copy them to a directory and open the project or solution file. Instead of writing over the older versions of AcmeEmployee, we'll copy the last project into a new directory and update that version. As a result, the first step in this sample is to create a new directory named AcmeEmployeeTwo and copy everything from AcmeEmployee into this new directory. Once the files are copied, you can double-click the AcmeEmployee.sln in the new directory and it will open your project. In addition, you needn't change the name of the project or make any more changes—it just works.

Sharing DataSets

As mentioned previously, we're planning to use the same `EmployeeDetailDS DataSet` in the control that we're using on the Form. To make this work, we need to be able to share the same `DataSet` reference in both projects. You can use several different approaches to accomplish this. You can create a separate library project that's shared by both the AcmeEmployee and AcmeControls projects. You can also move the reference to the AcmeControls project, and then use that reference in the

AcmeEmployee project. You can even add a Web reference to both projects that contain the `DataSet` references you need. Regardless of the approach used, the main consideration is to make sure you don't create circular references between two projects, which can cause dependency issues when you attempt to build the projects.

For this example, we'll take a middle-ground approach and move the `EmployeeDetailDS DataSet` to the AcmeControls project, and then share that reference in the AcmeEmployee project. The following steps can be used to accomplish this task:

1. Open the Directory Form Designer window and delete the `mDetailDS` object from the designer.

2. Select `EmployeeDetailDS` in the AcmeEmployee directory of the Solution Explorer, and then drag-and-drop it on to the AcmeControls project in the Solution Explorer. This moves all the necessary files to that directory.

3. Right-click `EmployeeDetailDS` in the AcmeControls project and select Run Custom Tool from the Context menu. This regenerates the typed `DataSet` and fixes any namespace differences.

4. Right-click the AcmeControls project in the Solution Explorer and choose Build from the Context menu. This adds the `DataSet` to the assembly, so you can reference it in the next step.

5. Open the Directory Form Designer window and drop a `DataSet` on to the form from the Data submenu of the toolbox. When the dialog box is displayed, choose Referenced DataSets… from the drop-down window, and then choose `AcmeControls.EmployeeDetailDS` from the list.

6. Rename the new `DataSet` to `mDetailDS`, which is the same name used for the old reference.

7. Update the binding information in the `lblManager` and `cboProject` controls on the Directory form. You needn't update any other controls because they will be removed later.

That's it! You successfully moved the `DataSet` to another project and updated the local references. The next step is to create the new User control and add it to our Directory form.

Creating the User Control

The actual process of adding a new User control to the AcmeControls project is the same as adding any other new item to a project. For this example, select Add | Add User Control from the AcmeControls Context menu or select the AcmeControls project and select Add New Item from the main File menu. When the New Item dialog box is displayed, make sure User control is selected and name it EmployeeInfo.cs. Once you select OK, Visual Studio will add the new control to the AcmeControls project and open the Designer window for the new control. As mentioned previously, the Designer window is the same window used to build forms, so the next step is to add controls on to the new form.

Because you're using the same controls from AcmeEmployee, all you need to do is cut the controls from the Directory Form, and then paste them on to the EmployeeInfo control form. The following screenshot shows the EmployeeInfo Designer window with the controls added. You still have two more tasks left before you can build the control. First, you need to add a `DataSet` to the designer, and then you need to add a new property used to set and get the control's `DataSet`.

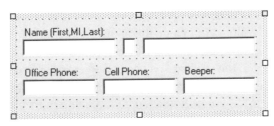

Using the same steps you've been using to add `DataSets` to the Windows Forms Designer windows, add a new `DataSet` to the EmployeeInfo Designer window, use the AcmeControls `EmployeeDetailDS` reference, and name the new `DataSet mDetailDS`. Next, you need to update all the binding information on the controls in the Designer window, using the same settings originally used. Once the `DataSet` has been added and bound to the controls, you need to add a property that can be used to update or retrieve the `DataSet`.

The following listing shows the property code added to your EmployeeInfo control. Remember, `mDetailDS` is the `DataSet` you just added in the last step. This property supports the capability to retrieve that `DataSet` when you need to update the data and you can update it with a new `DataSet` in the set operation. Notice the following set operation uses the same method of clearing the current `DataSet`, and then merging in the new data you used in the original form. When using this control, all you need to do is set the DataSource property to an `EmployeeDetailDS DataSet`, and then it automatically populates the controls through the data binding settings.

```
// Data Source for this Control
public EmployeeDetailDS DataSource
{
    get
    {
```

```
      mDetailDS.AcceptChanges();
      return mDetailDS;
   }
   set
   {
      mDetailDS.Clear();
      mDetailDS.Merge( value );
   }
}
```

Using the New Control

You're ready to build and use the new EmployeeInfo User control. The first step is to build the control by right-clicking the AcmeControls project and selecting Build. In addition, you can also build any project by selecting that project, and then selecting Build from the main Build menu. Once the control has been built, use the same, previously described, steps for adding a Custom control to add the new User control. With the control added to the toolbox, you can now open the Directory Form in the AcmeEmployee project and drop the User control on to the Form. Once the control is dropped on to the form, you need to change the name to `ucEmployeeInfo`.

The following screenshot shows the Directory Form's Designer window with the new User control added. When looking at the following Designer window, the only difference between this version and the original is you can't see gridlines around the Employee controls. Now that you have this control, you can add it to many forms and they'll all have the same look and feel for editing employee information.

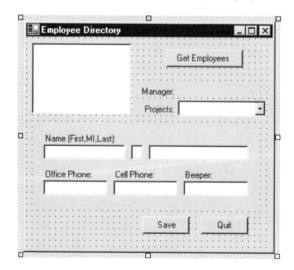

At this point, you still have two minor code changes to make before you're done. There isn't too much to do: you need to update the `DataSet` on the control when detail information is retrieved and you need to use the control's version of the `DataSet` for updates. The following code snippet shows the two changes made in Directory.cs.

```
[lstEmployees_SelectedIndexChanged]
// load the EmployeeInfo control
ucEmployeeInfo.DataSource = detailDS;
```

```
[btnSave_Click]
emp.EmployeUpdate( ucEmployeeInfo.DataSource );
```

The first change shown in the previous example was to add a line below the original merge call in the `SelectedIndexChanged` event handler that sets the DataSource property on the EmployeeInfo control. The second change was to pass EmployeeInfo's DataSource to the update function, instead of using the local `mDetailDS DataSet`.

With all these steps complete, you can do a full build of the solution and test the new control. The following screenshot shows the updated AcmeEmployee application running with the new User control. Notice it doesn't look any different from the original version, which is exactly what we wanted to accomplish.

Remote Deployment

With the new Microsoft .NET platform, you have many different deployment options available. The easiest way to deploy an application is to do an xcopy of the files from one directory to another. And, you can use Setup and Deployment projects available with Visual Studio.NET to build different types of setup programs. In addition, you can also deploy Windows Forms applications from the browser, which requires the .NET Framework to be installed on the remote client machine. We won't get into all the different deployment options here. Instead, the focus of this discussion is providing a method for remote client installations to interact with central servers.

When deploying an application to remote clients, you need to consider how that application will communicate with other application and database servers. This isn't an issue for stand-alone applications that don't interact with a server, but most business applications use some sort of central business objects and database. With firewalls and other security restrictions in place, you might be unable to interact with the servers from a remote client using standard protocols. This is the type of scenario that's perfect for Web services. As a result, we'll evolve our AcmeEmployee application to use Web services, instead of the business components that currently exist.

Before we begin with this new project, we'll need to copy some existing projects into new directories. The three projects we'll use for this example are AcmeControls, AcmeEmployee, and AcmeDirectory. The AcmeDirectory project can be found in the samples in Chapter 8. We've also added an updated version to the samples for this chapter. Just as we did with the last example, we're going to create new folders and copy the project files into those new folders. Start by creating a folder named AcmeControlsWeb and copy all the project files under AcmeControls to this new folder. *Don't* copy the bin and obj folders in the original AcmeControls folder. Next, create a folder named AcmeEmployeeWeb and copy the project files from your latest version, which is AcmeControlsTwo. Finally, create a new folder named AcmeDirectory and copy the project files from the Chapter 8 version of AcmeDirectory.

By now, it should start making sense why we decided to use the same `DataSets` defined for the Web service project in Chapter 8. In addition, by using a `DataSet`-based approach to building our AcmeEmployee application, it will be easy for you to convert the application into one that uses Web services with few code changes. Before we can get into the AcmeEmployee updates, though, you need to update the original Web service to add `Save` functionality.

Updating the Web Service

The first step in building this new application is to update the AcmeDirectory Web service, first developed in Chapter 8. Once again, the benefits of xcopy deployment in Microsoft .NET will make this easy for you to modify the original application. The first step is to update the Internet Information Server (IIS) settings to point to the new Web service directory. If you haven't installed the Chapter 8 examples, then you need to create a new Web site. Otherwise, you only need to update the directory the Web site references. In both cases, all you need is a virtual directory in IIS named AcmeDirectory that points to the new directory you just added.

To update IIS, open the IIS manager, found on the Administrative menu, and either create a new virtual site named AcmeDirectory or right-click the existing site and select Properties from the Context menu. When creating a new virtual site, you're prompted for the Web site location, which should be set to your new AcmeDirectory folder. In both cases, you'll see the following dialog box, which should have the same Local Path and Application Name properties as shown in the following.

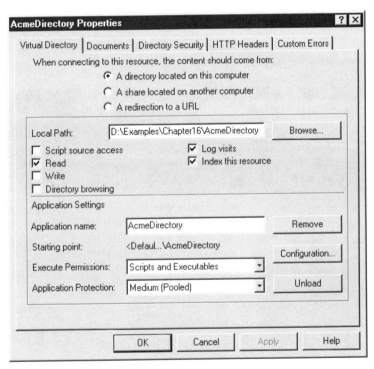

Once the Web settings are updated, you can double-click the AcmeDirectory.sln file in the AcmeDirectory folder to open the Visual Studio development environment for the Web service project. Because this project already contains methods for getting employees and employee details, the only thing you need to do is add the `Save` operation. This can be accomplished by copying the `EmployeeUpdate` and `Update` methods, shown in Listing 16-4, to the business and data access components in this project, and then adding a new WebMethod to the Directory.asmx.cs file. The following code snippet shows the new `EmployeeSave` method that was added.

```
[WebMethod]
public void EmployeeSave( EmployeeDetailDS detailDS )
{
   bcEmployee EmpBusiness = new bcEmployee();
   EmpBusiness.EmployeUpdate( detailDS );
}
```

We're done with the updates to the Web service. All that's left to do is build it and test the interfaces. You can review Chapters 8 and 14 for details on how you can fully test the interface but, for this example, all you need to do is open the Directory.asmx file in a browser. If the Web service was updated correctly, you should see the following in your browser.

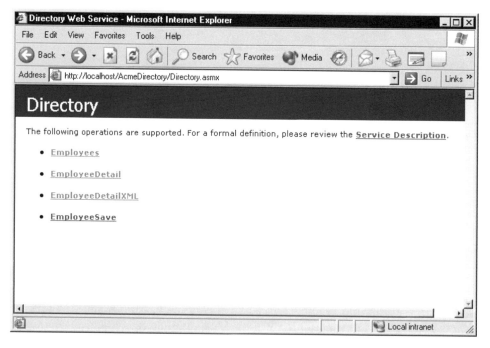

You can use the previous links to check the individual interface methods and even view the Web service contract information.

Adding the Web Reference

Now that you have the Web service updated, it's time to replace your existing
business components with Web service references. Before going any farther, though,
you need to open the new AcmeEmployee solution and fix project references. The
original solution you copied was set to reference the AcmeControls project in the
original folder. You need to remove that reference from AcmeEmployee and add a
new reference to the project in the AcmeControlsWeb Folder. Now you're ready to
start adding the Web reference.

Figure 16-6 shows the Add Web Reference dialog box that opens when you select
Add Web Reference from one of the Project menus. When the dialog box is first
displayed, you'll need to add the Address shown in Figure 16-6 to retrieve the Web
service description file for the Directory Web service. After you enter the URL to
your Directory service and press ENTER, the information shown in Figure 16-6 is
displayed.

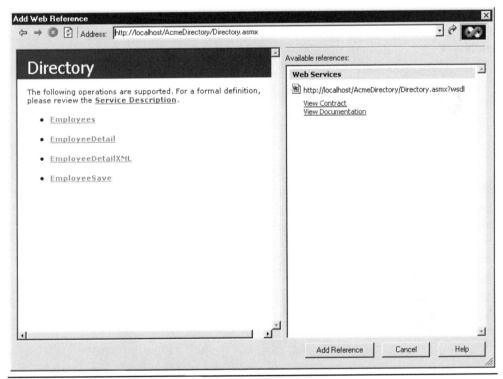

Figure 16-6   *Add Web Reference dialog box*

The window on the left in Figure 16-6 is the same screen you would see when you navigate to the Directory.asmx file in a browser. The window on the right in Figure 16-6 enables you to view additional information about the Web service. To add this reference to the project, all you need to do is click the Add Reference button, shown at the bottom, in Figure 16-6. Because both the AcmeControls and AcmeEmployee projects use the DataSet definitions from this Web service, you need to add the Web reference to both projects. When you add the Web reference, the default name given to it is localhost. Please change that to AcmeDirectory in both projects.

After adding the same Web reference to both the AcmeControls and AcmeDirectory projects, you need to remove the existing business classes and `DataSets`. Before removing the actual `DataSet` files, this will be easier to manage if you first remove the `DataSets` you added to the Form and User control designers. Figure 16-7 shows your Visual Studio development environment with both projects updated and the Web service reference expanded in the AcmeEmployee project. When looking through the Solution Explorer window, you can see all the `DataSets` have been removed from both projects. In addition, the `bcEmployee`, `dcEmployee`, and `DataManager` classes have been removed from AcmeEmployee. With this new implementation, you'll be using the Web service to get your `DataSet` references and invoke the commands.

When looking at the Web reference information, you can see the `DataSet` references along with the Directory.disco, Directory.wsdl, and Reference.map files. Once again, a complete description of Web services is beyond the scope of this chapter, however, the file we're interested in here is the WSDL file. This reference will be used in your Directory form code to access the Web service methods. Before updating the methods, you need to fix all the `DataSet` references and binding information. Using the same steps discussed throughout this chapter, you need to add both the `mEmployeesDS` and the `mDetailDS` DataSets to the Directory Form using the `DataSet` references from the Web service. Once the `DataSets` are added, you need to go back and check/fix the binding information on the controls.

Once the Directory form is updated, you need to use the same steps to add the `mDetailDS` DataSet to the EmployeeInfo User control and fix its binding information. In addition, you need to modify the DataSource property. Although you're using the same `DataSet` references for both projects, the actual project references for these are different. One is `AcmeControls.AcmeDirectory.EmployeeDetailDS` and the other is `AcmeEmployee.AcmeDirectory.EmployeeDetailDS`. Because the actual references are different, you can't assign the DataSource property on the control with the `DataSet` reference you're using in AcmeEmployee. The solution to this is to change the data type on the DataSource property from `EmployeeDetailDS`

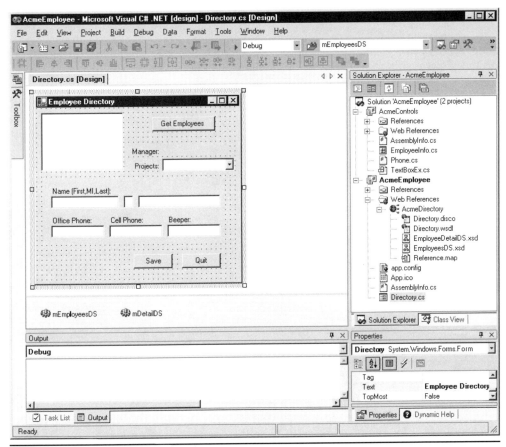

Figure 16-7   *Project with Web references*

to `DataSet`. The `Merge` operation will work the same and there won't be any data issues because they both use the same physical structure.

When all the `DataSet` references have been fixed and the EmployeeInfo User control is updated, the last step is to update some code. Listing 16-8 shows the updated code for the three main operations in your application. As you can see, these operations are similar to the ones in your original code but, instead of using a business component, we're using a Web service. Even the function names and parameters are the same and, because we used `DataSets`, the rest of the code didn't need to change. What you see in Listing 16-8 are the only changes made to the Directory code.

Listing 16-8   *Web Service Updates*

```
[Get Employees]
AcmeDirectory.Directory webDirectory = new AcmeDirectory.Directory();
EmployeesDS empDS = webDirectory.Employees();

[Get Details]
AcmeDirectory.Directory webDirectory = new AcmeDirectory.Directory();
EmployeeDetailDS detailDS = webDirectory.EmployeeDetail( empID );

[Save]
private void btnSave_Click(object sender, System.EventArgs e)
{
   // Call the update function... but only if we have data
   if( ucEmployeeInfo.DataSource != null )
   {
      // copy the control data into a DataSet the Web service understands
      EmployeeDetailDS saveDS = new EmployeeDetailDS();
      saveDS.Merge(ucEmployeeInfo.DataSource);
      // Initialize the Web service and make the call
      AcmeDirectory.Directory webDirectory = new AcmeDirectory.Directory();
      webDirectory.EmployeeSave( saveDS );
   }
}
```

The only section of code in Listing 16-8 that needed a little extra work was the Save operation. Because we're passing a DataSet to the Web service, you need to pass the specific type the Web service is expecting. Because the underlying type in the EmployeeInfo control is different from the one in AcmeEmployee, you need to convert it into the correct type. Once again, you're using exactly the same structures, so no issues occur with merging the data from one into another. As a result, all you need to do is create a new DataSet using the correct reference, and then merge the data from the control's DataSet into your new DataSet. Once this is done, you can pass the new DataSet into the Web service method.

Now you're done with all the changes. The last step is to build everything. You now have a new version of AcmeEmployee that uses Web services and can be deployed to remote locations. By taking advantage of DataSets and using the design principles discussed here and in Chapter 8, we were able to evolve our application from a stand-alone Windows application to a distributed Windows application. To close the loop on this, one more screenshot follows that shows the final application running. As you can see, the application looks the same and, something you can't see, it works the same. The only difference with this last implementation is the operations might be a little slower, which is dependant on the network connectivity between the application and the Web service.

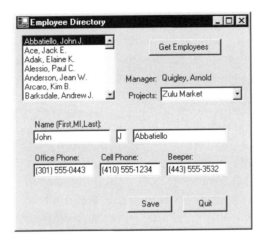

Integrating with Java

In the previous section, you saw how easy it was to integrate a Web service interface into a Windows Forms application. In this section, we use those same design patterns to integrate with a Java application. Because Web services use standard protocols, they're supported by multiple platforms, not only the Microsoft .NET platform. In fact, most of the vendors who provide Java solutions are also providing classes and libraries in Java to support Web services that use the same SOAP protocols the .NET platform uses. With the capability to integrate with Web services, using little effort, you can build new user interfaces into existing applications running on different platforms.

Chapter 7 provides in-depth information on the SOAP specification, along with examples on how to use SOAP in different applications. Chapter 8 focused more on the low-level aspects of Web services with discussions on the different protocols used, such as the Web Service Description Language (WSDL). By using the information from these two chapters, you are able to build a Web service interface into an existing Java server application, and then provide a Windows Forms user interface for that application. The application we're interfacing with is a timecard system, which is in use today at a consulting firm.

The timecard was developed using Java Applets for the user interface and Java Servlets on a middle tier. The middle-tier components interface with SQL-stored procedures developed as part of the original timecard system ten years ago. These stored procedures have been maintained and updated over the years and other applications are dependent on them. The original application was a SQL Windows application that wasn't year 2000 ready and needed to be replaced. The decision was made to provide a new Java interface into the existing SQL-stored procedures using applets and servlets. In addition, because the application needed to be available to a wide range of locations over the Internet, standard protocols were used to provide an interface between the applets and the servlets.

The interface between applets in a client browser and the servlets was XML over HTTPS. If you read Chapter 7, you know SOAP is nothing more than XML over HTTP and, even though our original XML structures didn't use SOAP, they can still be considered Web services. All we needed to do to make them SOAP-compliant was to wrap the existing XML structures with a `soap:Envelope` and `soap:Body`. Well, a little more work than that was required. We also had to create a WSDL file, but the overall effort was small and little code was modified.

Java Updates

The original design for the servlets in our timecard application supported two types of interfaces: XML and HTML. As a result, the code was already designed to support a parameter that indicated which type we wanted. All we needed to do was add support for a new type, which is SOAP. In fact, only two classes needed updating: one that handled reading parameters passed in and another that initialized an XML document that was loaded with data and returned to the client. The following snippet shows the code that initializes the XML document.

```
// Initialize document based on type of XML message
if( strOutput != null && strOutput.equals( "SOAP" ))
{
   StringBuffer strSoapBuff = new StringBuffer();
   strSoapBuff.append("<?xml version='1.0'?><soap:Envelope ");
   strSoapBuff.append("xmlns:soap=
                      'http://schemas.xmlsoap.org/soap/envelope/'>
                      <soap:Body>");
   strSoapBuff.append("<" + strName +
                      "xmlns='http://www.rdacorp.com/Merlin' />");
   strSoapBuff.append("</soap:Body></soap:Envelope>");
   xmlDocument.loadXML( strSoapBuff.toString());
```

```
    output = SOAP_TYPE;
}
else ...
```

When you look at the previous Java code, it probably looks familiar. Java and C# are both based on the C++ language, and they have similar characteristics. The important thing to note, however, is that all we did was add an `Envelope` and a `Body` with some namespace declarations. As we process the request, any data that needs to be returned will be inserted into the body of the SOAP message. SOAP isn't much more than a standard way to package XML data. The two main elements we added are all that's required.

Once the Java code is updated, all we need do is create a WSDL file that described the interfaces we want to access. The .NET Framework comes with several tools that help in the generation of WSDL files, but none of them will work with our servlets. Instead, we have to create the WSDL file by hand, which isn't too difficult. The first step is to create a text file that has sample XML data, which represents the XML interfaces to our servlets. Next, you use a tool from .NET named *xsd.exe*, which creates an XSD schema, based on the XML structures in the file. The last step is to add the generated schema to a WSDL file, and then define the different elements needed by the WSDL specifications. Once again, Chapter 8 covers the WSDL specifications in-depth if you want more information on the actual structure. Rather than look at the WSDL file right now, you'll have a chance to see it when you add the Web reference shortly.

Windows Forms Application

The application developed to interface with the new SOAP interfaces is a Windows Forms application. We've already been through the steps used to create a new application and add controls to that application. Instead, we'll focus on the operations that are specific to interfacing with the Java servlets. In reality, you've already seen most of these as well, but you haven't seen some of the different security requirements. The bottom line is this: interfacing with a Java Web service is identical to interfacing with the AcmeDirectory Web service you saw previously. Figure 16-8 shows the Add Web Reference dialog box for our new project with the MerlinEmployee.wsdl file loaded.

The window on the left in Figure 16-8 shows the actual WSDL file you created in the first step. Most of this is the XSD information you automatically generated. The WSDL file contains information about the XML structures passed back and forth, along with information used to locate the Web server that hosts the Web service.

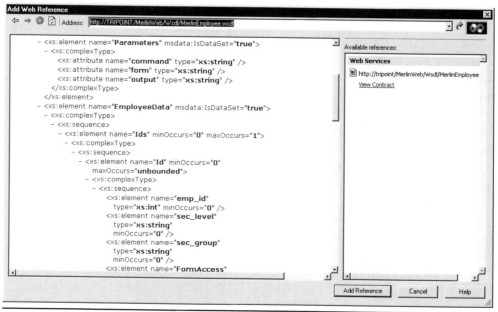

Figure 16-8 *MerlinEmployee Web Reference dialog box*

When the Add Reference button is clicked, a new Web reference is added that lets you programmatically interact with the Java servlets using SOAP. Listing 16-9 shows code used to interact with the Web reference and bind the result set to a DataGrid for display.

Listing 16-9 *Interfacing with the Java Web Reference*

```
private void button1_Click(object sender, System.EventArgs e)
{
   // instantiate the Web Service and set the credentials
   Merlin.MerlinEmployee employee = new Merlin.MerlinEmployee();
   CredentialCache credentialCache = new CredentialCache();
   NetworkCredential credentials =
      new NetworkCredential("wall","MerlinDemo");
   credentialCache.Add(new Uri(employee.Url), "Basic", credentials);
```

```
employee.Credentials = credentialCache;

// Initialize the parameters
Merlin.Parameters empParam = new Merlin.Parameters();
empParam.command = "selectEmployees";
empParam.form = "1";
empParam.output = "SOAP";
// Invoke the SelectEmployees command
Merlin.EmployeeData data = employee.SelectEmployees(empParam);

// serialize the result into XML
XmlSerializer serializer =
    new XmlSerializer(typeof(Merlin.EmployeeData));
Stream writer = new MemoryStream();
serializer.Serialize(writer, data);
writer.Seek(0,System.IO.SeekOrigin.Begin );

// load the results into a dataset and bind it to a grid
DataSet EmployeeDS = new DataSet("EmployeeData");
EmployeeDS.ReadXml(writer);
dataGrid1.SetDataBinding( EmployeeDS, "Employee" );
}
```

The first line of code in Listing 16-9 is where you instantiate the Web service, which is named Merlin.MerlinEmployee. Following the Web service creation is code used to set up security information that will be used to authenticate against the server where your servlets are hosted. The servlets are restricted to authenticated users and the authentication method used is *Basic Authentication*, which is standard for Web applications. Note, this is a sample application. You normally wouldn't hard code a user name and password like this. The next section of code in Listing 16-9 creates a parameter variable, which is a DataSet defined in the WSDL file, and initializes it with the parameters that will be passed into the application.

Once the parameters are initialized in Listing 16-9, it's time to call the actual Web service. The return value from the Web service is an XML structure with SOAP data named EmployeeData, which is converted into a DataSet you can bind to. Because you generated the WSDL by hand and didn't have all the information needed for strongly typed DataSets, the object returned from this call isn't a DataSet, which is the reason you need to create one. Once the `DataSet` is created and loaded with data, the last step is to bind it to a grid, which gives you the following output.

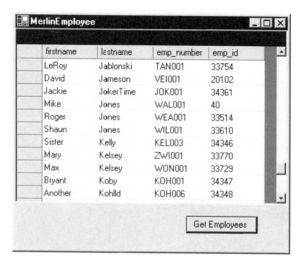

That's it! You now have a Windows Forms application that interfaces with a Java servlet using SOAP messages. The most difficult part about the entire previous exercise was creating the WSDL file but, once you've done one, the rest are easy. The .NET code created, along with the WSDL file it pulled into the Web Reference folder, will be available with all the samples on the McGraw-Hill/Osborne Web site (**www.osborne.com**). We won't be able to provide the Java code, which is a system in production today. The data we used in this demo was fake, but the Java code was real.

Summary

We covered a lot of ground in this chapter, starting with a stand-alone Windows application and finishing with an application that interfaces with Java servlets. Along the way, you learned how to develop and use Custom controls, as well as User controls. You also learned about good design techniques that support extensibility and maintainability through the use of `DataSets` and a layering technique in the code. Then you learned how easy it is to convert the application to a remote application using Web services, which was facilitated by the design approach used.

The last section in this chapter demonstrated how to write a Windows Forms application that can interact with other Web services. The example discussed was based on interfacing with an existing Java application in production today. You learned how easy it is to interface with that application and provide a new user interface to it.

The following list highlights some of the areas covered in this chapter:

► Creating new Windows Forms applications

► Design techniques

► Adding `DataSets` to a form

► Adding controls to a form

► Creating Custom controls

► Creating User controls

► Using OPENXML in SQL Server

► Interfacing with Web services

► Interfacing with other platforms

Debugging
.NET Applications

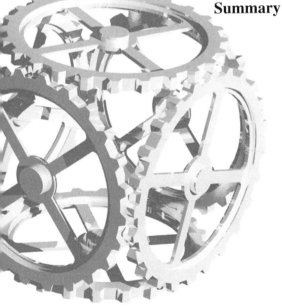

E very development experience requires some amount of debugging and Microsoft's Visual Studio .NET is no exception. This, though, might be the most pleasant debugging experience yet. For those developers who have used prior versions of Visual Studio, the debugger will be quite familiar. But the new features will also be welcome additions.

In this chapter, you learn about some of the new features .NET's debugger offers. You also look at how to debug ASP.NET applications, as well as multithreaded applications. And you'll try your hand at remote debugging. In the end, you'll be equipped to squash any type of bug an application might throw your way.

Debugging .NET Applications

If you've ever used Visual Studio's debugger before, the basic commands are still available. Pressing F9 toggles breakpoints on a selected line of source code. And the F5 key initiates a debug session for an application. Those are the basics needed to begin debugging a .NET application—nothing new or mysterious here.

However, before you dive into debugging proper, you must understand how .NET compiles applications. .NET uses a two-step process when it compiles source code. First, .NET compiles to Microsoft Intermediate Language (MSIL) code, using the appropriate .NET-compatible compiler. For example, when using C#, .NET uses a C# compiler to compile to MSIL. And, it uses a VB.NET compiler to compile VB.NET code into MSIL. Once the .NET compiler has produced the MSIL, the second step is to compile that to native machine code.

When debugging, .NET reverses this process. First, it decompiles the native code into MSIL. Then, using programmer's database (PDB) files, .NET can map the MSIL back to the original source code. The PDB files are separate from the application executables or the DLLs. The compiler can be configured to generate them as part of the compilation process. They're used by the debugger as small databases, containing enough information to map the MSIL-compiled code to lines in the original source code. Using both the PDB files and the original source code, Visual Studio provides a rich environment that enables the developer to completely manipulate and debug any .NET application.

The process of debugging a .NET application is simple enough. Visual Studio .NET has preserved the concept of Project Configurations from prior versions of Visual Studio. As a developer, you can define your own configuration but, usually, the two predefined configurations—Debug and Release—suit most project needs.

Project Configuration

To adjust the settings for these configurations, right-click the project in the Solution Explorer window and select the Properties menu item. This brings up the Property Pages dialog box for the project, as shown in Figure 17-1. From the Configuration Properties folder, select the Debugging settings. Here, you can modify a number of settings. In the top category—Debuggers—you have the capability to toggle various types of debugging on or off, including whether Visual Studio will debug ASP, ASP.NET, Unmanaged, and SQL code. When setting the option to debug ASP.NET code to true, an additional attribute is specified in the `compilation` element of the web.config file. This is discussed more in the next section. More important for the individual project, though, you can specify how Visual Studio will debug the application you're building within the Start Action category.

The Debug Mode option enables developers to determine what Visual Studio will start when it begins the debugging session. The choices available are shown in Table 17-1.

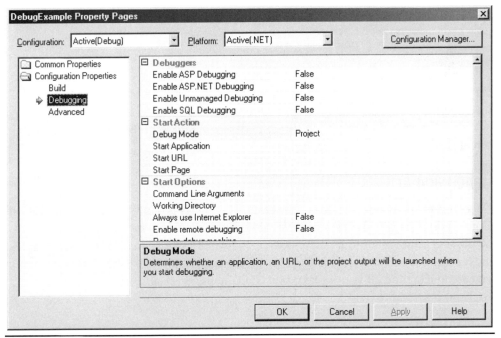

Figure 17-1 *Property Pages dialog box*

Setting	Description
Project	This is the default setting. It specifies Visual Studio will run the project's executable (for Windows Application and Console Application projects) or the page (for Web projects) when it initiates the debug session. Class Library projects can't be started directly.
Program	This setting specifies a particular application should be started when the debug session is initiated. This is often the case when you debug Class Library projects. You might have another project that consumes the library, so starting that application would be the appropriate choice. This option requires the Start Application setting be filled in with the command to launch the desired application.
URL	This setting tells Visual Studio to launch a particular URL when initiating a debug session. Again, this might be used when debugging a Class Library project. The Start URL setting must be assigned a URL when this option is selected.
Wait to Attach to an External Process	This option can only be used with Web Application and Web service projects. The debugger will wait for an external process to interact with the Web application (a browser, for example), or to call into the Web service.

Table 17-1 *Debug Mode Settings*

The remaining choices in the Start Options category are miscellaneous options that provide more control over how the application is started by Visual Studio. Included here is the capability to specify the parameters to debug on a remote machine. This is important when trying to debug a unique problem, say, on a Web server that has already been deployed.

Debugging Actions

Once you begin a debug session, the execution runs as it would normally, until it hits a breakpoint. As was the case in prior versions of Visual Studio, you set breakpoints by moving your cursor to a line of source code and pressing the F9 key. This toggles the breakpoint on and off. You can also do the same thing from the Debug menu. Or, you could examine all your breakpoints, and enable or disable them at will from the Breakpoints window.

NOTE

You can view the Breakpoints window at any time, while debugging an application or not, by clicking the Debug menu. Click the Windows menu item. From here, click the Breakpoints menu item to display the Breakpoints window. You can also display this window by pressing CTRL-ALT-B.

When you hit a breakpoint, you can inspect variables and objects, add and remove breakpoints, and even set your current line of execution to another line. These are powerful features you can use to improve your code and identify problems, but they're expected of any debugger today. To view values in variables and objects, position the mouse over the desired object in the code. Then with a right-click, you can choose to add the variable or object to your Watch window by selecting the Add Watch menu item. Or, you can display the variable or object in the QuickWatch dialog box by choosing the QuickWatch menu item, or by using the keyboard and pressing SHIFT-F9. You can also add the item to your Watch window from the QuickWatch dialog box, as shown in Figure 17-2.

NOTE

The debugger can only display values of variables and objects within the same scope as the breakpoint. Something is within the scope of the breakpoint when it's part of the same method or function currently being executed.

When you right-click your source code, you also have a number of other options. By choosing the Set Next Statement menu item, you can reassign the current line of execution to another line within the scope of the breakpoint. You can also select the Run To Cursor menu item so the debugger will continue execution until it reaches the specified line of source code. Again, it must be within the scope of the breakpoint.

Other options enable you to modify breakpoints, depending on whether the line beneath the cursor already has a breakpoint. In addition, you can invoke *IntelliSense* to examine classes and methods. You can also jump to other references and the current object's definition.

Figure 17-2   *QuickWatch dialog box*

Evaluating Expressions in the Debugger

One of the most important features a debugger must provide is its capability to inspect values during the execution of the application. As you saw in Figure17-2, you can view variables or objects when the application hits a breakpoint. You can also add them to your Watch window. But you can do much more using the Watch window.

For example, say you're looking at an object—foo—that has an integer—m_bar—as one of its data members. You can look at this value by adding foo to your Watch window, expanding the object, and viewing all its members. Or, you can simply enter the following expression into your Watch window:

```
foo.m_bar
```

This will display only the value of the m_bar data member. If a large number of properties and data members exist on the foo object, this makes watching only the one specific value much easier.

But what if you want to know if it equaled a specific value or another variable? You could also enter the following into the Watch window:

```
foo.m_bar == endOfList
```

where endOfList is another integer with a specific value. The result of this expression will either be true or false.

The debugger will also evaluate full-class derivations. If, for example, you have an instance of a Tiger class—say, objTiger—which derives from the class, Cat, which derives from the class, Animal, you can work your way up the class chain, and examine the data members of each class using the objTiger instance. Class inheritance is fully supported by the debugger.

The Watch window also supports function evaluation. You can invoke a function, passing in arguments, while stopped at a breakpoint. You can even invoke overloaded functions. If a function foo() takes no parameters and an overloaded function that takes one integer, the debugger will invoke the proper function based on the parameters provided.

```
foo()
foo(4)
```

The Watch window expression also handles arrays, string manipulations, typeof and sizeof operators, casts, and value assignments. It basically enables you to manipulate the variables and objects the way you would using code. Some limitations exist, of course. C/C++ code doesn't provide as many of these manipulations because they aren't built into the languages, as they are in C# and VB.NET. Also, the overloaded infix operators such as

```
|  ^  <<  >>  >  <  >=  <=
```

don't work. On the other hand, the following overloaded infix operators do work.

```
+  -  /  %  &  ==  !=
```

These overloaded prefix operators

```
+  -  ++  --  !  ~
```

are handled by the Watch window, as are the following overloaded suffix operators:

```
++  --
```

Even the overloaded `[]` operator is properly evaluated.

Basically, the Watch window is a versatile tool for evaluating and modifying the values and objects in an application, again within the scope of the breakpoint. By playing with these values, a developer can diagnose a problem and even determine the solution. The flexibility of this view enables the developer to fix the source code eventually and, after recompiling the code, eliminate the bug. The Watch window is an essential tool for any developer debugging an application using Visual Studio .NET and should be fully explored.

Debugging ASP.NET Applications

When you create an ASP.NET application, certain project settings are given values by default to allow debugging. Referring to the Project Property Page dialog box in Figure 17-1, the Enable ASP.NET Debugging setting must be set to true. Another important setting for debugging Web Applications, the Start Page property, isn't used by the values described in Table 17-1. Instead, it simply determines which of the pages is the starting page for the Web Application or service. Or, you can set this option by right-clicking an .aspx page in the Solution Explorer window and select the Set As Startup Page menu item.

Some of the files in an ASP.NET application, such as the .aspx and .ascx files, are compiled at run time. To tell the compiler to include debug symbols when compiling these files, Web Applications and Web services must have the following setting in the `system.web` element of their web.config file:

```
<compilation defaultLanguage="c#" debug="true"/>
```

NOTE

During compilation of the .aspx and .ascx files, .NET inserts debug symbols if the `debug` attribute of the `compilation` element is set to true. This makes the compiled files larger, decreasing performance. When deploying Web Applications, setting this attribute to false makes sense.

Once you select the startup page and enable ASP.NET debugging, you can initiate the debug session. When you start debugging a Web Application, a browser is opened to the Web Application's URL. The application runs until it hits a breakpoint.

NOTE

Given that Web Applications are so accessible, debugging them with breakpoints can have several side effects. First, any users of the Web site will be paused if they encounter a breakpoint. This can confuse users who aren't aware the site is involved in a debug session and it might cause the session to timeout. Second, debugging the application becomes difficult when more than one HTTP request is received by the Web site. The debugger will jump to each breakpoint as it is hit, which makes keeping track of your own debug session difficult. The best way to debug Web Applications is on an isolated Web server that is unavailable to the general public.

Tracing ASP.NET Applications

The .NET Framework offers another way to tap into the workings of Web Applications, allowing you, as a developer, to see what's going on while they're running. By turning on tracing, .NET displays a number of statistics each time a specific Web page is requested by the client's browser.

To enable tracing for a particular page in an ASP.NET application, you must go to the HTML view of the desired .aspx page. In the @Page directive, you add the Trace attribute, setting it to a value of true. To demonstrate how this works, we'll build a Web Application called WebAuto with one ASP.NET Web page, called MainPage.aspx. The following line is taken from that .aspx page:

```
<%@ Page language="c#" Codebehind="MainPage.aspx.cs"
AutoEventWireup="false"
    Inherits="WebAuto.MainPage" Trace="true" %>
```

As you can see in this example, the Trace attribute is set to true, specifying that tracing be performed for this page. If this attribute is omitted, ASP.NET defaults the value to false.

The WebAuto Web Application consists of only the one page and the page itself is quite simple. This is a static page that displays a label and an image of an automobile. When you run this application, you see the results in Figure 17-3. Following the HTML generated for this page is a considerable amount of information produced by the tracing option.

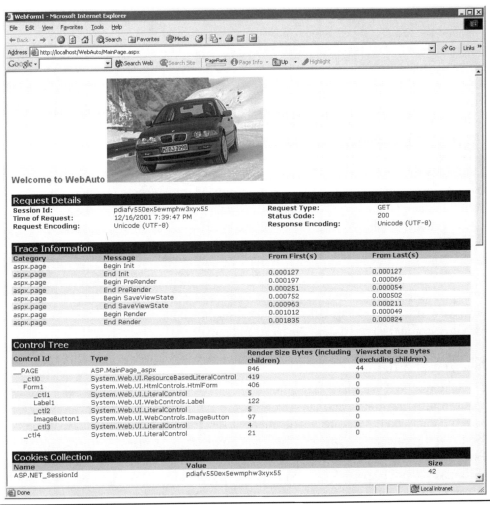

Figure 17-3   *Tracing Web pages in ASP.NET*

NOTE

The tracing information in this example appears below the actual HTML output of the Web page. However, if the page were designed with absolute positioning for its components, the trace output would have been overwritten with the HTML output from the page. This can make viewing the trace information difficult. Be aware of this caveat when you enable tracing for a particular Web page.

A significant amount of information is produced when tracing is used for a Web page. The first section provides details about the HTTP request for the page. This includes such information as the session identifier, the time of the request, the encoding type, and the request type.

If you were trying to obtain performance statistics, the next section lists critical information about building and rendering the page. The From First(s) column shows the amount of time, in seconds, it took from the first call to that step. The next column, From Last(s), also in seconds, shows the time it took for only that step. This is quite useful in determining if a page takes too long to render or if it contains too much ViewState information.

The other sections contain information about the Web controls on the page and the cookies used to manage session information. In addition, another section provides information about the HTTP headers used to request the page. And a final section imparts all the session variables and their values available to the Web page.

You can also enable tracing for the entire Web Application by adjusting the `trace` element in the web.config file. By setting the `enabled` attribute to true, you capture statistics for every page within the application. If the `pageOutput` attribute is set to true, the trace information will be displayed at the bottom of each page, just as it would if you had used the `Trace` attribute in the `@Page` directive. Otherwise, if it's left as false, then you can view the application's trace log using a Web browser and navigating to the trace.axd page.

Debug Client Script

Visual Studio .NET has made debugging client-side script easier than ever. This feature has been fully integrated into the Visual Studio IDE. Just as you would anywhere else, you can set a breakpoint on the client-side script and Visual Studio will enable you to hit this breakpoint when the script is invoked on the client's browser. While debugging the client-side script, only the stack frame of the browser is available. This makes sense because Visual Studio is attaching to the browser's process. While you can't follow the code from client to server, you can still easily debug the client-side script.

This is quite extraordinary because anyone who has ever written client-side script knows how hard it is to tell what's wrong when the code misbehaves. In the past, developers have had to make temporary kludges to the code, things like popping up little windows or alert dialog boxes to display values and other clues to determine what's happening within the client's browser. This feature enables developers to test their client-side script, exposing any issues before the code is deployed. And, it lets them easily determine the cause of bugs once the code has been deployed.

The first thing to do is enable client-side debugging in your browser. In Internet Explorer, go to the Tools menu and select the Internet Options menu item. From the Advanced tab, clear the Disable Script Debugging check box option.

Now, you can place breakpoints in the client script. When the application runs and the browser executes client-side script, the debugger will stop at the breakpoint. While the stack will only contain information for the browser, it does enable you to view and edit the client-side variables, and to determine the problem. Editing values will alter the execution of the script and let you resolve the issue.

Debugging Multithreaded Applications

You needn't do anything special to debug multithreaded applications. On the other hand, debugging multithreaded applications can become quite messy, quite fast. The key to debugging such applications successfully is to be aware that a multithreaded application has many threads executing simultaneously (or as close to simultaneously as a processor is capable), making the debugging experience unpredictable. This can create confusion when you expect certain objects to have certain values at certain times. Because threads run independently of each other, always being able to predict the state of the application is difficult.

One of the most improved aspects of the Visual Studio debugger is its capability to enable developers to have better control over the threads executing in an application. Using the Threads window during the debug session, a developer can see which threads have been instantiated, turn them on and off, and switch between them. To display this window, click the Debug menu, select the Windows menu item, and then select the Threads menu item. This window displays the currently instantiated threads in the application, as you see in Figure 17-4.

From this window, you can right-click a given thread and select the Freeze menu item. This suspends the thread. When you want to let the thread begin executing once more, select the Thaw menu item. Toggling threads on and off is an easy way to control execution of the application. By freezing one or more threads, you can allow the rest of the application to continue, essentially eliminating those threads from the process. Then, later, you can restore those threads by choosing to thaw them.

The Threads window also enables you to switch focus from one thread to another. This literally moves you to the spot in the code where the selected thread was executing before a breakpoint was hit. From here, you can examine variables and objects as if you'd hit a breakpoint within this thread. The scope of execution is now the thread switched to from the Threads window. The active thread is always the thread with the arrow positioned next to it on the left.

Using the Threads window, you can regain control of your multithreaded application and diminish the chaos of trying to debug threads running simultaneously. While setting breakpoints is still essential to debugging multithreaded applications, you

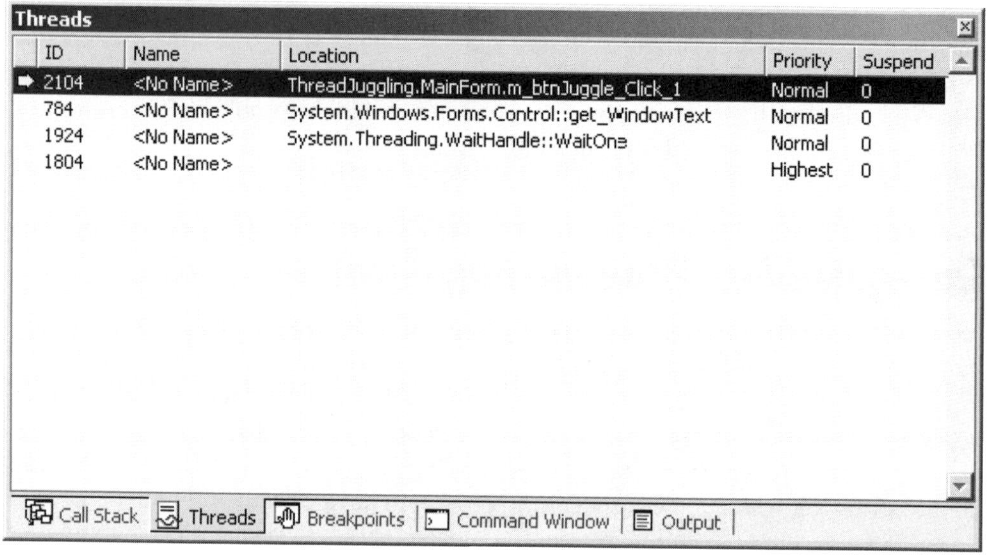

Figure 17-4   *Threads window*

now have a way of managing multiple threads. This makes debugging such applications as easy as debugging a regular, single-threaded application.

Remote Debugging

Remote debugging enables developers to debug an application on another machine across a network. This becomes necessary when you're trying to determine the cause of a problem on a machine that can't be accessed directly and it's encountering issues that cannot be reproduced on other machines. More specifically, this becomes critical when a production server is encountering a bug that can't be produced on a development or staging box, and access to the production machine is limited.

Typically, remote debugging is constrained, more or less, to working with machines in the same domain, unless the domains have a two-way trust. The target machine must be configured properly, so a debug session can be initiated by a remote computer. You can configure a machine for remote debugging in several ways, all of which include DCOM and the Machine Debug Manager (MDM) service.

Configuring a Machine for Remote Debugging

The easiest, but longest, route to configuring a machine for remote debugging is to perform a complete, licensed installation of Visual Studio .NET. This includes all the pieces required for remote debugging. If development isn't a requirement for this particular machine, however, it might be overkill to install the entire environment just for remote debugging, especially when other options exist.

Another option is to run the Visual Studio .NET Setup CD and select the Remote Components Setup from the options in the Setup wizard. This will install only the components needed for remote debugging. When the Setup wizard begins, there is a link to the Remote Components Setup link on the bottom of the form. Clicking the link displays the screen shown in Figure 17-5. When you select this option, you have

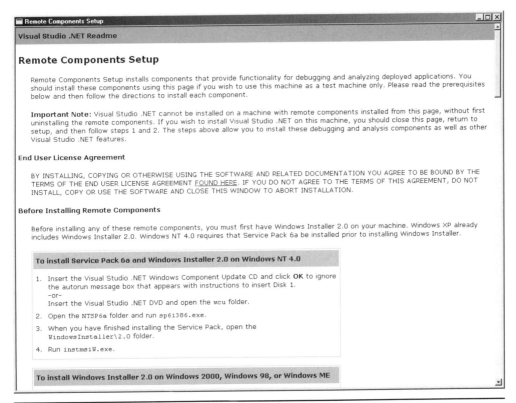

Figure 17-5   *Remote Components Setup dialog box*

two choices: install the components needed for Native remote debugging or install the components for Full remote debugging.

Scrolling down toward the bottom of this page, you'll find a button, Install Native, for Native-only debugging (see Figure 17-6). Clicking this button begins the installation. Native remote debugging installs only the files and components (as shown in Table 17-2) required for an external machine to connect for debugging of native code only. This limits the debugging session to native debugging only, eliminating other choices such as Common Language Runtime, Microsoft T-SQL (though this is discussed shortly), and Script.

Full remote debugging installs everything shown in Table 17-2. This enables the machine to be debugged remotely for all types of debugging, including native debugging, but also for Common Language Runtime, Script, and Microsoft T-SQL.

Another option is to install a minimal set of files to the target machine. These files are

- ▶ msvcmon.exe,
- ▶ msvcr70.dll
- ▶ natdbgtlnet.dll
- ▶ natdbgdm.dll
- ▶ psapi.dll—if the target machine is running NT4
- ▶ dbghelp.dll—optional component for dump support

All these files can be copied to the same location on the target machine or they can be run from a share on the local machine where Visual Studio .NET is running. Running from a share enables you to debug remote machines that don't allow installation of files.

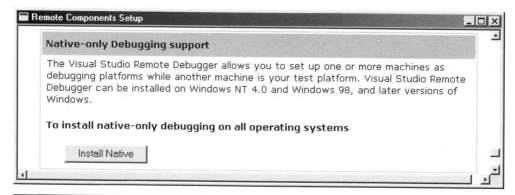

Figure 17-6 *Native remote debugging*

Component	Full Remote Debugging	Native Remote Debugging
msvcr70.dll	Required	Required
msvci70.dll	Required	Required
msvcp70.dll	Required	Required
psapi.dll	Required	Required
dbghelp.dll	Required	Required
msvcmon.exe	Required	Required
NatDbgDM.dll	Required	Required
NatDbgTLNet.dll	Required	Required
coloader.dll	Required	
coloader.tlb	Required	
mssdi98.dll	Required	
sqldbg.dll	Required	
dbgproxy.exe	Required	
mcee.dll	Required	
mcee_cs.dat	Required	
mcee_mc.dat	Required	
cpde.dll	Required	
vs7jit.exe	Required	
csm.dll	Required	
diasymreader.dll	Required	
mdm.exe	Required	
mdmui.dll	Required	
pdm.dll	Required	
msdbg2.dll	Required	
msdis130.dll	Required	
mspdb70.dll	Required	
shmetapdb.dll	Required	

Table 17-2   *Components Required for Remote Debugging*

SQL Server Remote Debugging

To debug SQL Server remotely, you can choose to install Full remote debugging or provide only the components needed for debugging SQL Server. Table 17-3 shows

Component	Installation Target	Installation Directory
sqlle.dll	Remote machine	\Program Files\Microsoft Visual Studio.NET\ Common7\Packages\Debugger
sqldbg.dll	Remote and Server machines	\Program Files\Common Files\ Microsoft Shared\SQL Debugging
mssdi98.dll	Server	\Program Files\Microsoft SQL Server\ MSSQL\Binn
sqldbreg2.exe	Remote machine	\Program Files\Common Files\ Microsoft Shared\SQL Debugging

Table 17-3 *SQL Server Remote Debugging Components*

the components that must be installed manually for a database server to enable remote debugging. Note, some files are meant for the remote machine and others are meant for the database server.

The sqldbg.dll and mssdi98.dll files can be found in the \ENGLISH\ENT\X86\ OTHER\SDI directory of the SQL Server 2000 Enterprise Edition CD. The others are installed from the Visual Studio installation CDs.

Initiating a Remote Debug Session

Now that the target machine has been configured for remote debugging, all you have to do is initiate a remote debug session. To do this, go to the Debug menu and select the Processes... menu item. Clicking this menu displays the Processes dialog box shown in Figure 17-7. The first thing to do is find the remote server you want to debug. This can either be typed in to the text box labeled Name: or discovered using the button to the right of the text box, labeled .... Once the machine has been entered, the Available Processes list box displays all the process on the remote computer that can be debugged. Clicking the Show System Processes check box displays more processes, most importantly, the *aspnet_wp.exe* process.

NOTE

It might be necessary to press Refresh to get the process list to update properly.

This process hosts any and all ASP.NET applications on a given server. In many ways, this is equivalent to the way Inetinfo.exe would host Web Applications. It runs as a system process, so the check box must be checked for it to appear in the available

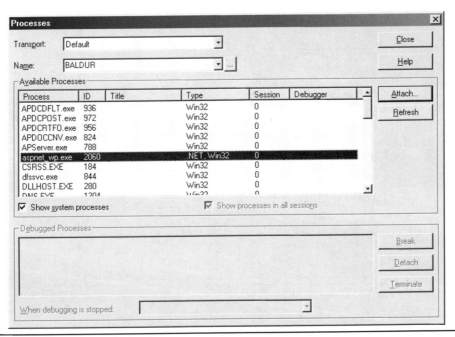

Figure 17-7   *Processes dialog box*

processes. Once the aspnet_wp.exe process is selected, click the Attach button. This displays the Attach To Process dialog box, shown in Figure 17-8. Based on the components installed on the target machine, you'll be able to choose from different program types.

NOTE

The Processes dialog box enables you to debug any of the applications displayed, not only aspnet_wp.exe. And, you can use this dialog to debug not only applications on remote servers, but also programs on the local server.

Selecting a program type displays the applications that will be debugged. As you can see in the example in Figure 17-8, you can debug a couple of ASP.NET applications running under the IIS service, such as the `FootballStats` Web service and the `FootballViewer` Web Application. Clicking the OK button of this dialog box, and then clicking the Close button of the Processes dialog box, begins the debug session. At this point, Visual Studio appears to be in Debug mode, but without starting Internet Explorer. Instead, it's debugging the Web Applications remotely.

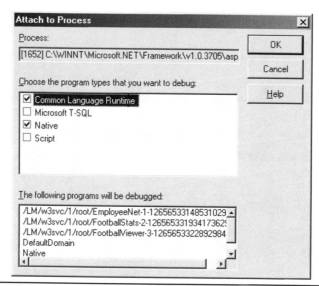

Figure 17-8   *Attach to Process dialog box*

You can set breakpoints within any of the Web Applications listed for the aspnet_wp.exe process, providing you have the source code, and then debug them as you would any other Web Application.

Summary

In this chapter, you took a tour through the various ways to debug applications using Visual Studio .NET. You've seen some of the new features this development environment offers developers. And you learned how to use some not-so-new features that are just as important to the debugging process. In summary, you explored the following:

▶ You learned how .NET compiles applications into MSIL, and then native machine code. Also, you saw how the debugger reverses this process to map back to the source code when debugging an application.

▶ The basic steps to initiate a debug session for a local application remain the same as prior versions of Visual Studio. You use the F5 key to begin the debug session and the F9 key to toggle breakpoints on and off.

▶ Debugging an ASP.NET Web Application with Visual Studio .NET is remarkably similar to debugging a regular Windows application. You can set breakpoints, and then examine variables and objects as needed.

▶ ASP.NET enables you to trace individual Web pages, displaying a great deal of statistical information about the page, such as load times and Web control information. You can also trace the entire Web Application using the trace element in the web.config file.

▶ Visual Studio .NET offers developers the capability to debug client-side script. Although you can't see the stack trace of the Web Application, you can explore the variables on the client side and discover the problems causing the script to fail.

▶ Visual Studio .NET makes it easy to debug multithreaded applications using the Threads window. From this window, you can pause and restart individual threads, and you can easily switch between the threads to inspect values and set breakpoints.

▶ Visual Studio .NET can debug remote applications. Once the target machine is properly configured, you can use Visual Studio to attach to, and debug, the remote process.

Index

INTERNATIONAL CONTACT INFORMATION

AUSTRALIA
McGraw-Hill Book Company Australia Pty. Ltd.
TEL +61-2-9417-9899
FAX +61-2-9417-5687
http://www.mcgraw-hill.com.au
books-it_sydney@mcgraw-hill.com

CANADA
McGraw-Hill Ryerson Ltd.
TEL +905-430-5000
FAX +905-430-5020
http://www.mcgrawhill.ca

GREECE, MIDDLE EAST, NORTHERN AFRICA
McGraw-Hill Hellas
TEL +30-1-656-0990-3-4
FAX +30-1-654-5525

MEXICO (Also serving Latin America)
McGraw-Hill Interamericana Editores S.A. de C.V.
TEL +525-117-1583
FAX +525-117-1589
http://www.mcgraw-hill.com.mx
fernando_castellanos@mcgraw-hill.com

SINGAPORE (Serving Asia)
McGraw-Hill Book Company
TEL +65-863-1580
FAX +65-862-3354
http://www.mcgraw-hill.com.sg
mghasia@mcgraw-hill.com

SOUTH AFRICA
McGraw-Hill South Africa
TEL +27-11-622-7512
FAX +27-11-622-9045
robyn_swanepoel@mcgraw-hill.com

UNITED KINGDOM & EUROPE (Excluding Southern Europe)
McGraw-Hill Education Europe
TEL +44-1-628-502500
FAX +44-1-628-770224
http://www.mcgraw-hill.co.uk
computing_neurope@mcgraw-hill.com

ALL OTHER INQUIRIES Contact:
Osborne/McGraw-Hill
TEL +1-510-549-6600
FAX +1-510-883-7600
http://www.osborne.com
omg_international@mcgraw-hill.com